Daniel Rathnakara Sadananda

The Johannine Exegesis of God

An Exploration into the
Johannine Understanding of God

Walter de Gruyter · Berlin · New York

⊚ Printed on acid-free paper which falls within
the guidelines of the ANSI to ensure permanence and durability.

ISBN 3-11-018248-3

Bibliographic information published by Die Deutsche Bibliothek

Die Deutsche Bibliothek lists this publication in the Deutsche Nationalbibliografie; detailed bibliographic data is available in the Internet at <http://dnb.ddb.de>.

© Copyright 2004 by Walter de Gruyter GmbH & Co. KG, D-10785 Berlin
All rights reserved, including those of translation into foreign languages. No part of this book may be reproduced or transmitted in any form or by any means, electronic or mechanical, including photocopy, recording, or any information storage and retrieval system, without permission in writing from the publisher.
Printed in Germany
Cover design: Christopher Schneider, Berlin

Dedicated to the loving memory of
my parents

Reverend James Lawrence Sadananda

and

Jessie Jemima Sadananda

in whose parental love and care
I got the first foretaste of
God's self-emptying love.

Acknowledgements

The "Johannine exegesis of God" – an exploration into the Johannine understanding of God – is a slightly revised and updated version of my inaugural dissertation accepted by the Kirchliche Hochschule, Bethel, Bielefeld, Germany in summer 1997.

I express my profound gratitude to Professor Dr. Andreas Lindemann, my 'Doktorvater', in whom I found a mentor and guide 'par excellence'. I treasure the stimulating and enriching discussions we shared, and the able supervision and faithful scholarship he offered. The cordial atmosphere and freedom he provided moulded this work. It is his understanding, advice, patience and personal involvement that are responsible in bringing this research to fruition. His perseverance, insistence, eagerness, and technical assistance have finally resulted in the publication of this work. I deem it a God-given gift that our academical partnership has evolved into an affectionate friendship.

My thanks are due to Professor Dr. François Vouga, the co-referent, for his comments and constructive criticism that have enriched the work. The fraternity of the Kirchliche Hochschule in Bethel provided a stimulating and congenial atmosphere for research. The faculty, library personnel and administrative staff have at all times extended a helping hand and friendship that was inspiring.

It was an educative and enriching, at the same time a humbling experience to read the multitude of authors who have worked on the Fourth Gospel. They provided new insights and opened up new perspectives to unravelling the mysteries of the Fourth Gospel. All that I could say on the subject is what I learnt from these Johannine experts, whose exegetical experiments greatly enhanced the outcome of this work.

I am indeed grateful to Dr. Gerhard Wehmeier, the then *Probst*, Evangelische Kirche Kurhessen-Waldeck, Kassel, Germany, who is responsible for bringing me in contact with Professor Lindemann at the Kirchliche Hochschule Bethel for doctoral research. My thanks are due to the Diakonisches Werk of the Evangelische Kirche in Deutschland (EKD) for making this study possible through the award of a scholarship between February 1993 and July 1997. Reverend Helmut Staudt, the then scholarship Secretary needs special mention for his concern and keen interest.

Professor Dr. Traugott Staehlin and Professorin Dr. Petra von Gemünden need special mention for their encouragement and support. I am grateful to Dr. Andreas Mueller for his readiness to read through and correct the manuscript before its submission as dissertation. My thanks are also due to Professor Dr. Hans-Joachim Bischof, University of Bielefeld for his interest and help extended during the final stages of editing.

A special thanks to Professor Dr. Michael Wolter, Professor Dr. James D. G. Dunn, Professor Dr. Richard B. Hays and Professor Dr. Hermann Lichtenberger, the editors of the "Beihefte zur Zeitschrift für die Neutestamentliche Wissenschaft" (BZNW) for accepting this work for publication. I am indeed indebted to Dr. Claus-Jürgen Thornton of the Walter de Gruyter Verlag, Berlin, who demonstrated enduring patience, and provided the most sophisticated professional expertise, guidance and help in getting this work through the process of publication. I am grateful to the publishers Walter de Gruyter, Berlin for beautiful printing and making this work available to a wide readership.

I am indebted to my uncle, Professor Dr. John Sadananda, who not only guided my theological journey, but also has always been a pillar of strength and inspiration to me.

Without the total commitment and involvement of my wife Monika this project would not have become a reality. Our daughter Sthuthi showed a lot of understanding, and was a source of inspiration while preparing this work for publication.

This work is dedicated to the loving memory of my parents, James and Jessie Sadananda in whose parental love and care I got the first foretaste of God's self-emptying love.

"Now to God who by the power at work within us is able to accomplish abundantly far more than all we can ask or imagine, to God be glory in the church and in Christ Jesus to all generations, forever and ever."

Pentecost 2004 D. R. Sadananda
Mangalore, India

Contents

Acknowledgements VII

Chapter One: Introduction

1.1 The Quest 1
1.2 The Problem of the Theology of the New Testament 1
1.3 The Theological Re-Reading 2
1.4 Theology in Christological Captivity? 4
1.5 Travails of a Theological Quest — Compositional History
    of the Fourth Gospel 6
1.6 Theologising History — Historicity of the Fourth Gospel 9
1.7 Theological Re-Reading of the Fourth Gospel —
    Towards Understanding the Johannine Exegesis of God 11

Chapter Two: Is Jesus God?
Thomas' Confession in the Light of the Passion Narrative

2.1 Introduction 13
2.2 Thomas' Confession — "My Lord, My God" 14
2.3 Self-Giving Jesus — Composure and Sovereignty in the
    Midst of Betrayal and Arrest 19
2.4 Jesus — The Pascal Lamb 21
2.5 The Trial of Jesus — The Man, The King 30
2.6 Mission Completed — Jesus Heralds Victory Even in Death 37
2.7 That You may Believe — Jesus the Christ, the Son of God 39
2.8 Summary and Conclusions 43

Chapter Three: Theology in Conflict — Is Jesus Equal to God?
(John 5:17–30)

3.1 Introduction 45
3.2 Order of Chapters Five and Six 46
3.3 The Pericope 47

3.4	The Structure	48
3.5	The Context	51
3.6	Exegesis	52

    3.6.1 Verses 17–18: Overture—Is Jesus Equal to God? 52
    3.6.2 Verses 19–30: The Father and the Son—
    Relationship Explained 59
        3.6.2.1 Verses 19–20: Theological Introduction—
        The Father's Self-Emptying in the Son and the
        Absolute Dependence of the Son upon the Father 59
        3.6.2.2 Verses 21–22: The Father's Self-Emptying—Basis
        of the Son's Authority to Give Life and to Judge 64
        3.6.2.3 Verse 23: Theological Reflection—The Honour Due
        the Son because of his Relationship with the Father 67
        3.6.2.4 Verses 24–25: The Son as Life-Giver and Judge—
        Eternal Life and Judgement as the Present Reality 69
        3.6.2.5 Verse 26: The Son has Life in Himself 70
        3.6.2.6 Verse 27: The Son's Authority to Judge
        as the Son of Man 71
        3.6.2.7 Verses 28–29: The Open Eschatology—
        The Son as Judge with Life-Giving as a Sub-Theme 74
        3.6.2.8 Verse 30: Theological Conclusion—
        The Absolute Dependence of the Son on the Father 79

3.7 Summary and Conclusions 79

Chapter Four: Theology in Conflict—Is Jesus Pre-existent? (John 8:12–59)

4.1	The Literary Structure	81
4.2	The Context	83
4.3	Exegesis	84

    4.3.1 Verses 12–20: Jesus the Light of the World—
    the Authority of Jesus' Witness 84
    4.3.2 Verses 21–30: Jesus the One from Above—
    The Origin of Jesus' Authority 89
        4.3.2.1 Verses 21–22: Jesus' going away—Jesus is sought 89
        4.3.2.2 Verse 23: Jesus is from above 90
        4.3.2.3 Verse 24: Belief in Jesus 91
        4.3.2.4 Verses 25–27: Jesus' Authority 92
        4.3.2.5 Verses 28–30: The revelation of the Son of man 94

Contents

- 4.3.3 Verses 31–34: Truth and Liberation 98
  - 4.3.3.1 Remaining in the Word 98
  - 4.3.3.2 Truth 99
  - 4.3.3.3 Freedom 103
- 4.3.4 Verses 35–36: Operation Liberation 107
- 4.3.5 Verses 37–47: God's Party and the Devil's Party 107
- 4.3.6 Verses 48–59: Jesus the Pre-existent Son is the Revealer and Embodiment of Salvation 108
  - 4.3.6.1 Verses 48–50: Jewish Allegation—Jesus a Samaritan, and Possessed 108
  - 4.3.6.2 Verses 51–55: Is Jesus greater than Abraham? 110
  - 4.3.6.3 Verses 56–57: Abraham's Joy to see the Day of Salvation 111
  - 4.3.6.4 Verses 58–59: Pre-existence of God's Universal Salvific Purpose 113
- 4.4 Summary and Conclusions 116

Chapter Five: Theology in Conflict—Are Jesus and the Father One? (John 10:22–39)

- 5.1 The Context 117
- 5.2 The Structure 117
- 5.3 Exegesis 118
  - 5.3.1 Verses 22–30: Oneness of the Father and the Son 118
    - 5.3.1.1 Verses 22–24: The Question 118
    - 5.3.1.2 Verses 24–30: The Claim 119
  - 5.3.2 Verses 31–39: Mutual In-dwelling of the Father and the Son 123
    - 5.3.2.1 Verses 31–33: The Jewish Anger 123
    - 5.3.2.2 Verses 34–36: Johannine Appeal to the Scripture 123
    - 5.3.2.3 Verses 37–39: The Second Claim 130
- 5.4 Summary and Conclusions 130

Chapter Six: The God of the Johannine Jesus: Characterisation of God in the Prayer of Jesus (John 17:1–26)

- 6.1 Introduction 133

Contents

- 6.2 Exegesis 134
  - 6.2.1 Verses 1–5: The True God 134
  - 6.2.2 Verses 6–10: The God who gives identity 139
  - 6.2.3 Verses 11–15: The God who protects 141
  - 6.2.4 Verses 16–19: The God who sanctifies 143
  - 6.2.5 Verses 20–23: The God who unites 145
  - 6.2.6 Verses 23b–26: The God who loves 148
- 6.3 Summary and Conclusions 149

Chapter Seven: Incarnate Logos as Historical Theophany (John 1:1–18)

- 7.1 Integrity of the Prologue 151
  - 7.1.1 In Search of a pre-Johannine Hymn 151
  - 7.1.2 The Prologue is a Unity 157
  - 7.1.3 Analysis 161
  - 7.1.4 A Possible Solution 163
- 7.2 The Logos—A Search for a Mythological Context 163
  - 7.2.1 The Origin 164
  - 7.2.2 Old Testament Wisdom Tradition? 164
  - 7.2.3 Philonic Exegesis of the Old Testament? 166
  - 7.2.4 Targumic Traditions? 167
  - 7.2.5 Gnosticism? 167
  - 7.2.6 Analysis 170
- 7.3 Exegesis 173
  - 7.3.1 Verses 1–2: The Logos and God 173
  - 7.3.2 Verses 3–5: The Logos and the World 180
  - 7.3.3 Verses 6–8: Witness to and Interpreter of God's Acts in the World—God's Human Instrument 'the Man' John 186
  - 7.3.4 Verses 9–13: God's A-historical Presence and Covenant with the World through the Logos 187
  - 7.3.5 Verses 14–18: The Incarnation and the Exegesis of God— a Historical Theophany 194
- 7.4 Summary and Conclusions 215

Chapter 8: Theology in Dialogue—Dialogue with the Considerate Jews (John 3:1–21)

- 8.1 Introduction 219

8.2 Exegesis 221
   8.2.1 Verses 3–6: God Creates a New Eschatological Community .. 221
   8.2.2 Verses 7–8: A New Community — The Sign of
         God's Freedom to Act 225
   8.2.3 Verses 9–15: Jesus — The Normative Determinant
         to Understand God's Action 226
   8.2.4 Verses 16–17: Jesus — The Metaphor of the
         Self-emptying God 227
   8.2.5 Verses 18–21: Only a Self-emptying Community
         Can Represent a Self-emptying God 229
8.3 Summary and Conclusions 230

Chapter Nine: Theology in Dialogue — Dialogue with the Samaritans (John 4:1–42)

9.1 Introduction 231
9.2 Exegesis 233
   9.2.1 Verses 5–6: The Place of the Dialogue 233
   9.2.2 Verses 7–15: Dialogue on God's Gift
         which Transcends all Traditions 235
   9.2.3 Verses 16–26: Dialogue on God's Worship,
         the Centre of a New Tradition 238
   9.2.4 Verses 27–38: Dialogue on God's Will —
         The Basis of New Traditions 251
   9.2.5 Verses 39–42: The Dialogue's Ultimate Goal —
         Recognising the God-sent Saviour and
         Confessing the Saviour-hood of God 253
9.3 Summary and Conclusions 254

Chapter Ten: Revelation Continued — the Authentic Theology: The Paraclete and the Understanding of God

10.1 Composition of the Farewell Discourses 255
10.2 The Paraclete — God's Comforting and Challenging Presence 256
10.3 The Paraclete — Re-enactor of God's Revelation in
     Teaching and Remembering 260
10.4 God Creates the Possibility of 'Authentic Witness' in the Face
     of the World's Vicious Contempt through Paraclete 264

10.5 The Paraclete Creates a 'Mirror Model' of God's World 266
10.6 The Paraclete—the Sign of God's Revelation Continued 269
10.7 Summary and Conclusions 272

Chapter Eleven: Conclusion: Johannine Exegesis of God

11.1 The Characterisation of God in the Fourth Gospel 275
11.2 Johannine Theo-centric Christology 280
    11.2.1 Agent Christology 280
    11.2.2 Mediator Christology 281
    11.2.3 'I am' Christology 282
    11.2.4 Oneness Christology 284
11.3 Theological Hermeneutic 285
11.4 Whither Theo-logy? 288

Bibliography 293

Select Index of References 339

Index of Modern Authors 351

Chapter One

Introduction

1.1 The Quest

My fascination with the Fourth Gospel began when, as an undergraduate I ventured into evaluating the ecumenical discussion related to the theme of the World Council of Churches Vancouver Assembly, "Jesus Christ, the life of the world" in the light of the New Testament concept of life. Naturally I was lured by the Johannine concept of 'eternal life' which I contended to signify human participation in God's very life, in His very self. But two questions lingered: Does the Johannine concept of 'life' refer to the participation in God's Being or/and function? Does the Fourth Evangelist's God-language have something radically new to convey? Working on my Master's thesis on Johannine Sacramentalism, I came to the inference that Jesus Christ himself is the eternal sacrament of God, and in him symbol and reality merge. But the question regarding God-language still remained. I queried: Does the Fourth Evangelist write Christology or Theology?

1.2 The Problem of the Theology of the New Testament

After Nils Alstrup Dahl's provocative and seminal essay "The Neglected Factor in New Testament Theology"[1] Andreas Lindemann ponders over the probable reasons for the lack of interest among New Testament scholars in the New Testament idea of God:

a) The widely held popular view is that the God of the New Testament is the replica of the Old Testament understanding of God! Therefore for

---

1 N. A. Dahl, "The Neglected Factor in New Testament Theology," *Reflection* 73/1 (1975): 5–8.

the Biblical understanding of God one looks more into the Old Testament as if the New Testament language of God is only secondary.²
b) In evaluating the Theology of the early church, the Jesus movement, it is often taken for granted that the early converts' (e.g. Paul) fundamental commitment to one God did not alter when they embraced Jesus. Their basic Theology therefore remained intact whereas their Christology naturally underwent a sea change. From the viewpoint of interpreters of New Testament Theology the early Christians were perceived to have become more christocentric, though God did not disappear entirely. He was however pushed to a back seat. Early Christian communities did change their attitude towards God because of their Christology, but they did not evolve a new Theology, a new teaching about God.³
c) Interpreters had always known that the New Testament writings were written to people who were in a theistic world, to whom the existence of God was never in doubt. And they perceived that the New Testament writers have been found to have considered it unnecessary to explore the concept of God elaborately. For them Christology and soteriology, and therefore, ethics and Eschatology were of importance, not Theology.⁴

In New Testament writings the question whether God exists was a non issue. New Testament documents seem to have taken God quite for granted. The New Testament community did believe in God, it recognised the One in whom we live, move and are (Acts 17:28). The New Testament Christians believed that God is their environment and perhaps this unshakeable, unquestioning assurance was primarily responsible for their apparent neglect of explicit explorations on the concept of God, as we find often in the Old Testament.

1.3 The Theological Re-Reading

In response to the plea to re-evaluate New Testament Theology in its all important/deciding narrower sense, there came studies exploring especially

---

2 A. Lindemann, "Die Rede von Gott in der paulinischen Theologie," in *Paulus: Apostel und Lehrer der Kirche. Studien zu Paulus und zum frühen Paulus-Verständnis* (Tübingen: J. C. B. Mohr [Paul Siebeck]), 11.
3 *Ibid.*, 11–12.
4 *Ibid.*, 12–13.

the Theology of Paul in triple-pack through Halvor Moxnes' *Theology in Conflict: Studies in Paul's Understanding of God in Romans*, Paul-Gerhard Klumbies' *Die Rede von Gott bei Paulus in ihrem zeitgeschichtlichen Kontext* and Neil G. Richardson's *Paul's Language about God*. Recently Nicholas T. Wright has started an ambitious five-volume series on "Christian origin and the question of God."[5] Kurt Erlemann's *Das Bild Gottes in den synoptischen Gleichnissen* and Douglas W. Kennard's *The Doctrine of God in Petrine Theology* are, to mention just two, notable monographs apart from a number of articles that explore the understanding of God outside the Pauline corpus.

Since Rudolf Bultmann, Johannine interpretation has moved in the direction of Christology. Hans Conzelmann opens his discussion on Johannine Christology, remarking that it could be said that the whole of Johannine Theology is Christology, though it could equally well be argued that it is soteriology or anthropology.[6] According to Ernst Käsemann epiphany Christology marks the pivotal point of Johannine Theology. The Christology of the Fourth Evangelist reaches the summit to point to a 'God who walks on the earth' whereby Käsemann contends that Johannine Christology itself becomes Theology.[7]

C. Kingsley Barrett, through two very lively essays, has tried to balance the christological discussion in the Fourth Gospel;[8] David A. Fennema[9] and Jerome H. Neyrey's socio-scientific criticism of the Fourth Gospel[10] end up proclaiming Jesus as God! However, venturing through new criticism, namely in literary criticism Gail R. O'Day[11] makes an attempt to counter Bultmann's dictum on the Fourth Gospel: 'Jesus as revealer of God reveals

---

5   N. T. Wright, *The New Testament and the People of God* (London: S.P.C.K., 1992).
6   H. Conzelmann, *Grundriß der Theologie des Neuen Testaments* (6th ed., rev. by A. Lindemann; Tübingen: J. C. B. Mohr [Paul Siebeck], 1997), 373.
7   E. Käsemann, *The Testament of Jesus: A Study of the Gospel of John in the Light of Chapter 17* (trans. G. Krodel; NTL; London: SCM, 1968).
8   C. K. Barrett, "'The Father is Greater than I' (Jn 14:28): Subordinationist Christology in the New Testament," in *Neues Testament und Kirche: Für Rudolf Schnackenburg* (ed. J. Gnilka; Freiburg/Basel: Herder, 1974), 144–59, and his "Christocentric or Theocentric? Observations on the Theological Method of the Fourth Gospel," in *Essays on John* (Philadelphia: Westminster, 1982), 1–18.
9   D. A. Fennema, *Jesus and God according to John: An Analysis of the Fourth Gospel's Father/Son Christology* (Diss. Duke University, Durham, N. C., 1979).
10 J. H. Neyrey, *An Ideology of Revolt: John's Christology in Social-Science Perspective* (Philadelphia: Fortress, 1988).
11 G. R. O'Day, *Revelation in the Fourth Gospel: Narrative Mode and Theological Claim* (Philadelphia: Fortress, 1986).

nothing, but that he is the revealer and that the Evangelist in his Gospel presents only the fact (*das Daß*) of revelation without describing its content (*ihr Was*).' In O'Day's opinion, not *"Was"* but *"Wie"* is the right question that has to be asked to the text. Affirming rightly that the narrative creates and communicates revelation, and that the locus of revelation lies in the biblical text and in the world created by the words of the text, she however comes to the thesis that the narrative itself is revelation! Finally we are not left with anything more than what Bultmann has already pointed to: a narrative and a Jesus—the revealer, as O'Day asks the reader to imbibe the revelation of Jesus through imaginative participation in the text.

Marianne M. Thompson's "God's Voice You Have Never Heard, God's Form You Have Never Seen: The Characterization of God in the Gospel of John"[12] is the only direct article published on the theme. Using Robert Alter's scale of characterisation, she analyses the Gospel narrative from the categories: actions of God, appearance, comment by other characters, direct speech, inward speech, and commentary of the narrator, to arrive at the conclusion that God is characterised as the One known through Jesus. But she queries in her conclusion: "if God makes no appearances how is any one to 'see' God at all?" Jesus reproves his audience: "you have never heard God's voice." And she complains: "However if God but seldom speaks, how are they to hear?" And the situation seems to be much the same for the reader. There is no dramatic description of the opening of the heavens, no vision of God, no theophany and only one instance of God speaking. What seems to characterise the plight of Jesus' audience applies to the reader as well. "God's voice you have never heard; God's form you have never seen, or, have you?" Bultmann's dictum seems to stand firm, the revealer reveals nothing, but that he is the revealer!

1.4 Theology in Christological Captivity?

Bultmann's opinion of 'God language' was very strikingly straightforward: "Es zeigt sich also: will man von Gott reden, so muß man offenbar von sich

---

12 M. M. Thompson, "God's Voice You Have Never Heard, God's Form You Have Never Seen: The Characterization of God in the Gospel of John," *Semeia* 63 (1993): 177–204.

selbst reden."[13] Although Bultmann insisted on theological anthropology, that God and man ought to always be spoken of/held together, the outcome of his Theology was a rather unilateral concentration on 'man.' Moxnes' criticism is credible. New Testament writers do not speak about 'man' in general, but speak of people, 'God's elected people' in a certain span and specific time.[14] Indeed in the New Testament the interaction of the people of God with the 'other people,' their cultural/socio-political interaction, and their experience with people, with or without God, create and develop the God-language.

Especially in the last few decades, since the Christian community has learnt to take its neighbours of faith seriously, inter-religious dialogue has opened our eyes to the bare fact that the 'Theology' stands close beside in our every interaction with our neighbours of other faiths. The language used, the very attitudes, exclusive/inclusive rhetoric not only create, but portray who our God is! "Love your neighbour" becomes the revelation command as it shows explicitly which God you belong to.

Moreover the christocentric approach to the New Testament and the exported christocentric theological system of the West have proclaimed 'God Jesus' in the religiously pluralistic societies. Thus the young missionary churches have (mis)understood the two nature doctrine or the teaching of Trinity, giving way to a Christo-theological system. In becoming increasingly christocentric the church has pushed itself to the verge of (indeed) christomonism! In the dialogue situations with the neighbours of our faith we strive for a christological approach instead of a theocentrical one, with the fear of failing to uphold the uniqueness of Jesus, we in fact shy away from speaking of the unique God. Today *God* has become a captive of Christology. To liberate God from the church's christological captivity, in fact to liberate our language of God, the time has come to re-read, to re-hear the New Testament witnesses in their struggle to liberate the God-language from Judaism's racial/political Theology. In the Old Testament the question of God was distinctly socio-political. Their belief in God gave Israel its social, religious and political identity. Their God-language did dictate and mould Israel's relationship with its neighbours.

The Fourth Gospel in fact reflects a sociological/theological struggle of a community for an authentic theological identity. It shows how the

---

13 R. Bultmann, "Welchen Sinn hat es, von Gott zu reden?," in *Glauben und Verstehen: Gesammelte Aufsätze*, vol. I (9th ed.; Tübingen: J. C. B. Mohr [Paul Siebeck], 1993), 28.

14 H. Moxnes, *Theology in Conflict: Studies in Paul's Understanding of God in Romans* (NovTSup 53; Leiden: E. J. Brill, 1980), 5.

community was involved in a tense, but rather creative theological debate not only with its neighbours of faith (inter-community), but also among its members (intra-community), among those who wished its demise, and those who wished to give it a gracious hearing. It reflects the attempts of a community's struggle towards formulating a Christology that is both credible, and faithful to its Theology

1.5 Travails of a Theological Quest — Compositional History of the Fourth Gospel

Wayne A. Meeks believes that in the Fourth Gospel we encounter a theological/ sociological struggle of a small group of believers isolated over against 'the world' that belongs intrinsically to the below, identifying with the man from heaven. The myth 'the man' functions both as a challenge and vindication of its theo-logical existence, as the group separated itself/was forced out from the social reality into an exclusive and totalistic community. Meeks opinions that the development of a language and a set of symbols peculiar to itself reinforced its exclusive outlook.[15] The question one should ask then is: does the theo-logical quest lead to isolation? Or did the fact that it was a sociological minority consciously force the community to loose its theological direction, to become christocentric thereby marginalising it to society's periphery and finally to its break-up?

D. Moody Smith too detects the sense of exclusiveness and a sharp delineation of the community from the world.[16] R. Alan Culpepper seeks to understand the Johannine community in terms of a 'school' and the Gospel as a 'letter,' a product of study, teaching, interpretation, and writing. He argues that the synagogal opposition spurred the study of the Scriptures and the interpretation of the traditions about Jesus in the Johannine community were for use against the Jews. Thus the 'school' developed a sectarian conscience.[17]

---

15 W. A. Meeks, "The Man from Heaven in Johannine Sectarianism," in *The Interpretation of John* (ed. J. Ashton; Philadelphia: Fortress, 1986), 141–73.
16 D. M. Smith, *Johannine Christianity: Essays on its Setting, Sources, and Theology* (Columbia, S. C.: University of South Carolina Press, 1984), 1–36 — an essay originally published in a shorter form in *NTS* 21 (1976): 222–48 under the title "Johannine Christianity. Some Reflections on its Character and Delineation."
17 R. A. Culpepper, *The Johannine School: An Evaluation of the Johannine-School Hypothesis Based on an Investigation of the Nature of Ancient Schools* (SBLDS 26; Missoula,

The studies of Smith and Culpepper portray the dangers of a theological enterprise if undertaken to be exclusive. Was the sectarian consciousness that the scholars point out, a product of exclusive Christology? Could it be possible to detect the community undertaking a theological correction in the Gospel to save what was to be saved, or to arrange a co-existence of christocentric exclusivists and theocentric universalists?

Among numerous composition theories[18] J. Louis Martyn,[19] Georg Richter[20] and Marie-Émile Boismard[21] make the Theology of the community a deciding factor, as the Gospel came into existence[22] after much editorial and redactional work.

Mont.: Scholars Press, 1975). In his dissertation he discusses and compares Johannine activity with other schools.

18 See W. Wilkens, *Die Entstehungsgeschichte des vierten Evangeliums* (Zollikon: Evangelischer Verlag, 1958), esp. 92–122, 127–64, 171–74; W. Langbrandtner, *Weltferner Gott oder Gott der Liebe: Der Ketzerstreit in der johanneischen Kirche; eine exegetisch-religionsgeschichtliche Untersuchung mit Berücksichtigung der koptisch-gnostischen Texte aus Nag-Hammadi* (BBET 6; Frankfurt am Main: Peter Lang, 1977); R. E. Brown, *The Gospel according to John* (2 vols.; AB 29.29A; Garden City, N. Y.: Doubleday, 1966–1970), 1:xxiv–xxxix; B. Lindars, *Behind the Fourth Gospel* (London: S.P.C.K., 1971), chapters 2 and 3, esp. 13–18, 38–78, and his *The Gospel of John* (NCB; London: Oliphants, 1972), 46–54; W. Schmithals, *Johannesevangelium und Johannesbriefe* (BZNW 64; Berlin and New York: de Gruyter, 1992).

19 See J. L. Martyn, "Glimpses into the History of the Johannine Community. From its Origin through the Period of its Life in which the Fourth Gospel was Composed," in *L'Évangile de Jean* (ed. M. de Jonge; BETL 44; Leuven: University Press, 1977), 149–75, and his *History and Theology in the Fourth Gospel* (2nd ed.; Nashville: Abingdon, 1979).

20 Georg Richter, "Präsentische und futurische Eschatologie im 4. Evangelium," in *Gegenwart und kommendes Reich: Schülergabe Anton Vögtle zum 65. Geburtstag* (ed. P. Fiedler & D. Zeller; SBB 6; Stuttgart: Katholisches Bibelwerk, 1975), 117–52. For an English summary and evaluation see A. J. Mattill Jr., "Johannine Communities Behind the Fourth Gospel: Georg Richter's Analysis," *TS* 38 (1977): 294–315.

21 I could not read M.-É. Boismard's *L'Évangile de Jean* (Paris: Cerf, 1977) for want of French knowledge, but could read a summary of his theory in R. E. Brown's *The Community of the Beloved Disciple* (New York: Paulist Press, 1979), 178–79, and read the English translation of *"The Evaluation of Christology"* in his *Moses or Jesus: An Essay in Johannine Christology* (trans. B. T. Viviano; Minneapolis: Fortress, and Leuven: Peeters, 1993), 127–33. See also J. Ashton, *Understanding the Fourth Gospel* (Oxford: Clarendon, 1991), 82–86.

22 K. Wengst in *Bedrängte Gemeinde und verherrlichter Christus* (3rd ed.; Munich: Kaiser, 1990) also argues for a dialectic between the life and struggles of a community and its theological reflections.

For Martyn 'the christological-theological debate with the Jewish Synagogue' plays the decisive role, as the Gospel refers to the community's theological perspective! Richter detects the tension between the proponents of 'low Christology' and 'high Christology' within the community, and the Gospel for him in its finished form is the work of a monotheistic mediator, a theologian! Boismard sees the implication of the Son–Logos–Preexistent Christology in the Theology of the community. The final redaction for him reflects the community's attempt to react to the apparent dangers of theologising Jesus as God and its theo-logical consequence.

Though Martyn's hypothesis is of profound value to Johannine research, his limiting of the Johannine community to Jewish Christians, and interpreting the Gospel Theology in the light of the Synagogue excommunication limits the effects of the hypothesis. Richter, ascribing the christological developments to 'inner community theologising dynamic,' and Boismard, transporting the final publication of the Gospel to Ephesus, thereby indicating a geographical shift to a sociological environment from an original Jewish background and a more primitive Christology to a Gentile setting and a higher Christology, are the strong points of the respective hypotheses.

Four issues stand out relevant for our discussion:

a) The Fourth Gospel is a product of a long theological quest of a complex Johannine community.

b) The Theology of the community did not have a uniform coded structure! The community allowed 'theological freedom' (a sect will/could not have). The theological discussions basically motivated and catalysed the creative interaction between the basic community and new entrants (Samaritans? Hellenists?).

c) The Theology of the community needed corrections, explanations and interpretations, as the christological evaluation catalysed theological tension within and without that are closely associated with identity issues and the community's environment.

d) Negatively the Fourth Gospel is an example of how contextual theologies, if we do not consider their theo-logical implications, could make/break communities. The Fourth Gospel is an example for the instance of how exclusive christology if not held within the universal parenthood of God could send destructive ripples and distort peace in the wider society.

1.6 Theologising History—Historicity of the Fourth Gospel

The genius of the Fourth Evangelist is well attested by the way he creatively shapes his narrative Theology, his Gospel. In the Fourth Gospel we encounter a Johannine Jesus speaking Johannine language. The community's faith expression finds authenticity in Jesus' words. Martyn has interpreted the Fourth Gospel as a two-level drama—on the primary level it expresses the bits of Christian traditions concerning the historical life of Jesus of Nazareth. This provides a backdrop for the secondary level which expresses in slightly disguised fashion the contextual situation of the Evangelist. In such a situation the Fourth Gospel is a complex intermingling of two time periods and historical situations. Jesus is at once the traditional Jesus of the Christian community's heritage and the contemporary Johannine missionary. The opponents of Jesus are at once both Jewish leaders of Palestine in the early 1st century, contemporary to the historical Jesus, and Jewish protagonists of the Evangelist's own day. Martyn finds in the Fourth Gospel a dynamic, creative, contextual theological interpretation of the Jesus tradition by the Johannine community.[23]

As a document of faith views history from the perspective of faith, the history that the Fourth Gospel presents is included in the history of suprahistorical faith. The scholarly world today increasingly agrees that there is little actual history in the Fourth Gospel. The new quest for the historical Jesus completely neglects Johannine presentation from consideration. Even attempts to find the sources behind the Fourth Gospel are now limited to the 'Sign Source' theory.[24] There is, however, a renewed interest in searching for 'Synoptic' parallels, although Percival Gardner-Smith, R. Bultmann and Charles Harold Dodd have long back declared the Fourth Gospel's indepen-

---

23 J. L. Martyn, *History and Theology in the Fourth Gospel*. Cf. C. L. Blomberg, *The Historical Reliability of John's Gospel: Issues and Commentary* (Leicester: Apollos, 2001).
24 See R. T. Fortna, *The Fourth Gospel and its Predecessor: From Narrative Source to Present Gospel* (Philadelphia: Fortress, 1988); W. Nicol, *The Semeia in the Fourth Gospel: Tradition and Redaction* (NovTSup 32; Leiden: E. J. Brill, 1972); U. C. von Wahlde, *The Earliest Version of John's Gospel: Recovering the Gospel of Signs* (Wilmington, Del.: Michael Glazier, 1989); R. Bultmann, *Das Evangelium des Johannes* (21st ed.; KEK 2; Göttingen: Vandenhoeck & Ruprecht, 1986); J. Becker, *Das Evangelium nach Johannes* (2 vols.; 3rd ed.; ÖTK 4/1–2; Gütersloh: Mohn, 1991); R. Schnackenburg, *The Gospel according to St. John* (trans. C. Hastings, et al.; 3 vols.; London: Burns and Oates, 1968–1980).

dence of the Synoptics. The Leuven School led by Frans Neirynck defends the position that the Fourth Evangelist knew, and was dependent on the three Synoptic Gospels.[25] Gardner-Smith is inclined to propose that the Fourth Evangelist must have been dependent on the Synoptic Gospels at least for its genre, particularly as it relates to the origin of the Gospels.[26] These on the other hand point out the Johannine drawing from early Christian heritage, but reworking it to contextualise the Jesus tradition for his community, thereby rendering the identity of 'source' affiliation beyond recognition.

The Fourth Evangelist uses his own creative hermeneutic. To be effective he needs to receive tradition and interpret it, in the process of which the time and horizon of the event, and interpretation merge. The Fourth Evangelist builds bridges between the time intervals and the distant horizons through the mode of symbols, teaching and remembering. When such an interpretive bridge is built, and time and horizon are merged, the past is not annulled but actualised for the present! The past is present and preserved in its entirety to make a past event a present reality, whereby the historical Jesus becomes visible in the kerygma of the community.

The Johannine Jesus, the proclaimer himself becomes the proclaimed. He steps out of mere historicity and addresses the community of the Evangelist in person. For the Fourth Gospel kerygma Jesus thus ceases to be a figure of the past, or even a past figure whose influence has extended into the present, but becomes a present reality. Here the Fourth Gospel uses history not as a means of confining Jesus within the set limits of his historical life, but makes it serve as an anchor for the factual reality of God's self-revelation within history. Thereby the Fourth Evangelist theologises history to interpret the breaking-in of God's eschaton!

---

25 See F. Neirynck, "John and the Synoptics," in *L'Évangile de Jean* (ed. M. de Jonge; BETL 44; Leuven: University Press, 1977), 73–106, and for a survey of the Fourth Gospel and the Synoptics see D. M. Smith, *John among the Gospels: The Relationship in Twentieth-Century Research* (2nd ed.; Columbia, S. C.: University of South Carolina Press, 2001).

26 P. Gardner-Smith, *St. John and the Synoptic Gospels* (Cambridge: Cambridge University Press, 1938).

1.7 Theological Re-Reading of the Fourth Gospel—Towards Understanding the Johannine Exegesis of God

To attempt the 'characterisation of God' in the Fourth Gospel, the study of the titles used for God such as ὁ πατήρ or ὁ θεός reduce God to abstract ideas and categories to say God is love, light, truth. It is not in the title or in the abstract categories, but in the text context that theological thinking enfolds and is expressed. The text context is not merely a linguistic one, it reflects the socio-cultural context. By way of exploring human experience, and understanding the concrete community context which created the 'text contexts,' we encounter not only in the explicit theological language, but also in silent implicit symbols, 'the God' of the community—the Johannine exegesis of God!

We approach the Johannine text context in order to explore the Johannine understanding of God with the following questions:
a) How does the Fourth Evangelist characterise God? What language does he use to characterise God? What is the relationship of his christological language to his God-language? What kind of interaction is seen between Christology and Theology in the Fourth Gospel?
b) Does the Johannine God-language benefit from, get enriched and enlarged through its dialogue/conflict with its pluralistic environment?
c) Is the Evangelist theocentric or christocentric? How does he expect us to approach and interpret his Gospel narrative?
d) What are the implications of Theology in the community's identity, existence, authority and legitimacy in its struggle for identity and existence?

In attempting an exegesis of God in the Fourth Gospel, one should clarify at the outset the all important christological question who Jesus is. Is Jesus God as reflected in Thomas' confession of the resurrected Jesus? We begin our exegetical exploration into the Theology of the Fourth Gospel with a close scrutiny of the Johannine passion narrative and indeed its Christology as to find the key to interpret Thomas' 'My Lord, my God.' Here we begin to perceive Johannine christological language and God-language interacting to elucidate each other, and are naturally confronted with the question of the relationship of 'the man' Jesus to God. The Fourth Gospel revels in the discussion of the relationship of God to 'the man' Jesus, in whom the community has seen God's mighty acts and the sign of the resurrection, and depicts the relationship by means of a distinctively Johannine Father–Son imagery.

Exactly at this point begins the community's theological conflict with the Synagogue. The Johannine Theology gets new interpretation in the conflict context. We concentrate our energies to attempt to understand the community's theological answer to the questions that the synagogue hurled at it—Is Jesus equal to God? Is Jesus pre-existent? Are the Father and Jesus one? The Evangelist tries his ultimate to inform the reader, as he portrays the departing Jesus praying to his Father that Jesus is theocentric. Here we have tried to emulate the narrative exegesis in order to allow the farewell prayer itself to open up before the reader the Johannine Jesus' characterisation of God.

The Prologue of the Fourth Gospel is the summit of theo-logical language! Our theological exegesis of it is an attempt to understand the Fourth Gospel's presentation of the incarnate Logos as the historical Theophany, where the original christological hymn has been tuned into an editorial masterpiece to dictate the Gospel's perspective, that Christology is the exegesis of Theology. Isolated and sidelined in spite of its efforts to clarify its Theology in its conflict with the Synagogue, the Johannine community now has no option but to assert itself.

Socially isolated, yet enriched in its theological insights, the community enters into a creative dialogue with considerate Jews and the Samaritans to clarify how its Theology envisages its role with those who stand outside the community. Our exegetical interpretation attempts to identify the dialogue dynamics of a theological conversation between those who do not share the same theological affirmations. The Johannine community's dialogue with its neighbours did create/bring into the fore-front questions regarding legitimacy and authority to decide, the community's understanding of how God authenticates its witness, and how the community can perceive the authenticity of God's continual revelation. Our re-reading of the Paraclete passages is an attempt to understand the community's theological construct, the Paraclete that lent authenticity and legitimacy to the community's theological endeavours and made its theological language clear and precise.

Chapter Two

Is Jesus God?

Thomas' Confession in the Light of the Passion Narrative

2.1 Introduction

Thomas' confession of Jesus "my Lord, my God" is considered to be the christological summit of New Testament Theology. In the whole of the New Testament writings it is unique, as nowhere but here Jesus is referred to explicitly as God! Generations of theologians who naturally read the Fourth Gospel from the perspective of the Trinitarian Doctrine, a later theological development in the history of the church, interpret Thomas' confession either as a confirmation of, or the seed of the Trinitarian understanding of God! Normally, since the narrative block explaining the appearance of the risen Jesus to the disciples with Thomas stands at the very end of the Fourth Gospel (chapter 21 being a later addition) interpreters intensively argue that Thomas' confession of Jesus holds the key required to interpret and understand Johannine Christology.

Without undermining the confessional character of Thomas' "My Lord, my God" one ought to risk an enquiry into the impact of such a faith affirmation on the Theology of the Johannine community. What did this narrative tradition actually intend to convey? Did it represent the 'theological perspective of a cross section of the community' in tension with the overall christological affirmations of the community? How did the community accommodate this narrative tradition in its evolving theological system? Did the community allow the whole of its Theology to be interpreted in terms of it? Or did it find the necessity to interpret Thomas' confession in terms of the community's Theology, especially in view of its distinctive Theology of the passion and resurrection of Jesus?

The Thomas pericope has no Synoptic parallel. It may be that the Thomas episode was either a Johannine construct, or an independent tradition floating in the Johannine community. It makes use of the 'doubt motif' reported in the Synoptic narratives (cf. Matt 28:17; Luke 24:11, 21ff., 37–38,

41) and the physical demonstration of the risen Jesus to overcome the doubt of the disciples (Luke 24:39–41). Nevertheless it builds upon the distinctly Johannine introduction of the Thomas persona in John 14:16 and 14:5, and refers to the characteristically Johannine pierced πλευρά of Jesus (19:34a). And most interestingly, the Thomas pericope in attempting a logical development from v. 23 excludes Thomas from the scene of the bestowal of the Spirit upon the disciples reported in vv. 19–23. But as such the passage with vv. 19–23 presupposes the presence of all disciples, and scarcely foresees the absence of a disciple, as the bestowal of the Spirit and granting of authority to forgive sins, applies to them as a whole. Used independently the pericope must have been making certain theological overtones in the community.

2.2 Thomas' Confession—"My Lord, My God"

Thomas' "unless I see" (v. 25) has always been interpreted as doubt and perhaps too easily characterised as moral failure on the disciple's part. Herbert Kohler suggests that Thomas had a very legitimate doubt, as he does not doubt the report of his brothers that they had seen the Lord, but in his mind their seeing is not unequivocal, and he would believe if the risen one were clearly identifiable with the crucified Jesus. In Kohler's view, by dramatising the theme of doubt in the character of Thomas, the Evangelist wants to point out the danger of that faith which can too quickly attach itself to the risen one, and thus exchange the powerlessness of the crucified for the omnipotence of the exalted victor over death, since that faith appears more drawn to the all powerful God than to the powerless crucified.[1]

The Evangelist's particular mention of Jesus' invitation to touch him, especially the wounds on his hands and the spear-pierced side (probably healed marks, not open wounds!) is to make clear to the reader that the manifesting risen Jesus is the crucified one himself. The basis of Kohler's observation lies probably in his taking for granted that the risen one is revered as 'God.' The critical narrative reading of the text plainly says Thomas had not believed the very fact of the resurrection! Note his emphatic οὐ μὴ πιστεύσω. Therefore, when the risen Jesus comes and stands in the

---

[1] H. Kohler, *Kreuz und Menschwerdung im Johannesevangelium: Ein exegetisch-hermeneutischer Versuch zur johanneischen Kreuzestheologie* (ATANT 72; Zurich: Theologischer Verlag, 1987), 175ff.

midst of his disciples greeting them Shalom and asking Thomas φέρε τὸν δάκτυλόν σου ὧδε, καὶ ἴδε τὰς χεῖράς μου καὶ φέρε τὴν χεῖρά σου καὶ βάλε εἰς τὴν πλευράν μου, καὶ μὴ γίνου ἄπιστος ἀλλὰ πιστός he does not venture into tangible verification, but immediately believes in the resurrection of Jesus. He becomes ecstatic, and spontaneously confesses—ὁ κύριός μου καὶ ὁ θεός μου.

Some possible interpretive helps to understand the Thomas confession are the following:

a) The collocation of κύριος and θεός appears in Gentile literature, among other sources in an Egyptian inscription of the year 24 B.C. which speaks of τῷ θεῷ καὶ κυρίῳ Σοκνοπαίῳ. In the Caesar cult, "*Dominus et deus noster*" was well known to have been an imperial title much affected by Domitian (Suetonius, *Domitian* 13) in A.D. 81–96. It has been suggested that the Fourth Gospel used these for Jesus in order to repudiate the emperor cult.[2]

b) Raymond Brown discerns in Thomas' words a combination of a covenantal confession ("you are my God"—Hos 2:25) and a baptismal profession/confession of faith—Jesus is the Lord.[3] John Suggit drafts a liturgical scene in John 20:19–29 as follows: the gathering of the believers on the first day of the week, the Lord's day (vv. 19, 26), the presence of Christ (vv. 19, 26), the blessing (vv. 19, 21, 26), the coming of the Spirit (v. 22), the absolution (v. 23), the confession of faith (v. 28) and the benediction (v. 29).[4] In his opinion "my Lord, my God" is the liturgical response of a worshipping community to Jesus who confronts and challenges them to recognise him in the Word. C. K. Barrett thinks the Thomas confession might have had a liturgical origin, or at least setting, whereas the common assumption is that the veneration of Jesus as κύριος in a worship context led to the expression of belief in the Deity of Christ in the early church.[5] C. H. Dodd observes that in Thomas' confession we have the Johannine community's struggle to express the

---

2 See R. Bultmann, *Das Evangelium des Johannes*, 538; C. K. Barrett, *The Gospel according to St. John: An Introduction with Commentary and Notes on the Greek Text* (2nd ed.; London: S.P.C.K., 1978), 573, and G. R. Beasley-Murray, *John* (WBC 36; Waco, Tex.: Word Books, 1987), 391.
3 See R. E. Brown, *The Gospel according to John*, 2:1047–48.
4 See J. Suggit, *The Sign of Life: Studies in the Fourth Gospel and the Liturgy of the Church* (Pietermaritzburg, South Africa: Cluster Publications, 1993), 150–57.
5 See C. K. Barrett, op. cit., 573.

identification of the historical Jesus ὁ κύριός μου with the incarnate Logos, the risen Christ ὁ θεός μου.[6]

c) The Septuagint frequently renders יְהוָה אֱלֹהִים as κύριος ὁ θεός. This combination usually occurs in worship, prayer, confession contexts— κύριε ὁ θεός (3 times),[7] κύριε ὁ θεός μου (20 times),[8] κύριε ὁ θεὸς ἡμῶν (14 times),[9] κύριος ὁ θεός σου (once),[10] also frequent are expressions of κύριος ὁ θεός μου,[11] and κύριος ὁ θεὸς ἡμῶν,[12] and those instances where σύ[13] or σὺ εἶ or εἶ σύ[14] accompanies a phrase such as θεός μου or κύριος ὁ θεός ἡμῶν. The closest Septuagint parallel is Ps 34:23—ὁ θεός μου καὶ ὁ κύριός μου. The inverted order in the Fourth Gospel may be due to the frequency of κύριε ὁ θεός μου in the Septuagint. Another close parallel is Ps 5:3, which has the vocational ὁ βασιλεύς μου καὶ ὁ θεός μου. If we closely examine Ps 34:23 in the Septuagint rendering—ἐξεγέρθητι, κύριε, καὶ πρόσχες τῇ κρίσει μου, ὁ θεός μου καὶ ὁ κύριός μου, εἰς τὴν δίκην μου, we see that it has not translated the second verb very accurately. It means 'awake' rather than 'attend' (the word is הָקִיצָה). If the phrase that Thomas uses was originally used in the Aramaic speaking community, this might have led some Christians to see a prophecy here, the call to arise and awake fit very well in a post-resurrection situation. Moreover the Psalm ends on a joyful note (v. 27c, d: Μεγαλυνθήτω ὁ κύριος οἱ θέλοντες τὴν εἰρήνην τοῦ δούλου αὐτοῦ). The word 'Shalom' (שָׁלוֹם) is rendered in the Septuagint with εἰρήνη, the word which Jesus uses to greet his disciples.[15]

---

6 See C. H. Dodd, *Interpretation of the Fourth Gospel* (Cambridge: Cambridge University Press, 1953), 430–31.
7 Ps 9:33; 85:15; 87:2.
8 2 Kgdms (2 Sam) 15:31; 3 Kgdms (1 Kgs) 17:21; Est 4:17; Tobit 3:11; Ps 7:2, 4, 7; 9:33; 12:4; 29:3, 13; 34:24; 37:16; 39:6; 85:12; 103:1; 108:26; Jonah 2:7; Hab 1:12; Isa 25:1.
9 4 Kgdms (2 Kgs) 19:19; 1 Chr 29:16; 2 Chr 14:10–11; 20:12; Ps 98:8; 105:47; Isa 26:12, 13; Bar 2:12, 19, 27; Dan 9:15, 17.
10 Ps 80:11.
11 Ps 143:1; Jer 38:18 among others.
12 2 Esd 9:9; Ps 98:9.
13 Jer 38:18; Bar 2:15; 3:6.
14 2 Macc 1:27; Ps 15:2; 96:9; 117:28; 139:7; 142:10; Hos 2:25; Isa 44:17; Jer 3:22.
15 See A. T. Hanson, *The Prophetic Gospel: A Study of John and the Old Testament* (Edinburgh: T&T Clark, 1991), 232ff.

Even then, interpreting ὁ κύριός μου καὶ ὁ θεός μου is not easy. Edwin Abbott suggested that it may be translated as "my Lord is *also my God.*"[16] According to him the omission of ἐστι might have been prompted by the Evangelist's desire to force his readers to think out the full import of the confession, while the emphatic καί (also) is frequent in the Fourth Gospel.[17] It may also be translated as an exclamation—and Thomas exclaimed, "My Lord and my God." It could be that Thomas was exclaiming and expressing his astonishment and wonder, and praising God for the sign of the resurrection of Jesus, meaning—"Praise be to my Lord and my God!"[18]

The most common translation is as addressed to Jesus: Thomas answered and said to him, "My lord and my God."[19] ἀπεκρίθη Θωμᾶς καὶ εἶπεν αὐτῷ implies a response to Jesus on the part of Thomas—'he spoke up.'[20] Given the context and presence of ἀπεκρίθη, αὐτῷ indicates that Thomas is reacting to Jesus' invitation in v. 27. As far as ὁ κύριος is concerned, although the pre-Christian Papyri seem to lack the instance of this *'enallage'* of case,[21] the articular nominative of address is an established New Testament usage.[22] It

---

16 See E. A. Abbott, *Johannine Grammar* (London: A. and C. Black, 1906), § 2049. He contends that κύριε should have been used if the vocative had been intended. For him the instance LXX-Ps 34:24 is explicable by its special context and with that one exceptional use ὁ κύριος is never vocational in the Septuagint. In classical Greek vocational nominative is: a) accompanied by οὗτος or σύ, b) found only in poetry, and c) while using κύριε freely the Papyri never have a vocatival ὁ κύριος.
17 *Ibid.*, §§ 2050–2051.
18 As proposed according to Theodore of Mopsuestia which was proscribed at the 5th ecumenical council in A.D. 553—see G. R. Beasley-Murray, *John*, 385, and M. J. Harris, *Jesus as God: The New Testament Use of theos in Reference to Jesus* (Grand Rapids: Baker Book House, 1992), 108–109.
19 W. Bauer, et al., *A Greek-English Lexicon of the New Testament and Other Early Christian Literature* (Chicago, Ill.: University of Chicago Press, 1979), 357b; W. Bauer, *Das Johannesevangelium* (3rd ed.; HNT 6; Tübingen: J. C. B. Mohr [Paul Siebeck], 1933), 222; E. C. Hoskyns, *The Fourth Gospel* (2 vols.; ed. Francis Noel Davey; London: Faber and Faber, 1940), 2:549; R. E. Brown, *The Gospel according to John*, 2:1026, 1047; L. Morris, *The Gospel according to John* (NICNT 4; London: Morgan & Scott, 1971), 853; G. R. Beasley-Murray, *John*, 385; R. Schnackenburg, *The Gospel according to St. John*, 3:333; B. Lindars, *The Gospel of John*, 615 among others.
20 This phrase probably represents the biblical Aramaic עָנֵה as in Dan 2:5, 8, 26; 3:14; 5:17 or the Hebrew וַיַּעַן . . . וַיֹּאמֶר. See Bauer, et al., *A Greek-English Lexicon*, 93c, and F. Büchsel, in *TDNT* 3:945.
21 J. H. Moulton and N. Turner, *A Grammar of New Testament Greek.* Vol. 3: *Syntax* (Edinburgh: T&T Clark, 1963), 34.
22 BDF, § 147—the New Testament can even say ὁ θεός, ὁ πατήρ in which arthrous Semitic vocative is being reproduced by a nominative with article.

is not easy to decide and conclude that the Evangelist through Thomas' statement exhorts his readers to the Deity of Jesus. C. F. D. Moule while writing about the problem of John 20:28 in his idiom book writes, "it is to be noted that a substantive in nominative case used in a vocative sense, and followed by a possessive could not be anarthrous," but adds that the article before θεός may not, therefore, be significant.[23]

Moreover, before we decide on the meaning of Thomas' statement we must ascertain the significance of μου. The presence of μου gives Thomas' statement a personal and confessional character. It is remarkable that μου and not ἡμῶν is found, since the other disciples were also present. Nor does Thomas say σύ εἶ ὁ θεός. Μου places Thomas' confession in perspective and works as an interpretive, exegetical help. The Evangelist's use of μου exhorts us not to absolutise the perception and not to use the confession as a universal acclamation of the deity of Jesus. Μου emphatically converts the perception into faith and personalises Thomas' confession, making supreme faith an act of personal experience in the language of adoring devotion.

There has always been a tendency to interpret Thomas' confession "My Lord and my God" with John 1:1; cf. 1:18 "and the Word was God," and to ascribe the risen Jesus as God. For such interpreters the risen Lord becomes the repudiation of the opposition's angry enquiring in 5:17—"he makes himself God"—and at 10:33—"you a mere man claim to be God?" In his "Überlegungen zu Joh. 20:24–29," J. Kremer rightly observes that "als Anrede hat das Bekenntnis »mein Herr und mein Gott« zwar nicht den Charakter einer Definition der Gottheit Christi (»wahrer Gott«) . . . ."[24] Does the Fourth Gospel ascribe absolute divinity to the risen Jesus? Does it propose ditheism? Why then, does the Evangelist two verses later not recommend his readers to believe Jesus as God, but just exhorts them to believe that Jesus is (only) the Christ, the Son of God?

Before attempting an answer to the above questions the interpreter should come to conclusions of certain issues raised below: Does the Fourth Evangelist's passion/resurrection narrative narrate the passion of a docetic Jesus whose God identity only becomes revealed at his resurrection? How

---

23 C. F. D. Moule, *An Idiom Book of New Testament Greek* (Cambridge: Cambridge University Press, 1953), 116.

24 J. Kremer, "»Nimm deine Hand und lege sie in meine Seite!«. Exegetische, hermeneutische und bibeltheologische Überlegungen zu Joh. 20, 24–29," in *The Four Gospels, 1992: Festschrift Frans Neirynck* (ed. F. van Segbroeck, et al.; 3 vols.; BETL 100; Leuven: University Press, 1992), 3:2167.

does the Evangelist characterise 'Jesus' in his passion/resurrection narratives? What does the Evangelist convey through this Thomas episode? What is his purpose in placing the Thomas episode at the climax of his passion/resurrection narratives? Since by placing the pericope as a climax to both his passion and resurrection narratives, and as an immediate prelude to his confessed purpose of writing the Gospel, the Fourth Evangelist exhorts us for a contextual interpretive exegesis of the Thomas pericope. A grammatical analysis of the sentence and search for a better translation and thereby a better interpretation of the confession cannot do justice to the Evangelist's intentions, purpose and goal. Therefore, we propose a contextual exegetical exploration of the distinctive/special features of the passion/resurrection narrative and his stated purpose (20:30–31) of writing his Gospel in our attempt to understand the Thomas confession "my Lord, my God."

2.3 Self-Giving Jesus—Composure and Sovereignty in the Midst of Betrayal and Arrest

The arrest scene at the Olive Groove which begins the passion narrative in the Fourth Gospel has no Synoptic parallel as to vv. 4–9 in its narrative structure. The passage dramatises the garden scene, as Jesus himself receives the enemy gang asking them whom they seek, as a result of which the gang looses its nerve. Finally at the end, when Jesus was arrested, the Evangelist brings in Peter's sword-slashing.

The most striking feature of this narration is the threefold repetition of ἐγώ εἰμι here in vv. 5, 6 and 8. It has been contended that the Fourth Evangelist uses this phrase in double meaning. On the one hand in vv. 5 and 8, when the soldiers and officers who have come to arrest Jesus tell him that they are seeking Jesus of Nazareth, he replies saying ἐγώ εἰμι. It is clear that here ἐγώ εἰμι is used as a simple self-identification formula,[25] meaning 'I am he, Jesus of Nazareth whom you are seeking.' In v. 6 however, the Evangelist narrates the effect of Jesus' ἐγώ εἰμι on the soldiers and officers in that "they drew back and fell to the ground."

---

25 See M. Davies, *Rhetoric and Reference in the Fourth Gospel* (Sheffield: JSOT Press, 1992), 83, and P. B. Harner, *The "I am" of the Fourth Gospel: A Study in Johannine Usage and Thought* (Philadelphia: Fortress, 1970), 45.

Is then the phrase ἐγώ εἰμι to be understood absolutely? Is this the way the Fourth Evangelist wishes to express his belief that such an attitude of awe and reverence is the only fitting response to Jesus who is the ἐγώ εἰμι?

Probably the exegetical key lies in vv. 9–11. In v. 9 the Evangelist ponders over a prophetic saying of Jesus—ὅτι οὓς δέδωκάς μοι οὐκ ἀπώλεσα ἐξ αὐτῶν οὐδένα (cf. 6:39; 17:12)—and reflects over its fulfilment. The reflected prophetic saying portrays Jesus as God's prophet/agent whose disciples/co-workers are God's gift to him. In v. 11 the Evangelist again brings into the limelight 'the agent' role of Jesus as he affirms, "shall I not drink the cup the Father has given me?"[26] Now one tends to ask: how could then a prophet/God's agent be the ἐγώ εἰμι—'he who he is'?"

If one interprets ἐγώ εἰμι in the absolute way only to explain the reaction of the audience, then we have probably a better explanation—Ps 56:10 (LXX 55:10); 27:2. In both instances the Psalmist appeals to God from deadly peril, expresses his confidence in God's aid. On both occasions the Psalms end with the verse which could well be understood of the resurrection.

LXX Ps 55:10	ἐπιστρέψουσιν οἱ ἐχθροί μου εἰς τὰ ὀπίσω, ἐν ᾗ ἂν ἡμέρᾳ ἐπικαλέσωμαί σε, ἰδοὺ ἔγνων ὅτι θεός μου εἶ σύ.
	(Then my enemies will fall back in the day when I call. This I know, that God is for me . . .)
LXX Ps 55:14	ὅτι ἐρρύσω τὴν ψυχήν μου ἐκ θανάτου καὶ τοὺς πόδας μου ἐξ ὀλισθήματος τοῦ εὐαρεστῆσαι ἐνώπιον τοῦ θεοῦ ἐν φωτὶ ζώντων.
	(For you have delivered my soul from death, and my feet from falling, so that I may walk before God in the light of life.)
LXX Ps 26:2	ἐν τῷ ἐγγίζειν ἐπ' ἐμὲ κακοῦντας τοῦ φαγεῖν τὰς σάρκας μου οἱ θλίβοντές με καὶ οἱ ἐχθροί μου αὐτοὶ ἠσθένησαν καὶ ἔπεσαν
	(When evildoers assail me, uttering slanders against me, my adversaries and foes, they shall stumble and fall.)
LXX Ps 26:13	πιστεύω τοῦ ἰδεῖν τὰ ἀγαθὰ κυρίου ἐν γῇ ζώντων.
	(I believe that I shall see the goodness of the Lord in the land of the living!)

The arrest scene at the garden therefore pictures Jesus as the righteous servant/agent of God doing His will, and under His protection. It is He who is in control of the situation, not his enemies. Though he stands alone, he is

---

26 See the echo of Ps 116:13; the drinking of the cup is an analogy which is also used in the Synoptics.

not alone, God stands by him. The enemies cannot stand before him or touch him, the suffering which the 'servant' Jesus is led to is the 'cup' the Father has given him. Although the soldiers take Jesus captive, they do so only as he gives himself up to them in willing submission. In fact he virtually dictates their actions, thrice identifying himself as the object of their search (vv. 5, 6 and 8), directing that the disciples be released (v. 8), and commanding Peter to permit his arrest (v. 11). The issue is that if these features of victory and sovereignty are any indication of the direction in which the Fourth Evangelist wishes his narrative interpretation of the event to be understood, then it undoubtedly expresses the fact that the righteous Servant of God need not fear, as God protects him (see exegesis of 17:11bff.—in his prayer Jesus affirms his belief in the God who protects).

2.4 Jesus—The Pascal Lamb

In the Johannine passion narrative we hear 'the Lamb of God' motif being echoed at three places. The first indication is found in the scene that portrays Jesus' trail before Pilate. He declares Jesus thrice to be innocent (18:38; 19:4, 6; cf. Exod 12:5). Is this a veiled pointer to the blamelessness of the Pascal lamb? John 19:14 records the time of Pilate's judgement which begins the crucifixion of Jesus. The Johannine narrative's preference for fixing Jesus' crucifixion/death in time sequence clearly emphasises the Evangelist's theological conviction of Jesus himself being the true Pascal Lamb. It appears as though the Evangelist has intentionally altered the Synoptic chronology.[27] When the Passover eve happened to fall on Sabbath eve (according to the Fourth Gospel that was exactly the case—Nisan 14th, Friday), the Rabbis interpreted that 'the evening' (of Exod 12:6) begins at noon (6th hour) when the sun begins its decline in order to allow the slaughtering of the large number of lambs required before Sabbath breaks at the evening.[28] Thus the Johannine editorial notice at v. 14 brings to the fore the theological reflection

---

27 The Synoptic chronology records that Jesus was only condemned and executed on the day after the Passover meal—Nisan 15th, Friday.

28 See H. L. Strack and P. Billerbeck, *Kommentar zum Neuen Testament aus Talmud und Midrasch* (7 vols.; Munich: C. H. Beck, 1922–1961), 2:836; R. E. Brown, *The Gospel according to John*, 2:833; G. Reim, *Studien zum alttestamentlichen Hintergrund des Johannesevangeliums* (SNTSMS 22; Cambridge: Cambridge University Press, 1974), 177.

that the true Pascal Lamb of God—Jesus—was on the cross, just at the time when the Pascal lambs were being slaughtered.

The second indication is found in v. 29 where Jesus who himself offers the 'water of life' that stills all thirst, reaches the deepest point of fleshy existence.[29] The incident where the sponge was lifted to Jesus' mouth on the hyssop stem appears to be another indication in support of the argument that the Johannine passion narrative presents Jesus as the Pascal Lamb. Purifying power was ascribed to the Hyssop as it was certainly used in cultic sprinkling (cf. Lev 14:6–7; Num 19:6; Ps 50:9), and it was the agent used to apply the blood of the Passover lamb to the door (Exod 12:22). Thus the mention of Hyssop may well be symbolically evocative of Jesus' dying as the Pascal Lamb of the new covenant.[30]

If we agree on ὑσσώπῳ as the original reading,[31] then the Fourth Gospel's deliberate departure from the Markan κάλαμος—the reed lifting the sponge attached to the Hyssop stem even when it lacked the necessary stiffness[32] making it therefore ill-suited to lift a heavy wet sponge—is an indication that the Evangelist may have been prompted by the motif of the Passover.[33] Even if one is uncertain to an extent, seen along with v. 14 and v. 36 (see

---

29 See R. Bultmann, *Das Evangelium des Johannes*, 522.
30 R. E. Brown, *The Gospel according to John*, 2:930.
31 The reading ὑσσώπῳ is attested by every major Greek manuscript. One minuscule manuscript 476 reads ὑσσῷ (a javelin), compare the it[b, ff2, n, v] use of *perticae* (a pole or long staff). A reading which may be more appropriate in the context, and makes the action more comprehensible has arisen accidentally through haplography with ΥCCΩΠΕΡΙΘΕΝΤΕC being written for ΥCCΩΠΩΠΕΡΙΘΕΝΤΕC. Whereas θ, 829, 1195, 2174 which reads μετὰ χολῆς καὶ ὑσσώπου and an old Latin version which reads merely *cum felle permixtum* both seem to have been influenced by Matt 27:34. See B. M. Metzger, *A Textual Commentary on the Greek New Testament* (London: United Bible Society, 1975), 253–54.
32 In the Old Testament, Hyssop is referred to as the humblest of shrubs (1 Kgs 4:33), it was very brittle and often grew from the cracks in stone walls which belonged most likely to 'Origanum maru' of the Labrial family, see R. E. Brown, *The Gospel according to John*, 2:929–30.
33 See C. K. Barrett, *The Gospel according to St. John*, 553. Referring to M. Para 12:1 he suggests that perhaps Hyssop was attached to a reed, as such a procedure was used if the Hyssop used for cultic sprinkling was so stubby that the priests' fingertips were in jeopardy of contacting the sacrificial blood or water. But Bultmann is sceptical for, as he says, it is scarcely believable that Jesus should be designated as the Passover lamb through a statement that a sponge with vinegar was stuck on a Hyssop stem (Bultmann, *Das Evangelium des Johannes*, 522).

below) a veiled pointer to portray Jesus as the 'Pascal Lamb' cannot escape being noticed.

The third indication of the Fourth Evangelist portraying Jesus as the Passover lamb might have been behind the very ironically depicted backroom manoeuvres of the opponents of Jesus even after he died. When the Jews did not wish to have Jesus' body remain on the cross overnight (John 19:31–32) even as the Passover lamb was not to be left over until the morning (Exod 12:10; Num 9:12), they specifically ask Pilate to have Jesus' legs broken and the body taken down. The Evangelist reports that the body was lowered, but creates yet another narrative scene to painstakingly inform his readers that 'no bones were broken.' The blamelessness of the lamb that already came to the fore during Pilate's trial is now confirmed through an Old Testament quotation in v. 36. Whether or not this verse is intended to evoke a Pascal allusion depends on the origin of the Old Testament quotation. If it comes from the Pentateuch (LXX: Exod 12:46; Num 9:12), then the Pascal allusion is quite clear. However, if the quotation stems from the Psalter (LXX: Ps 33:21) where God's protection of the righteous is spoken of, then the Pascal allusion need not be present.

LXX Exod 12:46—ὀστοῦν οὐ συντρίψετε ἀπ' αὐτοῦ.
LXX Num 9:12—ὀστοῦν οὐ συντρίψουσιν ἀπ' αὐτοῦ.
John 19:36b—ὀστοῦν οὐ συντριβήσεται αὐτοῦ.

Either of these citations could be sufficiently close to John 19:36b. If our observations, that in the Fourth Gospel's chronology of the passion Jesus was on the cross just at the time when the Pascal lambs were being slaughtered, and that the Johannine mention of Hyssop at 19:29 might have Pascal connotations are correct, then John 19:36b has Pentateuchal origin and therefore portrays Jesus as Pascal Lamb.

However LXX Ps 33:21 which reads κύριος φυλάσσει πάντα τὰ ὀστᾶ αὐτῶν, ἓν ἐξ αὐτῶν οὐ συντριβήσεται and John 19:36b both demonstrate the common passive form of the verb συντριβήσεται, though otherwise we find no word parallels. The Psalm has plural 'bones' rather than singular, and the term is not the subject of the passive verb as it is in the Fourth Gospel. Moreover this Psalm is the one in which the faithful Israelite is promised complete immunity from harm in this world. To apply the works of v. 21 to someone who has just been put to death with every circumstance of cruelty would seem outrageous. But with the Evangelist's penchant for the Psalms in his passion narrative and the LXX Ps 33:21 indicating a reference to the rescue from eternal death—resurrection—in its last verse, one cannot entirely dismiss the Psalter background of the quotation.³⁴

A meaningful decision in this case may not be a question of either/or, but of both/and. The linguistic considerations show that John 19:36 is/can be better identified with Num 9:12 and Exod 12:36.³⁵ If J. M. Ford's interpretation of 'spear thrust' in 19:34 is correct, then the Levitical rules that the blood of the victim must spurt forth intensifies the Pascal lamb reflection in 19:36.³⁶ It is indeed probable that the primary reference was to the Passover lamb, since Jesus died while it was being carried out and the early Christians must have also treasured LXX Psalm 33, as it is echoed at least eight times in the New Testament.³⁷ It is thanksgiving to God for preserving Jesus' body for the resurrection. The Fourth Gospel might have intended to refer to both the Psalter and the Pentateuch.³⁸

Those who read the Fourth Gospel cannot avoid paying attention to the passion framework which plays a significant role in the Gospel structure.³⁹

---

34 See C. H. Dodd, *Interpretation of the Fourth Gospel,* 230–38; J. T. Forestell, *The Word of the Cross: Salvation as Revelation in the Fourth Gospel* (AnBib 57; Rome: Biblical Institute Press, 1974), 90, n. 32.

35 Num 9:12 (Codex Alexandrinus) reads ὀστοῦν οὐ συντρίψεται ἀπ' αὐτοῦ. See E. D. Freed, *Old Testament Quotations in the Gospel of John* (NovTSup 11; Leiden: E. J. Brill, 1965), 113, who sees v. 36b echoing Num 9:12. The עֶצֶם corresponds to the singular ὀστοῦν. The phrase לֹא יִשְׁבְּרוּ could be translated as οὐ συντριβήσεται, and the αὐτοῦ of v. 36b is a very acceptable translation of the בּוֹ of the Masoretic Text. See B. H. Grigsby, "The Cross as an Expiatory Sacrifice in the Fourth Gospel," *JSNT* 15 (1982): 58–59; G. Reim, *Studien zum alttestamentlichen Hintergrund des Johannesevangeliums,* 52–54.

36 J. M. Ford, "Mingled Blood—From the Side of Christ: Jn. XIX:34," *NTS* 15 (1969): 337–39. She cites the frequent Rabbinic description of spurting forth זְבוֹק of the Pascal lambs blood—especially on the basis of the Tractate *Oholoth* in the Talmud.

37 See A. T. Hanson, *The Prophetic Gospel,* 219–20.

38 Bultmann, Barrett, Brown, Lindars and Schnackenburg (see their commentaries) all see both citations as relevant and coherent. Bultmann, Lindars and Schnackenburg think that the Fourth Evangelist's source understood the reference as a quotation from the Psalter and that the Evangelist must have been applying it to the 'Pascal lamb' citation from the Pentateuch.

39 W. Wilkens' thesis indicates that the Fourth Gospel evolved from, and still reflects an original Passover framework, see his *Die Entstehungsgeschichte des vierten Evangeliums*. W. A. Meeks proposes that 'Moses' served as a model for the Evangelist's prophet-king Christology and that the Johannine 'new Moses' accomplishes the new Exodus, see his *The Prophet-King: Moses Traditions and the Johannine Christology* (NovTSup 14; Leiden: E. J. Brill, 1967). R. T. Fortna thinks that the frequent references to the Passover in the Fourth Gospel are meant to remind the reader of the

It is surely more than a coincidence that the Fourth Evangelist alludes to Jesus' death at each of the three Passovers mentioned (2:13, 19–22; 6:4, 51; 11:50–53, 55; 12:20, 24). Thus his presentation of Jesus as the Pascal Lamb in his Passion narrative is not at all surprising. However, to understand the fuller significance of the Evangelist's presentation of Jesus as the 'Pascal Lamb' one needs to focus on the distinctive Johannine christological title: 'Lamb of God.'

What is the intention of the Fourth Gospel in making John the Baptist witness to Jesus as ὁ ἀμνὸς τοῦ θεοῦ ὁ αἴρων τὴν ἁμαρτίαν τοῦ κόσμου? If we observe the characterisation of the Baptist in the Synoptics it is impossible to believe that John could ever speak of Jesus who will die as the lamb that was to be slaughtered at Passover. The Baptist's preaching, as we read in the Synoptics, proclaims the nearness of the eschatological kingdom, with its emphasis on ethical revival. Later on in prison, John shows signs of doubt as to Jesus' messiahship, he seems to be disheartened by the delay of eschatological judgement through the eschatological Messiah. These quite surely point out that the Baptist was not alluding to a 'Messiah-Lamb of God' which would die an expiatory death to take away sin. Then what is the purpose of the Fourth Evangelist in narrating the christological title as the witness of John?

Further it may prove a grave mistake if interpretation becomes engrossed solely on the term 'the lamb,' for the title here given to Jesus is not just ὁ ἀμνός, but ὁ ἀμνὸς τοῦ θεοῦ. Then what is meant by ὁ ἀμνὸς τοῦ θεοῦ? Does the title foresee and encompass the question of the death of the lamb? What does αἴρειν signify? Does it denote sacrificial cleansing of sin or the representative bearing of the sin of the other, or the new order that the Lamb of God brings into existence? What then is the significance of τοῦ κόσμου in the argument?

The christological title 'the lamb' (τὸ ἀρνίον) appears 27 times in the Book of Revelation with reference to the lamb that was slain, but is now victorious and executing judgement upon the earth and reigning the eternal order. But the expression ὁ ἀμνὸς τοῦ θεοῦ figures only in John 1:29, 36. In Acts 8:32 we find the quotation from Isa 53:7–8 (LXX) including the expression καὶ ὡς ἀμνὸς ἐναντίον τοῦ κείραντος αὐτὸν ἄφωνος. . . . The dis-

---

fateful Passover on whose eve Jesus, designated from the start as the 'Lamb of God,' was slain; see R. T. Fortna, "Christology in the Fourth Gospel: A Redactional-Critical Perspective," *NTS* 21 (1975): 502.

cussion that follows the quote relates it to Jesus and interprets Jesus' death as victoriously fulfilling the prophecy. In 1 Pet 1:18–19 ὡς ἀμνοῦ ἀμώμου καὶ ἀσπίλου . . . points to the redemption by the blood of Christ comparing it to that of the lamb.

The 'lamb of God' imagery traditionally makes the interpreter think of the 'Pascal lamb' (Exod 12:6; Num 9:12) and the ritual that commemorates Israel's exodus and deliverance from Egypt. The 'Pascal lamb' motif is often interpreted in terms of the expiatory sacrifices of the Jewish religion. Actually in the Pascal celebration one finds no sacrifices. The lamb calls people to complete obedience to God, and to rely entirely on Him. It brings into focus the fact that they were liberated not by human might, but only through the mighty hand of God. People are called upon to accept this in their obedience, to 'see,' recognise and experience the deliverance. The ritual of killing/eating the lamb at the Passover meal is an anamnesis of God's call to be obedient, to be ready and to worship. The blood of the lamb is not an expiatory offering for liberation.

The expression ὁ ἀμνὸς τοῦ θεοῦ is often seen as the Evangelist's reference to the 'servant of the Lord' in Isaiah 53. Those who contend the Aramaic origin of the Fourth Gospel argue that the 'Lamb of God' is a mistranslation of the Aramaic original טליא דאלהא. The Aramaic טַלְיָא taken in the sense of the Hebrew טָלֶה means 'lamb,' but actually טַלְיָא in Aramaic corresponds to Greek παῖς, meaning servant. Therefore the expression of ὁ ἀμνὸς τοῦ θεοῦ represents an Aramaic original טליא דאלהא intended as the equivalent of the Isaianic phrase עבד יהוה 'the servant of the Lord.'[40] But the Septuagint never translates טָלֶה as ἀμνός, and no parallels are adduced to טַלְיָא as a rendering of עֶבֶד, even the Syriac versions go back from παῖς to עַבְדָּא except where they take it to mean 'son.'[41]

The seeming parallel between John 1:29, 36 and Isa 53:7 where the Septuagint reads ὡς ἀμνὸς ἐναντίον τοῦ κείροντος αὐτὸν ἄφωνος has been noted to seek identification in the idea of the meekness of the uncomplaining lamb, and Jesus' own meekness especially during his trail when he did not answer back and was silent. A narrative reading of the Gospel confirms that though the Fourth Gospel retains elements of this tradition, it actually portrays Jesus defending himself before Annas and Pilate (18:20–23, 34–37).

---

40 C. F. Burney, *The Aramaic Approach to the Fourth Gospel* (Oxford: Clarendon Press, 1922), 104–108; J. Jeremias, in *TDNT* 1:338–41.
41 See C. H. Dodd, *Interpretation of the Fourth Gospel*, 235–36.

However, it should be noted that although the Septuagint reads ἀμνός, the Masoretic Text has רָחֵל which actually means an ewe or merely a sheep. On the other hand, in the previous clause the Masoretic Text reads שֶׂה which is translated in the Septuagint as πρόβατον, although here ἀμνός would have been a better choice—in the Septuagint ἀμνός is sometimes used as a translation of רָחֵל, but sometimes of שֶׂה,[42] then in fact the Hebrew text here may be translated as "like a lamb that is led to the slaughter-house, like a sheep that is dumb before its shearers."[43] If this is the case the whole aspect of the connection between the christological title 'the Lamb of God' in the Fourth Gospel and that of the 'Servant of God' in Isaiah 53 is altered.

The servant will be silent like a 'sheep.' רָחֵל occurs only three other times in the Old Testament but never to denote a sacrificial animal. 'Like a lamb on the way to being slaughtered'—here the Hebrew word שֶׂה used for the Lamb also denotes the Passover lamb (Exod 12:3–5). It is not used to denote the sacrificial animal itself. Furthermore Isaiah is not referring to sacrificial slaughter. He uses טֶבַח which is slaughter for food, instead of זֶבַח, slaughter for sacrifice (cf. John 6:54—the Johannine Jesus calls to eat of his flesh, and drink of his blood). Isaiah does not provide therefore an intersection of the metaphor of lamb with sacrificial animal. But it portrays a 'prototype' servant who, like a lamb, obeys the will of God without questioning it, even in the midst of suffering, affliction and adversity. Through such a life of willing and complete obedience, he will see 'the light of life' (Isa 53:10ff.). Through this invaluable experience he becomes to many a role-model to overcome unjust suffering and affliction. It is not the atoning death of the servant, but his role-model in which he gives others/his community the key to overcome unjust suffering and affliction, and to see the light of life. The theme of the servant song in Isaiah is not the atoning death of the servant, but a call to the remnant to follow the role-model of the servant and to be servants of the Lord, to enable the world to see the light of life. Therefore instead of fixing one's eyes on Isa 53:7 and on the παῖς/ἀμνός debate to find a comparison, the interpreter is called to see the force of the metaphor in its totality—'the Lamb of God who takes away the sin of the world.'

---

42 J. Jeremias, in *TDNT* 1:338ff.
43 J. H. Roberts, "The Lamb of God," in *The Christ of John: Essays on the Christology of the Fourth Gospel* (Proceedings of the Fourth Meeting of Die Nuwe-Testamentiese werkgemeenskap van Suid-Afrika; Potchefstrom, South Africa: Pro Rege Press, 1971), 45–46.

In the Apocrypha and Pseudepigrapha 'sheep' is used as a metaphor for people: sheep are like God, devout among the nation (*Pss. Sol.* 8:23), out of many sheep the Lord chose one for Himself, which is Himself (2 Esd 5:26), Israel is like skipping lambs in the wilderness (Wis 19:9). In *1 Enoch* David is pictured as a lamb that became a ram and ruled the sheep. The history of conflicts and occasional successes of the 'sheep' against the wild animals projects a pictorial imagery of the history of the Jews in their conflict with the Gentiles. But Israel believed that when the Lord intervenes and raises up a ram to lead the sheep, the sheep would become victorious over all wild beasts in the land.[44]

The literary context for the lamb motif in Second Temple Judaism demonstrates an imagery rooted in the prophecies of Daniel 8 and Ezekiel 34. The link between the lamb metaphor and the Jewish deliverer, that a lamb can be a leader and even a conqueror, and a symbol of power is a significant development of the Second Temple period. The imagery of the lamb growing a horn, a power symbol, is seen as God's intervention, and comprises therefore a significant shift in this developing motif. In *T. Jos.* 19:8–11 we read of a vision in which a lamb is attacked by a lion, reptiles and other animals. The lamb conquers the wild animals and is praised by men and angels. In *T. Benj.* 3:8 the lamb metaphor is used for the Messiah.[45]

---

44   *1 En.* 85–90, esp. 89:41–50.
45   The apparent Christian elements in these passages raise a question of the date of the *Testaments of the Twelve Patriarchs* and/or the possibility of Christian interpolation. In the case of *T. Jos.* 19:8 the conquering lamb does not appear to be a Christian interpolation, the content of vv. 8–10 is compatible with the eschatological expectations of the *Testaments* and is not incongruous with the literary form of the passage. Further, if a Christian interpolator had inserted a lamb he would probably have removed the lion to avoid association with the dual Messiahship view of some Jews. However, v. 11b referring to the Lamb of God saving Gentiles may be a Christian interpolation. In the case of *T. Benj.* 3:8 it is unlikely that a Christian would have inserted a reference to the lamb descending from the tribe of Joseph; see D. B. Sandy, "John the Baptist's 'Lamb of God' Affirmation in its Canonical and Apocalyptic Milieu," *JETS* 34 (1991): 454–55; J. H. Charlesworth, "Christian and Jewish Self Definition in the Light of the Christian Additions to the Apocryphal Writings," in *Jewish and Christian Self-Definition* (ed. E. P. Sanders; 3 vols.; Philadelphia: Fortress, 1980–83), vol. 2: *Aspects of Judaism in the Graeco-Roman Period*, 1981, 27–55. In spite of the textual difficulties Dodd, Barrett, and Brown think that the apocalyptic messianic figure of the lamb must have been in the Fourth Evangelist's mind.

A lamb prevails over other animals, the victory of the lamb deserves a large celebration, the lamb is predicative of a future event in the last days, and the lamb represents the deliverer of the Jews. In the Rabbinic sources, the most vivid lamb metaphor stands for a lamb deliverer.

Widely associated with Messianic expectations were beliefs that the Messiah would remove from his kingdom the sinners and their sinful needs—"He will purge Jerusalem and make it holy as it was from the beginning" (*Pss. Sol.* 17:30), sinners shall be judged for their sins and driven from the face of the earth. He shall crush the teeth of the sinners (*1 En.* 38:1; 46:4), in his priesthood sin shall cease and lawless men shall rest from their evil deeds (*T. Levi* 18:9). Then, "who takes away the sin of the world" need not refer to Jesus' atoning death for sin. If the Lamb of God is a messianic deliverer, then the removal of sin and evil is inherent in, and consistent with, such a messianic concept. Support for this interpretation of αἴρω with ἁμαρτία comes from the Septuagint (cf. Odae 11:17; *Pss. Sol.* 17:20–21; Isa 38:17) and most significantly from 1 John 3:5, 8. There is an apparent parallel between the purpose clauses using αἴρω and λύω—ἵνα τὰς ἁμαρτίας ἄρῃ, καὶ ἁμαρτία ἐν αὐτῷ οὐκ ἔστιν and ἵνα λύσῃ τὰ ἔργα τοῦ διαβόλου. Therefore Semitic and contextual evidence during the Second Temple period suggest that the lamb motif imparted the belief that the Messiah as part of his messianic mission would remove the sins of the world.

In the Passover celebration the lamb is passive, its blood is a sign/symbol of the liberative activities of a liberator-God. In the symbol of the Passover lamb, however, the idea of an 'expiatory death' is completely absent. The blood of the lamb signifies 'the worth,' the value of liberation, and the suffering and thriving of the people for freedom, and the blood applied to the door was a constant reminder of their eager awaiting and obedient readiness in believing in the mighty hand of God, who alone can liberate. Now the portrayal of Jesus in the Baptist's witness as the 'Lamb of God' converts the passive Pascal lamb symbol into an active sign. The emphasis still lies on the genitive τοῦ θεοῦ, but the Fourth Evangelist brings into synthesis the 'servant of the Lord' and the Second Temple period's 'lamb' symbolism for the Messiah. Jesus according to him is the instrument of God's salvific work, in him God's will for His people is manifested. The theological emphasis of the Fourth Evangelist portraying Jesus as ὁ ἀμνὸς τοῦ θεοῦ does not lie in sacrificial atonement. It actually interprets the Messiah as a lamb—the meek/weak/powerless becomes the place where God's mighty works are manifested; but as to the horns that this 'Lamb of

God' grows, his 'power' does not lie in political activism, but in his complete obedience to the will of God and in his servanthood.

The ὁ ἀμνὸς τοῦ θεοῦ is therefore a radical reinterpretation of the Jewish Messiah concept. The 'Lamb of God,' whose power lies in his humbleness, meekness, loving obedience to the will of God even to the point of giving up his own life, is characterised by his self-emptying. For the Fourth Evangelist such a Messiah, 'the Lamb of God,' personifies Life which is the complete loving obedience to God. When such a Messiah is in the world, the forces of death and the sin of the world try to overcome the Life that he has! The Fourth Gospel perceives the suffering and affliction of the Lamb of God, the Messiah, as a result arising out of the bitter conflict between 'the sin of the world' and the 'Lamb of God.' The loving complete obedience of the lamb to the point of death crushes the suffering and affliction and releases the power of Life; the power of God which takes away the sin of the world. Sin in the Fourth Gospel is broken relationship (see the exegesis of the Paraclete passages, esp. John 16:7–8) The 'Lamb of God' as the perfect symbol of complete obedience shows the way to restore a creational relationship. The Lamb of God thus becomes the 'prototype' for the world to recognise God's way to Life and light, God's prototype for a new order! The 'Lamb of God' is thus God's sign for the world that God is the deliverer and the liberator, and He Himself takes away the sin of the world to give 'Life.'

2.5 The Trial of Jesus—The Man, The King

Pilate presents Jesus with the two-fold "Behold the Man! Behold your King!" Precisely parallel are not only these proclamations, but also the narrative build-up and the crowd's reaction to them.

John 18:33–38		John 19:9–11
King's duty	}Pilate's dialogue with Jesus{	King's power
John 19:5		John 19:14
ἰδοὺ ὁ ἄνθρωπος	} The proclamation {	ἴδε ὁ βασιλεὺς ὑμῶν
John 19:6		John 19:15
σταύρωσον σταύρωσον	} The crowd's response {	ἆρον ἆρον, σταύρωσον αὐτόν

Bultmann argues that the theological context of the trial narrative is explored in the two scenes in which Jesus and Pilate are in close-door conversations.⁴⁶ But in terms of literary structure itself the presentation of Jesus and the proclamation are the twin climaxes of the whole trial.⁴⁷

ἰδοὺ ὁ ἄνθρωπος

In the Fourth Gospel one finds sometimes the sarcastic and disparaging, sometimes innocent, but usually ironic references to Jesus as 'a man' (9:29), 'the man' (5:12), 'you being a man' (10:33), 'this man' (11:47). In the dramatic dialogue of chapter 9 we encounter 'the man' called Jesus who healed the blind man (v. 11), 'this man' called a sinner (vv. 16, 24), this man whose origins are unknown (v. 29) or who comes from God (v. 33). During Jesus' trial the servant of the High priest asks Peter whether he is not one of this man's disciples (18:27).

In the statement of the crippled at the pool of Beth-za'tha—"I have no man to put me into the pool"—the double-edged character of the term ὁ ἄνθρωπος is clear. Jesus is the man who helps him, but of course for the action he is subsequently accused as the one who made himself equal to God (5:18). Is ὁ ἄνθρωπος then only a sarcastic or ironic demonstration of Jesus' humanity, to awaken sympathy and demonstrate the ridiculousness of the Kingship claim and Jesus' harmlessness indeed,⁴⁸ or does one interpret ὁ ἄνθρωπος as a title?

Scholars have argued that we may have here an echo of LXX Zech 6:12 which reads, Ἰδοὺ ἀνήρ, Ἀνατολὴ ὄνομα αὐτῷ.⁴⁹ The objection that John uses ἄνθρωπος not ἀνήρ could easily be explained, because when Philo quotes this text he uses ἄνθρωπος instead of ἀνήρ.⁵⁰ Also Jesus appearing with a crown would suit the Zechariah context. In Zechariah 6 God commands him to crown 'Joshua' the High Priest as King. This might have later led to, and lent itself to, eschatological interpretation.⁵¹ Anthony T. Hanson draws attention

---

46 R. Bultmann, *Das Evangelium des Johannes*, 502.
47 W. A. Meeks, *The Prophet-King*, 70.
48 J. H. Bernard, *A Critical and Exegetical Commentary on the Gospel according to St. John* (2 vols.; ICC; Edinburgh: T&T Clark, 1928), 1:616; E. C. Hoskyns, *The Fourth Gospel*, 523; S. Schulz, *Das Evangelium nach Johannes* (4ᵗʰ ed.; NTD 4; Göttingen: Vandenhoeck & Ruprecht, 1983), 230–31; A. Wikenhauser, *Das Evangelium nach Johannes* (3ʳᵈ ed.; RNT 4; Regensburg: Pustet, 1961), 327.
49 The Hebrew rendering is: וְאָמַרְתָּ אֵלָיו לֵאמֹר כֹּה אָמַר יְהוָה צְבָאוֹת לֵאמֹר הִנֵּה־אִישׁ צֶמַח שְׁמוֹ וּמִתַּחְתָּיו יִצְמָח וּבָנָה אֶת־הֵיכַל יְהוָה.
50 *Conf.* 62: ἰδοὺ ἄνθρωπος ᾧ ὄνομα ἀνατολή. . . .
51 Barrett compares Zech 6:12 in his commentary, but sees no direct reference to the passage, Lindars believes a reference to Zech 6:12 and Brown and Meeks in his *The*

to Isa 53:3 where LXX Isa 53:3b, c reads ἄνθρωπος ἐν πληγῇ ὢν καὶ εἰδὼς φέρειν μαλακίαν, ὅτι ἀπέστραπται τὸ πρόσωπον αὐτοῦ, ἠτιμάσθη καὶ οὐκ ἐλογίσθη ... In the Fourth Gospel's narrative Jesus has just been scourged, insulted and shrunk.[52] The crowd's behaviour as against Jesus fits the Johannine context.

Pilate's first close-door dialogue with Jesus helps us to interpret the first proclamation of Pilate: "ἰδοὺ ὁ ἄνθρωπος;". His question—"are you the King of the Jews?" (v. 33)—belongs to the traditional passion account. In the dialogue (vv. 34–38) which surely is a handiwork of the Fourth Evangelist, we see the only direct statements on the nature of Jesus' kingship in the Fourth Gospel. Jesus does not speak of himself, rather he speaks of his βασιλεία. The first statement defines Jesus' kingship negatively: ἡ βασιλεία ἡ ἐμὴ οὐκ ἔστιν ἐκ τοῦ κόσμου ... ἡ βασιλεία ἡ ἐμὴ οὐκ ἔστιν ἐντεῦθεν (v. 36a), the second positively: βασιλεύς εἰμι. ἐγὼ εἰς τοῦτο γεγέννημαι καὶ εἰς τοῦτο ἐλήλυθα εἰς τὸν κόσμον, ἵνα μαρτυρήσω τῇ ἀληθείᾳ. πᾶς ὁ ὢν ἐκ τῆς ἀληθείας ἀκούει μου τῆς φωνῆς (v. 37).

The phrase οὐκ ἔστιν ἐκ τοῦ κόσμου must be understood first of all as a genitive of origin. Jesus' kingship does not derive from the world, but from God. Its origin corresponds to his own origin.[53] 'βασιλεία' does not locate the kingdom in terms of geographical boundaries since it does not originate in the world, rather it defines a sovereign rule, the dynamic activity and saving sovereignty of the saviour God. It is not established by worldly power (v. 36b), but only by the power of God. Therefore, Jesus' βασιλεία is based and governed by God.

After having explained what his βασιλεία is 'not,' Jesus declares what it is: his is the βασιλεία that makes God's reality effective in the world,[54] for Jesus is the King who testifies to the Truth (v. 37). The Fourth Gospel describes Jesus' ministry as that of bearing witness to the Truth. Bearing witness to the Truth in fact means bearing witness to God (see exegesis of chapter 8). It is interpreting for people the acts of God and thus helping/calling people to decide between what is true and false, between acts that do

---

Prophet-King, 70–71, refer to Zech 6:12 and Num 24:17. Hanson refers to Zech 6:12, but dismisses Num 24:17; see his *The Prophetic Gospel*, 204.

52 In Isa 53:3c the Masoretic Text has וּכְמַסְתֵּר פָּנִים מִמֶּנּוּ, a serious deviation of the Septuagint from the Masoretic Text is noticed.

53 Compare John 8:23—the opposite of ἐκ τοῦ κόσμου is ἐκ τοῦ ἄνω which means ἐκ τοῦ θεοῦ/ἄνωθεν. See W. A. Meeks, *The Prophet-King*, 63.

54 R. Bultmann, *Das Evangelium des Johannes*, 506–507.

and do not belong to God. In such a challenge Jesus brings judgement, as he discloses what is false and sinful. It is an act of creating opinion and conscientizing people to judge from God's perspective, to exhort people to have a theological perspective in their each and every act, and thus be guided ἄνωθεν. At this particular moment, law ceases to rule the kingdom, instead 'faith' becomes the deciding and abiding factor. And Jesus proclaims: "everyone on the side of the Truth (God!) listens to me" (v. 37c; cf. 8:40, 45–46, 47; and 10:3, 16, 27).

At this moment of ἀκούειν—constructed with genitive, it refers to listening with understanding, acceptance and decision—Jesus' kingdom becomes political as it confronts the earthly powers both of Chief Priests and officials (Jewish religious) and Pilate (Roman political). Though the Fourth Evangelist does not elaborate, v. 37 definitely points towards principles that governed the life of Jesus, as witness to the truth, such as willingness to die rather than escape at any price (cf. 12:24), service rather than dominion (13:13–17), respectability, love for others rather than egoism (13:34), freedom and courage to criticise the world order despite its enmity (7:7). Such principles have potential for inspiring political options and concrete political choices.

Therefore, Jesus' βασιλεία is not an isolated sphere of pure inwardness over against the world. It is not a private cocoon for integrating religious needs which could not come into conflict with the world. Jesus' βασιλεία unmasks the world and challenges it.[55] Pilate ends the dialogue with his now famous question—what is Truth? The Fourth Evangelist pictures Pilate's avoidance and thus rejection of the possibility to recognise, to accept and to stand by the truth.

In the scene that follows the first interrogation, Pilate sets 'Barabbas,' a criminal, free. This emphatically underlines the powerlessness of 'the Roman king' (Governor) and strikingly proclaims his captivity. Pilate now allows flogging, and the 'King of the Jews' is crowned with a crown of thorns and clothed in a purple robe. The mocking salutations and the dishonouring blows on the cheek remind the reader of what Pilate thought of Jesus. One would therefore expect a mocking proclamation 'see your king here' from Pilate as Jesus comes out arrayed in a parody of royal attire. Instead Pilate says: ἰδοὺ ὁ ἄνθρωπος.

---

55 *Ibid.*, 507–508.

Is ὁ ἄνθρωπος the counterpart of ὁ υἱὸς τοῦ ἀνθρώπου which disappears after 13:31 in the Johannine passion narrative? C. H. Dodd and Josef Blank track back to the Son of Man tradition in the Fourth Gospel in order to interpret ὁ ἄνθρωπος.[56] In addition Blank observes that in it is precisely the Son of Man to whom judgement is given. For C. K. Barrett, ὁ ἄνθρωπος calls to mind those Jewish Hellenistic myths of the heavenly or primal man which lie behind the Fourth Evangelist's phrase, ὁ υἱὸς τοῦ ἀνθρώπου.[57] The Johannine narrative scheme that takes up the christological titles introduced in the first chapter to bring them to logical, affirmative conclusions summons us to concur. It may be the intention of the Fourth Evangelist to affirm through Pilate's ἰδοὺ ὁ ἄνθρωπος, that the man who brought κρίσις as people encountered him throughout his life, is also the man who judges, even when Pilate and the others try to pass judgement on him: he is in every sense 'ὁ ἄνθρωπος' who said to Nathaniel: "I tell you the truth, you shall see heaven open and the angels of God ascending and descending on the Son of Man!" (John 1:51).

Nevertheless, Bultmann's remark that in Pilate's declaration, the Johannine kerygma ὁ λόγος σὰρξ ἐγένετο becomes visible in its extreme consequence seemed to take both the narrative structure and the trial context very seriously.[58] Pilate did not know who Jesus is in truth. But he knows that this man is not a claimant for the throne. He is merely a man! This is exactly the kerygma that the Fourth Gospel wants to proclaim, that God's revelation and the human confrontation of the relational face of God, the Logos, takes place in the flesh (see exegesis of John 1:14). Where humankind does not expect God to be, He is present in ὁ ἄνθρωπος, who does not want to transcend himself (18:36), who does not want to be more than he is, a witness to the Truth (18:37). Though this man is disfigured, mocked and in captivity, though he does not have much space for freedom, it is in him that the God of freedom is revealed, in him the almighty God confronts man, in him one has the exegesis of God Himself.

---

56 C. H. Dodd, *Interpretation of the Fourth Gospel*, 437, and J. Blank, *Krisis: Untersuchungen zur johanneischen Christologie und Eschatologie* (Freiburg: Lambertus-Verlag, 1964), 75.
57 C. K. Barrett, *The Gospel according to St. John*, 450.
58 R. Bultmann, *Das Evangelium des Johannes*, 510.

ἴδε ὁ βασιλεὺς ὑμῶν

When the Jews understood Pilate's intentions of mocking them through presenting a tragic/pitiful man, telling them symbolically that he is harmless and does not deserve the death sentence, they bring against Jesus the charges of blasphemy—"he claims himself to be the Son of God"—and thereby persist on the Governor to crucify him. Hearing the 'Son of God' charge Pilate rushes to a second close-door interrogation of Jesus. The question πόθεν εἶ σύ; is one of the leitmotifs of Johannine Christology asked repeatedly during Jesus' confrontation with the Jews (cf. 7:27; 8:14; 9:29–30). The question on Pilate's lips portrays his anxiety to know whether Jesus was of this earth or from heaven, whether he was a man or a god. His query receives no answer. Pilate's fear turns to annoyance, as he starts boasting of his ἐξουσία. Jesus answers indirectly hinting at his origin, and thereby placing Pilate's ἐξουσία in perspective!

Pilate was conscious of possessing authority from the most powerful Caesar and representing the most powerful Roman empire on earth. Jesus, however, using ἄνωθεν reminds him that human power/authority is merely delegated and derived. ἄνωθεν in the Fourth Gospel describes heavenly/divine realm (cf. 3:27, 31c). For the Fourth Evangelist Jesus is ἄνωθεν, which conditions his being and will (cf. 3:31; 8:23). Therefore ἄνωθεν in the Evangelist's understanding is God Himself, who is the supreme authority and source of all power.

Divine authority comes always with a responsibility—the one who has ἐξουσία is under obligation to hold firm to God (ἄνωθεν), to receive guidance from above to interpret, decide and judge. The object of such delegated power is to bear witness to the Truth (cf. 18:37). The delegated authority is not for self-propagation, but for common welfare without succumbing to external pressure, fear and prejudice. Behind Jesus' pregnant and somewhat cryptic statements that emphasise the limits of Pilate's power, the attempt to head the conflict between the church and the empire might have been reflected.[59] But the interpretation that Jesus has been given by God into Pilate's hands as a grand design[60] seems to be farfetched. Rather it must be seen as a call to Pilate to ponder over his given ἐξουσία and its responsibility.

---

59 W. A. Meeks, *The Prophet-King*, 73.
60 R. Bultmann, *Das Evangelium des Johannes*, 512–13; R. Schnackenburg, *The Gospel according to St. John*, 3:261, and G. R. Beasley-Murray, *John*, 340.

Deeply affected by the challenge thrown to his authority, Pilate attempts to secure Jesus' release. But as the shouts for Jesus' crucifixion rise, and as Jewish leaders play their trump card—that if Pilate releases Jesus he becomes Caesar's enemy—Pilate understands that the threat might even cost him his governorship. Not being able to wield his authority, and decisively defeated by the Jews, Pilate searches out a mode of revenging himself on the Jews for his humiliation at their hands. He presents Jesus once again—ἴδε ὁ βασιλεὺς ὑμῶν.

The real impact of the second public presentation of Jesus as King becomes plain as the chief priests declare: "we have no king but Caesar." At the time of the Passover, when Israel's great celebration remembered and commemorated God's almighty power that liberated them from slavery, when Israel bowed in reverence and worship, to renew the covenant that God is their King and they His people, the chief priests chanted נשמת from the Passover Haggadah, a hymn sung at the conclusion of the greater Hallel: "From everlasting to everlasting Thou art God; Beside Thee we have no king, redeemer or saviour, no liberator, deliverer, provider; None who takes pity in every time of distress and trouble; We have no king but Thee,"[61] they reject 'God' and the 'Sent One.'

The Fourth Gospel indicates that the notice on the cross that read "Jesus of Nazareth the King of the Jews" was written in three languages—Aramaic, Greek and Latin. This might be interpreted as Johannine narrative strategy to indicate the universality of the King's reign. Specific Johannine redaction highlighting the chief priests' unease, and Pilate's ironic insistence upon its irrevocability with ὃ γέγραφα, γέγραφα are perhaps the Johannine reinterpretation of the kingship of Jesus—the King reigns from the cross despite his rejection!

Apart from the passion narrative the title 'the king of Israel' appears twice: once in the confessional response of Nathaniel (1:49) and again in the acclamation of the pilgrims at Jesus' final entry into Jerusalem. The original connotation of the king of Israel title was determined by a distinctly Davidic Messianology. However, in both cases implicit reorientation of the title is suggested. For Nathaniel, the king of Israel is the one who has mysterious knowledge of him, he will see greater things through the one who is in continual communion with the above world, the one in whom the heaven opens (1:50–51). As in the case of the Pilgrims' acclamation, the editorial note of the

---

61　See for details W. A. Meeks, *The Prophet-King*, 77.

Evangelist makes it plain that Jesus' kingship should be understood from the perspective of Jesus' death on the cross and from the stand-point of the community's post-resurrection faith—the King who rules in obedience to the Father's will even unto death is glorified in his self-emptying.

In John 6:14–15 we encounter the implied association of the prophet who is to come into the world and the king. Meeks suggests that the Evangelist is making use of certain Moses traditions in which prophetic and royal functions combine. Jesus, says the Evangelist, does not accept the 'kingly' role as perceived by the crowd. Instead he withdraws to the hills (6:15b). In fact in John 4 Jesus does not reject the title prophet when the Samaritan woman confronts in him a prophet. The Evangelist seems to rework the understanding of Jesus' kingship radically in terms of a prophetic mission in constant communion with God![62]

Thus the 'kingship of Jesus' according to the Fourth Evangelist expresses God's kingship, God's authority. It originates, derives its ἐξουσία from above. It is a delegated power; its ἐξουσία lies in its ability to enable, its power lies in making people see the 'truth,' and thereby in judging and challenging people to decide from God's perspective. It is an ἐξουσία that liberates and sets free. Still the 'kingship' of Jesus and his authority lie in becoming captive in his obedience to God. Its sublime beauty lies in service—serving God's will to the point of his self-emptying on the cross.

2.6 Mission Completed—Jesus Heralds Victory Even in Death

'τετέλεσται' announces the completion of Jesus' earthly work. This reminds us of 17:4—ἐγώ σε ἐδόξασα ἐπὶ τῆς γῆς τὸ ἔργον τελειώσας ὃ δέδωκάς μοι ἵνα ποιήσω that which had been uttered 'sub specie,' of the completion of the work which has now become historical reality.[63] Dodd considers that τετέλεσται in its Johannine context conveys the notion of rites of sacrifice and initiation. He refers to Corp. herm. XIII 21 where, in the mystery of rebirth, the initiates say to the Mystagogue—σοῦ γὰρ βουλομένου πάντα τελεῖται.[64]

---

62 W. A. Meeks, The Prophet-King, 67–91, esp. 67, and M. de Jonge, Jesus: Stranger from Heaven and Son of God. Jesus Christ and the Christians in Johannine Perspective (ed. and trans. J. E. Steely; SBLSBS 11; Missoula, Mont.: Scholars Press, 1977), 49–76.
63 R. Bultmann, Das Evangelium des Johannes, 523.
64 C. H. Dodd, Interpretation of the Fourth Gospel, 421.

One cannot foresee that Jesus' τετέλεσται reflects his self-understanding as mysterious divinity, or that he himself has come to the τελείωσις, or has become τελειωθείς, since it is not written τετέλεσμαι or τετελείωμαι.⁶⁵

The verb τελέω fundamentally denotes 'to carry out' the will of somebody, and so fulfil obligations. The meaning of the term is therefore temporal and theological, it interprets Jesus' suffering and dying as the crowning climax and conclusion of the entrusted mission, and the work that he has performed—the obedience of the Son finds here its most radical expression.⁶⁶ It is interesting to note that Mark and Matthew record another 'loud cry' of Jesus before he dies, but do not report what it was (Mark 15:37; Matt 27:50). Mark/Matthew speak about the idea of Jesus having been forsaken by God (Matt 27:46; Mark 15:34)—as is hidden in Jesus' cry: ἠλι ἠλι λεμα σαβαχθανι; τοῦτ' ἔστιν· Θεέ μου Θεέ μου, ἱνατί με ἐγκατέλιπες; Luke had already altered the last words or the exclamation at death into the supplication πάτερ, εἰς χεῖράς σου παρατίθεμαι τὸ πνεῦμά μου (Luke 23:46). The Fourth Gospel's redaction of the passion narrative knows what exactly happened.

The narrative pictures Jesus, even to the very end, as the one taking the initiative and in control of the situation—in the exhortation of the beloved disciple (v. 27), in the request for the final drink (v. 28), and thus emphasises the force of 'τετέλεσται'—it was not an emotional outcry, but a conscious affirmation on the part of Jesus. When the eyes of the world saw the whole mission—when 'operation Jesus had been wrecked'— 'τετέλεσται' becomes in the pen of the Evangelist the cry of fulfilment and triumph. The victory it heralds is that of fulfilling the Father's will in obedience.⁶⁷

The Fourth Evangelist differs decisively in his choice of words in his description of Jesus' death from that of the Synoptic narratives. The Synoptic description of the event is through ἀφῆκεν τὸ πνεῦμα (Matthew), and ἐξέπνευσεν (Mark and Luke). The word παρέδωκεν that the Fourth Gospel uses reflects 10:18: οὐδεὶς αἴρει αὐτὴν ἀπ' ἐμοῦ, ἀλλ' ἐγὼ τίθημι αὐτὴν ἀπ' ἐμαυτοῦ. ἐξουσίαν ἔχω θεῖναι αὐτήν, καὶ ἐξουσίαν ἔχω πάλιν λαβεῖν αὐτήν· ταύτην τὴν ἐντολὴν ἔλαβον παρὰ τοῦ πατρός μου. It interprets the death of Jesus as a conscious act, as an act of reciprocation, for the complete self-

---

65 See R. Bultmann, *Das Evangelium des Johannes*, 523. But Bultmann holds Dodd's interpretation possible.
66 See G. R. Beasley-Murray, *John*, 352.
67 See M. M. Thompson, *The Humanity of Jesus in the Fourth Gospel* (Phildelphia: Fortress, 1988), 109; R. E. Brown, *The Gospel according to John*, 2:931; R. Schnackenburg, *The Gospel according to St. John*, 2:234.

emptying of the Father in giving His Son (ἔδωκεν—3:16, cf. 5:20). The Son empties himself even unto death in completing the mission entrusted to him by His Father.

2.7 That You may Believe—Jesus the Christ, the Son of God

Those who defend the idea that vv. 30–31 were originally the concluding summary of the sign source, and thereby argue that the 'Thomas confession' and the so called explicit pronouncement of the Evangelist's purpose of writing the Fourth Gospel should be kept at a critical distance for an effective exegesis and interpretation, should be able to recognise the fact that the Evangelist consciously made his choice of the concluding summary and its real relationship with 20:29.[68] Udo Schnelle interprets Thomas' story expressively as a Johannine sign which the Evangelist meant to be understood in direct connection with vv. 30–31. With these verses σημεῖον becomes the hermeneutical key to the entire presentation of Jesus' words and deeds.[69] The story of Thomas' confrontation/recognition of the risen one cannot be separated from the Evangelist's concluding statement in v. 30–31. The particle οὖν indicates a logical continuation from the previous verse.[70] Raymond Brown draws a connection between vv. 21 and 30, and rightly contends that the disciples mentioned in v. 30 were those commissioned in v. 21 to bring the challenge to those who were not eye witnesses. Thus in moving vv. 30–31 from the signs worked before the disciples to the faith of the reader, the Fourth Evangelist is carrying on the chain of thought forward in vv. 29a and 29b.[71]

---

[68] F. Neirynck, "The Sign Source in the Fourth Gospel: A Critique of the Hypothesis," in *Evangelica: Collected Essays*, vol. 2 (BETL 99; Leuven: University Press, 1991), 668–77, esp. 676.

[69] U. Schnelle, *Antidoketische Christologie im Johannesevangelium: Eine Untersuchung zur Stellung des 4. Evangeliums in der johanneischen Schule* (FRLANT 144; Göttingen: Vandenhoeck & Ruprecht, 1987), 155–56, and G. R. Beasley-Murray, *John*, 387.

[70] P. J. Judge, "A Note on Jn 20, 29," in *The Four Gospels, 1992: Festschrift Frans Neirynck* (ed. F. van Segbroeck, et al.; 3 vols.; BETL 100; Leuven: University Press, 1992), 3:2191, and D. A. Carson, *The Gospel according to John* (Leicester: InterVarsity Press, 1991), 660–61.

[71] R. E. Brown, *The Gospel according to John*, 2:1059.

To what does the Jesus beatitude—μακάριοι οἱ μὴ ἰδόντες καὶ πιστεύσαντες—refer? Does the Johannine Jesus commend the Thomas confession and acknowledge his "my Lord, my God" or does the Johannine Jesus take into account Thomas recognising the sign of the resurrection? The context seems to tell us that Thomas was not willing to believe the sign of resurrection without an experiential and factual verification (ἑώρακάς με πεπίστευκας; "did you believe me because you have seen?"). The immediate response of Jesus to Thomas' confession of belief is a question.[72] Here we see a strong criticism of Thomas' stiff-necked demand for a tangible proof of faith! Where tangible proofs are available, one is asked to evaluate, recognise and accept. But believing is committing oneself to the other (God), putting oneself at another's disposal without any reservations, questions and doubts.

In fact all the disciples and Mary Magdalene believed when they saw. Even Peter and the other disciples mentioned in vv. 3–8 were indeed convinced not through the appearance of the risen Lord, but through the sight of the empty grave—note καὶ εἶδεν καὶ ἐπίστευσεν in v. 8. Thomas in fact demanded no other proof than that which Jesus had freely offered the others (v. 20).

Thomas becomes for the Fourth Evangelist a representative of those whose faith relies entirely/completely on signs, such as those already rebuked/warned by Jesus during his earthly ministry (cf. 4:48). For the Fourth Evangelist, 'witnesses' to God's acts play a greater role in leading people to believe. The accusing tone in the Johannine Jesus' reaction to Thomas' confession therefore should be comprehended in the broader framework of Johannine Theology. One is reminded of 14:9 where Jesus says ὁ ἑωρακὼς ἐμὲ ἑώρακεν τὸν πατέρα. It is 'the witness' of Jesus that enables persons to 'see.' One should be careful not to oversimplify and equate the heard word as the proclaimed word in which recounted events have become symbolically picturised for the fellowship with the Lord,[73] for such are in danger of losing all contacts with the concrete tangible life of God present in the world. Such 'hearing' the word should be understood according to the

---

[72] Holtzmann, Bauer, Bernard, Bultmann, Sanders, Morris, Becker, Haenchen and Schnackenburg see in v. 29a a positive statement, though Schnackenburg detects an accusing tone! See for detailed arguments to consider v. 29a as a statement, U. Schnelle, *Antidoketische Christologie im Johannesevangelium*, 158, and G. R. Beasley-Murray, *John*, 386.

[73] R. Bultmann, *Das Evangelium des Johannes*, 539.

Johannine kerygma—ὁ λόγος σὰρξ ἐγένετο.⁷⁴ Therefore the risen one exhorts Thomas 'to experience him' in hearing 'the witness'—"we have seen the Lord"—and thus to see without seeing, and they are the ones pronounced blessed in v. 29, not those who confessed Jesus as "my Lord, my God."

The scholarly discussion of the Johannine purpose is usually tied up with the textual decision between the present subjunctive πιστεύητε supported by P⁶⁶ᵛⁱᵈ (probability) ℵ, B, Θ, 0250, 892 and aorist subjunctive πιστεύσητε supported by A, C, D, K, L, rell.⁷⁵ It has been argued that if the aorist subjunctive, strictly interpreted suggests that the Fourth Gospel was addressed to non-Christians 'so that they might come to believe that Jesus is the Christ . . .,' then the present subjunctive suggests that the aim of the writer was to strengthen the faith of those who already believe, 'that you may continue to believe.'⁷⁶ The early support, however, is clearly for the present subjunctive. Here, the primary Egyptian (P⁶⁶ ℵ B the earliest), some secondary witnesses of this tradition (0250, 892), and the non-Egyptian Θ form a considerable combination of evidence in favour of πιστεύητε. Whereas the earliest evidence for the aorist subjunctive stems from textual tradition of fifth century A, C, D, W etc., the aorist of πιστεύειν in the Fourth Gospel certainly has often an ingressive character, but not necessarily nor always (cf. 4:50; 7:39; 11:15, 40; 12:42; 14:29; 20:29).

The passages 11:15 and 14:29 are noteworthy where, in a similar ἵνα clause the certainly not unbelieving disciples are being addressed—they are to receive a new impulse of their faith. Furthermore, in 11:40, Martha who had already proclaimed her faith is reminded of the same with ἐὰν πιστεύσῃς. Therefore the aorist subjunctive does not necessarily have to indicate the commencement of new faith, or conversion to faith.⁷⁷ It could also refer to the simple act of believing without making a point when.⁷⁸

---

74 See P. J. Judge, "A Note on Jn 20, 29," 2190.
75 See the similar textual variant in 19:35 where again the other speaks directly to his readers—πιστεύητε P⁶⁶ᵛⁱᵈ ℵ* B, ψ Origen; πιστεύσητε rell.
76 B. M. Metzger, *A Textual Commentary on the Greek New Testament*, 256.
77 R. Schnackenburg, *The Gospel according to St. John*, 3:338.
78 G. D. Fee, "On the Text and Meaning of Jn 20, 30–31," in *The Four Gospels, 1992: Festschrift Frans Neirynck* (ed. F. van Segbroeck, et al.; 3 vols.; BETL 100; Leuven: University Press, 1992), 3:2199. He argues that the aorist is what an author would be expected to use if he had no specific kind of action in mind, and thus has no further significance at all. He contends that in the Johannine use of the aorist, most are strictly punctiliar, some of them are undoubtedly constative, for example John 1:8.

Therefore we need not be fanatical in choosing between the textual variants in order to detect whether the purpose of writing the Fourth Gospel was evangelistic, or for the members of a believing community.

So far as the Evangelist is concerned it is irrelevant whether the target readers are already Christians or as yet not. For him, believing (he does not use the noun πίστις, but the verb form πιστεύειν) is not a once-for-all decision, a static state of being, it is continual commitment, it must perpetually ascertain itself anew.[79] We need to add that several studies in the recent years, especially those centred around the themes of the community behind the Fourth Gospel, the traditions behind the Fourth Gospel, and the composition and order of the Fourth Gospel have enlightened our understanding to interpret the Gospel that was produced within, and for the sake of a believing community that stood over against various forces from within and without.[80]

The Johannine call to the reader is ὅτι Ἰησοῦς ἐστιν ὁ χριστὸς ὁ υἱὸς τοῦ θεοῦ. The χριστός title is used in the Fourth Gospel in order to discuss a number of issues in contemporary Messianic speculations. Using the title χριστός, the Evangelist joined the discussion regarding the traditions of the hiddenness of the Messiah (7:27b), messianic age and messianic signs and wonders (7:31), and the Davidic lineage of the Messiah (7:42; cf. 6:42; 7:52; 1:46).[81] The Johannine Jesus himself does not use the term χριστός nor deny its applicability. However, when confronted with the question in 10:24 whether he himself is the Christ he evades a direct answer to declare his oneness with the Father (see exegesis of 10:30). The attempt to explain χριστός through the Father–Son imagery and through his unique relationship with the Father is distinctly Johannine. It has perhaps though a Synoptic parallel, the Matthaean reworking of Peter's Caesarean confession of Jesus: σὺ εἶ ὁ χριστὸς ὁ υἱὸς τοῦ θεοῦ τοῦ ζῶντος.[82]

In Jewish Theology, too, the Messiah (ὁ χριστός) and Son of God were synonymous, ὁ χριστός as ὁ υἱὸς τοῦ θεοῦ being understood in adoptionist terms in line with the coronation in Psalm 2. It is interesting to find ὁ χριστός

---

79 See R. Bultmann, *Das Evangelium des Johannes*, 541.
80 G. D. Fee, "On the Text and Meaning of Jn 20, 30–31," 2205.
81 See M. L. Appold, *The Oneness Motif in the Fourth Gospel: Motif Analysis and Exegetical Probe into the Theology of John* (WUNT 2.1; Tübingen: J. C. B. Mohr [Paul Siebeck], 1991), 65–68; M. de Jonge, "Jewish Expectations about the Messiah According to the Fourth Gospel," *NTS* 19 (1972–73): 246–70.
82 Matt 16:16; cf. Mark 8:29; Luke 9:20.

(with the article) only here and on Martha's lips (11:27) in the Fourth Gospel, but each time in combination with ὁ υἱὸς τοῦ θεοῦ. Even where the designation χριστός is formalised and used as a proper name (1:17; 17:3) its contextual setting points beyond traditional messianic expectations by adding a qualifying statement to signify the Son's continual communion with the Father (1:18), and to relate co-ordinately 'the only true God' with Jesus Christ whom "You have sent" (17:3). Therefore the title ὁ χριστός in its co-ordination with ὁ υἱὸς τοῦ θεοῦ portrays Jesus as the Messiah, God's unique Agent with a mission. It signifies Jesus' unique relationship to God, his origin and his oneness with the Father (see for a further exploration of the oneness theme the following chapter). Nevertheless, it very consciously stops short of exhorting the community to believe and confess Jesus—My God!

2.8 Summary and Conclusions

a) The Thomas Pericope in isolation might have been affirming Jesus as God! Even in the arrest scene as compact tradition in itself, the ἐγώ εἰμι of Jesus could have been understood to proclaim Jesus' divinity. But the Fourth Evangelist in redacting the two independent traditional pericopes into his passion–resurrection narrative structure, gives them a theological re-orientation.
b) The Johannine passion narrative confidently characterises Jesus as God's righteous/obedient agent who fulfils his entrusted mission.
c) The christological titles, the Lamb of God, the Man, the King (of Jews), the Messiah, the Son of God all point to the mission entrusted to Jesus.
d) At the time of Jesus' betrayal and arrest—an unjust trial and an innocent's death for witnessing to the Truth—God is portrayed as the faithful companion and protector and source of strength. Jesus' belief in God's faithfulness gives him confidence as he commands control even in the face of grave adversity.
e) The confidence, courage, self-composure and control over the situation even in the face of death makes Jesus the 'King.' However Jesus redefines his kingship as the witness to the Truth, who helps his subjects to stand by and choose justice, and renounce injustice. He is a sign of God's power which enables people to decide from God's perspective, which liberates the innocent and sets free.

f) βασιλεία of God is universal. Jesus is the sign of God's kingship, he points to the saving sovereignty of the Saviour God. It makes God's reality effective in the world.
g) Jesus as the 'Pascal Lamb'/(lamb) of God symbolises not a sacrificial death, but God's call to unconditional obedience. In such obedience the meek/weak/powerless becomes the place where God's mighty works become manifest. Therefore the liberation is not in expiation, but is a sign of the restored creational relationship, through obedience which bridges broken relationships between the Creator and His creation.
h) ὁ ἄνθρωπος speaks not only of Jesus' true humanity, but of his being the sign of true humanity, as the crown of creation, as it ought to be, in the image of God—now in ὁ λόγος σὰρξ ἐγένετο.
i) A theocentric Jesus cannot himself become God! The ἐγώ εἰμι becomes the sovereignty and integrity of the righteous servant of God in the midst of betrayal and arrest. And "my Lord, my God" becomes a worshipping confession of joy for God's vindication of His Son, the Sent One, through the sign of the resurrection. Moreover, the Evangelist immediately relativises the Thomas confession in the text context through two conscious editorial notes: 1) through the beatitude which proclaims that the blessed are not those who confess Jesus as God, but those who believe the sign of resurrection without seeing, and 2) through a passionate exhortation to the community to continue to believe in Jesus as the Sent One (Christ) and the liberator who brings creation and the Creator back into creational relationship (Messiah). They are but the Evangelist's clear and explicit call to reinterpret the christological claim that Jesus is Lord and God within the monotheistic theological system.

Chapter Three

Theology in Conflict—Is Jesus Equal to God?

(John 5:17–30)

3.1 Introduction

The profundity of this section in the whole of the Fourth Gospel is evident. Jesus calling himself 'equal to God' and 'the Son' seems to be explained theologically in the light of his relationship with God, the Father. The Son carries out the function that is God's alone, namely, the giving of life in all its fullness and judging righteously. He is God's unique, ultimate, historical and eschatological revelation to the world. This discourse undoubtedly reveals the Fourth Evangelist's intimately connected Christology and Eschatology, but has often been read from the viewpoint of later dogmatic developments, and thus attempts so far have been to see the christological significance of the passage about Johannine Eschatology.

The following exegetical study departs from this approach to probe how the Theology (understanding of God) creates a new Christology, thereby trying to understand Johannine Christology-Eschatology as a product of a theological crisis. We no more ask the all important question: Who is Jesus? to the text, but try to understand how the language hereupon reserved only to speak of 'God' is now used to describe Jesus and his activities.

In other words, we ask the questions: How was Jesus 'theologised'? How was belief in God (Theology), in a new way related to the historical events that revolved around Jesus, thereby becoming the source of christological language? Can one explain the eschatological tension and the christological crisis as the product of the author's dilemma over his idea of, and belief in, God? Has the Fourth Evangelist's preconceived concept of God been a determining factor in his Christology and Eschatology to create a new Theology (new understanding of God)?

3.2 Order of Chapters Five and Six

Anyone who ventures into the exegesis of John 5 is faced with a decision regarding the scholarly opinion adduced by Rudolf Bultmann, that chapter 6 ought to be placed before chapter 5. The reasons[1] he gives for this interchange are substantial and impressive, they cannot be easily set aside. I do not intend to argue that Bultmann is demonstrably wrong in placing chapter 6 before 5, but would like to make one or two positive suggestions in support of the traditional view:

a) The discourse in chapter 5:17–18 follows two miracle stories: 4:46–54, where a Gentile is the principle figure, who believes and sees a miracle of 'healing,' and 5:1–16, where the principle figure is a Jew, the Jews see a miracle of healing and of liberation from sin (see v. 15), but apparently do not believe. If not coincidental, it indicates that the Evangelist has purposefully paired these two miracles, as these two 'healing' stories give a new dimension to the Sabbath controversy, a new understanding of the Sabbath celebration (see the exegesis below).

b) The discussion of the work of the Father and the Son in chapter 5, in my opinion, should form the proper background for the interpretation of chapter 6, especially 6:28ff.

In displacing chapters, Bultmann presupposes the orderliness and logical consistency of the Evangelist's mind. One needs to make a general judgement about whether the Evangelist's line of thought moved in an orderly progression, without sometimes or even frequently slipping from one theme to another. The Fourth Gospel as a whole permits us to presuppose that the Fourth Evangelist allowed himself a somewhat circular thought and expression pattern, and lacked logical progression. We should not presuppose that he wrote a good historical narrative and that his Gospel hangs by a single thread, but rather depends upon a number of factors: theological, thematic, geographical and chronological.[2]

---

1 See R. Bultmann, *Das Evangelium des Johannes*, 154ff.
2 For a good evaluation of Bultmann's position, see D. M. Smith, *The Composition and Order of the Fourth Gospel: Bultmann's Literary Theory* (New Haven: Yale University Press, 1965), 119–78, esp. 128–34.

3.3 The Pericope

There is some hesitation on the part of the scholars as to where the discourse begins. Some would like to see the beginning of the discourse at v. 16, where the Evangelist starts to speak of the Jews' refusal to accept Jesus' claim to have power over the law of the Sabbath,[3] while others see a division from v. 7, where a new start is made with Ὁ δὲ [Ἰησοῦς] ἀπεκρίνατο αὐτοῖς, thus making v. 16 the conclusion of all that has gone before.[4]

Actually, in vv. 9b–18 we have an editorial remark. Here we have comments of the Evangelist's (vv. 9b, 16, 18), words of Jesus in direct speech (vv. 14, 17), and a report of the proceedings between the cured man and the Jews once again in direct speech (vv. 10–13, 15). While v. 16 concludes the sign of the healing episode at the pool of the Beth-za'tha and recalls the immediate reaction of the Jews to it, vv. 17–18 lift the episode into another level of controversy giving rise to an important discourse.[5] Thus, vv. 17–18 play to perfection the role of a transitional note.[6] And a solemn ἀμὴν ἀμὴν λέγω ὑμῖν of v. 19 starts with a typical Johannine use of οὖν telling us to watch out, for something important is about to follow which is nevertheless connected to what has gone before.[7]

Where then does the division end: at v. 29 or v. 30? There seems to be a break between these two verses. But, if analysed carefully the argument changes only in v. 31. Here Jesus begins to speak about μαρτυρία. The noun or verb μαρτυρέω appears five times in vv. 31–32, while it has not appeared at all in vv. 19–30. The dominant themes of the discourse are: the giving of life and judgement. As v. 30 still concerns itself with the question of

---

3 R. Schnackenburg, *The Gospel according to St. John*, 2:90–91, and C. K. Barrett, *The Gospel according to St. John*, 214.
4 See G. H. C. Macgregor, *The Gospel of John* (MNTC; London: Hodder and Stoughton, 1928), 181.
5 The link between the words and ideas of vv. 17–18 and 19–30 is well shown by P. Gächter, "Zur Form von Joh 5:19–30," in *Neutestamentliche Aufsätze: Festschrift für Josef Schmid zum 70. Geburtstag* (ed. J. Blinzler; Regensburg: Pustet, 1963), 65ff.
6 See H. van Dyke Parunak, "Transitional Techniques in the Bible," *JBL* 102/4 (1983): 538–39. R. E. Brown, *The Gospel according to John*, 1:213, notes concerning John 5:17–18: "We treat these verses as an introduction to the discourse since there is a lapidary saying in v. 17 which supplies the subject for what follows." C. K. Barrett, *The Gospel according to St. John*, 213, observes that v. 17 is the seed out of which the discourse grows. Also see E. C. Hoskyns, *The Fourth Gospel*, 266.
7 See *BDF*, § 451.1.

judgement brought by Jesus, it, in all probability, belongs to the discourse which precedes it.[8] This is confirmed by the fact that there is a deliberate and classical linguistic parallel between vv. 19 and 30.

Thus, the discourse appears to be contained within two verses which speak of Jesus' absolute dependence on the Father. The Father–Son relationship which works out in their sharing the role of life-giving and judgement, and also in their sharing the honour, is put in the firm 'context' of the Son's absolute dependence upon and obedience to the Father.

3.4 The Structure

The internal structure of the discourse has been the source of another intense discussion. Charles Harold Dodd[9] and Paul Gächter[10] have claimed independently that a traditional parable stands behind vv. 19–20a.[11] Gächter however links v. 30 with the parable, and claims it to be the original application of the parable made by Jesus himself. He argues, that the Evangelist's original discourse was vv. 19–20, 24, 30, with him adding the clearly Johannine verse 24 to the traditional material. The rest of the discourse, according to him, has been gathered from various sources by the Evangelist, notably vv. 28 and 29 from a traditional apocalyptic source. He insists that behind the various elements of the discourse stands the figure of the Evangelist, who has structured this discourse chiastically with v. 24 as the central statement.[12]

---

8   Most scholars see a clear break at v. 30 and propose a new topic from v. 31. See J. Blank, *Krisis*, 109 n. 1; C. H. Dodd, *Interpretation of the Fourth Gospel*, 320; E. C. Hoskyns, *The Fourth Gospel*, 267; B. Lindars, *The Gospel of John*, 221–27; S. Schulz, *Untersuchungen zur Menschensohn-Christologie im Johannesevangelium: Zugleich ein Beitrag zur Methodengeschichte der Auslegung des 4. Evangeliums* (Göttingen: Vandenhoeck & Ruprecht, 1957), 109–10; A. Wikenhauser, *Das Evangelium nach Johannes*, 116–19; P. Gächter, "Zur Form von Joh 5:19–30," 65–68; R. H. Lightfoot, *St. John's Gospel* (Oxford: Clarendon Press, 1956), 141–45, and J. N. Sanders, *A Commentary on the Gospel according to St. John* (BNTC 4; London: Black, 1968), 166.
9   C. H. Dodd, "A Hidden Parable in the Fourth Gospel (Jn 5:19–20a)," in *More New Testament Studies* (Manchester: University Press, 1968), 30–40.
10   P. Gächter, "Zur Form von Joh 5:19–30," 67–68.
11   R. E. Brown and B. Lindars approve the suggestion, but the absolute use of ὁ υἱός has caused R. Schnackenburg to regard the theory as improbable, as he calls attention to the Johannine "Son" Christology, and as the title used theologically here is too far removed from a traditional background.
12   P. Gächter, "Zur Form von Joh 5:19–30," 65.

The problem of Eschatology of vv. 21–29 has caused further suggestions concerning the structure and redaction of the discourse. The simplest and most radical suggestion is that of Bultmann. He argues that vv. 28–29 reflect a later addition of 'final Eschatology' foreign to Johannine realised Eschatology, probably by an ecclesiastical redactor, and as such should be regarded as interpolation.[13] Therefore, the interpretive task should be focused on the genuine Johannine material.

Marie-Émile Boismard unwilling to make such a radical dissection of the text suggested a structure representing two stages of growth, namely: a) vv. 26–30 and b) vv. 19–25. According to him, vv. 19–25 are a "re-lecture" of vv. 26–30 representing a later stage in the development of tradition.[14] Raymond Brown follows this suggestion without committing himself to a judgement concerning the earlier or later development of two different eschatological motives,[15] his structure is simple and straightforward:

I	Division:	the two-fold Sabbath work of Jesus, namely to give life and to judge—realised Eschatology, vv. 19–25.[16]
II	Duplicate of Division I:	The same theme in terms of final Eschatology, vv. 26–30.[17]

In Brown's opinion the Johannine tradition has preserved two forms of the discourse as reflected in vv. 21–25 and vv. 26–29, with vv. 19–20 as a probable traditional parable introducing the discourse, and v. 30 as a probable original application summing up various themes in the discourse conclusion.[18]

---

13 R. Bultmann, *Das Evangelium des Johannes*, 196–97; see also S. Schulz, *Untersuchungen zur Menschensohn-Christologie im Johannesevangelium*, 109–11; idem, *Das Evangelium nach Johannes*, 89–90, and R. Schnackenburg, *The Gospel according to St. John*, 2:114–17.

14 According to M.-É. Boismard, there is no contact with 1 John in vv. 26–30. Jesus is represented as Danielic Son of Man as in the Synoptic tradition. VV. 28–29 clearly indicate a physical resurrection with no indication of time. In vv. 19–25, the contact with 1 John is strong. Jesus is presented in terms of Johannine Father–Son relationship. V. 25 speaks of a spiritual resurrection here and now. Boismard seems to make the issue of contact with 1 John all important, but one wonders how he would explain such "future" sayings as 1 John 2:28; 3:2 and 4:17.

15 R. E. Brown, *The Gospel according to John*, 1:218–20.

16 *Ibid.*, 218–19.

17 *Ibid*, 219.

18 According to Brown, the final redaction takes place in the last stage of his reconstructed 'five stage theory'; *ibid.*, xxiv–xxxix.

A. C. Sundberg has argued that the discourse should be rearranged with vv. 17–20, 26, 21; 22 and 27 forming couplets. VV. 23–24 and 25 are a couplet with vv. 28–29, 30.[19] This rearrangement eliminates any subordination of Jesus, making him equal to God. Apart from lack of any objective proof for such a rearrangement, the passage must be understood in the light of the rest of the Gospel where Jesus is subject to the will of the Father.[20]

J. H. Neyrey claims that 5:19–30 supports the distinctive Johannine high Christology. In explaining Jesus' equality with God the Evangelist collected older Johannine and traditional materials as well, to which he added special new material. The purpose of this collection was not to domesticate Johannine Eschatology, but to powerfully promote the Fourth Evangelist's high christological confession that Jesus is equal to God. According to him, 5:19–21, 24, 25, 30 are older Johannine material, 5:22, 27, 28 and 29 are traditional futuristic material and vv. 23 and 26 are distinctive eschatological material.[21]

The rearrangements, the attempts to layer out traditions, the chiastic formations and their results are often complicated or artificial. Perhaps, we should divert our attention towards the Fourth Evangelist's self-contained allusiveness in his movements from theme to theme and back and forth. The discourse appears to be moving in the following fashion:

vv. 17–18   The Overture—Is Jesus equal to God?
vv. 19–30   The Father and the Son—Relationship explained.
vv. 19–20   Theological introduction: The Father's self-emptying in the Son and the absolute dependence of the Son upon the Father.
vv. 21–22   The Father's self-emptying—Basis of the Son's authority to give life and judge.
v. 23   Theological reflection: the honour due the Son because of his relationship with the Father.
vv. 24–25   The Son as the Life-Giver and the Judge—Eternal life and judgement as the present reality.

---

19 A. C. Sundberg Jr, "Isos to Theo Christology in John 5:17–30," in *Papers of the Chicago Society of Biblical Research* 15 (1970): 19–31.
20 See John 6:38; 10:18; 12:49; 14:31; 15:10.
21 See J. H. Neyrey, *An Ideology of Revolt*, 9–35. Neyrey considers final Eschatology an integral part of the discourse and gives it due place in the exegesis. But a question worth asking is, whether one can so easily layer out different traditions from the Johannine discourse and try to rearrange it in order to prove Jesus' equality to God. Also see J. Frey, *Die johanneische Eschatologie*. Vol. III: *Die eschatologische Verkündigung in den johanneischen Texten* (WUNT 117; Tübingen: J. C. B. Mohr [Paul Siebeck], 2000), 326–41.

v. 26   The Son has life in himself.
v. 27   The Son's authority to judge as the Son of Man.
vv. 28–29 The open Eschatology—the Son as judge with life-giving as a subtheme.
v. 30   The Theological conclusion: the absolute dependence of the Son upon the Father.

3.5 The Context

Verse 16—"So because Jesus was doing these things on the Sabbath, the Jews persecuted him"—is wholly understandable in the *'einmalig'* Palestinian frame of Jesus' life. But in v. 17 Jesus defends his breaking of the Sabbath law by uttering words which clearly imply a quasi-divine claim on his own part, and the reasons given again in v. 18 are surely the same allegations put forward to kill Jesus in his earthly lifetime. And then, v. 19 onwards, we are confronted with a discourse explaining the claim made in v. 17.

Here we see a reflection of the community's experience with/against the Jewish synagogue. A radical reworking of the Jesus tradition is seen with reference to the persecution and the identity crisis.[22] If we take J. Louis Martyn's thesis which rightly calls the Fourth Gospel a two-level drama,[23] then the connection between the tradition and the contemporary community experience is not random and defective, but essentially and consciously constructed. The very 'anamnesis' of episodes in the *'einmalig'* Palestinian life of Jesus now become signs and the story of the community. They are not just narrated to indicate mere anticipation of the sovereignty of God, but its reality in their own midst.

Thus, Jesus' breaking of the Sabbath raises not only a legal discussion, but also the central issue of his relationship with the Torah/prophets and

---

22 In an attempt to find a Synoptic parallel to the healing at Beth-za'tha, scholars point towards Mark 2:1–12—the healing of the paralytic. True, there seem to be a lot of deducible parallels and it is also noteworthy that it was Jesus' forgiving the sins of the paralytic that made the Pharisees and Herodians (the Fourth Evangelist makes it the rejection of the whole Jewish nation!) allege that Jesus usurped divine power and authority. But one should admit that, given the masterly editorial work, the separation of traditional materials from a tightly knit Fourth Gospel is almost an impossibility; see L. Th. Witkamp, "The Use of Traditions in John 5:1–18," *JSNT* 25 (1985): 19–47.

23 See his *History and Theology in the Fourth Gospel*, 68–73.

most importantly to the only, one God. The litigation now snowballs into a theological crisis and the discussion of religious identity, thereby calling it to question the community's theological identification, its faith and belief in the Jewish Scriptures and its most treasured Monotheism. Thus, it is but natural that such a situation, where tradition and contemporary experience interpret and reinforce each other, leads to a new theological perspective and development.

3.6 Exegesis

3.6.1 Verses 17–18: Overture—Is Jesus Equal to God?

Verse 17 begins with the phrase Ὁ δὲ ['Ιησοῦς] ἀπεκρίνατο αὐτοῖς. The aorist middle form of the verb ἀποκρίνομαι (ἀπεκρινάμην) is used instead of the passive form ἀπεκρίθην as a middle. Ἀπεκρίνατο occurs here and in v. 19, twice out of seventy-eight occurrences of ἀποκρίνομαι in the Fourth Gospel. Ἀπεκρίνατο is the Jewish historian Josephus' usual form of writing. However, it occurs seven times in the whole of the New Testament, always reserved for solemn or legal utterances.[24] Here Jesus makes a 'claim'—a declaration not in response to any particular question posed to him, but only to the ascribed thoughts of the audience. It sounds like a typical and formal defence of his own behaviour.[25] ἀπεκρίνατο here means 'he made answer to the charge,' 'he defended himself.'[26]

The Synoptics report the Sabbath controversies, but the claim ὁ πατήρ μου ἕως ἄρτι ἐργάζεται κἀγὼ ἐργάζομαι made here by Jesus lifts the Sabbath controversy to a higher level of defence, usually not found in the Synoptics. The breaking of the Sabbath is normally defended on the following counts in the Synoptic Gospels:

a) by arguing about the precedence of David breaking the Sabbath—if great David had himself broken the Sabbath, why cannot great David's greater Son!

---

24 W. Bauer, et al., *A Greek-English Lexicon*, 93.
25 A good analogy to John 5:17, 19 is Luke 3:16.
26 J. H. Moulton & G. Milligan, *The Vocabulary of the Greek Testament: Illustrated from the Papyri and Other Non-Literary Sources* (London: Hodder and Stoughton, 1930), 29, also say that the aorist middle are frequent in papyri, but they are without exception legal reports. See also E. A. Abbott, *Johannine Grammar*, § 2537.

b) by citing humanitarian reasons and acts of mercy—Sabbath is made for man (human), not man for the Sabbath. Is it lawful to do good on Sabbath?

c) by claiming special prophetic authority to reform and correct the Sabbath—'God prefers mercy to sacrifice,' 'The Son of Man is the Lord of the Sabbath.'[27]

The Fourth Evangelist seems to rework the implicit theological force of the Son of Man being the Lord of the Sabbath, and makes it explicit by not only invoking Jesus' special relationship with God the Father, but also by directly alluding to God's continuous working. What does ἐργάζεται mean? In making this claim the Evangelist exhibits knowledge of contemporary Jewish discussions. It was clear that God could not rest on the Sabbath. But this caused serious theological difficulties for them. On the one hand the Torah taught clearly that God rested on the Sabbath (Gen 2:2; Exod 20:11; 31:17), yet on the other hand the faith of Israel preserved the belief that God never left the world to follow its own destiny. God always directs history.

Therefore, the Rabbis gave special attention to explain the Sabbath rest of God, maintaining on the one hand that God does not 'rest' on the Sabbath, and arguing on the other that the constancy of God's working also on Sabbath should not create an ethical dichotomy between the position of God and that of humankind, since the Creator Himself would then disregard the very precept He entrusted upon His creatures. Though their answers varied argumentatively from one another, they appealed to the fact that God's providence remained active on the Sabbath, for otherwise the universe would cease to exist. God rested from the work of creating His world, but not from His work of moral judgement. Thus God's working on the Sabbath was an acknowledged factor in Jewish Theology.[28]

The Hellenistic Jewish philosopher Philo too argued that God never ceases to act.[29] Even in the classical Greek thought form, for example

---

27 See Mark 2:23–3:6; Luke 6:1–11; 13:15 and Matt 12:1–14.

28 See especially Midrashim *Genesis Rabbah* 11:10; *Exodus Rabbah* 30:6, 9. These discussions are found in detail in H. L. Strack & P. Billerbeck, *Kommentar zum Neuen Testament aus Talmud und Midrasch*, 2:461–62. See also C. H. Dodd, *Interpretation of the Fourth Gospel*, 321–22; J. H. Bernard, *Commentary on the Gospel according to St. John*, 1:232; C. K. Barrett, *The Gospel according to St. John*, 255–56; W. Bauer, *Das Johannesevangelium*, 82, and E. Haenchen, *John: A Commentary on the Gospel of John* (trans. R. W. Funk; 2 vols.; Hermeneia; Philadelphia: Fortress, 1984), 1:248–49.

29 See Philo, *Leg. All.* 1.5–6: "God never ceases to act; but as it is the property of fire to warm and of snow to chill, so it is the property of God to make... He causes to

Aristotle's doctrine that God is pure activity (ἐνέργεια) this is of cardinal importance.³⁰ Hermetic writers too adopt this view when they write that the sense and thought of God is this, that He is always moving all things.³¹ Therefore, that God continues His work even on the Sabbath was an agreed theological principle among Jews and Greeks though their God concepts varied to a great extent. But the question we now need to ask is whether the Fourth Evangelist here alludes to the Sabbath celebration as a memorial to God's rest at creation, or to the Sabbath as a celebration of the Exodus experience and liberation?

The deuteronomical version of the Decalogue describes the Sabbath celebration as the commemoration of Israel's liberation from Egypt: "Remember that you were slaves in Egypt and that the Lord your God brought you out of there with a mighty hand and an outstretched arm. Therefore, the Lord your God has commanded you to observe the Sabbath day." The acknowledged theological fact that the Israelites first experienced God as the liberator God led to the belief that the Liberator Himself is the Creator. This then led to what may probably be extended to the fact that the Sabbath was first connected with liberation.

The Genesis creation stories and the Theology probably indicate that on the 7th day God did not do anything, but that He enjoyed/celebrated the completion of creation, which He saw as 'good.' But the Pentateuch editors then led us to the theological depiction of the 'fall' and the 'bondage' it brought about. We should, therefore, ask the question: can God really enjoy and celebrate Sabbath when the creation He saw as 'good' is 'fallen' and no more considered to be good?

---

rest that which... He is apparently making, but He Himself never ceases making." In *Cher.* 87 Philo explains that God's rest does not mean that He ceases to do good since that which is the cause of all things is by nature active and never has any respite from doing the best. In *Leg. All.* 1.16 he distinguishes between the creation of mortal things which was completed with the divine Sabbath rest and the creation of divine things which still continues.

30   There is something which moves without being moved, that it is eternal and is both substance and activity—ἔστι τι ὃ οὐ κρινούμενον κινεῖ ἀίδιον καὶ οὐσία καὶ ἐνέργεια οὖσα (Aristotle, *Metaphysics* Λ 1072a, 25, 26). This unmoved mover is God whom he defines as the eternal best living being—φαμὲν δὴ τὸν θεὸν εἶναι ζῷον ἀίδιον ἄριστον (*Metaphysics* Λ1072b, 29, 30)—quoted in J. N. Sanders, *A Commentary on the Gospel according to St. John*, 163.

31   *Corp. herm.* IX:9: καὶ τοῦτο ἔστιν ἡ αἴσθησις καὶ νόησις τοῦ θεοῦ τὸ τὰ πάντα ἀεὶ κινεῖν.

Interestingly in John 7:22–24 to silence the echo of the controversy over the Sabbath and to further establish the legality of Jesus' action, the Fourth Evangelist wisely uses the example of circumcision. It was legitimate to circumcise a child on the Sabbath, if it happened to be the 8th day after his birth (Lev 12:3), because circumcision was regarded as a redemptive act which mediated the liberation covenant. It was, in other words, legitimate to make a person 'whole.' This theory also receives interesting backing from the 2nd century Gnostic Tractate *The Gospel of Truth* 1:32 where Jesus says, "... what is the Sabbath, on which it is not fitting for salvation to be idle...." This allows us to conveniently conclude that the Evangelist is referring to the two healing stories as acts of 'bringing wholeness' and 'liberation,' and that the Evangelist draws the Jews' attention to the reality of the Sabbath—a celebration of the continuing search for the Exodus experience, liberation and the wholeness.

The translation of the adverb ἕως ἄρτι has been a problem. ἕως ἄρτι has been translated as 'even until now,' 'to this very day,' 'until now,' 'until this very hour,' but traditionally it has been understood as 'continually and always.' 'Until now,' 'even until now,' 'to this very hour' may refer to the culmination of God's work, whereas 'continually,' 'always' may suggest constancy or continuity. The implications of constancy and culmination are radically different. In my opinion, the emphasis should be on constancy rather than culmination because there is no implication in the text to deduce that the time has now come or soon will come for work to stop. Moreover, the verb that follows the adverb ἕως ἄρτι is in the present tense and describes an action continuing.[32]

---

[32] C. K. Barrett, *The Gospel according to St. John*, 255; J. N. Sanders, *A Commentary on the Gospel according to St. John*, 163; also J. H. Moulton, *A Grammar of New Testament Greek*. Vol. 1: *Prolegomena* (2nd ed.; Edinburgh: T&T Clark, 1906), 119; J. Frey, *Die johanneische Eschatologie*, 3:342–43. But, for a contrary opinion, see O. Cullmann, *Early Christian Worship* (trans. A. S. Todd and J. B. Torrance; London: SCM Press, 1954), 88–90, who considers Jesus' death and resurrection as the culmination of God's work and contends that now we are called upon to enter His rest. The whole discussion appears in the pre-context of observing the Fourth Gospel as a liturgy and John 5:17 as a negation of the Sabbath in favour of Sunday celebration. See also O. Cullmann, "Sabbat und Sonntag nach dem Johannesevangelium Joh 5:17," in *Vorträge und Aufsätze 1925–1962* (Tübingen: J. C. B. Mohr [Paul Siebeck], 1966), 187–91. The interpretive arguments are too hard to concur with, as they do not indicate the contextual thrust. See also, E. C. Hoskyns, *The Fourth Gospel*, 266–67, who argues: "However, the emphasis lies not on the continuous and unbroken invisible work of God, but on the visible work of the Son of God. This work involves not the

ὁ πατήρ μου is an important phrase. The Fourth Evangelist uses 'Father' almost as a pronoun to God. Israel as a covenant community called God 'Father,' but no individual was worthy enough to call God his father in a generic sense. Even if they used 'Father' to call God, they would immediately add the phrase 'in heaven.' By calling God 'my father' Jesus seems to be claiming a special, intimate relationship of 'the Son' with God. And having a direct corollary of this special relationship, Jesus claims: κἀγὼ ἐργάζομαι. If Jesus had only spoken of God's continuous working in order to bring wholeness and liberation, that would not have been contemptuous, but Jesus' assertion 'as my Father,' κἀγὼ ἐργάζομαι puts the Jews into a theological confusion.

It seems probable that v. 17b is inspired by a passage from Wis 8:4–6. In these verses the author describes the close relation that exists between Wisdom and God.[33] VV. 4–6 run thus:

V. 4   She is an initiate in the knowledge of God and an associate in his works.

(μύστις γάρ ἐστιν τῆς τοῦ θεοῦ ἐπιστήμης καὶ αἱρετὶς τῶν ἔργων αὐτοῦ.)

V. 5   If riches are a desirable possession in life, what is richer than wisdom who effects all things.

(εἰ δὲ πλοῦτός ἐστιν ἐπιθυμητὸν κτῆμα ἐν βίῳ, τί σοφίας πλουσιώτερον τῆς τὰ πάντα ἐργαζομένης)

V. 6   And if understanding is effective, who more than she is fashioner of what exists.

(εἰ δὲ φρόνησις ἐργάζεται, τίς αὐτῆς τῶν ὄντων μᾶλλόν ἐστιν τεχνῖτις)

Wisdom is initiated into all of God's work; she takes part in all He does and effects everything.

---

violation of the law of the Sabbath, but the complete overthrow and fulfilment of Sabbath. . ." This in my opinion looks at the Jewish tradition in contempt. He probably tries to stamp the superiority of Christianity over the Jewish religion. This is an erroneous perspective for a New Testament exegesis. In the passage, 'Sabbath celebration' is not questioned, but its ritualistic interpretation is confronted. S. Bacchiocchi in his article "John 5:17: Negation or Clarification of the Sabbath," *AUSS* 19 (1981): 3–19, esp. 11–13, interprets ἕως ἄρτι as having culminate emphasis. But again, the interpretive perspective and the questions asked to the text are unwarranted.

33   See A. T. Hanson, *The Prophetic Gospel*, 69–71, also G. Reim, *Studien zum alttestamentlichen Hintergrund des Johannesevangeliums*, 194.

The αἱρετίς of v. 4b is the key to the interpretation! It apparently occurs only here in the whole extent of ancient Greek literature. The Vulgate translates it as *electrix*. But the verb αἱρετίζω occurs in the rendering of Isa 42:1 and in Matt 12:18, where it means 'choose.' It also occurs in the Septuagint of 1 Chr 29:1, Hag 2:23, Mal 3:17 where it probably means adopt.[34] But the context of Wis 8:4b remains a mystery. Anthony Hanson queries: "Does it mean that Wisdom has made God's wishes her own?"[35]

The Book of Wisdom may well be one source of the Fourth Evangelist's Theology, because irrespective of whether he regarded the Book of Wisdom as canonical or not, he was quite capable of using it as a quarry for his theological construction. From whichever background the Evangelist spoke, Jesus' claiming of divine prerogative to be above the Sabbath naturally made the Jews very angry, for it amounted, in a strict sense, to nothing less than usurping divine power and authority.

The result of the claim made in v. 17 is the plot to kill Jesus. In v. 18 the Jews make two concrete allegations against Jesus:
a) Sabbath illegality, but this allegation is slowly sidelined in order to focus the readers' attention to the claim and its theological implication.
b) Blasphemy of calling God his own father and making himself equal to God.

Calling God his own father does not really constitute a culpable act of blasphemy. The law of blasphemy is so strictly constituted and defined, that only the one who pronounced the ineffable name of the four consonants יהוה could be punished by a death penalty.[36] Only if in further debate Jesus went on to use language which did amount to technical blasphemy, could he be convicted on a capital charge.

Therefore, the Jews stress that Jesus made himself equal to God. In a world where emperors began to claim divine honours and natures, it had been a special task of the Jews to explore such blasphemies for what they were worth. The Greeks found nothing extraordinary in such claims. They habitually thought of certain outstanding men as god-like or divinely inspired (θεῖοι ἄνθρωποι or θεῖοι ἄνδρες) in the sense that they were endowed with an unusually generous share of the divine nature.[37]

---

34 See H. Schlier, "αἱρετίζω," in *TDNT* 1:180–85.
35 See A. T. Hanson, *The Prophetic Gospel*, 70.
36 Mishnah Tractate *Sanhedrin* 7:5.
37 For a detailed discussion see, C. H. Dodd, *Interpretation of the Fourth Gospel*, 325–27.

Jews were willing to recognise that in certain conditions God had bestowed the title on men as a mark of favour (Ps 82:6 quoted again in John 10:34), and they glorified in the fact that God made Moses to be a 'god' to Pharaoh (Exod 7:1, cf. 4:16).[38] But to claim the title or make oneself God always brought retribution. Philo said that the mind is self-centred and godless when it deems itself equal to God.[39] In Jewish Theology, the demarcation between the Divine and human, Creator and creature, is strictly laid down, for the hope of becoming 'like God' was the temptation to which Eve succumbed (Gen 3:5, 22). This is a major theological position, as we read from the treatment accorded to Babylon in II Isaiah, for Babylon took upon herself to speak as God only can speak—"I am and there is none beside me" (Isa 47:8, 10)—, or the condemnation of Lucifer who said "I will make myself like the most high" (Isa 14:12–21).[40]

Therefore, the Jews considered Jesus' claim as blasphemy of the highest order. It was unthinkable for them that a human is comparable to God and that as such a being constituted danger not only for himself but for the whole community, he ought to be eliminated. Here, we see in the Fourth Evangelist the expert editor in action! He uses here his literary categories of misunderstanding and irony both together to bring about a thrilling turn in the drama of theological controversy: "He has made himself—equal to God."

In the following verses, the Evangelist laughs at his opponents' misunderstanding, as he clarifies that Jesus did not make himself God, but that God has 'made' him—and watch carefully, ironically he makes the Jews say—'equal' to God. He uses these two literary categories of irony and misunderstanding to clarify and drive in hard his Theology—his belief in God. The discussion of vv. 17–18 makes it clear that ὁ πατήρ μου ἕως ἄρτι ἐργάζεται κἀγὼ ἐργάζομαι is a statement of faith. It confesses God as creator, preserver and liberator. God is not the absolute who is faraway from, but with His creation. He does not create and leave the universe to run its destiny, instead He works continuously to bring wholeness and liberation. This is surely a Jewish God concept, but the attempt for a radical change appears in the second part of the confession. The Evangelist transfers all that he said about God to Jesus—as God is, so is Jesus also, as God continually

---

38 See H. L. Strack & P. Billerbeck, *Kommentar zum Neuen Testament aus Talmud und Midrasch*, 2:462ff.

39 Philo, *Leg. All.* 1.49: φίλαυτος δὲ καὶ ἄθεος ὁ νοῦς οἰόμενος ἴσος εἶναι θεῷ . . .

40 This probably alludes to the "kenosis hymn" of Phil 2:6ff.: ὃς ἐν μορφῇ θεοῦ ὑπάρχων οὐχ ἁρπαγμὸν ἡγήσατο τὸ εἶναι ἴσα θεῷ, ἀλλὰ ἑαυτὸν ἐκένωσεν . . .

works, Jesus works also. Now the two preceding acts of healing become God's continuous acts of bringing wholeness and liberation in and through Jesus. They are the signs to discern God's continuous working in the world. Making use of Jewish theological categories like σοφία, the Evangelist tries to interpret the Jesus phenomenon. Jewish theological language now becomes christological language.

The Evangelist however still tries to remain within the limits of Jewish monotheism. But the break between the Johannine community and the Jewish synagogue is so intense that he is misunderstood and not given a patient hearing. It is to the credit of the early community that it rightly understood Jesus, not as drastically different, but as the continuation of God's historic revelation to Israel and the whole world in its fullness. It tried to interpret Jesus in terms of Jewish theological language and even if other religious categories were used they were distilled through Jewish categories. Therefore, Jewish God language and related theological categories became determining factors in interpreting the evolving Christology of the early church.

3.6.2 Verses 19–30: The Father and the Son—Relationship Explained

3.6.2.1 Verses 19–20: Theological Introduction—The Father's Self-Emptying in the Son and the Absolute Dependence of the Son upon the Father

To proclaim that Jesus is not the rebellious Son who makes himself equal to his Father, the Fourth Evangelist uses a human analogy of the father–son relationship: οὐ δύναται ὁ υἱὸς ποιεῖν ἀφ' ἑαυτοῦ οὐδὲν ἐὰν μή τι βλέπῃ τὸν πατέρα ποιοῦντα· ἃ γὰρ ἂν ἐκεῖνος ποιῇ, ταῦτα καὶ ὁ υἱὸς ὁμοίως ποιεῖ. ὁ γὰρ πατὴρ φιλεῖ τὸν υἱὸν καὶ πάντα δείκνυσιν αὐτῷ ἃ αὐτὸς ποιεῖ, καὶ μείζονα τούτων δείξει αὐτῷ ἔργα.

Dodd is of the opinion that there lies a parable in vv. 19–20a. There is nothing necessarily christological here. We have rather the simple picture of a son apprenticed to his fathers trade. He thinks the article with father and son is generic, indicating that the statement applies to any father or any son. Here, the son watches his father at work and imitates him. The father shows the son several operations of his craft, so that, by closely following the father's example rather than by experimenting with his own techniques, the son himself becomes a master of the craft.[41]

---

41 The background of this picture is to be sought in a society where crafts are hereditary and techniques are handed down from the father to the son. C. H. Dodd

It is argued that the parable here follows the Synoptic parable format. There is,
a) a negation—a son cannot do anything by himself, only what he sees his father doing,
b) an affirmation—whatever the father does, the son does likewise,
c) and an explanation—for the father loves his son and shows him everything he is doing.[42]

Dodd contends that these two verses were not originally composed by the Fourth Evangelist and that they belong to primary traditions.

We see here probably an echo of Jesus' words, where he remembers his youth when he might have learnt his trade in the family workshop from his father at Nazareth. But in vv. 19ff. the picture is allegorised—the father and the son become God, the Father and Jesus, the Son. Undoubtedly once the allegorical approach is established in the reader's mind, he will surely be led to discover symbolic meanings in all possible details. So here the words 'sees the Father' will remind us of the very high theological doctrine of John 6:46 and this is probably intended on the Evangelist's part. Even if there lies a parable it will not reflect the early tradition of the self-consciousness of Jesus, but the masterly editorial hand of the Evangelist who might have used a parable or a proverb in this context to explain the relationship of Jesus and God, thereby repelling Jewish allegations against the Christian church of making Jesus God. Here, the parable's original meaning is not as important as its significance in the Johannine context.

Rudolf Schnackenburg is surely right in pointing out that the Son and the Father here are not used generically. Father and Son are Johannine technical words, where Son is a christological title and the Father for the Evangelist is God Himself.[43] The Son used in this exclusive sense and demanding the definite article cannot be compared with any human sons. And this way of speaking confirms the Jewish judgement which after all is objectively quite valid namely that Jesus deliberately calls God his Father.

---

in his article, "A Hidden Parable in the Fourth Gospel (Jn 5:19–20a)," in *More New Testament Studies* (Manchester: University Press, 1968), 30–40, refers to a papyrus from Oxyrhynchus (dated approx. A.D. 25–26), Hermetic literature, Hebrew prophetic tradition, Jewish wisdom and Rabbinic traditions.

42 Compare Luke 8:16 (cf. Matt 5:15); Luke 6:40; 9:21–22; 12:47–48.

43 The absolute Son is found 18 times in the Fourth Gospel, including 8 times in vv. 19–26, in 1 John 5 times, and in 2 John twice.

The Evangelist strongly emphasises in this verse that Jesus does not, in using the word Son or Father (my Father, in v. 17), aim to usurp God's power and authority, but rather makes himself thereby subject to God. οὐ δύναται ὁ υἱὸς ποιεῖν ἀφ' ἑαυτοῦ—to do nothing without prompting—is a common Johannine idiom (cf. John 7:18; 11:5; 15:4; 16:13; 18:34). The Son cannot take his own initiative, carry out his own self determined action. He cannot take independent decision. One is here reminded of the words of Moses, "The Lord has sent me to do all these works and it has not been of myself" (Num 16:28). The prophetic tradition was always forthright in proclaiming that a prophet could do nothing, but only that which God empowered him to do. Herein stems probably the clue that the Fourth Evangelist makes use of to explain the 'Jesus' phenomena, but goes far beyond it.

The Son sees/looks at what his Father does (ἐὰν μή τι βλέπῃ τὸν πατέρα ποιοῦντα), he discerns, gets impetus and acts. Thus he reproduces and reflects the Father's acts. In him then we have the revelation of the Father's thought and act. ἃ γὰρ ἂν ἐκεῖνος ποιῇ, ταῦτα καὶ ὁ υἱὸς ὁμοίως ποιεῖ. Here ἐκεῖνος, that is the Father, lays stress on a separate person pointing to a contrast in ὁ υἱός.[44] For "whatever the Father does, the Son does likewise"—here we should note that the verse does not speak about 'like substance' of the Father and the Son, but only their 'like action.'

ὁ γὰρ πατὴρ φιλεῖ τὸν υἱόν. The Father's love towards the Son is often discussed in the Fourth Gospel (John 3:35; 10:17; 15:19; 17:24, 26), but elsewhere the word used for love is ἀγαπᾶν. Therefore, P. Gächter suggests that the presence of φιλεῖν points towards a traditional parable.[45] But it is possible to deduce from the use of the verb φιλεῖν here that the Evangelist wants to emphasise personal love.[46]

πάντα δείκνυσιν αὐτῷ ἃ αὐτὸς ποιεῖ, the Father shows everything—the Father opens himself to the Son. H. Odeberg has seen a possible parallel to the Johannine picture of the relation between the Father and the Son in the Hebrew book of 3 *Enoch*, when the mutual relationship between the Holy One and the Metatron is depicted. It unfolds as follows:

---

44 C. K. Barrett, *The Gospel according to St. John*, 259.
45 P. Gächter, "Zur Form von Joh 5:19–30," 68.
46 R. Schnackenburg, *The Gospel according to St. John*, 2:104. According to Bultmann, Barrett and Schnackenburg no difference in meaning can be attributed to the use of a different word. φιλεῖν and ἀγαπᾶν are interchangeable for the Fourth Evangelist. It may be that in employing φιλεῖν the Evangelist wants to strongly suggest affective love.

a) The Holy One shows, teaches and reveals to Metatron all secrets and all the works (*3 En.* 11:1–3, 48 C. 20). Metatron watches intently 'to behold' what the Holy one shows him (*3 En.* 11:2).
b) Whatever word, whatever utterance that goes forth before the Holy one, Metatron carries out (*3 En.* 48 C. 10).
c) The Holy one commissions Metatron with the authority of judgement (*3 En.* 10:4–5, 48 C. 10).
d) Metatron performs the continual work of the Holy one and also has the function of taking care of all, conferring eternal life upon the spirits of the deceased (*3 En.* 16:1, 48 C. 11).
e) It is strongly emphasised that all his authority is conferred upon him by the Holy one. He does not do his will but the will of the Holy one (*3 En.* 16).[47]

As to whether the Fourth Evangelist had this passage from the Book of Enoch in mind is difficult to deduce. The whole analogy of Father and Son speaks of a perfect communication and a loving relationship where the 'seeing of the Son' and 'showing of the Father' are complimentary. This love relationship is so intimate that the whole person of the Son is the expression of the Father's will, thought and action. We cannot really divide the actions as that of the Father's and that of the Son's, since the Evangelist with his ὁμοίως makes it clear that it does not mean that the Son acts alongside or after the Father, but their mode of action is similar—they act at the same time and at once. It is suggested that this 'seeing and showing' speak of the pre-existence of Jesus. We do not have clear indications to say so, but v. 17 hints at this connection. It puts the Father and the Son in a continuous and timeless working span.

Is the Son a prophet in the hands of the Father? No, for it is the Son's voluntary 'seeing and doing,' the Father does not 'make' him see and learn. Thus we have here probably a mission analogy—the Son learns, the Father shows, trains and equips him for the mission. In this mission the Son becomes the self-expression of the Father. The action of the Son reveals the will of the Father and accomplishes what the Father wants him to do. The Father's will is archetype of the Son's action. The Son gives effect to the Father's will. Here we see the perfect, absolute dependence of the Son revealing itself in the oneness (equality–unity) with the Father.

---

47   H. Odeberg, *The Fourth Gospel Interpreted in its Relation to Contemporaneous Religious Currents in Palestine and the Hellenistic-Oriental World* (Uppsala: Almqvist & Wiksell, 1929), 205–206.

The Father and the Son analogy can also be interpreted as one which binds the 'otherness' and immanence of God. The presence of the Son in the midst of humankind may be interpreted as a sign of God's nearness or of God's being with His people whereby the invisible becomes visible and concrete. Thus, the Father–Son analogy not only binds God's otherness and immanence, but also points to their oneness. If the Son is the immanence of God at hand and the reflection of the invisible Father, then he should be one with the Father.

This oneness of the Father and the Son in the Son's perfect dependence and in the Father's 'showing' of all could probably be explained as 'the Father emptying (ἑαυτὸν κενόω) Himself in the Son' (clue taken from the Pauline [?] idea of Christ's self-emptying). The Father's showing is so full, so complete, so unreserved to the point that He becomes 'empty' in order to fill the Son. The Son is the self-expression of the Father. In the Father's emptying of Himself, the Son gets his identity. The Father on the other hand, in giving of Himself to the Son, finds Himself. Thus the Father's will and thought now become that of the Son's. And the Son reflects perfectly the thought and action of the Father.

In the following verses the Father gives the Son His authority over life and judgement. When He gives all that He has to the Son, He has nothing, but His own Son belongs to Him and, in a totally dependent Son, He has everything. Probably the whole incarnation framework of the Fourth Gospel can be described as the Father's emptying of Himself in His Son for the salvation of the world. And their oneness is reflected in the Father's emptying Himself in His Son and the Son's emptying himself for humankind. It is a oneness of belonging, a perfect relationship and a 'one-like' action.

καὶ μείζονα τούτων δείξει αὐτῷ ἔργα poses a very difficult problem. What do the (future) greater works mean? An all too easy suggestion is that of Bultmann: As this sentence is an addition to the 'source' of discourses in the Fourth Gospel, it should therefore be put between brackets.[48] If all the other statements are true and authentic then, why should one dismiss only v. 20c? Moreover, the whole hypothesis of the 'discourse source' for the Fourth Gospel is itself problematic and indefinable. It is suggested by scholars that the greater works
a) are simply the miracles that are to follow in the Gospel—perhaps, the resurrection of Lazarus and even that of Jesus himself,

---

48 See R. Bultmann, *Das Evangelium des Johannes*, 253, n. 1.

b) refer to the spiritual/ethical resurrection and the non-resurrection that is equated with Judgement,
c) are Jesus' eschatological works as mentioned in vv. 28ff.,
d) refer to the exclusive works of the exalted Christ—through his disciples (since 14:2 also has μείζονα [ἔργα]).

While suggestions b) and c) overlook the element of 'marvelling' which is a present experience, d) supposes that the phrase used each time by the writer has the same meaning, no matter what the context. I feel each context should be considered separately, though a) nevertheless remains an open possibility.

According to Josef Blank, v. 20b marks the transition from Christology to Eschatology, the words "show him all" in the first half of v. 20 being a personal ontological statement and the "will show him greater things" being an expression of the functional historical mode of being of the Son as the one who reveals God. This brings together the related sign of revelation in John 5:1–6 and its parallel, the reality of revelation in John 5:21ff.[49]

It is true that there is a clear reference to the sign of healing, however the greater works should be understood also in their relation to vv. 19–20a and v. 21ff. This points to the marvellous act of God's self-emptying which is made known by the Son. True, the life-giving and judging activities give greater works concrete and explicit form, but greater works are not just the signs and deeds of Jesus. They refer to the total historical phenomena of Jesus of Nazareth in whom God's self-emptying and the Son's total obedience is witnessed. The signs and the teaching are nothing but parts of this phenomenon. When God's true and living power reaches out and its righteous judgement confronts humankind, humankind can do nothing but marvel.

3.6.2.2 Verses 21–22: The Father's Self-Emptying—Basis of the Son's Authority to Give Life and to Judge

The Fourth Evangelist describes in concrete terms God's self-emptying. God delegates His two basic powers of life-giving and judgement to His Son. The Jewish tradition speaks about two measures of God. In the great revelation to Moses, God was described as merciful and just, and these two attributes were labelled in Rabbinic literature as God's two measures. God deals with the world in two ways according to the measure of mercy or goodness and according to the measure of the Law and punishment. Each measure is itself

---

49 See J. Blank, *Krisis*, 119.

generic for a host of God's actions, for example the measure of mercy is creative activity,[50] the measure of justice is known in His acts of judgement for the cause of the righteous.[51]

In Philo's opinion, one can know God through His acts and operations. God's operations in the world may be broadly classified as creative, and that of ruling. Philo calls God's two powers, δύναμις ποιητική and δύναμις βασιλική.[52] He explains δύναμις ποιητική by ἀγαθότης (goodness), εὐεργεσία (kindness), χαριστική (beneficent), and ποιητική (creative).[53] It is through δύναμις ποιητική that God creates and operates the world.[54]. He explains δύναμις βασιλική as ἀρχή (sovereignty), ἐξουσία (authority), ἀρχική (governing), and

---

50   In Jewish Theology, life-giving is a prerogative of God Himself. He is the Lord of life and death (1 Sam 2:6; 2 Kgs 5:7). The Jews' conviction that God will raise them to life again gains strength in the prophetic books (Hos 6:2; Ezek 37:1–14). All Jews except the Sadducees did believe in the resurrection, either as a resurrection of the righteous or a general resurrection, but only at the end of time (Isa 26:19; Dan 12:2). The Jews' continued hope in the resurrection finds place in the second benediction of the eighteen prayers—"You are the eternally living One who raises the dead to life, cares for the living and resurrects the dead" (quoted from R. Schnackenburg, *The Gospel according to St. John*, 2:106). But there is no evidence for the belief that the Messiah would be entrusted with the authority to raise the dead, since in their belief even God Himself would not raise the dead in this age. The resurrection was a phenomenon that belonged to the age to come. The Rabbinic literature contended that three keys are in God's hand and are not given to any representative, namely the key of the rain (Deut 28:12), the key of the womb (Gen 30:22) and the key of the resurrection of the dead (Ezek 37:13). C. K. Barrett quotes Rabbi Johanan in his *The Gospel according to St. John*, 206. Elijah was considered as an exemption to this rule, not as one who was endowed with the power to raise the dead but as an instrument in God's hand.
51   Again according to Jewish thought, judgement is considered to be one of God's supreme acts of sovereignty. Although God makes use of His angels to execute punishment, the power to judge belonged only to God. According to the earthly and national expectation of the Jews, the Messiah would not carry out God's judgement on His enemies, or on sinners of this world. (H. L. Strack and P. Billerbeck, *Kommentar zum Neuen Testament aus Talmud und Midrasch*, 4:1104ff. say that no text unambiguously attributes to the Messiah the function of judging the world on the last day.) Even in the Danielic vision the one like the Son of Man is not permitted to judge. Only in the figurative discourses of Enoch the Son of Man or the elect is entrusted by God with judgement (*1 En.* 37–41 and esp. 49:4; 61:9; 62:2ff.; 63:11 and 69:27).
52   See Philo, *Plant.* 85–89 and *Abr.* 121–122.
53   See Philo, *Cher.* 27; *Sacr.* 59; *Somn.* 1.162–163; *Abr.* 124–125; *Plant.* 86–87; *Spec. Leg.* 1.59, 209, 307; *Her.* 166; *Fug.* 95, 100; *Mos.* 2.99 etc.
54   Philo, *Qu. Gen.* 4.2.

κολαστική (punitive power).⁵⁵ By this δύναμις βασιλική God rules what has come into being.⁵⁶ These two powers, therefore, represent the complete and fundamental aspects of the deity, creation and judgement. And significantly for Philo, Logos in consort with the deity exercises the two powers of God.⁵⁷ Thus in Philo the two powers of God include all of God's action. God's creation and ruling of the world are two powers which adhere to God's divine Logos, flow from that source and are governed by it.⁵⁸

Seen against this background, the phenomenon of the Father's self-emptying in the Son becomes more complete. The Fourth Evangelist in elucidating and developing the Son's activities makes the phenomenon distinct. The Father entrusts and delegates the power of giving life and judgement to the Son. ὥσπερ . . . οὕτως (just as . . . so also) in v. 21 is used to express the oneness of the Father and the Son, but then οὓς θέλει (to whom he wishes) speaks of the Son's complete freedom. But this should not be understood as arbitrariness, but as 'authority' surely to carry out the will of the Father. Then v. 21 says "the Father judges no one" (οὐδένα). He has entrusted all (πᾶσαν) judgement to the Son. In v. 22 the Father determines the authority. The Father in fact pronounces judgement through the Son. One should understand that the Evangelist here demonstrates in the light of God's self-emptying the oneness of the Father and the Son, although consciously maintaining the Son's subordination.

It is very striking that all the verbs in these verses occur in their present tense. They clearly point to the fact that Jesus' activities of life-giving and judgement take place here and now in the present. Schnackenburg thinks that the Fourth Evangelist here connects the future expectations of the eschaton in the early Christian catechese, by making it into an event fulfilled in the present.⁵⁹ Evangelical scholars interpret the present tense as 'spiritual life,' 'spiritual resurrection' provided by Jesus here and now, thereby diluting the reality of the 'life experience' to a mere feeling. The ἐγείρει reminds the reader of v. 8 when Jesus says to the lame man, ἔγειρε. A relationship between this event and v. 21 immediately emerge. The sign of the raising of

---

55 Philo, *Sacr.* 59; *Abr.* 124–125; *Cher.* 27–28; *Her.* 166; *Congr.* 171; *Qu. Exod.* 2.68; *Fug.* 95, 98, 100; *Mos.* 2.99 etc.
56 Philo, *Qu. Gen.* 4.2.
57 Philo, *Qu. Exod.* 2.68 and *Fug.* 101.
58 C. H. Dodd, *Interpretation of the Fourth Gospel*, 322–23, and J. H. Neyrey, *An Ideology of Revolt*, 24–25.
59 R. Schnackenburg, *The Gospel according to St. John*, 2:106.

the lame man is not only a matter of feeling and spiritual awakening but a concrete life experience in this very world. To a community 'struggling for its existence' a 'feeling' of life or a spiritual awakening is not of much help. Such a community needs the guarantee of the experience of life and a foretaste that gives clear indication that the forces of death are being crushed! Therefore v. 21 should not be understood in terms of a spiritual resurrection, but as a confession of faith that, in and with Jesus, humankind has episodes of resurrection in every day life. It experiences God's help in defeating the forces of death and rising to 'life' with Him through His Son.

Bultmann claims that these verses (along with v. 23) set forth a single thought—Jesus fulfils, on behalf of the Father, the office of the eschatological judge with power to bestow life and condemn. But this does not do justice to the emphasis of the passage on the redemptive action of the Son. In Bultmann's opinion the judgement in v. 22 means condemnation and is not a decision between life and death. This interpretation though not entirely wrong, is insufficient and narrow. Κρίσις should be comprehended as judicial, since according to the Fourth Evangelist, God's judgement is not negative, but takes on a rather positive form. God's judgement is to send His Son into the world, to reveal Himself and His salvific plan. Judgement is in other words God's way of bringing justice. It may not necessarily be a negative condemnation, but also atoning and quickening, while the two signs in John 4:46–5:9 moreover exemplify the power of the Son to quicken the helpless, and to give life, strength and wholeness to those close to death. So here the Son performs the primary work of the Father in giving life. This is that aspect of the work which is again emphasised in vv. 24–25 too. The Father has certainly committed the entire eschatological process to the Son's hands, but the emphasis is on the divine will for salvation, not condemnation (cf. John 3:16, 36).

3.6.2.3 Verse 23: Theological Reflection—The Honour Due the Son because of his Relationship with the Father

The Father gives the Son His power to give life and judge, so that (ἵνα) is consecutive rather than purposive here. The Son will be honoured just as the Father is honoured. This is anthropomorphic language. Here one notices the Evangelist's familiarity with the concept of agency in Halakah, rather than that of the heavenly envoy of the Gnostic myth. The concept of agency in Halakah gives some clues to make clear the Johannine Father–Son relationship. The basic principles of agency in Halakah are as follows:

a) The agent is like the one who sent him.
b) To deal with the agent is the same as dealing with the sender.
c) Accepting and honouring the agent is in reality honouring the sender himself.
d) The agent is subordinate to the sender.
e) The agent is obedient to the will of the sender.
f) The sender commissions the agent, who can do only that which he has been authorised to, he cannot do anything on his own accord. However, in a legal agency the sender transfers his own right and property concerned to the agent. Thus he has the title and authority to secure legal claims on behalf of the sender.
g) The Son as agent emphasises the importance of the agency. The Son as an agent is considered to be a replica of the visible form of the Sender-Father. The Son as an agent also emphasises that he is partner to the sender, that is concerned in the undertaking.
h) The agent has to return and report back to the sender.
i) The agent can extend agency by appointing sub-agents.[60]

In v. 23 the Evangelist does suggest 'agency' for it emphasises the Son's subordination. But he, as is typical of him, goes far beyond making Jesus a mere agent, while

a) the concept of agency in the Fourth Gospel should be understood along with, and as a corollary to, the hereupon described phenomenon of the Father's self-emptying in His Son. Moreover,
b) one can very well understand "he who does not honour the Son does not honour the Father who sent him" in line with the concept of agency. But the honour given to an agent is never the same as that given to the principal. The Evangelist here breaks away from the concept of agency in envisaging and stating that the Son is given just the same honour (καθὼς τιμάω) as the Father. Again oneness of the Father and the Son is emphasised.

---

60 A. E. Harvey, "Christ as Agent," in *The Glory of Christ in the New Testament: Studies in Christology in Memory of George Bradford Caird* (ed. L. D. Hurst and Nicholas T. Wright; Oxford: Clarendon Press, 1987), 239–50. P. Borgen, "God's Agent in the Fourth Gospel," in *The Interpretation of John* (ed. J. Ashton; Philadelphia: Fortress, 1986), 67–78, and H. S. Friend, "Like Father, like Son—A Discussion of the Concept of Agency in Halakha and John," *ATJ* 21 (1990): 18–28, discuss in length the principles of agency in Halakah and its implications in the Fourth Gospel.

3.6.2.4 Verses 24–25: The Son as Life-Giver and Judge—Eternal Life and Judgement as the Present Reality

This verse contains the Johannine kerygma, that "whosoever believes the Son has eternal life" (cf. John 3:16, 36). This kerygma is adopted here to the context and the Fourth Evangelist's theocentricity is made evident. ". . . believes in Him who sent me has eternal life . . . (ὁ τὸν λόγον μου ἀκούων καὶ πιστεύων τῷ πέμψαντί με ἔχει ζωὴν αἰώνιον. . .)." ἀκούω in the Evangelist's opinion is not just simple listening or hearing. Instead it means to receive, to react positively, to be obedient, to discern, to appreciate, to open oneself. Hearing is not passive but active and carries the notion of invitation, challenge and acceptance of his call. πιστεύειν for the Evangelist is an active commitment to a person. It is not an emotional outbreak but willingness to respond to God's challenge and invitation presented in His Son. Here the Evangelist calls for faith in the Father through hearing Jesus' words.

Those who hear the word of the Son and believe in Him who sent Jesus have eternal life. These words bring back memories of the signs mentioned in 4:46–5:9, Jesus' words bring healing and life. In the Fourth Evangelist's opinion life is sharing in God's very life which brings wholeness to humankind, and puts right the relationship between God and humankind. Again the Evangelist stresses the present reality of 'life' which the believer can enjoy here and now.

"Those who have life will not be condemned as they have crossed over from death to life." Here the translation of κρίσις as 'condemned' is wrong. The judicial language should be noted. κρίσις here should be understood as that those who have life need have no apprehensions about the judicial process since it will not harm them. They will come to judgement but leave acquitted. The better translation would be, 'will not be judged' or 'passed judgement.' In the Fourth Evangelist's language life and judgement are complementary and they condition each other.

Life and death are part of Johannine dualistic scheme, where life is that which belongs to the above realm and death is characteristic of the world below. The Fourth Evangelist asserts that those who believed and thus have life have already passed onto life from death. Note the perfect tense μεταβέβηκεν! They belong to the realm of life permanently. The forces of death can neither hold fast nor tie. This life is not just a spiritual feeling or dream, but a concrete reality, yet truly a mystery. It is visible in the activity of the person. This should be understood with the Johannine community's struggle against persecution and simultaneous experience of life.

In my opinion v. 24 is more than a mere statement in the argument to explain the Father–Son relationship. It is a confession of faith in the 'One' who sent Jesus, and for humankind to share in His 'own life' is a present reality. As a matter of fact this 'life' is a mystery to be received as God Himself is a mystery. (Here mystery should not be understood as *'Geheimnis.'* The mystery has, and is still being revealed to humankind, but it contains elements that are beyond human comprehension.) It is to be understood in day to day life where one learns to live in the world without succumbing to the world (cf. John 17:14ff.; 16:33). One learns to overcome the forces of death, although what threatens does not disappear. Thus the sharing of the 'mysterious life' of God who is Himself a mystery transposes those who believe from the mystery of time to the mystery of eternity.

In v. 25 the 'Son' is recognised and declared as the Son of God. (The Fourth Evangelist uses the title 'Son of God' only three times for Jesus—cf. 10:36; 11:4 and 20:31). "The hour is coming and has now come" virtually declares eschaton a present reality. The voice of the Son of God sounds the inauguration of eschaton. The dead live. The dead here should not necessarily be understood as those who are dead and sleep in the tomb, or are spiritually dead. Though in apocalyptic language, this should be understood as those who are under the forces of death, live as dead ones, those who have lost their creativity, energy, strength and hope. Those who live in inhuman conditions will regain 'life,' will be liberated, gathered and organised. And 'this hour' is the hour of liberation and salvation. This understanding of present eschatological activity of God through the Son challenges the reader to see every small act of liberation in the history of humankind, of God's sovereign acts as a sign of God's presence in their midst, and a guarantee for the hope that God hears the cry of those under the forces of death.[61]

3.6.2.5 Verse 26: The Son has Life in Himself

"For as the Father has life in Himself, so He has granted the Son to have life in himself" is a timeless statement of faith. It confesses that God is a self-subsistent being and author of all life. He is a living God (Deut 5:26; Ps 42:2; Jer 10:10 etc.) who has the fountain of life (Ps 36:9). It also in the same breath confesses that the Son has derivative capacity to create and to give life. The idea of the Prologue that the Word is the agent of God in the creation is

---

61 J. Frey, *Die johanneische Eschatologie,* 3:380.

omitted, yet not contradicted. This verse also proclaims the Son as principle of life and new creation in a derivative sense.

The common possession of life by the Father and the Son was used in Patristic citations as an anti-Arian argument. They contended that the verse primarily described the internal life of the Trinity. This interpretation should be viewed in the light of later theological controversies. They do not really reflect the mind of the Evangelist.⁶²

3.6.2.6 Verse 27: The Son's Authority to Judge as the Son of Man

After fully developing the idea of the life-giving power of the Son, the Evangelist now goes on to consider the Son's full power to pass judgement. V. 27 is directly linked to v. 22 and also to v. 24. The Judgement mentioned here is undoubtedly the present judgement. But strangely the Evangelist says καὶ ἐξουσίαν ἔδωκεν αὐτῷ κρίσιν ποιεῖν, ὅτι υἱὸς ἀνθρώπου ἐστίν. In every other occurrence of the title 'the Son of Man' in the New Testament there is the use of a pair of articles—ὁ υἱὸς τοῦ ἀνθρώπου. It is only here that the anarthrous υἱὸς ἀνθρώπου is used. It is contended that υἱὸς ἀνθρώπου is not a title, but the semantic idiom meaning 'a man,' 'a human being.' Therefore the delegation of the authority to judge to the Son implicitly means that the Son has the authority to judge because he is a human being. As a participant in human nature the Son is uniquely qualified to act as the judge of humankind.⁶³

But it could very well be argued using grammatical grounds that the expression in question is no different from the articular title 'the Son of Man,' since the expression here precedes the copulative verb ἐστίν, the absence of the article is explained by pointing to E. C. Colwell's rule, according to which the article may be committed from a definite predicate noun which precedes the copula. Or in other words a predicative nominative noun which precedes the verb should be understood in a definite sense.⁶⁴

---

62 See R. E. Brown, *The Gospel according to John*, 1:215ff., for a detailed discussion.
63 See D. Burkett, *The Son of Man in the Gospel of John* (JSNTSup 56; Sheffield: JSOT Press, 1991), 44; A. M. Hunter, *The Gospel according to John* (CBC; Cambridge: Cambridge University Press, 1965), 60; G. H. C. Macgregor, *The Gospel of John*, 179, and R. H. Lightfoot, *St. John's Gospel*, 144.
64 E. C. Colwell, "A Definite Rule for the Use of the Article in the Greek New Testament," *JBL* 52 (1933): 12–21, esp. 14; C. F. D. Moule, *An Idiom Book of New Testament Greek*, 177, mentions Colwell's article with approval.

Philip Harner argued that the question of a noun being definite or indefinite has probably been correctly defined by Colwell, but that its being qualitative or not is a question which must be examined on its own. The categories of qualitativeness and definiteness are not mutually exclusive and frequently it is a delicate exegetical issue for the interpreter to decide which is the emphasis that the Greek had in mind.[65] It appears that 'Son of Man' in its present context of v. 27 is definite and titular, but it may well retain a 'qualitative' sense.[66]

Moreover, the anarthrous υἱὸς ἀνθρώπου may be because of the influence of Dan 7:13 in both the Septuagint and the Theodotion Greek versions of the Old Testament.

V. 27b—	ὅτι υἱὸς ἀνθρώπου ἐστίν
LXX Dan 7:13—	ὡς υἱὸς ἀνθρώπου ἤρχετο
Theodotion Dan 7:13—	ὡς υἱὸς ἀνθρώπου ἐρχόμενος
V. 27a—	καὶ ἐξουσίαν ἔδωκεν αὐτῷ
LXX Dan 7:14—	καὶ ἐδόθη αὐτῷ ἐξουσία,
Theodotion Dan 7:14—	καὶ αὐτῷ ἐδόθη ἡ ἀρχή

Dan 7:13ff. is considered to be the well-spring of the New Testament 'Son of Man' concept. The author of Daniel portrays a heavenly figure "like a Son of Man," to whom God grants awesome authority—"and to him was given authority and glory and kingdoms that all nations and languages should serve him. His dominion is an everlasting dominion, which shall not pass away and his kingdom one that shall not be destroyed" (Dan 7:13–14). The Danielic Son of Man does not sit on judgement and he is just 'like' a Son of Man.[67]

But one should not loose sight of the fact that later writers depending on Daniel speak of the Son of Man who is empowered by God to be the cosmic judge at the end of time. God appoints him to annihilate the sinners and to

---

65 P. B. Harner, "Qualitative anarthrous predicate nouns—Mark 15:3 and Jn. 1:1," *JBL* 92 (1973): 75–87, esp. 76, 85ff.
66 This view is suggested by E. C. Hoskyns, *The Fourth Gospel*, 270ff. Also see J. N. Sanders, *A Commentary on the Gospel according to St. John*, 168–78; L. Morris, *The Gospel according to John*, 320; G. R. Beasley-Murray, *John*, 87; E. Haenchen, *John*, 1:253, and F. J. Moloney, *The Johannine Son of Man* (Rome: LAS, 1976), 82.
67 For an opinion against using Dan 7:13 as background see, D. Burkett, *The Son of the Man in the Gospel of John*, 43.

lead those who are elect and righteous to a super-terrestrial salvation.[68] The Son of Man is therefore a figure whose proper place is in heaven, but who also is a figure of judgement and of the future. His activity will match the cosmic crisis which will terminate the earthly course of events. The Synoptics also manifestly have in view the vision of the one like a Son of Man in Daniel 7. But the Synoptic Jesus goes far beyond it in assuming the whole eschatological process of mediating the kingdom of God and the judgement in the present and the future under the function of the Son of Man (see for example, Matt 8:20; 11:18–19; Mark 8:31, 38; Luke 12:8–9 and Mark 14:62; Matt 25:31–46).

It is true that there exists a literary parallel between v. 27 and Dan 7:13ff. It is also true that the Christian delegation of Jesus as the Son of Man is very much influenced by the Danielic vision. But the decision as to whether the Fourth Evangelist incorporates the traditional Son of Man concept or not, is closely linked to the problem of the sudden appearance of the title in v. 27. All through the discourse Jesus has been referred to as the 'Son' and with the appearance of the term 'Son of Man' in v. 27 the former title disappears, although the person being referred to is surely Jesus. Some scholars feel the title 'Son of Man' is to be regarded as synonymous with the Son.[69] The use of Son of Man could have come about through a natural tendency to use this apocalyptic term in the context of vv. 28–29.[70] Some other scholars are of the opinion that the title is redactional.[71] Yet it should be maintained[72] and

---

68 See J. L. Martyn, *History and Theology in the Fourth Gospel*, 137–39. He quotes the Ethiopic book 1 *En.* 62 which points to a picture of heaven at the end of time when the separation of righteous from the sinners takes place: "And the righteous and the elect shall be saved on that day and they shall never thenceforth see the face of the sinners and the unrighteous. And the Lord of Spirit will abide over them and with that Son of Man they shall eat and lie down and rise up forever and ever" (Martyn's translation).
69 J. Blank, *Krisis*, 163–64; R. Bultmann, *Das Evangelium des Johannes*, 195–96; B. Lindars, "The Son of Man in the Theology of John," in *Essays on John* (ed. C. M. Tuckett; SNTA 17; Leuven: University Press, 1992), 153–66.
70 C. K. Barrett, *The Gospel according to St. John*, 262.
71 J. H. Bernard, *Commentary on the Gospel according to St. John*, 1:244; R. E. Brown, *The Gospel according to John*, 1:220; O. Cullmann, *The Christology of the New Testament* (trans. S. C. Guthrie and Ch. A. M. Hall; 2nd ed.; London: SCM Press, 1963), 186, and J. Marsh, *The Gospel of St. John* (Pelican Gospel Commentaries; Harmondsworth: Penguin, 1968), 264.
72 R. Schnackenburg, *The Gospel according to St. John*, 2:112–13; S. Schulz, *Untersuchungen zur Menschensohn-Christologie im Johannesevangelium*, 109–11.

understood in the light of its traditional use closely tied to the apocalyptic judgement which follows in vv. 28–29.

It can be said that the Evangelist has not used the title merely as a synonym to Son, as can be observed through his explanation of some theological insights using a combination of the titles. If one reads the Gospel, the Fourth Evangelist specifically stresses that the Son did not come into the world to judge (John 3:17; 5:24; 8:15; 12:47). But it is crystal clear that the presence of the incarnate Son brings judgement into the world (3:19–21; 5:22; 8:24; 9:39 and 12:31). Perhaps in the light of this apparent contradiction we need to understand the Evangelist's use of the title 'Son of Man' in our present context. V. 27 belongs to what follows in vv. 28–29 and this combination of verses clearly indicate traditional apocalyptic beliefs. It is an important indication that the Evangelist alludes to the traditional Son of Man saying. But in what sense the Johannine Son of Man is a continuity/discontinuity of the traditional Danielic figure should be discussed in order to find its theological importance.

The sequence of the verses and their thematic integration indicate that the Son of Man of v. 27 is to be understood in the light of the dominant Son motif. In the statement, 'the Son is given the authority to judge because he is the Son of Man,' the Fourth Evangelist sees the fulfilment of the traditional Son of Man figure in the Son. It conversely says that the 'Son of Man' is not just a heavenly figure, but the 'Son' himself. And in the Son this heavenly figure is accessible. Though the judicial office is fulfilled by the Son, the Son of Man is no longer to be considered a horrifying judge, but brings salvation. He has the authority of judgement, not to destroy, but to give life. God's justice is His giving of life. In this sense Son—Son of Man of v. 27—is 'the place of judgement,' conversely 'the place of God's revelation' where we are led to the right understanding of God present in our midst.[73] In fact the Johannine Son and Son of Man share oneness with God as he shares in God's mission of justice through the giving of life.

3.6.2.7 Verses 28–29: The Open Eschatology—The Son as Judge with Life-Giving as a Sub-Theme

These verses bring us to the very heart of the problem of Johannine Eschatology, since we are concerned with the relationship of Johannine Eschatology

---

73 Cf. John 1:51 and the 'lifting up' passages in the Fourth Gospel.

and the understanding of God. The futuristic Eschatology that we are here confronted with, is a matter of intense debate in Johannine scholarship. To arrive at a solution as to how a predominantly realised eschatological structure can have verses like 28–29, many suggestions have been put forward.

Firstly, the solution provided is to dilute the eschatological tension to spiritual and actual resurrection. According to the proponents, the time in vv. 28–29 refers not to the distant end of the times, but to the near future and denotes the physical raising of Lazarus (they consider that μὴ θαυμάζετε refers to the healings) and eventually to the resurrection of Jesus. For them the issue at v. 25 is spiritual death, while in vv. 28–29 physical death is under consideration. These verses taken together according to their contention illustrate the Son's power over spiritual as well as physical death.[74]

Secondly, a very popular suggestion is to simply do away with vv. 28–29. Scholars proposing this solution share the conviction that, since the nature of the elements mentioned here cannot be reconciled with the rest of the Gospel, it cannot form part of the original thought pattern. According to Bultmann, the most popular proponent of this view, the reason for the addition of these verses by an ecclesiastical redactor was to introduce by way of correction the popular traditional Eschatology which expected the raising of the dead in the eschatological future. This was to play down the radically realised Eschatology found in the Fourth Gospel. As to how the redactor was supposed to envisage the integration of these verses with the rest of the context is according to Bultmann difficult to say.[75]

Thirdly, another suggestion is to consider these verses as redactional, 'interpret them on their own' so that it makes sense. Schnackenburg can be called the torchbearer of this view. He says, vv. 28–29 are intended to reassert the importance of the future judgement, as the Evangelist has no interest either in the future of the world or in the earthly journey of the church. Although Schnackenburg finds no evidence of Johannine polemic against this kind of traditional futuristic Eschatology, he does find evidence of a radical intellectual reorientation which uses different intellectual categories, namely that of the vertical replacing the horizontal and temporal perspective. This reorientation expresses a concern within the existential situation and the ultimate fate of the individual. According to him, with the

---

74 See especially J. Marsh, *The Gospel of St. John*, 264, and W. Hendriksen, *New Testament Commentary: Exposition of the Gospel according to John* (2 vols.; Grand Rapids: Baker Book House, 1953–1954), 1:200–201.
75 See R. Bultmann, *Das Evangelium des Johannes*, 196.

familiar idea of an earthly and heavenly realm and with a clear descent and ascent motif what interests the Evangelist most is the search for a meaning of human existence—where does it come from and where does it go?

In the Fourth Gospel, Eschatology is the function of Christology—the fullness of salvation is present in Jesus Christ offered to humankind definitely and permanently. Therefore, Schnackenburg argues that the present union of believers with their Lord is the primary and controlling factor. The resurrection is present in the enduring fellowship of the disciples with Jesus. He contends that the Fourth Evangelist does not distinguish between periods of time, but concentrates all things in the person of Jesus.[76]

While on the one hand, the presentation of the 'get rid' option, and the dilution of the problem to either a mere spiritual or an actual explanation are not acceptable, on the other, Schnackenburg's arguments too are hard to accept at least on three counts, especially when one wants to argue that the Evangelist has, along with his much-talked-about explicit vertical view, an implicit horizontal view.

a) The Evangelist uses the language of resurrection. The resurrection of Jesus is for him a representative event. The resurrection of Jesus and "I am the resurrection and the life" are to be viewed as the Johannine confession of faith in the resurrection. It is certain that the Evangelist has a concept of the vertical above–below, heavenly–worldly movement. Accordingly he speaks of Jesus' coming and Jesus' return to the Father and the disciples' following him to be with him. Evidently, he does write explicitly about the second coming. Yet he does not believe in the immortality of the soul. Rather he believes in the resurrection of the body. This should be considered as an implicit horizontal view of history.

b) The Fourth Evangelist traces history from creation to the history of Israel, Abraham, Moses, the Prophets, John the Baptist and Jesus and the continued history of the community. He thrives to be part of Israel's religious ethos.[77] For him history cannot stop with Jesus, the very concept of mission in the Fourth Gospel confesses his hope for a continued history of humankind. (He does not preach a cocooned cult, he exhorts his community to be in the world in spite of tribulations.) He has interest in the future of the world. According to him, κόσμος is not the whole

---

76 R. Schnackenburg, *The Gospel according to St. John*, 2:114–17, and also especially, 426–37.
77 See below pp. 221–29.

creation but the human world. (In the Fourth Evangelist's opinion, creation is from God and therefore cannot be negative, but 'the world' as humankind, which tries to be on its own and therefore is in opposition to God.) To be "of this world" for him means to be against God. The very coming of the Son is to give the κόσμος, humankind the right direction in which it can find life, its goal of being with God. The Fourth Evangelist wants to see his faith confession "there shall be one flock, one shepherd" and "that all may be one" come true.

c) It is true that the Fourth Evangelist decidedly lays the emphasis on a person's decision. This may seem (if accepted without his teaching on community life), that the Fourth Evangelist is the most individualistic among the New Testament writers. According to him, in believing, a person passes over into life. This does not mean that the realised experience of life is final, conclusive and static. If that is the case, the concept of the Paraclete is virtually of no significance. The Evangelist believes that the Paraclete helps the 'life' experience to blossom out and, to use a Johannine phrase, be fruitful. The life received should move and grow to its fulfilment that it may be experienced in all fullness. I believe that the use of the categories, 'realised Eschatology' and/or 'the tension between realised and final Eschatology' in order to explain the Johannine concept of the future/end times, is misleading. In my opinion the Evangelist has an 'open Eschatology' and therefore refuses to speculate about the future. He follows Jesus and the early church's restraint in this regard, but his mention of the coming of the Paraclete in his eschatological scheme exhorts us to be open to God's initiative and working instead of speculating. (Further see our discussion on the Paraclete in Chapter Ten.)

In vv. 28–29 we see this open Eschatology. In fact, they do speak in terms of contemporary apocalyptic language (as in v. 27—Son of Man), but are now clothed in Johannine style. These verses speak about the concern of the community for those who do not believe. They question: what will happen to them? We see two groups of people,[78] those who have done good and

---

[78] The Jews except for the Sadducees believed in the resurrection. The context immediate to our discussion is the Christian concept of Jesus as Son of Man and his second coming—especially the grouping of the good/evil and the judgement according to works. It is identical with the Matthaean story of the last judgement in chapter 25. Also see Rom 2:6–10; 2 Cor 2:10; Acts 17:31; 1 Pet 4:5; 2 Tim 4:1 etc.

those who have done evil. However, it is not as simple as said. We may interpret them in two different ways:

a) we may consider the first group as those who did good works, as equivalent to those who believe[79] and the other group as those who did not believe and therefore did evil works, or

b) we may not include the believers at all! (they have already passed onto life). These are the two groups which comprise those non-believers who did good/evil.

We cannot really come to a consensus about these options. We do not need to decide at all for all will experience resurrection irrespective of their grouping. We come now to the crux of the problem: life and judgement now seem to oppose one another. Judgement for the Fourth Evangelist is generally an option, not necessarily condemnation or destruction. Even if it does mean destruction, it is hard to believe that 'they will be resurrected' and then immediately put to death again. To the question, what would be the fate of those who do not believe, the Fourth Evangelist does not seem to try to answer like the Synoptics or Paul, but keeps the options open. This should not be interpreted as a lack of interest in the future, but rather to be open to God's ways, allowing Him the decision instead of dictating and speculating.[80]

Finally we are confronted with the significance of this discussion to our investigation of the Evangelist's understanding of God. If we cling to the more explicit realised/vertical structure rather than the more implicit open and horizontal, then 'God' may become a principle which could be ignored without any real consequence. It thereby becomes a matter of perspective

---

79 The other futuristic utterances speak only of those who believe—and their resurrection, see John 6:39, 40, 44, 54; 12:48.

80 J. Frey, *Die johanneische Eschatologie*, 3:381–91. In his article on Johannine Eschatology, J. G. van der Watt, "A New Look at John 5:25–9 in the Light of the Use of the Term 'Eternal Life' in the Gospel According to John," *Neot* 19 (1985): 71–86, writes that vv. 28–29 spring from the Fourth Evangelist's concern regarding the people who died before the incarnation, the people who are still outside the divine reality, the people who had not yet had a chance to enter the divine reality as well as those who had rejected Jesus. He proposes that the verses be understood as the Fourth Evangelist's conception of the last day, the general idea of the way in which the eschatological events will take place when those who did not believe as well as those who lived before the incarnation will be judged as those who had believed and already passed onto life. This for me is a farfetched hypothesis—speculating on what the Fourth Evangelist did not want to speculate.

that only if one believes, God has control over him/her. It conversely means that He does not have control over everyone, which would thereby make Him a God of a chosen few. God does not force His way, but rather confronts humankind with an option. It is the horizontal, open Eschatology which really balances the vertical, realised Eschatology. Here whether one believes or not, acknowledges or not, God is a reality. He has power and control over individuals, over the world. He is the Lord of history who will bring it to a fitting conclusion, that all may have life in its fullness. It also assures that God cares, is a God of justice who judges and gives life. It is only in Him that we are secure, in Him that we have hope. Lastly it also challenges people to be open to God's ways.[81]

3.6.2.8 Verse 30: Theological Conclusion — The Absolute Dependence of the Son on the Father

The theological discussion over the relationship of the Father and the Son concludes by returning to its beginning (v. 19). It recapitulates the previous arguments. The dependence of the Son on his Father applies to every activity of the Son. The Son does only the Father's will. The Father's will determines the judgement by the Son. Therefore, it is always just and reveals the truth.

3.7 Summary and Conclusions

a) Chapter 5:17–30 which is the springboard for the Johannine Theology contains his understanding of God in a nutshell.
b) He confesses his belief in God in the common Jewish theological categories — God is Creator, Preserver and Liberator who works continually to bring wholeness to His creation.
c) The Evangelist identifies this continuous working of God in Jesus whom he calls the Son. In doing this he does not create ditheism, or make Jesus God, instead he unfolds in front of us the relationship of the Father and

---

81 For a detailed discussion and evaluation of research of Johannine eschatology see J. Frey, *Die johanneische Eschatologie*. Vol. I: *Ihre Probleme im Spiegel der Forschung seit Reimarus* (WUNT 96; Tübingen: J. C. B. Mohr [Paul Siebeck], 1997).

the Son through a phenomenon which we may call God's self-emptying reciprocated by the Son's obedience and dependence.
d) God's self-emptying is explained further, as God the Father delegating His inaccessible power of life and judgement to His Son. As the Father has life in Himself and is Judge, so also the Son. The Fourth Evangelist uses the Jewish concept of divine agency creatively as a corollary to the hereupon described phenomenon of God's self-emptying, and claims that the Son should be honoured just as one honours the Father.
e) In the Son's mission God's very life and God's judgement which are redemptive by nature, confront humankind and bring wholeness to it.
f) Johannine Eschatology speaks loudly of his understanding of God. The open Eschatology which balances both the horizontal and vertical Eschatology in the Fourth Gospel proclaims that God is a reality whether one acknowledges it or not. He is a God who cares and One of justice. It challenges people to be open to God's working with hope.
g) The Jewish tradition looked forward to a Son of Man to whom God would delegate the eschatological power of judgement. The Fourth Evangelist now identifies and theologically projects the Son himself in whom God's self-emptying is witnessed as the Son of Man.

In all, in this passage the Fourth Evangelist challenges us to confront the God of relationships, who thus far revealed Himself in the history of Israel, and now reveals Himself in a unique relationship with His Son.

Chapter Four

Theology in Conflict—Is Jesus Pre-existent?
(John 8:12–59)

4.1 The Literary Structure

This discourse-like dialogue that Jesus carries out with his opponents develops within the context of the Feast of the Tabernacles and begins at John 7:14, where it is said that Jesus "went up to the temple and taught" and ends with 8:59, when the Jews took stones to kill Jesus. The πάλιν of 8:12 is a continuation of what has proceeded before in chapter 7, as it is universally acknowledged that the passage between 7:53 to 8:11 did not belong in the original text.

Rudolf Bultmann, Heinz Becker and George Macgregor understand the present state of the text as a result of a series of dislocations. Bultmann detaches v. 12 from the discourse and places it before 12:44–50 that is followed by 8:21–29 and 12:34–36. Bultmann entitles this regrouped material the 'Light of the World.' However, even in this reconstruction vv. 26–27 are to be regarded as a misplaced fragment, inserted here incorrectly by the redactor, who has been misled by the occurrence of ταῦτα λαλῶ in vv. 26 and 28.

The section 8:13–20 is also foreign to this present context. It belongs to another division of the original gospel that Bultmann calls 'the Judge' (5:19–47; 7:15–24 and 8:13–20). While 8:30–40 has been sandwiched between 11:55–12:33 and 6:60–71 with the subheading 'Way to the Cross,' 8:48–50, 54–55 has been grouped with 7:14, 25–29; 8:48–50, 54–55; 7:30 under the subtitle 'the Dependence of the Revealer.' 8:41–47, 51–53 and 56–59 according to Bultmann comprise a fragment that speaks about two sub-themes, namely, 'Jews as the devil's children' and 'Abraham and Jesus.' Thus, chapter eight as it stands in the traditional gospel is the result of confusing editorial work and cannot be properly understood in the present order.[1]

---

1 R. Bultmann, *Das Evangelium des Johannes*, 222, 236, 260, 315. For a criticism, see D. M. Smith, *The Composition and Order of the Fourth Gospel*, 156–63.

Becker follows Bultmann in his rearrangement of the text and attempts to reconstruct a Gnostic source for the whole discourse.² Macgregor is less radical in his approach, but attempts to integrate chapter 8 more closely with chapter 7. The following sequence results: 7:15–24; 8:12–20; 7:1–14, 25–52, and 8:12–59.³ Joseph Sanders also suggests that chapters seven and eight should follow 5:47 and be rearranged as follows: 7:15–24; 8:12–20; 7:1–14, 25–52; 8:21–59.⁴

It is very much doubtful whether they belonged in the original discourse. I do agree that the discourse material in chapter 8 is 'put together' by the Evangelist, but I think that the text itself provides an indication as to how one could divide the material. There is a clear break at v. 20, where the Evangelist concludes his first section by telling his readers the place of the discussion that took place in vv. 12–20. The second section of the discourse starts at v. 21 where we again find πάλιν. However, it is not clear whether it should end after or before the editorial comment at v. 30.

Several factors point to the choice of v. 30 as the end of the division. The ταῦτα of v. 30 should be seen in close connection to the discussion which immediately precedes it. We are also told after these words, "many believed in him" (v. 30). This is a positive expression of faith. V. 31 too begins with Jesus speaking to the Jews who believed in him. The 'many' of v. 30 appear to fade out of the picture as 'the Jews' of v. 31 will not demonstrate true faith in Jesus as the encounter proceeds.⁵ But, this section which includes vv. 31–59 is knit together because the discussion centres around 'Abraham' and in v. 59, we see the claim: "before Abraham was, I am."

Therefore we propose to exegetise this text under the following structure:

---

2   H. Becker, *Die Reden des Johannesevangeliums und der Stil der gnostischen Offenbarungsrede* (FRLANT 68; Göttingen: Vandenhoeck & Ruprecht, 1956), 114–16 and 132–33.
3   G. H. C. Macgregor, *The Gospel of John*, 192–224.
4   J. N. Sanders, *A Commentary on the Gospel according to St. John*, 3.
5   Some scholars make a grammatical distinction—in v. 30 the verb πιστεύειν is used with εἰς while in v. 31 it is followed by a dative. Could this be an indication of the two different types of faith, the second one in v. 31 being insufficient? Yes, says R. E. Brown, *The Gospel according to John*, 1:513–15, but Bultmann refuses to agree in *TDNT* 6:197–228.

vv. 12–20   Jesus the light of the world—the authority of Jesus' testimony
vv. 21–30   Jesus the one from above—the origin of Jesus' authority
vv. 31–34   Truth and Liberation
vv. 35–36   Operation Liberation
vv. 37–47   God's party and devil's party
vv. 48–59   Jesus the pre-existent Son is the revealer and embodiment of salvation

4.2 The Context

The discourse that takes place in the context of the Feast of Tabernacles is typically Johannine. The dialogue between Jesus and his hearers is a dialectic of escalating divine claims and recurrent misapprehensions. The puzzling anomaly however is that the whole interchange is introduced as a discussion between Jesus and Jews who believed in him (vv. 30–31) since only a few verses later the same hearers are said to wish to kill Jesus.

We might probably in fact be able to detect some historical background for this interpretation between Jesus and his audience. Leaving the question of the historicity of this particular episode (or any other for that matter) aside, and without arguing for or against connections between the thoughts of the Evangelist and those of Paul, we notice that the role assigned to Abraham in this dialogue (esp. in vv. 31–59) is reminiscent of the central place he takes in Paul's argument for the antiquity of Christianity. Perhaps Jesus' audience appearing at this point in the Fourth Gospel represents and reflects the condition of Jews who were initially attracted to the Johannine community's message by its appeal to the first of the Patriarchs, but who later rejected it because of the community's claim to do more that just turn the Jewish faith in the 'one true God' upside down.

Until now they were persuaded to believe in Jesus, on the basis of the apostolic teaching that Jesus' mission was to restore the religion of Abraham. But when it became clear that the exaltation of Abraham was merely a foil to 'glorify Jesus' they drew back. The dialogue in John 8 may be a dramatic and highly compressed summary of a complex historical process, wherein the Jews who were initially attracted to the Christian 'reformation' of Judaism gradually become aware of the movement's implications. Thus, the whole chapter should be viewed as a protocol of a 'theological' crisis where the theological beliefs of one community are at loggerheads with those of the other, and they try to overcome one another by displaying superiority.

4.3 Exegesis

4.3.1 Verses 12–20: Jesus the Light of the World—the Authority of Jesus' Witness

The declaration "I am the Light of the world" is one of the ἐγώ εἰμι sayings of the Fourth Gospel (v. 12). It is a revelatory declaration.[6] ἐγώ εἰμι statements with an image have a similar structure. This structure is so formulated that each saying can be divided into several constituent parts. Siegfried Schulz[7] observes two main parts, the saying itself, and a sub-clause which shows soteriological implications of Jesus' claim:

A) 'self predication,' 'the revelatory word' or the predication of ontological nature;
B) the 'soteriological sub-clause' or 'the word of promise.'

According to Schulz there is an additional sub-division of the saying:

A) breaks down further into:
   a) the presentation (ἐγώ and εἰμι);
   b) the image word with article.
B) can be divided into
   a) the invitation or call to decision;
   b) the promise for the believers as the assurance of salvation or the threat against unbelievers.

---

6   Bultmann regards this as a kind of recognition formula—ἐγώ εἰμι as an answer to the question, Who is the expected one? Who is the light of the world? Here, then, ἐγώ is the predicate. But ἐγώ in this context is surely the subject. Thus the saying cannot be translated as 'the true light I am,' but only as 'I am the light.' It is a presentation of the speaking I, and therefore a revelatory statement.

7   S. Schulz, *Komposition und Herkunft der Johanneischen Reden* (BWANT 5; Stuttgart: Kohlhammer, 1960), 86–87; E. Schweizer, *Ego Eimi: Die religionsgeschichtliche Herkunft und theologische Bedeutung der johanneischen Bildreden. Zugleich ein Beitrag zur Quellenfrage des vierten Evangeliums* (FRLANT 56; Göttingen: Vandenhoeck & Ruprecht, 1939), 33, and D. M. Ball, *'I am' in John's Gospel: Literary Function, Background and Theological Implications* (JSNTSup 124; Sheffield: Sheffield Academic Press, 1996), 162–63.

The 'I am' sayings with an image such as 'light of the world' broadly display what Jesus is in regard to humankind. The image normally represents the gift of God, through Jesus to humankind, and therefore reveal the identity and role of Jesus. 'I am' sayings with an image are prophetic as they foreshadow the breaking in of the power/gift of God, they are parabolic as they encapsulate the salvific intentions of God in Jesus. When Jesus says 'I am' he basically proclaims the very presence of God.[8]

But the context is of vital importance in order to understand it. The last utterance of Jesus is recorded in 7:37–38. Jesus has no part in the discussion recorded in vv. 40–52. The setting is the Feast of Tabernacles. 7:37–38 has immediate reference to the water drawing ceremony of the festival. It shows Jesus fulfilling all that it signified of Israel's experience and hope for salvation. John 8:12 has immediate reference to the joyous celebration of each night in the light of the lamps as a part of the Feast of Tabernacles with all that it denotes in reference to Israel's experience of the shining of God upon them for their deliverance and hope of future salvation.[9]

The water drawing ceremony and the celebration of the light of the lamps would have been associated with recollections of the nation's experience at Exodus and the hope for a final liberation and redemption. In the wilderness wanderings, the presence of the Lord with His people was manifested in the 'shekinah'—the pillar of cloud by day and the pillar of fire by night. It saved them from their immediate destroyers (Exod 14:19–25) and guided them through the wilderness to the promised land (Exod 13:21–22). It is linked with the Old Testament faith in the Lord as the light of His people (Ps 27:1), which for the Jews denoted both the being of God and His saving activity. "Light is Yahweh in action," says Hans Conzelmann.[10] Ps 44:3 gives a remarkable expression of this concept of light. This was ever before the eyes of the Israelites in the representation of theophany, both for revelation (Ezek 1:4; 3:26–28), and for salvation (Hab 3:3–4). God's 'shining' for their salvation at the Exodus encouraged prayers for the like 'shining' of His face in the predicaments of the faithful (for example, Ps 80:1–7, 14–19), and was matched by their expectation of that same light shining for their

---

8 Ibid., 172–77, 276–84; also M. Davies, *Rhetoric and Reference in the Fourth Gospel*, 197–208.
9 See H. L. Strack & P. Billerbeck, *Kommentar zum Neuen Testament aus Talmud und Midrasch*, 2:805–807, and Rabbinic texts for a detailed discussion.
10 See *TDNT*, s.v. φῶς.

salvation in the coming kingdom of God (Isa 60:19–22). Zech 14:5b–7 is especially significant here, where the continued light of 'that day' is described followed by that of the living waters, which are to flow from Jerusalem. This is a passage read at the Tabernacles and one of those assumed in the saying of John 7:37–38.[11]

This festival background for 8:12 does not, however, exhaust the meaning of the saying, but it does indicate the starting point for its comprehension. Had it been uttered in a synagogue, it would have awakened in the people familiar associations (not to say of astonishment and outrage!), since contemporary Judaism spoke not only of God as the light of the world but also of the Torah, the Temple, Adam (to whom Prov 20:27 was applied), and even of at least one of its great teachers, Johanan ben Zakkai.[12] However, since the utterance is set in the celebration of salvation history and the eschatological expectations of the Tabernacle, the application assumes greater proportions and its relation to the cry of 7:37–38 is clear.

In the context of the Fourth Gospel the saying takes on a cosmic scope. It expresses the universal saving character of the revelation, and the universal saving significance of the person of Jesus.[13] This would have been quite comprehensible to the readers of the Fourth Gospel reared in the faiths of the Hellenistic world, since for them the thought of God as light belonged to the 'above.' They believed that only those from 'above' could bring light to the world below.[14] This revelatory statement makes plain the origin of Jesus, his mission of bringing crisis, judgement and life. It also makes clear that for people belonging to the 'below' world to pass into the 'above,' Jesus is indispensable. Thus, the Jews would have recognised in this exclusive claim, and in the doctrine of the Logos, that Jesus is the realisation of their former glimpses of truth, and the fulfilment of their earlier hopes and longings.

---

11 For a detailed Old Testament background see G. R. Beasley-Murray, *John*, 127–28, and A. T. Hanson, *The Prophetic Gospel*, 116–20.
12 See H. L. Strack & P. Billerbeck, *Kommentar zum Neuen Testament aus Talmud und Midrasch*, 1:237, for citations.
13 J. Blank, *Krisis*, 184.
14 For the probable Hellenistic background, see C. H. Dodd, *Interpretation of the Fourth Gospel*, 201–208; H. Odeberg, *The Fourth Gospel*, 268–92, and R. Bultmann, *Das Evangelium des Johannes*, 260–61.

When the original setting of 8:12 is seen in the context of the Feast of Tabernacles, it is understood why the imagery of 'following' the light is employed instead of 'receiving' or 'walking in' or the like. Probably this is because of what Israel did in the wilderness! A person's life is frequently thought of as a journey under the guidance and rule of God.[15] The people followed the light as it led them from the land of slavery through the perils of the wilderness to the promised land. The picture harmonises perfectly with the call of Jesus to follow him as disciples, but makes plain its soteriological and eschatological dimensions. Following Jesus, the light of the world gives the believer the assurance of avoiding the perils and snares of darkness, the promise of possessing the light of life and the liberation from the realm of death for a life with the Light (God Himself). The 'following' should be in the path towards exaltation and lifting up.[16] In following the light one passes from the below to the above. Since Jesus is the light of life (cf. 1:14) the promise carries the reality of passing from below to the above, here and now[17] in anticipation of its fullness.

The assertive effect of the saying can be perceived at once (vv. 13–18). It belongs to the function of light to discriminate, bring crisis and judge (cf. 3:19–20). But Jesus clarifies that he does not judge (v. 15) as that is not the purpose of his ministry as revealer and redeemer (cf. 3:17), but that judgement forms an inevitable consequence of revelation. The Pharisees object vehemently saying, "no person is authenticated through his own testimony." Jesus' reply is unexpected. His witness concerning himself is valid because he knows his origin and his destiny, whereas his opponents do not. "Even if I testify on my own behalf" (v. 14) and "even if I judge" (v. 16) should be held together. The testimony and judgement of Jesus are grounded in his 'from above origin' and in God from whom his mission is derived.

---

15 For a resumé of similar ideas in Jewish Gnostic thought, see R. Schnackenburg, *The Gospel according to St. John*, 2:191.

16 The 'lifting up' passage follows closely at 8:28. Also see the relationship between 'from above' and 'lifting up' in 3:13ff.

17 The genitive τῆς ζωῆς (exegetically) defines the promised light more specifically as the life which frees a person from the sphere of death. The future ἕξει is a language of promise not for a distant future but for one that begins immediately and never ends. The saying confers with the basic formula "whoever believes has eternal life and will live forever" (cf. 3:16; 6:51, 58 etc.) For a detailed discussion of the phrase 'light of life' in Jewish, Gnostic and Qumran texts see, R. Schnackenburg, *The Gospel according to St. John*, 2:191–92.

ὅτι μόνος οὐκ εἰμί, ἀλλ᾽ ἐγὼ καὶ ὁ πέμψας με πατήρ should be understood with vv. 19–30 in the background. It neither speaks of two powers in heaven, nor moves towards ditheism. It should still be understood as Jesus the 'Sent One.' Perhaps Isa 43:10 that refers to the Messiah, the king anointed, may be alluded to in v. 18. The Septuagint translates Isa 43:10 as γένεσθέ μοι μάρτυρες, κἀγὼ μάρτυς, λέγει κύριος ὁ θεός, καὶ ὁ παῖς, ὃν ἐξελεξάμην, ἵνα γνῶτε καὶ πιστεύσητε καὶ συνῆτε ὅτι ἐγώ εἰμι, ἔμπροσθέν μου οὐκ ἐγένετο ἄλλος θεὸς καὶ μετ᾽ ἐμὲ οὐκ ἔσται. It is a part of a 'servant song.' Here we find the people addressed, God Himself and His servant as three witnesses to the uniqueness of the Hebrew deity. It would be easy for the Fourth Evangelist to make a transition from servant to Messiah since in his view Jesus surely filled both roles. It was a foregone conclusion in all Jewish messianic belief that the Messiah would be chosen and sent by God to be His special agent. Thus in John 8 "the father who sent me" may correspond to "the servant I have chosen."[18]

Two complementary ideas are presented here, on the one hand the oneness of the Son and the Father in the testimony and judgement declared by the Son, and on the other their distinction. The agreement between two different persons, the Father and the Son, is an absolute necessity and the condition for a logical revelatory structure.[19] The Father who sent the Son is with him to reveal to him what to say in judgement and in testimony (see 5:30 and 7:16–17).

Where is your Father? expresses another Johannine misunderstanding (vv. 19–20)—we cannot see Him and we do not have His evidence (cf. also the allegation that Jesus is a Samaritan). The mutual involvement of the Father and the Son, their word and their work are the keynotes of the Johannine revelation of God. It is in fact an invitation to 'know God' better. The charge that the Jews do not know God (cf. 7:28, 8:55) is a bitter attack on Judaism's proudest possessions. How can the people who reject the 'Sent One,' 'the eschatological Messiah,' 'the Agent-Son' of God know 'God'? Their knowledge and understanding of God is faulty.

In the name of Jesus the Johannine community contests Judaism's claim of knowing the only true God, its obedience to His will, love for Him and living in union with God. They were not open enough to know God's way

---

18 A. T. Hanson, *The Prophetic Gospel*, 119–20.
19 J. Blank, *Krisis*, 223.

of working. It was not as Bultmann says, that "God shut himself off from them,"[20] but it was the people who shut themselves away from God and His working. The supposed knowledge about God and salvation becomes shattering ignorance when they place no faith in and love him, Jesus who possesses the true knowledge of God and reveals the way to salvation.[21]

According to the Fourth Evangelist, knowing God demands that they go beyond what they have learnt and understood from their own Jewish tradition. God is beyond religious traditions. Considering the bitter struggle between the Johannine community and the Synagogue as the context in which the Gospel was written, it is inevitable that, "when the hour comes," many controversies and differences of opinion are bound to arise in comprehending God's revelation in Jesus.

4.3.2 Verses 21–30: Jesus the One from Above—The Origin of Jesus' Authority

4.3.2.1 Verses 21–22: Jesus' going away—Jesus is sought

This passage begins on a threatening note. Jesus is to depart and the Jews who opposed him will seek him. This means ironically that they will seek what he proclaims as God's gift through him, but in vain, because they will die in their sins. The two terms 'sin' and 'death' now become a little clear. Sin is walking in darkness in the dominion of death and to die means to be finally subject to the realm below. In the Fourth Gospel we see an unbreakable link between human sinfulness, unbelief and death.

The Jews think that Jesus might kill himself and therefore put him 'beyond finding.' Suicide was regarded in Judaism as a serious sin resulting in exclusion from the future age.[22] It is not an ordinary misunderstanding, but a deliberate misinterpretation and a sarcastic comment. For if there is an ironical reflection of the mission of Jesus in John 7:35, then it is possibly an unwitting prophecy or at least a caricature of Jesus laying down his life for others.[23]

---

20 R. Bultmann, *Das Evangelium des Johannes*, 213.
21 R. Schnackenburg, *The Gospel according to St. John*, 2:195.
22 See *ibid.*, 198.
23 E. C. Hoskyns, *The Fourth Gospel*, 334; R. Bultmann, *Das Evangelium des Johannes*, 264, and C. K. Barrett, *The Gospel according to St. John*, 341.

4.3.2.2 Verse 23: Jesus is from above

The crisp dualism of ἐκ τῶν κάτω and ἐκ τῶν ἄνω speaks of the contrast between the 'upper' or 'heavenly' and the 'below,' 'lower' or earthly things. This vertical dualism was not foreign to Judaism. The Rabbinic literature speaks about 'no evil thing coming from above,' or about people being made according to the manner of both above and below, who will die if they sin and live if they do not sin. (While the 'above' realm was considered the realm of life, the 'below' was regarded as the place of judgement and death.[24])

One also finds this sharp dualism in Gnosticism where the 'lower,' 'earthly' realm is of darkness and death, and the 'upper' world is of life and light. Thus the Gospel of Truth presents parallels to the Johannine language. According to the Gospel of Truth, if a person has knowledge he is from above. Judgement and redemption come from above.[25] The Johannine vertical dualism with ἐκ τῶν ἄνω and ἐκ τῶν κάτω has ethical and moral designations, though we also encounter a very well balanced horizontal dualism between this age and the age to come. According to the Fourth Evangelist this ἐκ τῶν ἄνω is the divine sphere and 'below' is the creation created by the above. This 'created below' is moving horizontally, the movement being controlled by the 'above.' Technically ἐκ τῶν ἄνω means God in the Evangelist's understanding and ἐκ τῶν κάτω the creation. It is only in acknowledging and recognising this ἐκ τῶν ἄνω that ἐκ τῶν κάτω has existence and meaning.

And through Jesus' words "you are from below, I am from above, you are of this world, I am not of this world," the Fourth Evangelist wants his readers to acknowledge Jesus' divine origin and asserts that only in recognising the 'above' which confronts them in Jesus, will people 'live.' This is very much in line with the Johannine understanding of eternal life as a gift from above (see the exegesis of John 3:3–6, 9–15).

---

24 See R. Schnackenburg, *The Gospel according to St. John*, 2:198; H. Odeberg, *The Fourth Gospel*, 293–94, and H. L. Strack & P. Billerbeck, *Kommentar zum Neuen Testament aus Talmud und Midrasch*, 2:430–31.
25 *Gospel of Truth* 22:3ff.; 25:35–36; 35:1–2 in *NHL*, 37–49.

4.3.2.3 Verse 24: Belief in Jesus

The choice confronting the Jews here is expressed in terms of its negative consequence and therefore takes the form of a threat: "if you do not believe what I have just said (if you do not believe that I am not of this world/that I am from above) then you will die still being a sinner" (ἐὰν γὰρ μὴ πιστεύσητε ὅτι ἐγώ εἰμι, ἀποθανεῖσθε ἐν ταῖς ἁμαρτίαις ὑμῶν). The first half of the threat raises a problem as to what is meant by πιστεύσητε ὅτι ἐγώ εἰμι. In the Fourth Gospel the expression ἐγώ εἰμι occurs thirty-three times on the lips of Jesus.[26] Of those it has a predicate in twenty-three cases. In only ten occurrences we find ἐγώ εἰμι in the absolute state (without an explicit predicate) and three of them occur in this chapter now under investigation, namely in vv. 24, 28 and 58. Along with these three occurrences 13:19 is also considered to be the verse where we confront a truly absolute ἐγώ εἰμι. Johannine scholarship has tended to find a Jewish background for this unnatural expression, especially in the Septuagint translation of the Hebrew אני יהוה, where ἐγώ εἰμι becomes a presentation formula, with revelatory significance as a surrogate for the divine name.[27]

Harner thinks that in v. 24 ἐγώ εἰμι is intended to be understood as complete and meaningful in itself. It should apparently be understood as "I am the one."[28] But in the case of 8:24, I believe the context supplies the implied predicate. Here Jesus is saying, "unless you believe that I am not of this world/that I am from above, you will die in your sins." He has just been talking about the fact that he is ἐκ τῶν ἄνω and not ἐκ τοῦ κόσμου τούτου. The meaning of 8:24 is determined by that of 8:28. How can the Evangelist make Jesus claim to be God in v. 24 and in v. 28 make Jesus confess that "I do nothing of myself, but speak as the Father taught me . . .?" It is simply intolerable that Jesus should be made to say 'I am God, the supreme God of the Old Testament and being God I do as I am told'!

It may be that this ἐγώ εἰμι (vv. 24) should be understood as a reference to 'Jesus the sent one from above' that is, the Messiah! In v. 24 ἐγώ εἰμι is the explicit object of belief. Here the proposition of faith is emphatically and

---

[26] Besides three times on the lips of John the Baptist (1:20, 27; 3:38) and once on the lips of Pilate (18:35).

[27] For a full discussion of the use of ἐγώ εἰμι in the Fourth Gospel, see R. E. Brown, *The Gospel According to John*, 1:533–38; P. B. Harner, *The "I am" of the Fourth Gospel*, and D. M. Ball, *'I am' in John's Gospel*, 48–59, 188–94.

[28] P. B. Harner, op. cit., 43ff.

categorically stated, that Jesus is from God.²⁹ In the immediate and larger context of v. 24 especially chapters 7 and 8, which have as their setting controversies with Jews at the Feast of Tabernacles, the Evangelist displays familiarity with several aspects of the Jewish messianic belief. This supports the suggestion that ἐγώ εἰμι in v. 24 refers to the messiahship of Jesus. The following reasons could be highlighted:

a) In the Jewish messianic thought the chief function of the Messiah was that of a judge.
b) He was expected to reprove sinners.
c) V. 23 which states that Jesus is from above and not of this world can be interpreted in the light of 12:34 where the Jews from Jerusalem ask, "But we know where this man comes from," and when the Christ comes no one knows from where he is!
d) And also it appears that in his development of the themes of Jesus' coming and going away and his being from above, the Evangelist has used Jewish ideas of a hidden and dying Messiah in a highly creative fashion. The Johannine device of misunderstanding regularly accompanies this idea.³⁰

The ἐγώ εἰμι in 8:24 probably reveals the Evangelist's unique concept of Jesus as Messiah, which puts the Jews in utter confusion—the Messiah remains hidden to Jewish understanding and panic struck Jews enquire, "Who are you?"

4.3.2.4 Verses 25–27: Jesus' Authority

Are we here dealing with a question or a statement? It is clear that ἡ ἀρχή may be used adverbially.³¹ It is almost impossible to make sense out of the phrase, if τὴν ἀρχήν is taken as an accusative noun, unless one adds some-

---

29 Remember this was precisely the confession of Jesus' messiahship which led to excommunication from the synagogue during the time of controversy between the institution and the community—John 9:22; 12:42; 16:2. See also J. L. Martyn, *History and Theology in the Fourth Gospel*.

30 Cf. C. H. Dodd, *Interpretation of the Fourth Gospel*, 89, 91–92; W. A. Meeks, "The Man from Heaven in Johannine Sectarianism," 141–73, esp. 154–60, and M. D. Hooker, "The Johannine Prologue and the Messianic Secret," *NTS* 21 (1975): 44. She maintains that the hiddenness, which the Jews do not understand, is Jesus' divine, 'from above' origin.

31 This adverbial use is quite frequent. See H. G. Liddell & R. Scott, *A Greek-English Lexicon*, 252, s.v. ἀρχή i.b.c.

thing further. If it is a question, then τὴν ἀρχήν is translated as 'at all' and ὅτι is simply 'why.' This leaves us with a translation, "why am I speaking to you at all?"[32] Though there are variations on the exact form of the question, most grammarians and commentators consider it a satisfactory solution.[33] In translating the phrase as a statement, several words have to be supplied. It is generally translated as an affirmation about the nature of Jesus, so an ἐγώ εἰμι is added. ἀπό is understood as governing τὴν ἀρχήν and ὅτι as a relative ὅ τι, 'that which.'

These additions again give rise to various possibilities, "I am from the beginning what I told you" or "I am what I told you from the beginning."[34] Another suggestion is that the τὴν ἀρχήν remains adverbial, giving the translation, "primarily (I am) what I am telling you."[35] These suggestions see v. 25b as a continuation of its discussion concerning the nature of Jesus. The main argument for this interpretation is that it fits the context better than a question.[36] Raymond Brown tentatively followed by Barnabas Lindars and Leon Morris uses the evidence of P66[37] which contains "I am telling you from the beginning what I am also telling you now," and translates the phrase as "what I have been telling you from the beginning."[38]

While the arguments for the interpretation of v. 25b as a statement do have some very important advocates,[39] the necessary additions appear too

---

32 Very close to the question is probably an exasperated remark that translated the ὅτι as 'that': "that I speak to you at all."
33 M. Zerwick & J. Smith, *Biblical Greek* (Rome, 1963), § 222; J. H. Moulton & G. Milligan, *The Vocabulary of the Greek Testament*, 81, s.v. ἀρχή; BDF, § 300(2); W. Bauer et al., *A Greek-English Lexicon*, 111, s.v. ἀρχή; W. Bauer, *Das Johannesevangelium*, 123; J. Blank, *Krisis*, 228; R. Schnackenburg, *The Gospel according to St. John*, 2:200–201; C. H. Dodd, *Historical Tradition in the Fourth Gospel* (Cambridge: Cambridge University Press, 1963), 230, n. 1; R. Bultmann, *Das Evangelium des Johannes*, 276ff.
34 See C. K. Barrett, *The Gospel according to St. John*, 342ff.
35 J. H. Bernard, *Commentary on the Gospel according to St. John*, 2:301–302.
36 See C. K. Barrett, op. cit., 342ff.; also J. Marsh, *The Gospel of St. John*, 360. Marsh rules out the interpretation of the phrase in the form of a question as quite unacceptable on account of the context.
37 See R. W. Funk, "Papyrus Bodmer II P66 and John 8:25," *HTR* 51 (1958): 95–100, and E. R. Smothers, "Two Readings in Papyrus Bodmer II," *HTR* 51 (1958): 111–22.
38 R. E. Brown, *The Gospel according to John*, 1:347–48; B. Lindars, *The Gospel of John*, 321, and L. Morris, *The Gospel according to John*, 448–50.
39 See E. C. Hoskyns, *The Fourth Gospel*, 335–36; R. H. Lightfoot, *St. John's Gospel*, 191, and H. Odeberg, *The Fourth Gospel*, 294–95.

demanding. Perhaps the ἐγώ εἰμι could be carried over from v. 24, although this is a little forced. The accusative (ἀπό) τὴν ἀρχήν would be extraordinary in the Fourth Gospel, where one finds ἀπ' (ἐξ) ἀρχῆς to express 'from the beginning' (see John 8:44; 15:27; 16:4). Finally the present tense of λαλῶ is handled violently when one translates it as "what I have told from the beginning."[40] Although the translation as a statement may appear to suit the context better than the question, it runs the risk of being a 'tour de force' on the part of the interpreter to make it do so.[41]

However, I prefer to translate it as a statement: "what I am saying from the beginning." Here I sense a common human expression of furious impatience, and therefore ἀρχή or the presence of "I am" has nothing to do with the christological discussion of pre-existence. Here, Jesus says, and of course confirms what he has already told them during the course of the discussion (vv. 12–24). He adds nothing new, at the same time refuses to repeat what he has already said.

Jesus, who does not want to say anything more about himself to the stubborn Jews, could still say 'many things' about them and judge (cf. v. 16). He however sees his task not in judging, but in redeeming.[42] For we see Jesus calling their attention to the faithfulness of the One who sent him and continuing to tell them that he tells the world only what he hears from the Father. Incomprehension again greets him (v. 27). Jesus now informs them of the time and the event when they will know the meaning and content of ἐγώ εἰμι.

4.3.2.5 Verses 28–30: The revelation of the Son of man

The revelation seems to reach a high point in v. 28. The use of οὖν is a logical link to what has gone before. While the Jewish listeners still have not understood him up to this point, the Fourth Evangelist introduces a more solemn statement: "when you have lifted up the Son of Man, then you will

---

40 R. Schnackenburg, *The Gospel according to St. John*, 2:201. See that the tense of the verb is λαλῶ and not εἶπον or λελάληκα.
41 The Latin fathers generally understood it as a statement, while the Greek fathers almost universally read it as a question. For summaries of Patristic evidence, see R. Bultmann, *Das Evangelium des Johannes*, 267–68, and R. E. Brown, *The Gospel according to John*, 1:347ff.
42 The idea of judgement is not essential to the context and tends to disrupt it, but the Evangelist likes to let particular ideas keep recurring.

know that I am he." However, there are several problems involved in this apparently clearly stated fact. The commentators have observed that the form of the verb ὑψόω is in the active voice and in the second person plural. Jesus will be 'lifted up' by "you"—who forms the subject of the verb ὑψώσητε. We have no indication that the Evangelist has changed the audience of Jesus.

Instead, it would seem that we need to carry over the οἱ Ἰουδαῖοι from 8:22 to act as subject. In other places where the 'lifting up' is mentioned (John 3:14; 12:34) the verb is passive and closely linked with δεῖ, expressing a divine necessity, similar to the passion predictions of the Synoptic Gospels (see Mark 8:31; 9:31; 10:33 and parallels). Here in saying "when you have lifted up the Son of Man" the Evangelist almost makes an accusation. The reference here is clearly to the activity of the Jews in crucifying Jesus. It is the Jews, Jesus' interlocutors throughout the discussion who will come to the knowledge that he is 'I am,' but what is the object of γνώσεσθε? What does ἐγώ εἰμι mean here?

Bultmann has attempted to base the authority of Jesus' claims in v. 28 in his being the Son of Man. To do this he makes the Son of Man the predicate of ἐγώ εἰμι. It is at the moment of Jesus' elevation on the cross that the Jews will understand that he is the Son of Man.[43] While this would be linguistically possible, it seems hardly probable. The Son of Man in the Fourth Gospel is linked with the theme of 'lifting up' (cf. 3:14, 12:34) and not with the "I am" statements. He never says "I am the Son of Man." The ἐγώ εἰμι of v. 28a seems to catch up and repeat what has already been said in v. 24. To make the 'Son of Man' the predicate of v. 28a would cause the loss of the obviously intended repetition.[44]

The predicate of ἐγώ εἰμι is implicit in the context as in v. 24. Jesus says to the Jews following their obtusity in v. 26, "you will come to know that I am the one sent by the Father." This is in continuation with the Christology of the Fourth Gospel, where Jesus is subordinate to the Father, not just in an economic sense but also in essentiality. The Jews will come to know that Jesus came from above and had to return above and that he is divine in that sense. Hence, "the one sent by the Father" as the predicate of ἐγώ εἰμι does make a great deal of sense in terms of what went before and what is to follow.

---

43 R. Bultmann, *Das Evangelium des Johannes*, 265–66, and A. Wikenhauser, *Das Evangelium nach Johannes*, 140.
44 See R. Schnackenburg, *The Gospel according to St. John*, 2:202.

Verse 29 continues with the assertion of the validity of Jesus' revelation. The revelation of the Son of Man lifted up on the cross is valid not only because Jesus has spoken what he has heard from the Father (v. 28b) but also because the Father remains continually with him and has not left him alone. After the present tense μετ' ἐμοῦ ἐστιν, one expects a perfect tense which would logically claim that the Father has never left Jesus alone—He was with him before all things and remains with him. Instead we find the aorist ἀφῆκεν. This could refer to the incarnation. When the pre-existent Logos who had been with God (John 1:1–2) entered the world of flesh (John 1:14), the Father did not abandon him, but was even then with him. It could also be the Evangelist's way of telling his readers that even in the apparent solitude of the cross, the Father was with Jesus. It is because of this continual presence of the Father with Jesus that he can claim to be the 'I am,' the authentic revelation of God.

The ὅτι of v. 29c may explain why the Father never left Jesus: "because I always do what is pleasing to him." It is better understood, however as the introduction to a clause of consequence.[45] The logic of this passage then is as follows: only after the Jews have lifted up the Son of Man on the cross, will they be able to understand that he is the authentic revelation of God (v. 28a). For Jesus, the Son of Man reveals what he has learnt from the Father, as the faithful Son (agent?) in accordance with the terms of commission.

Therefore his revelation is uniquely valid (v. 28b). But there is more to it than this. There is unity between the Son and the Father which extends to their very presence with one another in that the Father did not leave him to work out his task alone. The Father is with him (v. 29a, b), and because of this, all that the Son does is pleasing to the Father, as it is in perfect concurrence with His will (v. 29c). Therefore, he is the ἐγώ εἰμι.[46]

We must note that, when the Fourth Evangelist relates ἐγώ εἰμι, the Old Testament Jewish designation for God, to Jesus, it could mean that he puts Jesus in the place of God. But even here the humanness of Jesus is not actually eliminated. With the introduction of the ἐγώ εἰμι of Jesus, the Evangelist does make the claim that God Himself appears in the man Jesus. However, even in his context he has not forgotten that God is making Him-

---

45 See W. Bauer et al., *A Greek-English Lexicon*, 593 on ὅτι.
46 See C. H. Dodd, *Interpretation of the Fourth Gospel*, 93–96 and 349–50, where he suggests that Jesus' being sent by the Father is involved in his being "I am" which the Rabbis sometimes rendered as אֲנִי וָהוּא—"I am and the One who sent me."

self perfectly visible in the man Jesus, and therefore even here the Evangelist has not simply equated Jesus with God, but presented him as a divine being, while the emphasis here is precisely placed on the utter dependence upon the Father of the exalted Son of Man, who can say of himself ἐγώ εἰμι.[47]

There is another question concerning the knowledge mentioned in vv. 28–29. Will it be positive or negative in its effect? Will it be the knowledge that will lead to salvation, or the knowledge that will come too late? Will this knowledge vitiate, or confirm the threat contained in v. 24? Bultmann who is followed by Barrett takes the effect of the knowledge as negative, that they will know when it is too late. Those who refuse to believe in him now will see him not as the revealer, but as the judge, then, and as those who seek in vain, they will realise that it is too late and their knowledge will in some form be knowledge of despair.[48]

But I tend to argue with Schnackenburg and others who understand knowledge in a positive sense since γινώσκω tends to be a positive word in the Fourth Gospel (see John 7:17, 26; 8:37; 10:38; 14:31 and 17:23). In fact, it is continually linked with the Johannine idea of faith.[49] The very similar passage in 12:32 is also positive: "and when I am lifted up from the earth, I will draw all people to myself." It would appear that John 8:28 may be understood in a more positive light.[50] This is further indicated by the result of the discussion as reported in v. 30: "many believed in him." What is promised in v. 28a is therefore not condemnation but hope.

But this hope of course depends on a 'decision.' According to v. 28a, it is when Jesus the Son of Man is raised upon the cross that they will know that Jesus the Son of Man is the revealer and the revelation of God. His revelation in itself is neither salvation nor condemnation. It is the possibility of both. Perhaps as Schnackenburg holds, the Evangelist wanted to extend

---

47 W. G. Kümmel, *Theology of the New Testament according to its Major Witnesses: Jesus, Paul and John* (trans. J. E. Steely; London: SCM Press, 1974), 267–77.
48 R. Bultmann, *Das Evangelium des Johannes*, 266–68, and C. K. Barrett, *The Gospel according to St. John*, 344.
49 See John 6:69; 8:31–32; 10:38; 16:30 and 17:7–8, and also E. K. Lee, *The Religious Thought of St. John* (London: S.P.C.K., 1950), 220–25, and also the only other place where the activity of people in the death of Jesus is mentioned, in John 19:37: "They shall look upon him whom they have pierced." This is not a negative condemnation, but by quoting Zech. 12:10, the Fourth Evangelist refers to the saving power of the cross.
50 R. Schnackenburg, *The Gospel according to St. John*, 2:202.

the horizon to his own time period during the community–synagogue crisis. Thus the promise of v. 28a is neither about salvation nor about condemnation, but rather the possibility of both, offered to the Jews in the time of Jesus and in the time of the Johannine church.[51]

In his discussion of Jesus' relationship to his Father, the Evangelist clearly presents Jesus as the Son of Man, the unique, authentic revealer of the Father, while he is 'from above' and sent by the Father (cf. vv. 14, 16, 18, 19, 21, 23, 26–29). But despite their obtuseness (cf. vv. 25–27) the Jews will be able to look upon the Son of Man whom they have lifted upon the cross, and they will find God's revelation to humankind. Note that the Son of Man title occurs once again in the context of revelation and judgement and this revelation for the Evangelist will not be limited to any historical moment, rather the glory of God will always shine forth from Christ crucified. As such the cross will always be the place where people can find God's revelation, and consequently the knowledge of God's revelation that comes through the elevated Son of Man depends entirely upon the peoples' acceptance or rejection!

The problem that confronts the Evangelist is probably to bring together two facts into one story, namely,
a) that the vast majority of Jews rejected the message of the earthly Jesus,
b) and that the majority of the Johannine community were Jews who had come to faith after Jesus had been 'lifted up.'

The reference at v. 30 to 'many believing in Jesus' is hard to concur with, when one reads it as the conclusion to a story about the earthly Jesus speaking to a group of stubborn Jews, who did not understand who he was, and what he was about. It does make sense, however, if read as a comment relating to the time of the Johannine church when some Jews believed Jesus after he was 'lifted up.'

4.3.3 Verses 31–34: Truth and Liberation

4.3.3.1 Remaining in the Word

The primary duty of a believer is indicated in the exhortation of Jesus, "remain in my word" (v. 31). μένειν signifies a settled determination to live

---

51 E. C. Hoskyns, *The Fourth Gospel*, 336.

in the word. It entails a perpetual listening to it, reflection on it, holding fast to it and carrying out its bidding. In John 15:7 it is represented as letting the Word abide in us, which leads to living in Christ and Christ in us. The "Word" itself means the presence of God for the Fourth Evangelist (Jesus speaks what he heard from the Father). By remaining in the word one can become learners in the presence of God. This process entails a coming to know or dawning of the truth.

ἡ ἀλήθεια is a technical word with revelatory significance for the Fourth Evangelist. Truth and freedom, which mean revelation and salvation, are put together in a very unique manner (vv. 31b–34). In an attempt to understand this unique revelatory structure, we need to focus our attention on two key words of this passage, ἡ ἀλήθεια and ἐλευθερόω.

4.3.3.2 Truth

In the Old Testament the word truth (אֱמֶת) is applied to God. God is a God of Truth—"the Lord is the true God" (Jer 10:10). He is not 'the true God' in contrast to false ones, but rather one on whom His people can rely and can rightly be called a fortress, a refuge or a rock. Truth means essentially 'reliability,' 'dependability,' 'the ability to perform what is required.' In itself truth is a fact or a state which is unalterable and has to be accepted (cf. Ps 31:5; 146:6). Truth denotes the quality of God's activity, for instance, His judging (cf. Ps 96:13; 57:3). His 'Truth' is the reason as to why people can trust in Him. In a universe that is influx and constantly changing, He proves to be the only unchanging reality. And the truth is also what God demands of people. He desires it in inward parts (Ps 51:6), one must speak it (Ps 15:2), seek it (Jer 5:1) and walk in it (2 Kgs 20:3). Here truth means unwavering conformity with God's will as made known in the law (Psalms 119, 142, 151). In a more general sense it means faithfulness, trustworthiness.

In classical Greek, the meaning of the term is summed up by Bultmann as follows: "ἡ ἀλήθεια originally signifies a content of fact or a state of affairs, in so far as it is seen, indicated or expressed and is completely manifested in such seeing, indication or expression, with special reference to the fact that it might be concealed, falsified or diminished. ἡ ἀλήθεια is the complete or real state of affairs. As in forensic language, ἡ ἀλήθεια is the state of affairs to be proved over against the various assertions of the parties, so in the historian's perspective, it is the historical state of affairs over against the myth and in the philosopher's that which really is in the absolute sense."[52]

The Septuagint translates אֱמֶת as ἡ ἀλήθεια, but the Hebrew אֱמֶת differs in meaning from the classical Greek ἡ ἀλήθεια. While the Hebrew word has the meaning of 'faithfulness,' 'trustworthiness,' 'sureness' and 'permanence,' the Greek ἡ ἀλήθεια has the meaning opposed to falsehood or, of reality as opposed to mere appearance. The Hebrew אֱמֶת is moral rather than intellectual. In Hebrew the ontological element is emphasised, while in the classical Greek the cognitive element is dominant. The former word refers to verity, to that which is ideally true and the latter to veracity, to that which is factually true. The Hebrew words deal with persons or things as realities that one can lean upon. The classical Greek connotation deals with ideas or their expression in relation to facts.[53]

In the Apocalyptic and Wisdom traditions, 'truth' has a moral significance but, with a different shade of meaning, it is righteousness or rectitude, rather than faithfulness. In fact the word 'truth' is often synonymous with mystery and accordingly anticipates the revealed truth or the divine plan revealed to people. Dan 10:21 mentions the 'Book of Truth' as that which contains the divine plan for the time of salvation. The association of the truth mystery is distinctly found in Wis 3:9. This verse describes the case of the just at the moment of judgement. V. 9 continues: "those who trust in him will understand the truth." This cannot be explained either in terms of אֱמֶת that they will experience the faithfulness of God, or in the Greek platonic sense that they will contemplate the very reality of God, but rather in all probability in an apocalyptic sense, that they will comprehend the divine plan where wisdom will eventually be revealed to them.[54]

Comparable Rabbinic parallels show that in their circles, truth was identified with the Torah and the study of its precepts was believed to make people free.[55] One of the parallels quoted most often from Qumran is 1QS IV,

---

52 For a detailed discussion see R. Bultmann in *TDNT* 1:231–58. Also C. H. Dodd, *Interpretation of the Fourth Gospel*, 170–86; E. K. Lee, *The Religious Thought of St. John*, 38ff., and *NIDNTT* 3:874–902.
53 See B. H. Jackayya, "ἀλήθεια (Truth) in the Johannine Corpus," *CTM* 41 (1970): 171–75.
54 See I. de la Potterie, "The Truth in Saint John," in *The Interpretation of John* (ed. J. Ashton; Philadelphia: Fortress, 1986), 53–55.
55 For detailed quotes see, C. K. Barrett, *The Gospel according to St. John*, 344; H. L. Strack and P. Billerbeck, *Kommentar zum Neuen Testament aus Talmud und Midrasch*,

20–22, where it is said that on the day of the judgement, God will purify by His truth all the deeds of people and that He will sprinkle upon them the spirit of truth. It is observed by some scholars that the function of אֱמֶת in these verses is closely related to that of ἡ ἀλήθεια in John 8:32. These two passages however have little in common. In 1QS IV, 20–22 an aspect of the last judgement is described and the truth has no liberating function, whereas John 8 is clearly concerned with liberation by truth here and now in this era.[56]

R. Bultmann[57] and C. H. Dodd[58] are convinced that the sense of ἡ ἀλήθεια in the Fourth Gospel has evolved from the Hellenistic dualistic usage of the term. In these circles truth carries the connotation of true authentic reality in contrast to εἴδωλον. ἡ ἀλήθεια in the Fourth Gospel is therefore taken to mean the divine reality, which at the same time implies revelation. In contrast to the pseudo-reality of the world (ψεῦδος), truth reveals the only true possibility for human existence that leads to ζωή. Truth must therefore be understood to mean a life-giving power that illuminates the being of humankind by revealing the only true possibility of existence.[59]

It must be realised that Bultmann's argument that the combination of ἡ ἀλήθεια—πιστεύειν—γινώσκειν in John 8:30ff. proves the Hellenistic Gnostic character of the passage and therefore, interpreted accordingly, is not at all conclusive. For, the use of γινώσκειν in this context could only be well interpreted from the Old Testament ידע concept, which Bultmann too concedes.[60]

ἡ ἀλήθεια as implying revelation is also valid, but we should ask whether it means only the 'bare fact of revelation' or its content too! It is important to note the other occurrences of ἡ ἀλήθεια in the Fourth Gospel and build a comprehensive structure in order to interpret it. Let us begin with the passage under discussion. It is clear that the truth that sets free (8:22) is identical with the Son (8:36) who is none other than Jesus himself (14:6). Further, the truth will not be known (8:32) while the unbeliever knows neither Jesus nor the Father (8:19; cf. 8:55). Jesus tells the truth (8:45) which

---

2:522ff. These examples offer no sufficient explanation of ἡ ἀλήθεια as used in John 8.
56 B. C. Lategan, "The Truth that Sets Man Free: John 8:31–36," *Neot* 2 (1968): 72–73.
57 R. Bultmann, in *TDNT* 1:231–58.
58 C. H. Dodd, *Interpretation of the Fourth Gospel*, 176ff.
59 R. Bultmann, *Das Evangelium des Johannes*, 333ff.
60 R. Bultmann, in *TDNT* 1:231–58.

is the Word of God (17:17) and this he was taught by the Father (8:40). But Jesus himself is the truth (14:6). Therefore, John the Baptist was witness to the truth (5:33) and this was also the reason why Jesus came into the world (18:37). Therefore, those who are of the truth listen to his voice (18:37). Satan, however, is a liar and is not rooted in the truth (8:44). He who does the truth comes out into the light (3:21) and is sanctified by the truth (17:17–19).

In view of the above explanatory structure we may surely say that ἡ ἀλήθεια means revelation. This case is strengthened by the fact that ἡ ἀλήθεια is used with the ἐγώ εἰμι formula in the Fourth Gospel, whereas the different attributes must be understood as being on the same level and mutually interchangeable. Along with 14:6 we should note that in the passage under discussion ἐγώ εἰμι is used three times (8:24, 28, 58). It is clear that ἐγώ εἰμι is a revelatory formula whose interpretive key should be sought in the emphatic Old Testament revelation formula אֲנִי הוּא, and especially in 'Abraham' who is in the centre of the argument structure of the passage as the ancestor of all Israel, as the recipient of God's promises and as partner in the divine covenant. By saying "before Abraham was, I am," the Fourth Evangelist in no antiquated way puts Jesus in the divine history of Israel (see the exegesis of vv. 56–58).

It is not suggested that we follow the 'salvation history' mode of interpretation prescribed by Oscar Cullmann. He lays stress on the Johannine literature's interpretation in terms of the salvation history model, which is probably strongly influenced by his understanding of Luke.[61] Perhaps Schnackenburg is more correct in stating that the Evangelist nowhere recites explicitly the Old Testament history of salvation, but that the Old Testament forms the basis and treasure house of Johannine Theology. It is clear that Johannine Theology is inconceivable without Old Testament foundation and background. This follows quickly that if ἡ ἀλήθεια which means revelation could be interpreted following tips from the Old Testament אֱמֶת then we do not merely have the bare fact of revelation here, but the content explanation too.

What then does ἡ ἀλήθεια mean? It means 'the ultimate reality,' God Himself (not a principle but a living God—Old Testament concept). This God is not only real, He is also veritable. This constitutes the deepest sense

---

[61] See also R. E. Brown, "The Kerygma of the Gospel According to John," *Int* 21 (1967):394ff.

of אֱמֶת–ἡ ἀλήθεια where legal and ethical aspects are combined to describe the hallmark and aim of God's actions.[62] This explains the faithfulness of God with regard to Himself and consequently with regard to His covenant and His promises. Therefore, when we say that ἡ ἀλήθεια indicates divine revelation it may be said that revelation consists in bringing to light the trueness, the truthfulness and the trustworthiness of God's covenant and His promises. ἡ ἀλήθεια cannot be held or possessed. It is not a matter of contemplation or speculation but it is something to be received, obeyed and done or rejected and disobeyed! ἡ ἀλήθεια is not a concrete conception of God to be apprehended by intellectuals, but a revelation of reality to be received in a personal relationship. Then we can say that the Johannine ἡ ἀλήθεια means that in the process of this personal relationship God's plan for the cosmos is revealed, known and entered into.

4.3.3.3 Freedom

If ἀλήθεια understood as above sets people free, attention must also be given to the second part of this theological statement in v. 32. The word ἐλευθερόω or its substantive ἐλεύθερος occurs only here in the Johannine literature, where it is used in a legal sense in contrast to δοῦλος. When inquiring into the text as to the exact meaning of ἐλευθερόω in the Fourth Gospel, one is encountered with the difficulty that the idea of freedom occurs in all patterns of thought that constitute the possible background of the Johannine statement. It is necessary, therefore, to ask in what way freedom is attained according to the different systems and especially from what matter, object or condition humankind is free?

The Hellenistic idea of freedom (where the political concept developed into a philosophical one)[63] as expressed in particular by the stoics (and later taken up again by the idealists) rests on the fundamental division of all matter into two categories: those objects that are ἐφ' ἡμῖν and those that are οὐκ ἐφ' ἡμῖν. Sin is the result of the fact that a human being does not restrict himself/herself to that which is ἐφ' ἡμῖν but strives after objects that are οὐκ ἐφ' ἡμῖν. Freedom requires the correct insight that man/woman must restrict

---

62 It is remarkable in this respect that in John 1:14, 17 a combination of χάρις and ἀλήθεια occur together, see the exegesis of 1:14, 17.
63 See for a detailed discussion, H. Schlier, in *TDNT* 2:487ff., and R. Bultmann, *Das Evangelium des Johannes*, 335ff.

himself/herself to the sphere of his/her own spirit where matters from ἔξω have no influence. For this reason human beings can never be enslaved to sin. At the most it can be said that he 'errs,' in so far as the true nature of freedom is not understood correctly. The way to freedom is seen here as the way to independence and self realisation. By returning to the original self, freedom is attained.

Typical of various Gnostic tendencies with their dualistic structure is the liberation of the (higher) soul from the (lower) matter in which it is held captive. Well known is the metaphor of the soul caught in the prison of the body. Liberation from the σῶμα is effected by the right γνῶσις that is, the knowledge of the way to freedom as revealed in the myth of salvation. This myth tells how the so called 'redeemed Redeemer' descends from high, is himself held captive by the matter, triumphs over it in the end and thus opens up the way to freedom for all.

Gnostics seek freedom from the lower realms of darkness and death and want to win the authenticity of humanity in order to be fulfilled by the fullness of true being. It is no accident that the *Gospel of Philip* from the Gnostic Nag Hammadi Library pays particular attention to it in Logia 110, 123.[64] The Gnostic Tract accepts the Johannine text, but gives a particular interpretation of its own of freedom which leads to Gnosis. Knowledge of truth raises the souls and allows them to rise above the whole scene that is this world. Freedom requires primarily a detachment from this world, detachment from ties to other people. The means to achieve this detachment is increasing Gnosis. It also says that truth when revealed in Gnosis is more powerful than ignorance and error, ignorance is enslavement, knowledge is freedom.[65]

It is important to note a common thought in both the Hellenistic and Gnostic systems that is, that the freedom of a person is essentially something that cannot be lost. Through ignorance or sin the person may be alienated from his freedom, but by discovering the correct insight and knowledge, he

---

64 The word said, "If you know the truth, the truth will make you free. Ignorance is a slave, knowledge is freedom. If we know the truth, we shall find the fruits of the truth within us. If we are joined to it it will bring our fulfilment." See *Gospel According To Philip* in *NHL*, esp. 149–50.

65 See *Gospel According To Philip* in *NHL*, 150: ". . . but those who are in the truth will be perfect when all the truth is revealed. For the truth is like ignorance, while it is hidden, it rests in itself but when it is revealed and recognised it is praised in as much as it is stronger than ignorance and error. It gives freedom."

himself is able to regain it on his own accord and by his own efforts.⁶⁶ The remarkable fact one notices now is that basically the same attitude towards freedom is discernible in the answer of the Jews in John 8:33, when they react to his suggestion that they are in need of liberation. This similarity does not necessarily indicate mutual dependence, but shows that there is a formal resemblance in structure of thought on the idea of freedom in these various mid-east thought systems. The Jews claim that they are the descendants of Abraham and therefore have never rendered slave duties to any one. It is a clear reference to their 'inner' freedom. As the chosen people they have treasured this 'feeling of freedom' throughout their history.

For them the descent from Abraham ensures retention of inner freedom even to the poor and oppressed Israelites. This spiritual nobility is the unalienable right that belongs to the members of the chosen people. In addition to this, the Evangelist's acquaintance with the contemporary situation in Jerusalem probably plays a role in the interpretation. The zealots looked upon the Jewish subservience to the Romans as a form of δουλεία while the Pharisees claimed that their δουλεία existed only in the worship of God. But here the Evangelist exploits the faulty premise of the Jews. According to him real freedom is possible only where freedom from sin is attained.

In contrast to the above mentioned ideas of freedom the Evangelist wishes to make clear that a person enslaved by sin itself has consequently and irrevocably lost his freedom. Freedom does not form an inherent part of a person to which he can lay a claim or which he can manipulate. Therefore as a slave to sin he has no command over his own freedom. The Johannine concept of sin can be defined as apartness from God.⁶⁷ The apartness or the fallenness surely reflects the Jewish Theology of creation and fall! And to explain this, the Fourth Evangelist uses his dualistic language of darkness and light, death and life. And if we understand the Johannine concept of life as sharing in the very life of God, then naturally in such a life with God, sin has no place.

'Sin' here in the context may also mean refusal to see ἀλήθεια, reliance on status (Abraham's free children), self-enslavement and self-imposed limitations and barriers. According to the Fourth Evangelist human beings

---

66 R. Bultmann, *Das Evangelium des Johannes*, 334ff.
67 The Johannine understanding of the 'world' as one which is against God or fallen apart from God is very important here.

cannot work their freedom out from this state. Instead it can only be effected by the intervention of a higher power outside of oneself. Freedom, therefore, in the Evangelist's opinion is always a gift of grace and can never be achieved by human beings for themselves.

The liberation in this context surely means the readiness of God's faithfulness to make people free even when they are unfaithful. In making a person whole by offering him life God opens an opportunity to be in right relationship with Him, thereby humankind is helped in the successive discovery of new dimensions of 'that relationship' which frees from self-imposed limitations. In the light of the ἀλήθεια offered and the true relationship established, humankind discovers its road to freedom.

Although Bultmann clearly recognises this, he, nonetheless, believes that 8:32ff. is of Gnostic origin where the Redeemer is also pictured as the liberator of the imprisoned soul.[68] He attempts to remove the evangelical idea of freedom according to the existentialistic concepts. Freedom is the eschatological gift that exists in the opening up of the future. In this process man is renewed, he himself becomes part of the future and at the same time is released from his past, his *'woher'* — his sinful past and his own world. He is liberated from himself, from the world and from the past in general, and is now linked up with the future. It is clear that based on these precepts the past as such attains a negative and the future a positive connotation.

We cannot enter into the detailed discussion of this construction. Its implication for the exegesis of our pericope must however be made clear. In our discussion on the meaning of the ἀλήθεια we said that it should be understood as God's revelation, His promises, faithfulness, trustworthiness as attested in the 'past' — in the history of Israel — and made anew now in the present for our future.

Even the Jewish concept of liberation is very much based on their past Exodus experience. In fact ἀλήθεια brings into remembrance God's deeds of salvation in the past, and this alludes to the great act of God in liberating His people out of the slave house of Egypt. The Jewish folk always looked forward to liberation in hope, for they were convinced that their God of liberation who brought them out of Egypt is able to give liberation in the present. But in the existentialistic interpretation, the focus is shifted from the past to the future and the 'essential' dimension of the past is lost to a great

---

68 See R. Bultmann, *Das Evangelium des Johannes*, 334ff.

extent in interpreting v. 32ff. It is true that Bultmann does recognise the value of the past, but this is surely not reflected in his exegesis.[69]

4.3.4 Verses 35–36: Operation Liberation

The Fourth Evangelist uses the parable of the slave and the son to explain 'operation liberation.'[70] It is the son who can set the slave free. The slave has no legal personality and has no control over his existence. He has no claim to be liberated. It must come from outside. The slave does not have authority and his position in the house is always a precarious one. Only the Son of the house is assured of his freedom. We are expected to see "the son" as "the Son," who is in special relationship with the Father (5:19ff.). And only this Son offers the slaves (who have forfeited their freedom) a new relationship with the Father and a share in the inheritance that is his in the Father's house. Slaves redeemed into that relationship should surely know freedom.

A by-product of this interpretation should also be noted, in that the 'Son' has the freedom; he has the power to freedom (probably an intended addition to the Father–Son analogy of chapter 5:19ff.). This in my opinion begins an intended theological development towards the absolute ἐγώ εἰμί of v. 58.

4.3.5 Verses 37–47: God's Party and the Devil's Party

Here we see the traditional theistic language; those who belong to God are in His party and those who are against by action or default are the devils. The Fourth Evangelist speaks about the choice that confronts humankind and speaks of the primary criteria to belong to God's party:
a) To recognise God's Sent One and the acts of God in the Sent One (Jesus does what the Father tells him)—v. 42.
b) To hear God's voice through the words of the sent one (Jesus speaks what he heard from the Father)—v. 38.
c) To be open to God's salvific operations (v. 43).
d) To love God's sent one (v. 42).

---

69 *Ibid.*, 336–37.
70 See C. H. Dodd, *Historical Tradition in the Fourth Gospel*, 381–88; B. Lindars, *The Gospel of John*, 325, and his "Slave and the Son in John 8:31–36," in *Essays on John*, 168–81, and F. F. Bruce, *The Gospel of John: Introduction, Exposition and Notes* (Grand Rapids: Eerdmans, 1983), 197.

e) To share the freedom and from above origin (v. 47) by believing and remaining in the word (which has living force of movement χωρεῖν)—v. 37. Those who do not fulfil these conditions belong to the devil's party. They reproduce the character of the devil, who is a murderer from the beginning (who took life away and broke relationships), a liar, and the father of lying (the Jewish Theology of 'fall' is very much in the background). Children of the devil oppose and shut themselves from the Word and works of God that are revealed through the Sent One.

The argument in these verses is to make clear that God's covenant with Abraham is not limited to one clan or tradition. It is God's universal covenant with humankind. Abraham is the representative not only of one clan, Israel, but of the whole of humankind. Those who follow Abraham's obedience and faith irrespective of their religious traditions and human dependence belong to the covenant and therefore are of God's party. Those who do not follow Abraham, even though they are by birth his descendants and share in his religious ethos, cannot belong to God's party. God is a God of the universe. He is the One who chooses and frees people to be a source of blessing to humankind and makes Himself known.

He does not want certain people to 'keep' Him as their own and form traditions, to deny accessibility and freedom to others. Those who try to limit God's infinity and His mode of operation belong in the devil's party, while those who recognise the universality of God's plan for salvation (even in other traditions) and are willing to be His fellow workers belong in God's party. Here we see a struggle between Judaism and the emerging Christian community for a share in the rich tradition of the religious ethos. The arguments put forward by the early church to show God's universality should be a reminder today to our contemporary Christendom.

4.3.6 Verses 48–59: Jesus the Pre-existent Son is the Revealer and Embodiment of Salvation

4.3.6.1 Verses 48–50: Jewish Allegation—Jesus a Samaritan, and Possessed

The charge that Jesus is a Samaritan is unique in this passage. Its precise significance however, is not known. We do however know that,
a) the Samaritans were viewed by the Jews as heretics since they rejected the worship at Jerusalem and asserted their own, as God ordained.

b) the Jews seem to have associated Samaritans with magic. It may probably be a Jewish allegation that Jesus was a magician and deceiver of the people.[71]
c) It is clear that the charges of being a Samaritan and of being possessed were linked with and prompted by the denials of Jesus, that Jews were children of God and Abraham, a charge that the Samaritans hurled perpetually against the Jews.
d) It may have had significance in the life of the Johannine community that had Samaritan members. The ethnic Jewish community considered the teaching of the Johannine community as Samaritan.

Jesus ignores the charge "you are a Samaritan" and denies that he is possessed. Instead he says, he honours his Father by carrying out his commission to declare the truth he has been given. The Jews are unaware that by rejecting Jesus and his words, they are in reality dishonouring God (vv. 49–50). "I honour my Father and you dishonour me" should be understood along with John 5:23. According to the rules of agency,[72] in receiving and honouring an agent one receives and honours the agent's sender. According to Johannine logic honouring Jesus equally to God is functionally equivalent to believing in Him.[73] However, Jesus' honour and glory are more than that of an agent. Twice we are told that Jesus enjoyed glory with God before being sent as an agent (cf. 17:5, 24). Can we describe it as the glory of Christ within the godhead and his glory as God, and as pointing up to the Pauline kenosis hymn (Phil 2:5–11)? Probably we may, for the Evangelist emphatically concludes this passage with a firm confession of the pre-existence of Jesus.

But there is another possibility. In v. 51 the Evangelist puts the case against the Jews in God's court. "He is the one who judges" is reminiscent of Old Testament passages in which the righteous commit their cause to God, the Judge that He may vindicate them and condemn their unjust oppressors (see Ps 7:9–11; 35:22–28; the servant songs of Isaiah). Here the Evangelist depicts the paradox when the world judged and ridiculed Jesus by crucifying him. God used the same—'lifting up' as a place to reveal His glory (see v. 28).

---

71 J. L. Martyn, *History and Theology in the Fourth Gospel*, 77–78.
72 P. Borgen, "God's Agent in the Fourth Gospel," in *The Interpretation of John*, 67–75.
73 See J. Neyrey, *An Ideology of Revolt*, 55–56.

4.3.6.2 Verses 51–55: Is Jesus greater than Abraham?

Verse 51 seems at first sight to be out of place,[74] but if we consider here that the Fourth Evangelist is preparing a way to v. 58, then it has a very important role to play. It should be read with 5:21 and 8:31 in mind. The promise relates to one who keeps the 'word' of Jesus. Such a person will not see death (θάνατον οὐ μὴ θεωρήσῃ εἰς τὸν αἰῶνα). The assurance clearly relates to life which physical death cannot extinguish. The believer receives eternal life. Only the one who has 'life' can give life to others (cf. 5:26).

The Jews misunderstand the saying as relating to physical death and so find in it a confirmation of their charge of madness or of being possessed. Their νῦν ἐγνώκαμεν as we know now is probably the counterpart of ἐγνώκαμεν of the Johannine community. In the reply of the Jews θεωρέω becomes γεύομαι ('to see' becomes 'to taste').[75] The Jews found Jesus' saying absurd while, according to their knowledge the holiest of their forefathers, Abraham and all who had spoken in God's name tasted death like the rest of humankind. In other words, they question: Are you greater than our father Abraham? Eventually they ask: Who is Jesus making himself out to be? (see 5:18) This query veils the other ridicule of him being a Samaritan (cf. 4:12).

To the question whom are you making yourself to be, Jesus answers, "I am not making myself anybody" (see response to 5:18 in vv. 19–30). Jesus is not seeking his own glory (v. 50) and if he were to do so, it would be worthless (v. 54). It is the Father who glorifies him (see exegesis of v. 50). The reader perceives the gulf between the Jews and Jesus in their understanding of God. A God who reveals Himself prepares salvation for the world through the self-sacrifice of His Son in a shameful death on the cross (cf. 3:14; 8:28; 12:23–24, 31–33). It is this incomprehension of God's ways that makes Jesus say: "you do not know Him" and affirm, "I do know Him and I keep His Word." The Fourth Evangelist never speaks of Jesus as 'believing in God' but always of his knowing Him. Here he asserts solemnly that to say Jesus did not know God would make him a liar like the Jews, which implies that they are not merely mistaken about their supposed knowledge of God,

---

74 Some scholars see a Synoptic echo of Mark 9:1 here: E. Haenchen, *John*, 1:32, and B. Lindars, *The Gospel of John*, 332.
75 This coincides with the related saying that occurs at the beginning of the *Gospel of Thomas*, "everyone who finds the explanation of these words will not taste death." But the two terms are interchangeable in the *Gospel of Thomas* as we find to "see death" in Logia 18, 19 and 85. Also see, G. R. Beasley-Murray, *John*, 137.

Exegesis

but lying. This only manifests their limited knowledge about the revelation of God and their hatred for the authentic revealer of God.

4.3.6.3 Verses 56–57: Abraham's Joy to see the Day of Salvation

In sharp contrast to the rage of the Jews, Jesus says Ἀβραὰμ ὁ πατὴρ ὑμῶν ἠγαλλιάσατο ἵνα ἴδῃ τὴν ἡμέραν τὴν ἐμήν, καὶ εἶδεν καὶ ἐχάρη. The first part of the verse signifies the anticipatory joy while the next half states, "he saw it and was glad." The question whether this seeing which makes Abraham's joy complete is to be attributed to him in his life-time or understood as taking place now at the time of Jesus, is very fundamental to the exegesis. Six different solutions have been proposed:

a) "Abraham rejoiced" could be alluded to his joy at the prospect of his having a son (a plain reading of Genesis 17). The visit of the three men at Mamre to announce a second time the birth of Isaac is also closely linked to this proposal (Genesis 18). The Theophany is interpreted at least by Philo as Abraham having the vision of the divine Logos.[76]

b) It could relate to the birth of Isaac whose name means laughter.

c) Abraham finding the lamb to sacrifice in place of Isaac (Genesis 22) is also alluded to, since the event is important to the Jewish understanding of atonement. Our attention is drawn to the fact that when Abraham saw the substitute lamb provided by God Himself he saw the vision of greater atonement and was glad.[77]

d) A host of Rabbinic literature, especially the Haggadah's claim that Abraham was given a vision to see the future. This suggestion is grounded in the covenant between the pieces found in Gen 15:17–21.[78] Another slightly different version of the same argument is based on the Evangelist's allusion to Isaiah's vision in Isa 12:37–41, where he concludes that the failure of the people to believe in Jesus was a fulfilment of the inaugural vision of Isaiah. With an eye on this clear example of

---

76 L. Urban & P. Henry, "'Before Abraham was, I am': Does Philo explain Jn. 8:56–58?" *SPhilo* 6 (1979–80): 171–76. This article provides an extensive range of quotations from Philo about Abraham.

77 See F. F. Bruce, *The Gospel of John*, 204–205.

78 See H. L. Strack & P. Billerbeck, *Kommentar zum Neuen Testament aus Talmud und Midrasch*, 2:525–26; G. R. Beasley-Murray, *John*, 138, and C. K. Barrett, *The Gospel according to St. John*, 352.

prophetic vision in the Fourth Gospel, it is assumed that Abraham is being treated as a prophet in chapter 8 and that in his role as a prophet he was granted a vision of the future and especially of the Messianic days. The Rabbinic literature mentioned above is again cited as supportive evidence.

e) It is also suggested that Abraham is currently seeing and witnessing Jesus in his ministry from paradise. The Synoptic story of 'poor Lazarus' is mentioned as supportive evidence.[79]

f) Charles Burney attempts to make ἠγαλλιάσατο a mistranslation of the Aramaic verb meaning 'to long for.' He is of the notion that, "Abraham saw it and rejoiced" is a tautology that cannot be in the original. The author's original writing is probably, "Abraham desired or longed to see my day."[80] J. de Zwaan contends that what the Fourth Evangelist actually wrote should have been translated Ἀβραὰμ ὤξυνε τὸν νοῦν αὐτοῦ ἵνα ἴδῃ τὴν ἡμέραν . . . ("Abraham our father sharpened his mind in order to know my day and he saw and was glad.")[81].

It should be observed that the ἵνα clause following "he rejoiced" can be stretched to some kind of conditional "he rejoiced that he was to see" (RSV) or ἠγαλλιάσατο ἵνα ἴδῃ can perhaps be made to mean 'longed to see' or 'desired to see.' But if one were simply reading the text the ἵνα would be one of the explanations giving grounds for rejoicing. "He rejoiced to see my day."[82] It should also be noticed that in καὶ εἶδεν καὶ ἐχάρη the tense is not perfect to mean a contemporary experience, but aorist. The patriarch was very much alive to God's liberation and his saving purpose. The birth of a child and the promise it brought along, or any covenant for that matter made Abraham visualise God's greater plans for him. A sign was enough for him to rejoice, be glad and be open to God's way of working.

---

79 See B. Lindars, *The Gospel of John*, 335, and E. Haenchen, *John*, 371.

80 C. F. Burney, *The Aramaic Approach to the Fourth Gospel*, 111. Burney's long footnote on 111–12 argues unconvincingly that the Jerusalem Targum on Genesis 15 provides a proper background for an understanding of the exegesis that would have been familiar to Jesus and his hearers.

81 J. de Zwaan, "John wrote in Aramaic," *JBL* 57 (1938): 164–65, quoted by L. Urban & P. Henry, "'Before Abraham was, I am': Does Philo explain John 8:56–58?" *SPhilo* 6 (1979–80): 164.

82 *BDF*, § 392, 1.1. render 'he longed with desire,' 'rejoiced that he was to . . .'; C. K. Barrett, *The Gospel according to St. John*, 351, considers ἵνα as explanatory.

The Jews looked forward to the fulfilment of God's promise to Abraham in the messianic age. In Jewish terminology 'the day' usually signifies the appearance of the Messiah in the last days and the eschatological vision. Now the Evangelist claims that in the ministry of Jesus the saving sovereignty of God comes in its totality because He is the revealer and redeemer. Therefore for him 'the day' has become 'my day' in order to make a messianic claim for Jesus. And the Fourth Evangelist makes it clear that for Abraham a sign, a promise was sufficient to be overjoyed (χαίρειν), anticipate and visualise how it would be when the promise is finally fulfilled. And the Evangelist ironically condemns the Jews by saying that they who called themselves Abraham's descendants cannot even recognise 'the day' of the Messiah and God's saving plan working in the midst of them. In other words, he says, "How can you call yourselves descendants of Abraham?"

The Jews realised that v. 56 goes beyond a mere deduction from the Scriptures or Haggadah. They understood that it implied Abraham's faith and his openness, as well as his hope and capacity to visualise the fulfilment of promise, hence their shocked question, "how can you at your age presume to see Abraham?" (probably even, "you boy!") But the Fourth Evangelist uses the objection to make the greatest claim for Jesus.

4.3.6.4 Verses 58–59: Pre-existence of God's Universal Salvific Purpose

πρὶν 'Αβραὰμ γενέσθαι ἐγώ εἰμι ("Before Abraham came into existence/was born, I am") expresses the contrast between the existence initiated by birth and an absolute existence.[83] Jesus speaking εἰμί in the present places him in the eternal present, probably the Evangelist means in God's eternal presence. Seen in the background of the Fourth Gospel's Logos and Son Christology it is nothing extraordinary. In his eternally existent being, Jesus has an absolute precedent over Abraham, who came into existence at a specific moment in time.

Is then the statement an assertion that Jesus is God? Surely it carries more than an affirmation that Jesus is the revelation of God. Probably it is a fresh expression of the Logos Theology. As such it entails the relational face of God that was from the beginning, as in John 1:1. Bultmann says the

---

83 E. C. Hoskyns, *The Fourth Gospel*, 349.

ἐγώ which Jesus speaks as revealer is the 'I' of the eternal Logos, which was in the beginning, the 'I' of the eternal God Himself.[84] V. 58 is no doubt one of the best passages in support of such pre-existence. This also forms a reminiscent of Ps 90:2 (LXX 89:2), "before the mountains were born or you brought forth the earth and the world, from the everlasting to everlasting σὺ εἶ you are!"

But Edwin Freed observes that the 'I am' of v. 58 relates to the idea of the pre-existence of 'the name,' as the representative of the person of Messiah. Therefore, ἐγώ εἰμι here must indicate specifically that he fulfilled the role of Messiah and thus inaugurated the coming of redemption and salvation. Following our discussion through chapter 8 we may possibly agree with Freed to the extent that ἐγώ εἰμι here may include messianic connotations, but should immediately add that the Jews did not regard the Messiah equivalent to the divine.[85]

The use of ἐγώ εἰμι here is slightly different from that in vv. 24 and 28. It is probably one of the clearest absolute uses of ἐγώ εἰμι where no predicate is intended. It is as if Jesus said "I am who I am." I am the place of divine presence and revelation in history, I am the revelation of God. The ἐγώ εἰμι here is not only the expression of revelation, but also the embodiment of revelation here and now. Those who debate with Jesus are arguing with the ἐγώ εἰμι Himself, with the historical revealer and representative of Yahweh, and thus with Yahweh Himself.[86]

The saying's intention lies primarily not in his being, but rather on his salvific activity. Schnackenburg rightly points out the Old Testament passage underlying Jesus' claim as Exod 3:14, where God declares himself as "I am the I am" (LXX—Ἐγώ εἰμι ὁ ὤν). With the announcement of His name, Yahweh revealed to His chosen people Israel not His metaphysical nature, but His steadfastness and faithfulness and promised them His help

---

84 R. Bultmann, *Das Evangelium des Johannes*, 248–49.
85 See E. D. Freed, "Who or what was before Abraham in John 8.58?" *JSNT* 17 (1983): 52–59. Freed's attempt to distinguish between the Messiah himself and the 'name' of the Messiah is questionable for the Hebrew concept of 'name' is not just a 'principle' or 'tag,' but the person himself. Compare D. M. Ball, *'I am' in John's Gospel*, 194–98.
86 J. Blank, *Krisis*, 246.

and protection.[87] The same is more apparent in the "I am he" sayings of Deutero-Isaiah (esp. 43:11–13; 46:4; 48:12). In this context, the assertion "Before Abraham was I am" forms the basis of the promise of salvation to God's people. This is why Jesus can give true freedom (v. 31) and the life that overcomes death (v. 51).

Also, the Evangelist probably connects vv. 56–58 to justify that in the person of Jesus, the ἐγώ εἰμι, 'that day' or the fulfilment of the 'promise' given to Abraham, the promise of a fuller liberation and redemption is realised. Here we may note that 'the name,' 'the promise' and 'the word' cannot be separated from 'the person' in Hebrew Theology (see also the exegesis of John 17). It should also be noted here that the Hebrews first experienced Yahweh as the liberator God, then their Theology projected and confessed Him also as the creator. Here too Jesus the one who had been depicted as 'the liberator' (v. 31) is now proclaimed as 'the pre-existent' (v. 58). The Son who embodies God's salvation, and in whom the community experiences liberation, becomes the sign of God's universal salvific purpose that existed even before creation came into existence, if we interpret the very act of creation as an act of liberation from chaos. Jesus' pre-existence is therefore the community's affirmation of the pre-existence of God's universal salvific purpose.

The recorded reaction clearly shows that the Jews could not comprehend the theological projections contained and intentions involved in the affirmation of Jesus' pre-existence: "they took stones." The same reaction is recorded in John 10:31 when Jesus said "I and my Father are one." The Jews always understood "I am" as the name of the Yahweh. They considered the statement "before Abraham was I am" as a direct claim to divinity and therefore, blasphemy. It is true, that the community's christological language at times speaks of Jesus as if he is God, but treads back to balance it by using a combination of both messianic language and the concept of divine agency. But in some places the community seems to be making the claim that Jesus is God (John 1:1; 8:58). This inconsistency is what the Jews probably found difficult to digest and thus the reason for the tension and theological crisis between the Johannine community and the synagogue.

---

87 R. Schnackenburg, *The Gospel according to St. John*, 1:224.

4.4 Summary and Conclusions

From the analysis above we may gather the following conclusions:

a) The passage challenges us to identify God in His historical relationship with Israel.
b) Dualistic language is used to express the understanding of God. Though God belongs to the above realm, He wants to relate Himself to the below world which He created. The themes of light, truth, revelation, liberation and freedom all point in this direction.
c) God establishes this relationship through His Son who is from above and the light of the world. In him the world below confronts truth, in him God's liberation operates.
d) God cannot be understood apart from His relationship with the Son. He is always with the Son, He authenticates the Son and therefore the Son can say, "I am."
e) The 'I am' of Jesus the Son is not an act of self-propagation, but obedient revelation! The 'I am' in absolute sense represents the salvific, relational intention of God. It has precedence to all of the historical revelations of God through Abraham, Moses and the prophets.
f) In proclaiming Jesus as the 'I am,'—'the light of the world' the Fourth Evangelist indeed confesses faith in God and His salvific-relational intention and in its parabolic confrontation in and through the Son.
g) The Fourth Evangelist experiences this God of relationships in Jesus through belief and openness, and calls others to follow him in experiencing Jesus, the liberator and with him venture into a theological projection to confess Jesus as pre-existent, which is in fact an affirmation of the eternity of God's universal salvific purpose.
h) This God who reveals Himself in relationships cannot be tied up within a tradition. He is beyond traditions and creates new ones.

Chapter Five

Theology in Conflict — Are Jesus and the Father One?
(John 10:22–39)

5.1 The Context

The passage is set in the context of Hanukkah, the festival of dedication that celebrated the Jewish independence, the reconstruction and the re-consecration of the temple in 165 B.C. under Judas Maccabee (1 Macc 1:54; 2 Macc 6:1–7). The festival, a commemoration of political independence was no longer a reality, but rather the only hope for all the militant Jewish activists and common people of regaining independence was the appearance of the Messiah.

The Fourth Evangelist ironically sets the stage for a trial of Jesus by the Jews. A gathering in the Stoa of Solomon asks Jesus, "Are you the Messiah?" And the Evangelist portrays Jesus as the defender.[1] He tells the readers that a community that eagerly waited for the Messiah did not recognise him when he appeared, but was rather intent on embarrassing Jesus by asking, "Are you the Messiah?" Jesus' answer to their question acquires greater proportions than the Jewish messianic concept, as he prefers to explain the Father-Son relationship. This surely highlights the trial of the community by the Synagogue authorities — "Who do you claim Jesus to be?"

5.2 The Structure

For a proper exegesis of chapter 10, J. H. Bernard proposes the following order, which according to him is original, namely, chapter 9, 10:19–29, 1–18,

---

1 Some suggestions have been made about the relationship between John 10:29–39 and the trial of Jesus before the Sanhedrin in the Synoptics; see R. E. Brown, *The Gospel according to John*, 1:404–406; R. Schnackenburg, *The Gospel according to St. John*, 2:306, and J. H. Neyrey, "I said: You are gods: Psalm 82:6 and John 10," *JBL* 108 (1989): 650.

30–39.² Rudolf Bultmann's rearrangement sequence is considerably more complex, namely, 10:22–26, 11–13, 1–10, 14–18, 27–39 with 19–21 forming the conclusion of the preceding section "Light of the world." Apart from disclosing inner connections and thought patterns the value and the validity of the rearrangement hypothesis remains highly questionable. But keeping in mind these inner connections and thought patterns one can even interpret 10:22–39 in canonical order without much difference in the outcome.³ Therefore we propose the following structure:

VV. 22–30   Oneness of the Father and the Son
VV. 31–39   Mutual in-dwelling of the Father and the Son

5.3 Exegesis

5.3.1 Verses 22–30: Oneness of the Father and the Son

5.3.1.1 Verses 22–24: The Question

In the cold wintry weather the Fourth Evangelist moves Jesus into Solomon's porch, probably to get shelter from the wind. It may, however, signify that the great deliverance from antichrist and the triumph of true religion was being celebrated. The 'Jews' were in "frozen" spirits. For them there was no sign of liberation even when Jesus, God's sign of deliverance, stood right in their midst. Jesus who did not observe the law as the tradition did demand, and whose speech and action (chapters 9, 10) were tantalising causing ripples of turmoil and confusion among the Jews, leads them to ask—ἕως πότε τὴν ψυχὴν ἡμῶν αἴρεις; εἰ σὺ εἶ ὁ χριστός, εἰπὲ ἡμῖν παρρησίᾳ. It is unlikely that they wished to know Jesus' answer in order to acknowledge him as Messiah, if he so confessed it. The clause is commonly translated as: "How long are you keeping us in suspense?," but Barrett cites authorities in both ancient and modern Greek to mean: "How long do you intend to annoy or provoke us?"⁴

---

2   J. H. Bernard, *Commentary on the Gospel according to St. John*, 1:341, see also xxix–xxx.
3   C. H. Dodd, J. Schneider, R. E. Brown and R. Schnackenburg agree that the present order is a purposeful arrangement and not a product of accident or confusion.
4   C. K. Barrett, *The Gospel according to St. John*, 380.

5.3.1.2 Verses 24–30: The Claim

In v. 24, the Evangelist calls the attention of the Jews to Jesus' teaching and works. This affirmation that εἶπον ὑμῖν means that his teaching makes the answer clear enough for those with eyes to see and ears to hear, or in other words, that his words and works set forth who he is,[5] that the works done in the Father's name tell the Jews what they want to know since they bear clear witness to Him.[6]

Verses 26–30 connect us back to the discourse on the theme 'Good Shepherd,' where the Fourth Evangelist makes a brilliant claim for Jesus. ἐγὼ καὶ ὁ πατὴρ ἕν ἐσμεν. ἐσμεν refers to the plural subject and therefore to two distinct personalities, ἐγώ (Jesus) and ὁ πατήρ. It is said "I and the Father are ἕν not εἷς." The two masculine subjects are ἕν (neuter)—one thing. This has given rise to different interpretations; that the Father and the Son are one in action not in person; that it refers to harmony, sharing, mutual coherence and likeness.

It is argued mostly in Patristic writings that it refers to the unity of essence or of will and love. But it is evident that the conclusions drawn by the church fathers were far from the mind of the Evangelist, and are out of context and anachronistic as they reflect the controversies of later Christendom.[7]

It is also argued that ἕν refers to moral unity between the Father and the Son. Jesus' obedience to the Father and the Father's love towards Jesus is the shared idea of every covenant member. To become holy, as God is holy was the apex of Jewish piety and each Israelite's life's goal. In this the Israelites were not striving for divinity or to become like God, but for moral unity to

---

5 See E. C. Hoskyns, *The Fourth Gospel*, 387.
6 See R. Bultmann, *Das Evangelium des Johannes*, 275; R. Schnackenburg, *The Gospel according to St. John*, 1:305–306, and C. K. Barrett, op. cit., 380.
7 Athanasius interprets ἕν as unity of essence. To press the meaning of ἕν as to identify essence or οὐσία is to introduce thoughts not present in the Fourth Gospel. Origen interprets ἕν as εἷς θεῖος, I and my Father are one God. But his view of the unity is impaired by the pluralism implicit in his subordinistic view of the divinity of the Son. The Son for Origen is θεός not ὁ θεός and as θεός he is inferior to ὁ θεός. He is God in a derivative sense and his divinity is by communication from God and the Father of the universe; for a detail of the Patristic interpretations of John 10:30, see T. E. Pollard, "The Exegesis of John X.30 in the Early Trinitarian Controversies," *NTS* 3 (1956–57): 334–49, and his *Johannine Christology and the Early Church* (SNTSMS 13; Cambridge: Cambridge University Press, 1970), and M. F. Wiles, *The Spiritual Gospel: The Interpretation of the Fourth Gospel in the Early Church* (Cambridge: Cambridge University Press, 1960), 112–47.

be in the image of God. "As your God is holy you should also . . ."—this was the covenant obligation and mission entrusted to each covenant member. But for the Fourth Evangelist the relationship of the Father and the Son is much more than moral unity.

It has been suggested that ἕν be translated not as 'one' but 'equal,' "I and the Father are equal."[8] Attention is drawn to a similar use of ἕν in 1 Cor 3:8 in which the status of Paul and Apollos are compared[9] in a conciliatory move. Paul insists that he and Apollos while quite different in Paul's eyes, are on par when confronted with God. Here ἕν must be translated as 'equal to,' or 'on par with.' It does not refer to moral unity or metaphysical identity but to equality of power, role and status.[10]

The context of v. 30 suggests that ἕν relates to the shepherding activity of the Father. In v. 28 Jesus says, "No one can snatch them out of my hand." V. 29b says, "no one can snatch them out of my Father's hand." Thus v. 30 is primarily related to the work of pastoral caring. To be in the hands of the Son is to be in the hands of the Father. It is contended that the disciples are safe only because being in the hands of the Son also means being in the hands of the Father. The identity of pastoral caring is bound to the dependence of the Son on the Father. The Father guarantees that the Son's caring is His caring. In this sense the Father and the Son are one.

The dependence of the Son in his oneness with the Father can also be argued with the affirmation in v. 29a. But over this text there is considerable scholarly discussion. The majority of the scholars agree that μείζων not μεῖζον is the correct reading.[11] So then the text says, "My Father is greater

---

8 J. H. Neyrey, *An Ideology of Revolt*, 69.
9 See J. H. Bernard, *Commentary on the Gospel according to St. John*, 1:365.
10 In the conflict of Corinth, Paul senses that in many ways Apollos is perceived as superior to him while Paul lacked eloquence, wisdom and power (1 Cor 1:17; 2:1, 4; 4:9–12). Yet he claims the superior place at Corinth as its skilled master builder (1 Cor 3:10), but for quelling the factions and strife he will agree that he and Apollos are equal in regard to their mission to the people. 1 Cor 3:8 is by no means a parallel but an internal clue as to how ἕν was understood in the early Christian church.
11 The text of v. 29a is a confusion. The words between μου and ἐστιν appear in these forms:
    a) ὃ δέδωκέν μοι πάντων μεῖζόν ἐστιν—B* VL (except d) Vg bo, Ambrose, Jerome
    b) ὃ δέδωκέν μοι πάντων μείζων ἐστιν—ℵ L W Ψ D (ὁ δεδωκώς)
    c) ὃς δέδωκέν μοι μείζων πάντων ἐστιν—P66* (omits μοι) K Δ Π Λ 33
    d) ὃς δέδωκέν μοι μεῖζόν πάντων ἐστιν—A Θ (X) sy[pal]

than all." That God is greater than all has considerable relevance for the argument in vv. 28–30, where it means that God is more powerful than the snatchers. John Whittaker suggests that "greater than all" in the context of Hellenistic Jewish writings refers to the supreme deity, and that πάντων

J. N. Birdsall prefers reading b) since it is the most difficult. True it is untranslatable and could probably be translated as "My Father with regard to what He has given me is greater than all." But Birdsall himself regards that it should be read as ὅς rather than ὅ since the relative that follows is the masculine πατήρ. C. K. Barrett prefers d) but runs into difficulty on account of the predicate which is in neuter gender. The variant a) is adopted by both the Bible Society text and Nestle-Aland[26], but has a suspicious look because of the congruence of the relative clause with μεῖζον. It could be translated as "O my Father what he has given me is greater than all this," but it does not fit into the context as ὃ δέδωκέν μοι means "sheep" and these cannot be said to be greater than all. That leaves us with variant c) which is best attested and appears to capture the meaning.

Bultmann and Dodd support this variant. However there are objections that this is the simplest among the manuscript variants and as Barrett puts it, it is impossible to explain how this ὅς . . . μείζων reading came to be changed into the difficult ὅ . . . μεῖζον! One can only point to the fact that the transition from ὅς . . . μείζων to ὅ . . . μείζων or ὅ . . . μεῖζον is in fact well within the bounds of transcriptional probability. In the case of the transition to ὅ . . . μείζων it is not difficult to conceive the scribe as motivated, whether consciously or unconsciously by the desire to provide an explicit object to δέδωκε. The notion of the Father giving to the Son, it may be recalled, occurs frequently: John 5:36 (ἃ δέδωκέν μοι . . .), 6:37 (ὃ δίδωσίν μοι . . .), 6:39 (ὃ δέδωκέν μοι . . .), 17:2 (ὃ δέδωκας αὐτῷ . . .), 17:4 (ὃ δέδωκάς μοι . . .), 17:9 (ᾧ δέδωκάς μοι , . .), 17:24 (ἣν δέδωκάς μοι . . .) and 18:11 (ὃ δέδωκέν μοι . . .). But if ὅ ... μείζων is correct then 10:29 is one of the few instances in this Gospel (other examples are 14:27 and 16:23) in which δίδωμι occurs without an expressed grammatical object. It is surely difficult to deny the possibility of a scribe failing to note that the object of δέδωκεν was to be supplied from the previous sentence and in consequence succumbed to the urge to bring the language of 10:29 into line with the formulations occurring elsewhere in the Gospel by substituting ὅ for ὅς.

It is very difficult to decide how the deterioration from μείζων to μεῖζον took place within the evidence available, but it could reasonably be accounted that the transition to μείζων (a mere orthographical slip) preceded and provoked the alteration of ὅς to ὅ than the scribe altered ὅς to ὅ in front of μείζων at the expense of the logic of the sentence as a whole. Then this c) variant could be translated as "My Father who gave them to me is greater than any (all) power." J. Whittaker supports this variant and goes further to provide a convincing Hellenistic setting. For a full discussion see B. M. Metzger, *A Textual Commentary on the Greek New Testament*, 232; C. K. Barrett, *The Gospel according to St. John*, 381–82; R. Schnackenburg, *The Gospel according to St. John*, 2:307–308, J. N. Birdsall, "John X.29," *JTS* n.s. 11 (1960): 342–45, and J. Whittaker, "A Hellenistic context for John 10,29," *VC* 24 (1970): 241–60.

μείζων signifies God's superiority and transcendence over the created universe and everything.¹² If the Father is greater than all, if the Son's pastoral care is dependent on God's all powerfulness, then to say "I and my Father are one" is a paradox. Can we really take this paradox rationally?

To explain this paradox of dependence and oneness one should again go back to the 'shepherd' metaphor. The Fourth Evangelist confesses that Jesus is the good shepherd. In the Old Testament the shepherd metaphor is applied only to 'God' who leads, protects and gathers His people, looking after them solicitously and lovingly. The shepherd metaphor was not only used to speak of God's providence, but also of His liberative activities (Ezek 34:23–24; Mic 5:1–3; Psalm 23). It is exactly here that the Fourth Evangelist speaks of oneness of the Father and the Son, Jesus is the good shepherd not only because he gives perfect pastoral care but because he liberates his sheep risking his own life.

J. H. Bernard and R. Bultmann in their rearrangement scheme have shown us the inner thought form/structure of the shepherd discourse. Bernard thinks that v. 30 should immediately succeed v. 18. Bultmann feels that v. 18 should be followed by vv. 27–30. Even if one rearranges the order, one should be open to the inner structural connections. In v. 18 Jesus speaks of his laying down his own life for the sake of his sheep. In other words the Evangelist speaks of Jesus giving himself, or in other words Jesus' self-emptying.

Most commentators find v. 30 and 5:17–30 to be closely related. I agree with them.¹³ In 5:17–30 we identified a phenomenon that may be called the Father's self-emptying in the Son.¹⁴ Therefore, I see the oneness of the Father

---

12 See J. Whittaker, art. cit. He says that in Hellenistic Jewish liturgical formula found frequently in a magical papyrus at Leiden one can see the πάντων μείζων as an ἐπίκλησις. He exegetises this formula at length and concludes that πάντων combines the theme of God as creator and ruler of the universe. It combines both what Philo called δύναμις ποιητική and δύναμις βασιλική. It is Whittaker's well-attested hypothesis that the Evangelist should have been familiar with the liturgical flavor of πάντων μείζων.
13 See J. N. Sanders, *A commentary on the Gospel according to St. John*, 258; E. Haenchen, *John*, 1:49–50 contends the oneness in action, namely that of life-giving and judgement.
14 That the Father has given all to His Son is a clear message in the Fourth Gospel:
    3:35 : The Father loves the Son and has given all into his hands.
    5:20 : The Father loves the Son and shows him all that He Himself is doing.
    5:27 : The Father has given all judgement to the Son.
    13:3 : Jesus knowing that the Father had given all into his hands . . .

and the Son not only as the shepherd who gives life (10:10) or as judge (the gate allegory—the one who regulates the option of life and death) or as the redeemer-liberator, but as their 'oneness in self-emptying.' As the Father emptied Himself in the Son for the salvation of the world, so also the Son imitating the Father empties himself for the salvation of the world on the cross.[15]

5.3.2 Verses 31–39: Mutual In-dwelling of the Father and the Son

5.3.2.1 Verses 31–33: The Jewish Anger

The oneness claim here is misunderstood as the Jews take stones to throw at Jesus. Here the Johannine Jesus does not withdraw, but challenges their violent action. V. 32 is deeply ironical: Jesus performed many ἔργα καλά from the Father. Which of them did the Jews call blasphemous? The intention of the question is clear. These works were done at the command of and by the power of the Father through the Son. Therefore, they bear witness to the oneness of the Father and the Son.

The Fourth Evangelist brings out sharply the full force of the blasphemous accusation, "You being a man make yourself to be God?" In the Evangelist's own age this reading could have played a role in the Jewish-Christian debate over the person of Jesus. While the witness borne by the ἔργα was disregarded the Evangelist now follows an argument from the Scripture to perfection in Rabbinical style.

5.3.2.2 Verses 34–36: Johannine Appeal to the Scripture

Here we have one of the most difficult Old Testament references, not because its source is obscure, but because the argument it enshrines seems rather puzzling on the surface. The Jews accuse Jesus of making himself God and Jesus replies by quoting Ps 82:6, "Is it not written in your Law, 'I have said you are gods'?" The Fourth Evangelist continues, "if he called them 'gods,' to whom the word of God came (and the Scripture cannot be broken),

---

This giving of all might be 'words of God' (3:33)—heavenly revelation (words and the person's being cannot be separated in Hebrew Theology) and his creative and eschatological power (5:19–30).

15 Cf. v. 15.

do you say of him whom the Father has consecrated and sent into the world, 'you are blaspheming' because I said, 'I am the Son of God'?"

First of all it is difficult to understand why the Evangelist, a Jew, would use the expression 'in your law' (ἐν τῷ νόμῳ ὑμῶν). The phrase 'your law' was characteristic of Gentile speakers when referring to the Jewish law, used also by Pilate in John 18:31. The reading ὑμῶν omitted in P⁴⁵ and by some other authorities, but included in P⁶⁶ is to be retained as the appropriate one in the light of the Evangelist's whole treatment of the subject.[16] In every instance where he refers to the Torah, the Law, he speaks of it as "your law" (8:17; 10:34; 15:25). He means that the Torah has been diluted to mere legislative rules and traditions, and thereby become slavery and death.

Jewish Scripture was also the Bible of the early community. ὑμῶν should not be understood as derogatory or as the Evangelist being against it. Instead, it points to the community's emerging self-identification, and its God language. While he honours and cherishes his religious tradition, treasures the God who reveals Himself and thrives hard to belong to that religious ethos, he is of the opinion that the law helps him to better understand the revelation of God in Jesus of Nazareth. He presents Jesus as being above the law and the fulfilment of it. The Fourth Evangelist sees the Torah as a sign of life and freedom and as its becoming a reality in Jesus.[17] Thus the community here is in the process of reinterpreting theological categories and thereby reaffirms its identity.

ὁ νόμος strictly means Torah, but in the broadest sense covers the whole Old Testament. It is certainly the contextual meaning here at v. 35 that also refers to ἡ γραφή. Nevertheless it is used to cover the Psalter (cf. 12:34; 15:25).[18] ὅτι that usually introduces direct speech here introduces a quotation from the Old Testament. The task of isolating the quotation is simple, as v. 34 reproduces word to word the text of Ps 82 (81):6.[19] Scholars have

---

16 C. K. Barrett thinks otherwise; see his *The Gospel according to St. John*, 384.
17 See exegesis "For the law was given through Moses; grace and truth came through Jesus Christ"—John 1:17 (below pp. 207–208).
18 See C. K. Barrett, op. cit., 384.
19 C. F. Burney in his *The Aramaic Approach to the Fourth Gospel*, 118, says that the verbal agreement between the Fourth Gospel and the Septuagint has no special significance since the Hebrew could hardly be rendered otherwise. E. D. Freed in his *Old Testament Quotations in the Gospel of John*, 66, notes that the Hebrew second person plural pronoun (אתם) is not translated in Greek (cf. Isa 41:23). B. G. Schuchard in his *Scripture within Scripture: The Interrelationship of Form and Function*

traditionally identified Israel's judges as the addressees of Psalm 82. These judges appointed by Moses are referred to as gods by virtue of their role in the extraordinary divine function of judgement and because of an identity and authority derived from Moses (who himself is like God, Exod 12:1). The judges however have failed to faithfully execute justice in Israel. Therefore the Psalm indicates that they will die like ordinary mortals. The relevance of Ps 82:6 is however that if the unfaithful and unjust judges could be called gods, and if Moses' (the one who appointed them) identity surpasses that of gods then Jesus' identity surpasses that of Moses. Jesus is able to speak as he does of his unity with the Father and is worthy of the title Son of God.[20]

The 'Word of God came to' is typical of the Old Testament and of Judaism in general.[21] The phrase appears with Abraham (Gen 15:1), Moses (Exod 12:1), Solomon (1 Kgs 6:11), David (1 Chr 22:8), but it is prominent in references to Old Testament prophets (Jer 1:4, 11; Mic 1:1; Zech 1:1; Ezek 6:1; 17:1; 31:1; Hos 1:1; Joel 1:1 and Zeph 1:1). In the Old Testament, if the Word of God came to a prophet, it was not to the individuals but to the whole nation. But the prophets are not Israel's judges. Moreover, the Old Testament never speaks of the Word coming to Israel's judges. In Deut 1:15–18, there is no clear word of God coming but what is said is spoken by Moses. Moreover, there is no obvious continuity between Moses' time and the Judges of Israel, and therefore the suggestion that the term 'gods' refers to the judges is improbable.

As an alternative to a more traditional interpretation, scholars suggest that gods are superhuman figures or angels who have divine commission and have been designated with the affairs of the nations. But these super-

---

in the Explicit Old Testament Citations in the Gospel of John (SBLDS 133; Atlanta: Scholars Press, 1992), 61, notes that the Septuagint is in fact the Evangelist's most probable source, as only in v. 34 does he use εἶπα. Elsewhere he always uses εἶπον (cf. v. 36) for the first person aorist indicative active, εἶπα. It would seem that the quotation has come from Ps 81:6 (LXX).

20 See B. G. Schuchard, op. cit, 60–70; J. H. Bernard, *Commentary on the Gospel according to St. John*, 1:367; R. E. Brown, *The Gospel according to John*, 1:409–11; L. Morris, *The Gospel according to John*, 525–26; B. Lindars, *The Gospel of John*, 374; F. F. Bruce, *The Gospel of John*, 235; R. Kysar, *John* (ACNT; Minneapolis: Augsburg, 1986), 168–69, and W. G. Phillips, "An Apologetic Study of John 10:34–36," *BSac* 146 (1989): 405–19.
21 See R. Bultmann, *Das Evangelium des Johannes*, 296–97, and H. L. Strack & P. Billerbeck, *Kommentar zum Neuen Testament aus Talmud und Midrasch*, 2:543.

126   Theology in Conflict—Are Jesus and the Father One? (John 10:22–39)

human beings failed to execute their trust and as punishment they became mortal beings subjected to death.²² The relevance of Ps 82:6 to the context of John 10 lies therefore in the argument that if one can call evil angelic beings as gods, then how much more is Jesus, the one consecrated and sent by God, eligible to be called the Son of God. But this proposal could be quickly dismissed, as it is most unlikely that the Fourth Evangelist refers to angels. The context of his citation of the Psalm makes no reference to angels. Even the larger context of his Gospel lacks similar references to such heavenly beings playing roles of comparable significance.²³

Yet another interpretation which I personally prefer has emerged and has attracted a considerable amount of support in recent times. It asserts that the Evangelist understands the Psalm as being an address to the nation of Israel after its reception of the law at Mt. Sinai when God gave them the Torah making Israel holy and the people of the covenant.²⁴

---

22 See J. A. Emerton, "Melchizedek and the Gods: Fresh evidence for the Jewish background of John X.34–36," *JTS* n.s. 17 (1966): 399–401. He uses *11Q Melchizedek*, a Qumran text in support of his contention. He contends that the speaker in Psalm 82 is Melchizedek, an angelic being and God's representative and those addressed are the evil angels—Belial and his host. The Psalm indicates the coming of the eschatological judgement in which Melchizedek is to execute God's punishment on the evil angels. See also M. de Jonge & A. S. van der Woude, "11 Q Melchizedek and the New Testament," *NTS* 12 (1966): 301–26. This interpretation that gods denote angels probably stems from the fact that a Targum of Ps 82:6 differs radically from the Masoretic Text and the Septuagint perhaps with a view to avoid any human equality with God—"I said you were reckoned just as angels and you all are just as angels on high"; see E. D. Freed, *Old Testament Quotations in the Gospel of John*, 63.

23 See B. G. Schuchard, *Scripture within Scripture*, 63; A. T. Hanson, "John's citation of Psalm LXXXII," and "John's citation of Psalm LXXXII reconsidered," *NTS* 11 (1964–65): 158–62 and 13 (1966–67): 363–67 respectively, is of the opinion that the Evangelist would have no sympathy with the identification of Melchizedek with the angels.

24 See H. L. Strack & P. Billerbeck, *Kommentar zum Neuen Testament aus Talmud und Midrasch*, 2:543; R. Schnackenburg, *The Gospel according to St. John*, 2:311; C. K. Barrett, *The Gospel according to St. John*, 384–85, and N. A. Dahl, "The Johannine Church and History," in *The Interpretation of John* (ed. J. Ashton; Philadelphia: Fortress, 1986), 130.

By considering Israel as the addressees of the Psalm, some scholars have ventured to propose at least three different interpretations (to which I do not subscribe). J. S. Ackerman argues that Israel experienced a new creation at Sinai because God gave the word of Torah to which it became obedient and thus Israel became deathless once more, as it resembled the image and likeness of God given

To interpret what the Fourth Evangelist is trying to aim at by quoting Ps 82:6 one should first answer the question whether he is receding from his

---

at creation. And pointing to the relevance of John 10:34–36, he says that the Johannine Prologue bears striking resemblance to the Sinai myth indication of how wisdom once dwelt on earth with humankind (Ps 82:6) thus making it immortal. Because wisdom was rejected and returned to the Father, the sinful and mortals now die (Ps 82:7). Here Israel is being reproached for rejecting once more God's revelation to it (J. S. Ackerman, "The Rabbinic Interpretation of Psalm 82 and the Gospel of John [John 10:34]," *HTR* 59 [1966]: 186–91).

A. T. Hanson suggests that "the word of God" in v. 35 is to be understood as "the pre-existent Logos" and the phrase "to whom the word of God came" should then be understood as "to whom the pre-existent Logos spoke." The Evangelist's argument, therefore, is to be paraphrased thus: if to be addressed by the pre-existent word justifies men in being called gods, far more is the Johannine community justified in applying the title Son of God to the human bearer of the pre-existent word. Hanson speculates further that v. 7 of the Psalm should be understood as prophecy of the resurrection of Christ (Arise O God) and the accession of the Gentiles (A. T. Hanson, "John's citation of Psalm LXXXII" and "John's citation of Psalm LXXXII reconsidered," *NTS* 11 [1964–65]: 158–62 and 13 [1966–67]: 363–67 respectively and his *The Prophetic Gospel*, 144–49).

J. H. Neyrey in his article, "I said: You are gods: Psalm 82:6 and John 10," *JBL* 108 (1989): 647–63, attempts a Christian Midrash in John 10:34–36 in order to understand Ps 82:6. He says:

a) "I said you are gods" refers to Israel at Sinai when it received the Torah (cf. John 10:35).
b) It implied the intimate link between holiness, immortality and godliness. The Evangelist abbreviates only holiness and god-likeness.
c) Ps 82:6b—Son of the most high is Son of God in John 10:36 and refers to Jesus' godlikeness in terms of holiness, in being consecrated and sent.
d) Jesus is not making himself God, but God makes him the Son of God.
e) John 10 claims Jesus as not just a human being being proclaimed as God/Son of God, but a heavenly figure who is equal to God with full eschatological power.
f) Because of his God-given eschatological power over death he is equal to God.
g) John 10:34–36 probably echoes what the Midrash of Ps 82:6 discusses in terms of the angel of death whose power over God's people was retained—the angel of death cannot snatch Jesus' sheep either from his or God's hands.

Though provocative, it is very difficult to agree with these interpretations since Ackerman and Hanson speculate too much. It is unlikely that here the Evangelist all of a sudden brings his Logos in disguise and refers to it as the mere "word of God." As far as Neyrey's suggestion is concerned, though attractive, it tries to prove "Jesus as equal to God" and according to his own admission the Midrashim on which he has based his arguments were written considerably later than the Fourth Gospel.

first claim about Jesus in v. 30, "I and my Father are one," or clarifying it. Wayne Meeks rightly notes that when something claimed for Jesus caused a reaction from the synagogue, the Johannine community tended not to moderate its claim but to rephrase it in such a way as to cause even greater offence.²⁵ In chapters 5 and 8 we observed that the literary techniques of misunderstanding and irony were used to optimal effect to clarify the claims and in the course of it make it more offensive. Once again here in John 10:34–35, the Evangelist treads the same line. He clarifies that Jesus is not a second God as the Jews understood and that the oneness should be understood in terms of a relationship between the Father and the Son and thus brings the offence into a sharper contrast.

By quoting "I said you are gods" from Psalm 82, he makes it clear to his opponents that "you" refers to people—human beings, the ones chosen and made holy (through a covenant), Israel who lost it almost immediately as they chose to worship the golden calf. He shrewdly uses the guilt conscience of the Jews against them. Bultmann says this is a sort of argument intended by the Evangelist as a parody of Jewish theological method with the scripture. He seems to take the Rabbis on their own game.²⁶ With clever sophistry and an argumentative play of words, he challenges the Jews to open their scriptures (which they themselves regarded as the "authority" to judge).

The Johannine Jesus' tone of argument may be paraphrased as: 'You refuse to believe what I claim, and accuse me of blasphemy, let me remind you that, incredible though it may seem, the Scripture which cannot be broken, and which you regard as absolutely truthful says that wicked human beings (you Israel who proudly boast of yourselves) were called by divine title simply because Israel was chosen and made holy. It was not blasphemous for Israel to bear the divine label, then why do you get so upset and accuse me of blasphemy when I only claim to be the Son of God?'²⁷

The Johannine specific use of Psalm 82 allows him to draw a sharp contrast between "sons of God" and the anarthrous Son of God. The Evangelist's comparison of Jesus with the people of Israel is only limited to the level of principle, that both received a divine commission. The relative

---

25 W. A. Meeks, "The Man from Heaven in Johannine Sectarianism," 161–62.
26 R. Bultmann, *Das Evangelium des Johannes*, 296–97.
27 See exegesis of v. 30—moral arguments of oneness of the Father and the Son as moral likeness with regard to holiness that was the aim of every Israelite, as one also thrives hard to be sons and daughters of God.

clause (πρὸς οὕς) contains Israel's commission. Likewise the second relative clause (introduced by ὅν) highlights Jesus' divine commission. When one follows the Evangelist's own note on the Jewish reaction—"that they tried to seize him"—it specifically conveys that the Jews understood quite correctly what the implicit claim of the Fourth Evangelist's anarthrous title "Son of God" contained.[28]

In the context of Psalm 82, the Johannine claim that Jesus is the Son of God conveyed the following:

a) the Israelites were human beings and of the 'from below' origin. They were given the title "gods" by grace, whereas Jesus is the one from above, the pre-existent (see chapters 5 and 8) in whom one sees God's very own self-disclosure. In their self-emptying they are one! And therefore he is rightly the Son of God.

b) the Israelites are judged for their wickedness and will die. Jesus himself has been given the authority of judgement and he has life in himself (chapters 5 and 8).

It is worth noting that the quote in John 10:34 does not continue so as to include Ps 82:6b and 7. C. H. Dodd has rightly emphasised that the whole of the Psalm is essential to the Evangelist's argument.[29] If his opponents the Jews were familiar with Psalm 82 it would seem that their thoughts would have continued through v. 7 even though the quote in the Fourth Gospel does not contain it. This means that the Evangelist puts his case in God's court! He asks God to judge the theological struggle between the two communities in conflict. It then follows that he is calling upon the 'same one God' who is revealed in the Old Testament to enlighten the minds of his opposing community that they also know God's movement as revealed fully in Jesus instead of clinging to traditions and making their God stagnant! It

---

28 The anarthrous use of Son is not a convincing argument that Jesus placed himself below the people of Israel of Psalm 82. Some see this passage as a good example of Colwell's rule that definite predicate nouns that precede the verb usually lack the article. When translating the phrase, the article should be supplied. While this may be true in this case it is so because of the contextual indicators rather than of grammatical requirements. The Jews themselves regarded the anarthrous claim to be blasphemous (cf. 19:79) and worthy of death.

29 C. H. Dodd, *Interpretation of the Fourth Gospel*, 271; S. L. Homcy, "You are gods? Spirituality and a Difficult Text," *JETS* 32 (1989): 490, and A. T. Hanson, "John's Citation of Psalm LXXXII," *NTS* 11 (1964–65): 160–61 concur.

speaks of a continuation as well as a drastic mobility of theological categories and language!

5.3.2.3 Verses 37–39: The Second Claim

Here a renewed appeal is made to recognise the testimony of τὰ ἔργα of Jesus as pointing to his oneness with the Father. The expression ἵνα γνῶτε καὶ γινώσκητε intimates that the knowledge in view is no mere cognisance of a dogma, but an experience attainable only in faith. The awareness of the Son's living oneness with the Father is the commencement (γνῶτε: ingressive aorist) and the abiding task (γινώσκητε: enduring present) of Faith's journey. The oneness however is now expressed in terms of mutual in-dwelling ἐν ἐμοὶ ὁ πατὴρ κἀγὼ ἐν τῷ πατρί. This expression conveys the thought of complete oneness. But one should understand it from the point of view of God's self-emptying in the Son. This formula of mutual/reciprocal immanence is as Rudolf Schnackenburg puts it "a linguistic way of describing the complete unity between Jesus and the Father."[30] This formula challenges us to see the Son as the perfect expression and revelation of the Father, because of God's self-emptying taking place in the Son. The Fourth Evangelist probably boldly attempts a theological projection into the being of God to visualise a unique, revelatory relationship between the Father and the Son that is beyond all comparison, a oneness whereby the word and action of the Son are that of the Father and the Father's word and actions come to a fulfilment in him.

5.4 Summary and Conclusions

John 10:22–39 brings to a climax the Fourth Evangelist's theological reflections on the unique relationship between the Father and the Son. He uses two different, yet complementary models to explain his theological convictions:
a) He proclaims the oneness of the Father and the Son in what may be called the self-emptying phenomenon that enables him to balance both the Father's greatness and the Son's dependence.

---

30 R. Schnackenburg, *The Gospel according to St. John*, 3:69.

b) He proclaims a relationship of mutual in-dwelling between the Father and the Son to challenge his readers to recognise the Son as the Father's perfect and complete expression.

Through these two models the Evangelist probably attempts a bold theological projection into the being of God. He quotes Israel's Scriptures in order to exhort people to recognise that the same God who revealed Himself in the history of Israel, also revealed Himself in the phenomenon of the historical Jesus. He warns however against stagnating the God language and calls for a creative sensitivity for theological categories and language.

Chapter Six

The God of the Johannine Jesus
Characterisation of God in the Prayer of Jesus (John 17:1–26)

6.1 Introduction

The Prayer of the Johannine Jesus in chapter 17 is conditioned by its position at the conclusion of the farewell discourses of Jesus. A 'prayer' concluding the descriptive farewell discourses in the Old Testament and in later Jewish writings is not uncommon. In the Book of Deuteronomy, a Psalm—the song of Moses (chapter 32)—and a prophetic prayer—Moses' blessing of the tribes (chapter 33)—conclude a series of farewell discourses.[1] In Jewish apocalyptic literature, we may note the prayer of Ezra (4 Ezra 8:19b–36), of Baruch (2 Bar. 48) and in the Book of Jubilees the prayers ascribed to Moses (Jub. 1:19–21), Noah (Jub. 10:3–6), Abraham (Jub. 20–22) and Israel (Jub. 36:11). We also come across the 'last prayers of Moses' (Ps.-Philo 19:8), of Joshua (Ps.-Philo 24:3) and of Jacob (Josephus, Ant. 2.8). These instances show that in the apocalyptic literature the idea of a farewell prayer such as John 17 was already forming a sort of literary genius.[2]

In the farewell prayer of Jesus we find 'faith' finding its expression in word language. The literary genre of the farewell prayer is effectively made use of to portray the Johannine Jesus' understanding of God, to exhort the community to believe and remain in Him who sent Jesus. We propose to interpret the farewell prayer of Jesus in the following scheme:

vv. 1–5	The Only True God
vv. 6–11a	The God who Gives Identity
vv. 11b–15	The God who Protects

---

[1] M. Winter, *Das Vermächtnis Jesu und die Abschiedsworte der Väter: Gattungsgeschichtliche Untersuchung der Vermächtnisrede im Blick auf Joh. 13–17* (FRLANT 161; Göttingen: Vandenhoeck & Ruprecht, 1994), 65–86, esp. 77.
[2] G. R. Beasley-Murray, *John*, 293; J. F. Randall, "The Theme of Unity in John 17:20–23," *ETL* 41 (1965): 376–79, and M. Winter, op. cit., 149–60, 187–97.

vv. 16–19	The God who Sanctifies
vv. 20–23a	The God who Unites
vv. 23b–26	The God who Loves

6.2 Exegesis

6.2.1 Verses 1–5: The True God

The prayer begins with Jesus 'lifting up his eyes to heaven,' a natural posture for prayer among the Jews (cf. 11:41). Heaven symbolises the transcendent space of God.³ Using the address form πάτερ Jesus enters praying into the familiar space that is close to God—the space from which he had never been released, even in his 'coming down.' The address form πάτερ occurs 6 times, is pronounced at vv. 1, 5, 21, 24 πάτερ, at v. 11b πάτερ ἅγιε, then at v. 25 πάτερ δίκαιε. The prayer is thus structured as 'a communication process' between the Son and the Father. Jesus looks back on his earthly life in retrospection, he comes up with requests and needs at the ὥρα, and he looks beyond his earthly life, to God's eternal future in hope and anticipation.

The retrospection begins as Jesus looks back on his life and work, and sees it from God's perspective—all that he has is not his own, but is 'given' to him, he has been given power over all flesh/humanity and power to give eternal life. The Evangelist recapitulates what he has already discussed in 5:20–21 (see exegesis below). The recognition of the fact that those who are with him and the community built around him are a gift of the Father, is the Evangelist's way of affirming that his community has been created by God, is dependent upon and is guided by God Himself.

While affirming and confessing his own God-based, God-guided life, the Johannine Jesus requests God: δόξασόν σου τὸν υἱόν, ἵνα ὁ υἱὸς δοξάσῃ σέ. Δόξα is one of the keywords in the prayer. It is the essence of the ἄνωθεν, the sphere of God. Δόξα is not only the substance and appearance of the heavenly existence, but also divine power in action.⁴ It is the visible

---

3 R. Schnackenburg, *The Gospel according to St. John*, 3:170.
4 R. Bultmann, *Das Evangelium des Johannes*, 375.

manifestation of the majesty through acts of power.⁵ One is reminded here of the exchange of ὑψωθῆναι for δοξασθῆναι in 3:14. For the Fourth Evangelist in the 'lifting up' one could see the glorification.⁶ If so, then Rudolf Bultmann is right in perceiving Jesus' δοξασθῆναι as his being equipped with power and thus becoming fully effectual.⁷ Δόξα also means honour, the worth that is due. Therefore δοξασθῆναι could mean his being recognised, who he is, what he is, and be accorded the honour that he was denied previously.

What then is the relationship between the δόξα and the work and mission of Jesus? If Jesus' work consists of his being able to give eternal life to his own (v. 29), then he is the δοξασθείς at work in his community. When he 'works' and carries out the mission of the Father, he honours Him and makes God's power effectual—he glorifies God. Therefore Jesus' request 'to glorify the Son' in effect reflects the theocentricity of the Son.

Ernst Käsemann contends that, in Jesus being granted power over all flesh (v. 2, cf. v. 27) and in the Johannine Jesus' insistence on God being glorified in the Son, a kenosis as that found in Phil 2:7 is not to be detected.⁸ Raymond Brown nods in agreement, saying that the Fourth Gospel attributes a universal power, which normally is ascribed only to the risen Christ, to the earthly ministry of Jesus. Through the exposition of δόξα, the Fourth Evangelist in fact ventures beyond Jesus' kenosis. According to him, the kenosis of God forms the basis of Jesus' kenosis. In giving His 'power' to the Son, God empties Himself. This means that Jesus' δόξα is not something already existent, seen apart from God's δόξα, rather it is brought about in his work as God's Sent One, and in the human response to that work within the framework of history. His δόξα consists in the fact that history has the possibility of belief (and unbelief) and thus of life (and death) through his work.⁹

---

5   R. E. Brown, *The Gospel according to John*, 2:740.
6   For a detailed discussion on δόξα in the Fourth Gospel see, C. H. Dodd, *Interpretation of the Fourth Gospel*, 206–208; M. Pamment, "The Meaning of *Doxa* in the Fourth Gospel," *ZNW* 74 (1983): 12–16; P. E. Robertson, "Glory in the Fourth Gospel," *TTE* 38 (1988): 121–31; J. McHugh, "The Glory of the Cross: The Passion According to St John," *The Clergy Review* 67 (1982): 117–27, and W. R. Cook, "The 'Glory' Motif in the Johannine Corpus," *JETS* 27 (1984): 291–97.
7   R. Bultmann, *Das Evangelium des Johannes*, 375.
8   E. Käsemann, *The Testament of Jesus*, 10.
9   R. Bultmann, op. cit., 376.

God in His kenosis has made the transcendent δόξα to become tangible—in the life and work of His Son. And now in his ὥρα, in his being lifted up, in Jesus' giving his own life in obedience to the will of God, in fulfilling his entrusted mission, in Jesus' kenosis after the model of God's self-emptying, God is glorified. The Evangelist has depicted the work of Jesus in such a way that it can only, and ought only to be understood in the light of the seeming end, the ὥρα of self-emptying—as the eschatological event. In the ὥρα past and future are bound together, so that the latter gives meaning to the former! God creates a sign, where transcendent and tangible meet, where kenosis becomes the key to δοξασθῆναι. Bultmann strikingly formulates that Jesus' work does not come to an end with the end of his earthly life, but begins precisely then, in its real sense. He is glorified, he has become the eschatological event, beyond which history cannot go.[10] In the acknowledgement or rejection of this sign a decision is called for, as to whether history is life or death!

Verse 3 is not essential in its present context. It is a parenthesis, the structure of the prayer flows better even without it, the presence of the name Jesus Christ is unsuitable and contrary to the style of the prayer as a whole spoken by Jesus. It is only here in the whole of the Gospel that 'Eternal Life' has an article and the adjective is placed in the noun form.[11] This verse has often been cited as an example of Johannine Gnosticism, as it defines the gift of Eternal Life in terms of 'knowing.' For Rudolf Schnackenburg it is a gloss, which might have come from the circle responsible for the first Epistle.[12] C. Kingsley Barrett remarks that it would have been a footnote had such been available to the Fourth Evangelist.[13] Why then has the Evangelist placed it in the farewell prayer of Jesus? We note that ὁ μόνος ἀληθινὸς θεός and Ἰησοῦς Χριστός are not identified. This verse running contrary to the other verses that seemingly call Jesus 'God' makes the Evangelist's theological intention crystal clear. It contains the clearest terms of the Johannine conscious rejection of all forms of polytheism. It may also be a polemical scorn directed against the other redeemer figures, as it declares Jesus Christ as the One sent by God.

---

10 R. Bultmann, op cit., 376.
11 R. Schnackenburg, *The Gospel according to St. John*, 3:172.
12 *Ibid.*, 572.
13 C. K. Barrett, *The Gospel according to St. John*, 503.

What does the Evangelist mean when he says that Eternal life consists in the knowledge of the true God and in Jesus whom He sent? Γινώσκειν for the Greeks was a process analogous to seeing, a process of contemplation (θεωρεῖν) and grasping (καταλαβεῖν) the reality (ἀλήθεια) in which the knower and the known stand apart from each other! Γινώσκειν for them was purely cognitive. Likewise they interpreted the knowledge of God as abstract contemplation of the ultimate reality, in its changeless essence.

In contrast to the Greeks, the Hebrew concept of knowledge (ידע) consists in experience and intimate relationship. The knowledge of God for them consisted in acknowledging God in His works, responding to His claims. It is in entering into a personal relationship with God that humankind can understand His dealings with the world in time and hear and obey His commands.[14] In the prophetic tradition, knowledge of God was seen as one of the fruits of the renewed covenant (Jer 24:7; 31:33–34), and the knowledge of God was also seen as a characteristic of the eschatological period (Hab 2:14). Israel however rarely affirms that it knows God, for it the knowledge of God is the object of exhortation, aspiration or promise.[15] The expectations of the life-giving knowledge of God are found in Wis 15:3. At Qumran, the author of the hymn that concludes the *Community Rule* speaks of his being justified because he had been granted the knowledge of God: "For my light has sprung from the source of His knowledge: my eyes have beheld His marvellous deeds and the light of my heart is in the mystery to come" (1QS XI, 3–4).

For Paul the fuller knowledge of God is eschatological, as he writes "I know in part, but then I shall know even as I am known" (1 Cor 13:12). A parallel of Johannine thought may also be found in the saying preserved in the 'Q' source: καὶ οὐδεὶς ἐπιγινώσκει τὸν υἱὸν εἰ μὴ ὁ πατήρ, οὐδὲ τὸν πατέρα τις ἐπιγινώσκει εἰ μὴ ὁ υἱὸς καὶ ᾧ ἐὰν βούληται ὁ υἱὸς ἀποκαλύψαι (Matt 11:27 parallel Luke 10:22) that emphasises the importance of knowing the Father through the revelation given by the Son.[16]

---

14 For a detailed exploration of the subject, see C. H. Dodd, *Interpretation of the Fourth Gospel*, 151–69; K. J. Carl, "Knowing in St. John: Background of the Theme," *Indian Theological Studies* 21 (1984): 68–82; J. Gaffney, "Believing and Knowing in the Fourth Gospel," *TS* 26 (1965): 215–41.
15 C. H. Dodd, *Interpretation of the Fourth Gospel*, 164.
16 R. E. Brown, *The Gospel according to John*, 2:753.

The Fourth Evangelist proclaims that the Eternal Life consists in the knowledge of the only true God and Jesus Christ whom He has sent. Μόνος (Isa 37:20; John 5:44) and ἀληθινός (Exod 34:6) are traditional attributes of God. They are also found in the confession of faith in cultic formulas (cf. 1 Tim 1:17; 6:15–16; Rev 6:10). It splendidly voices monotheism, but the Fourth Evangelist understands 'the one true God' as a special connotation, He is the God who is known through and in His 'Sent One' Jesus Christ. The community's coming into the knowledge of God depends on its knowledge of the 'Sent One' who is in the bosom of the Father. It reminds us of John 1:18: "no one has seen God but the only Son who has made him known." The knowledge of God that the Sent One has is associated here with his origin ἄνωθεν, his 'sent'-ness—his commission and his complete obedience. In the relationship of the 'Father and the Son' one has the exegesis of God. This archetypal relationship is both a challenge and motivation for the community to enter into such a relationship and thereby 'know' God. The only true God is a God of relationship, who not only calls humankind into a knowing relationship, but also creates an eschatological model of such a relationship through his Sent One. The relationship of love, faithfulness, commission and obedience which one enters into is itself the Eternal Life (see exegesis of 3:16), as one learns through all such relationships what Life actually is!

Verse 4 affirms again that Jesus has glorified God having accomplished the work, which the Father gave him to do (cf. 4:34; 5:36; also 19:30). Jesus' ἔργον stands beyond the category of achievement. He does what he has been entrusted with; his most compelling obligation is the act of his free will.[17] Jesus glorifies God through his acts of supreme obedience. Here we have a glimpse into the Johannine Jesus' understanding of God—the God who entrusts us with a mission expects responsible obedience. A God-given mission is not a burden, but a challenge to give one's very best in order to share the joy of accomplishment, which is itself God's glory.

Verse 5 seems to be referring to the glory of the λόγος, the glory that is his by nature and right.[18] Καὶ νῦν that begins the sentence can introduce a decisive repetition of a request already made.[19] Καὶ νῦν then takes us back

---

17 R. Bultmann, *Das Evangelium des Johannes*, 379.
18 R. H. Lightfoot, *St. John's Gospel*, 300–301.
19 καὶ νῦν is used 9 times in the Johannine writings, it is often a Semitism rendering ועתה, a Hebrew phrase which is both a conjunction and an interjection. In the Old

to v. 1, to the 'now' of the ὥρα. V. 5 and v. 1 are therefore not in contradiction, the Johannine Jesus does not demand what is his by right from the beginning. Jesus explains 'the glory from the beginning' in terms of his returning to ἄνωθεν through his self-sacrificial obedience in accomplishing the entrusted mission. Whereby the transcendent glory that became tangible in his coming down (see the exegesis of v. 2), now at the ὥρα—through the eschatological event—becomes both tangible and transcendent at once.

Bultmann underlines the differences in the language of v. 5 and that of the hymn to Christ in Phil 2:6–11 in that the ascended Christ receives an honour that extends that of his equality with God in his pre-existence, namely of the κύριος.[20] The Johannine Jesus however does not anticipate a higher glory. Bultmann seems to be interpreting the text correctly (though his attempt to see it from the Gnostic background need not be correct). He says that the glory the Johannine Jesus speaks of, as he experienced with the Father before the world was made, appears to be the relational face of God reflected in 'His creative power' (see Ps 8:23, 30; Wis 7:25; 9:10). The Logos incarnated who came from above reflected the relational face of God in its judgemental power, which made it possible to understand 'world' as God's creation.[21] Therefore the Johannine Jesus' δοξασθῆναι at the ὥρα means judgement of the world and rediscovery of the world as creation, which itself is God's glory! If this theological interpretation is correct, then the Johannine Jesus' Theology perceives δοξασθῆναι as the restoration and renewal of the broken relationship between the Creator and His creation.

6.2.2 Verses 6–10: The God who gives identity

Φανερόω brings in the concept of revelation. Φανεροῦν in the Fourth Gospel combines the teaching and making known of the act of revelation.[22] Ἐφανέρωσα, a complexive aorist,[23] looks retrospectively on the revelatory mission of Jesus among the people. What Jesus reveals is now identified as

---

Testament it appears in judicial formulas, related to covenant demands and liturgical petitions. Often followed by an imperative the Hebrew expression can mark the transition from the summary of a situation to the demand for some result that should follow. See R. E. Brown, *The Gospel according to John*, 2:742.

20 R. Bultmann, *Das Evangelium des Johannes*, 380.
21 *Ibid*.
22 R. Bultmann and D. Lührmann, "φαίνω," in *TDNT* 9:1–10, esp. 5ff.
23 *BDF*, § 332.

'the name of God.' Does 'the name' simply point to the Name of the Father? Or does it point to the Being of God which makes people conscious of their being?[24]

In Judaism the expression 'name' was a way to avoid the tetragammaton. 'Name' was an expression of one's personality and power! Through a 'name' it is that relationships begin and grow. In Exod 3:14ff. by revealing His Name to Moses and through him to Israel, God called them to a relationship. This 'Name' stood for all that God did for His people. Disclosure of His Name thus meant the revelation of God Himself. Therefore God's Name is great and is to be 'recognised' (Isa 52:6; Ezek 39:7).

Certain Gnostic Texts, such as *Corp. herm.* V:10–11 which are linguistically close to the Fourth Gospel, declare God's Name to be 'inexpressible' or claim God to be superior to every name and indeed ultimately to be nameless.[25] Among Nag Hammadi Tractates, the *Prayer of Thanksgiving* VI:7, the *Gospel of Truth* 38:6–31; *The Gospel of Philip* 54:5–13 and *Od. Sol.* 41:16; 42:20 show certain similarities to the Fourth Gospel, but go beyond it in identifying the Son and the Father, and in stressing the unspeakable character of the name. Only certain men (the Gnostics) have the Name (the Being and Mystery) of God revealed to them and through that revelation they acquire a share in God's life, light and joy. It is impossible to deny that the language and mode of presentation are similar, but Judaism did exert a considerable influence on Gnosticism especially in regard to the speculation about the name.[26] The direct derivation of 'name' from the Gnostic background is however not possible.

Jesus gives those people that God has given to him τὸ ὄνομα. These were God's own possession from the beginning (v. 6b), but these are the elect, as they are taken out of the world. In giving them the τὸ ὄνομα, God calls them back into His relationship. Through the 'name' they come to a knowledge of their origin (that they are not from the world) that they belong to God. Through τὸ ὄνομα, they get their identity. Once they know their identity, they recognise that Jesus is sent by God, he is God's gift to them (v. 18).

---

24 F. Büchsel, *Das Evangelium nach Johannes* (NTD 4; Göttingen: Vandenhoeck & Ruprecht, 1934), 160.
25 H. Bietenhard, in *TDNT* 5:242ff. See also F. G. Untergaßmair, *Im Namen Jesu: Der Namensbegriff im Johannesevangelium* (FB 13; Stuttgart: Katholisches Bibelwerk, 1973), 245–305.
26 R. Schnackenburg, *The Gospel according to St. John*, 3:176.

Through this gift-giving, God calls them to grasp their relationship to Him. In hearing, accepting and obeying (v. 6) Jesus' words, which are God's own words they will be able to interpret their being, their relationship to God and to one another. Thus they rediscover their identity.

The community has its identity only in imbibing the gift of God in Jesus. Only so far as it remains in relationship with Jesus can the community remember that it is from God, and belongs to God. Through the eschatological event of δοξασθῆναι, Jesus now entrusts the community that has been given to him back to God. The community which finds itself in a conflict situation; in a situation where the synagogue tries to deny its identity, reflects a certainty of knowledge that Jesus is from God, and God through this gift of Jesus stands by on its behalf. When the community realises through its hearing, obeying relationship with Jesus that it belongs to God from the beginning, and that God has given it His τὸ ὄνομα through Jesus, the feeling of insecurity and lostness disappear to make way for an assurance of being a sign of the people of God. Here one can detect the community's consciousness of itself.

6.2.3 Verses 11–15: The God who protects

Πάτερ ἅγιε (v. 11b) in being addressed to God is striking as it is found here alone in this combination of adjective and noun in the Fourth Gospel. God is called the Holy One (of Israel) in the Old Testament and addressed as holy in the Jewish prayers—'O Holy Lord of all Holiness' (2 Macc 14:36), 'O Holy One among the Holy' (3 Macc 2:2). Πάτερ ἅγιε might have been derived from the Christian liturgical usage (*Didache* 10:2). In view of the element of otherness, awesomeness and splendour conveyed as the biblical concept of holiness, the expression πάτερ ἅγιε combines transcendence and intimacy, awesomeness, distantness and relationship in the Johannine Jesus' understanding of God.[27]

Jesus' Prayer is τήρησον αὐτοὺς ἐν τῷ ὀνόματί σου ᾧ δέδωκάς μοι (v. 11b). This petition should be understood within the framework of the impending departure of Jesus. His earthly presence with them was 'God's sign' and assurance that He was with them, He was their protector and keeper, as Jesus through his being and teaching constantly reminded them of their

---

27 G. R. Beasley-Murray, *John*, 288.

origin, their election, their mission. Through Jesus they were protected and kept safe from being engulfed by the world. His being with them reminded them of the τὸ ὄνομα, the new relationship and their identity thus worked as a safeguard! φυλάσσω has a military connotation[28] which suggests protection against any enemy. Here Jesus is not speaking about his power and strength that protected and preserved his disciples, but note ἐν τῷ ὀνόματί σου. He speaks of his given mission 'to be the sign of God's complete protection and salvation,' τὸ ὄνομα, God Himself has been their protector!

Now the 'sign' being taken away, they should experience God's special protection, so as to themselves become 'eschatological signs' of God in the world. Χαρά (like εἰρήνη in 14:27; 16:33)[29] is to be shared by the disciples. Πεπληρωμένην emphatically denotes that the joy they have received through him (cf. 15:11) will be brought to culmination. The 'fullness of joy' which is their eschatological existence, that no one can take away (16:22) becomes a sign of God's protection! The χαρά that God's protection brings is not a 'safe area' where no harm/evil exists, rather it is the joy of being in the world, in the midst of its hatred and persecution, and still be assured of being God's own ἄνωθεν, and enjoying God's personal relationship.

Verse 15 brings out emphatically the challenge and promise of God's protection to an eschatological community. 'In the world,' 'not in the world' in fact makes plain God's protecting purpose for human beings. The community, God's eschatological sign in the world, cannot be 'taken out'/ alienated. Only through its being in the world does the community have meaning, purpose and existence. Only in being threatened and being open to all kinds of assaults and danger, can the community present itself as God's alternative for a rebellious world. For God will protect it from evil ἐκ τοῦ πονηροῦ. Proclaiming God's protection in the midst of all adversities is the good news that the community has to offer.

The genitive τοῦ πονηροῦ can be either masculine or neuter ('deliverance from the evil one' or 'deliverance from evil' as possible allusion to the Lord's prayer, cf. 6:13). Here τοῦ πονηροῦ whether personal or impersonal denotes the active power of evil in the world. It is the community's mission to be in the world, in God's protection to become God's transforming community!

---

28 R. Kysar, *John*, 259.
29 R. Bultmann observes that χαρά and εἰρήνη are used together to portray the eschatological salvation in Isa 55:12; Rom 14:17; Gal 5:22; cf. Job 23:29; *1 En.* 5:9; Philo's *Leg. All.* 1.45; 3.81 and *Cher.* 86. See R. Bultmann, *Das Evangelium des Johannes*, 386.

The radicality of the petition lies in portraying God declining to create a 'safe haven' for the community, instead, challenging it to risk itself in the world in order to transform it. God protects those who make themselves open to assault, in their obedience to the τὸ ὄνομα, trying to build relationships that create God's eschatological community.

6.2.4 Verses 16–19: The God who sanctifies

The verb ἁγιάζειν (v. 17) means 'to make holy,' to take out of the sphere of the profane and place in the sphere of the divine.[30] In the Old Testament ἁγιάζειν is used for the consecration of sacrificial animals (Exod 13:2; Deut 15:19). It is also employed for the consecration of priests, for the performance of their sacred duties (Exod 28:41; 40:13; Lev 8:30; 2 Chr 5:11). A prophet's being consecrated for a special task was also seen as ἁγιάζειν (Jer 1:5; cf. Isaiah 6). A prophet had to be made holy because he was the bearer of God's mission. Thus the Jews firmly believed that sanctification comes from God, and that He grants it through the Torah, His commandments given to Israel.[31] The Rule of the Qumran community interestingly looks to the eschaton and declares that God will then purify by His truth all the works of human . . . (1QS IV, 20–21).

The petition for the sanctification of the disciples was formulated in a strictly theo-centric way. Sanctification proceeds from God. His truth is the sphere of that sanctification and His Word mediates it.[32] 'Sanctification in the Truth' is indeed a process of self-discovery.[33] The sanctification is ἐν τῇ ἀληθείᾳ. Truth symbolises God as He is, God in reality. In the light of the Truth human beings are seen as they are and as they ought to be (see exegesis at 8:31). It is in the Truth therefore that the disciples have an encounter with the liberating power of God! In the Truth they are equipped to see the world, their life and their personality from the perspective of God Himself. It is a process of 'theologising'—discovering oneself from God's standpoint.

---

30 R. Bultmann, *Das Evangelium des Johannes*, 389–90.
31 H. L. Strack & P. Billerbeck, *Kommentar zum Neuen Testament aus Talmud und Midrasch*, 2:566.
32 R. Schnackenburg, *The Gospel according to St. John*, 3:187.
33 See *Mandaean Literature* 165: "you are set up and established my chosen ones by the discourse of the truth that has come to you." The unmistakable closeness to Gnostic ideas should be noted; R. Bultmann, op. cit., 389–92; R. Schnackenburg, op. cit., 185–86.

The parallel construction ἐν τῷ ὀνόματί σου (v. 12) and ἐν τῇ ἀληθείᾳ (v. 17b) should be noted. In the Name one gets identity, communal and social. Now in the Truth one is sanctified—one discovers oneself. Both the giving of identity to and sanctifying of the disciples are wrought by the Word (vv. 14a, 17b), 'the Word' that Jesus himself is as he embodies the gift of God.[34]

The sanctification equips disciples for mission (v. 18). Now they, as separated and sanctified, bear 'the name' and the Truth in all its power! What was true of Jesus 'the Sent One' is also true for those 'sent by Jesus'; as the disciples' sending is modelled after Jesus' own sending (καθώς). The community continues the mission of the 'Sent one' bringing their gift of God—'the Word'—to the world, thus calling it to question and demanding a decision. Bultmann interprets correctly that the community takes over Jesus' role of presenting the world a continual possibility of faith, not by missionary enterprise, but by its very existence.[35]

Now Jesus 'sanctifies himself.' The Fourth Gospel speaks of Jesus being equipped and sanctified (10:36) and thus prepared and sent by God. Peter confesses Jesus as the 'Holy one of God' (ὁ ἅγιος τοῦ θεοῦ, 6:69) who has the words of life eternal (ῥήματα ζωῆς αἰωνίου ἔχεις). Since God has given him His 'Name' (vv. 11, 12), His 'Word' (v. 8), His 'Glory' (v. 22), Jesus can now speak of ἐγὼ ἁγιάζω ἐμαυτόν. But ὑπέρ leaves us in no doubt that Jesus 'emptying death' is meant here! The formula with ὑπέρ expresses his giving his life for others (6:51; 10:11, 15; 15:13).[36] It is interesting to note that for the Fourth Evangelist Jesus cannot sanctify the disciples in the community. Sanctification comes from God and God alone, whereas Jesus speaks of 'sanctifying himself' which however is to be understood as he fulfilling the entrusted task through his obedient self-sacrifice. Thus ἐγὼ ἁγιάζω ἐμαυτόν of Jesus creates an environment for the sanctification of the community. The Fourth Evangelist's emphatic perfect construction καὶ αὐτοὶ ἡγιασμένοι ἐν

---

34 Here the Fourth Gospel distinguishes itself from Gnostic ideas. Jesus discloses 'the Word' to the disciples in person and in history. The Jewish Torah-indicated 'cultic sanctification' is now replaced by Jesus, who is God's 'Sent One' and in whom God creates a new separated, sanctified community.
35 See R. Bultmann, *Das Evangelium des Johannes*, 391.
36 ὑπὲρ αὐτῶν reminds one of Jesus' words at the Last Supper recorded by the Synoptics and Paul—ὑπὲρ ὑμῶν (Luke 22:19; 1 Cor 11:24) and ὑπὲρ πολλῶν (Mark 14:24). These are the words relating to his death.

6.2.5 Verses 20–23: The God who unites

The sentences that constitute the verses are carefully constructed to balance each other in synonymous parallelism,[37] a pattern typical of Semitic thought.

First Sentence: VV. 20–21[38]	Second Sentence: VV. 22–23
Οὐ περὶ τούτων δὲ ἐρωτῶ μόνον, ἀλλὰ καὶ περὶ τῶν πιστευόντων διὰ τοῦ λόγου αὐτῶν εἰς ἐμέ,	κἀγὼ τὴν δόξαν ἣν δέδωκάς μοι δέδωκα αὐτοῖς,
"I ask not only on behalf of these, but also on behalf of those who will believe in me through their word,	The glory that you have given me I have given them,
ἵνα πάντες ἓν ὦσιν,	ἵνα ὦσιν ἕν
that they may all be one.	that they may be one,
καθὼς σύ, πάτερ, ἐν ἐμοὶ κἀγὼ ἐν σοί,	καθὼς ἡμεῖς ἕν· ἐγὼ ἐν αὐτοῖς καὶ σὺ ἐν ἐμοί,
As you, Father, are in me and I am in you,	as we are one, I in them and you in me,
ἵνα καὶ αὐτοὶ ἐν ἡμῖν ὦσιν,	ἵνα ὦσιν τετελειωμένοι εἰς ἕν,
may they also be one in us,	may they become completely one,
ἵνα ὁ κόσμος πιστεύῃ ὅτι σύ με ἀπέστειλας.	ἵνα γινώσκῃ ὁ κόσμος ὅτι σύ με ἀπέστειλας καὶ ἠγάπησας αὐτοὺς καθὼς ἐμὲ ἠγάπησας.
so that the world may believe that you have sent me.	so that the world may know that you have sent me and have loved them even as you have loved me.

---

37 M. L. Appold, *The Oneness Motif in the Fourth Gospel*, 157ff.
38 Some scholars contend that the prayer for 'all' (for future believers) in vv. 20–21 is a later editorial addition; see J. Becker, *Das Evangelium nach Johannes*, 2:509, and R. Schnackenburg, *The Gospel according to St. John*, 3:188–89. The main argument is that the entire prayer up to v. 19 has in view the disciples who are manifest representatives of the church to be and in v. 22–23 the prayer reverts to the disciples. The argument however overstates the position, in vv. 1–5, esp. v. 2 the prayer has in view all believers (πᾶν ὃ δέδωκας αὐτῷ), v. 24 again refers to those whom the Father has given to the Son (ὃ δέδωκάς μοι) which is the prayer context; see G. R. Beasley-Murray, *John*, 303–304, and R. Bultmann, *Das Evangelium des Johannes*, 392–93.

In each sentence there is a single major clause that deals with the work of Jesus—his prayer and his gift of glory. Six ἵνα clauses indicate the object and purpose of Jesus' work. The first two sets of ἵνα clauses deal with the unity and oneness, the object of Jesus' prayer. The third set of ἵνα clauses expresses the purpose of Jesus' prayer—that the world may believe/know. The measure of oneness along with its preconditions are defined by two καθώς clauses and the ultimate goal of Jesus' work is stated by two ὅτι clauses.[39]

Mark Appold following Ernst Käsemann argues that 'oneness' of the Father and the Son is a theological abbreviation to that which is eternally secure, pre-existently present and never relinquished.[40] Does the Fourth Gospel refer to the divinity of Jesus and the divine oneness of the Father and the Son? 'The Son is nothing by himself' is perhaps the theological rejoinder for such an attempt of a dogmatic exegesis. ἕν of the Fourth Evangelist is not 'alone' or a detached 'one.' It refers to a oneness of relationship, as we argued in our chapters on Theology in Conflict. ἕν here signifies oneness of the Father and Son in self-emptying and their oneness of mutuality, σὺ ἐν ἐμοί ... κἀγὼ ἐν σοί, it is a oneness of solidarity and representation. καθώς has both comparative and causative effect.[41] ἕν has therefore a significant paradigmatic value and a motivating force. The oneness of the Father and the Son which has its origin in the Father's 'giving' and thus relating everything to the Son (see exegesis of chapter 5) is the basis for the 'oneness' of the community. ἕν is not a mystical amalgamation, but denotes a network of relationships that reflect the self-emptying, self-giving relationship of the Father and the Son for the salvation of the world (see exegesis on 3:16). Therefore, ἕν has soteriological significance for the existence of the community.

The Johannine ἕν thus has its origin in divine action. The very fact that Jesus prays to the Father for this unity indicates that the key to oneness lies in God's power. It is God who can bring about oneness. The oneness that the Fourth Evangelist strives for is not a simple fellowship and harmonious interaction. Jesus is the chain link between the Father and the believers, he is the 'sent one' (coming from above) and going to the Father (v. 13). His

---

39 See R. Bultmann, op. cit., 394, and J. F. Randall, "The Theme of Unity in John 17:20–23," *ETL* 41 (1965): 388–89.
40 M. L. Appold, *The Oneness Motif in the Fourth Gospel*, 280–89.
41 *BDF*, § 453.

crossing the line between the below and the above realm meant abolition of a barrier! 'The unity with the Father' is the fundamental goodness that Jesus has come to bring to the world.

'Oneness' described in terms of καθὼς σύ, πάτερ, ἐν ἐμοὶ κἀγὼ ἐν σοί, and καθὼς ἡμεῖς ἕν· ἐγὼ ἐν αὐτοῖς καὶ σὺ ἐν ἐμοί, should not be seen as residue of mysticism. Actually such a mutual in-dwelling is the interpretation of identities. "As you, Father, are in me and I am in you," and "I in them and you in me," envisages the deepest level of 'peace'—Shalom. It is to be at peace with all—with God, with fellow human beings—at the core of being and identities. If our interpretation of v. 5ff is plausible, then when the believers know their 'identity,' then the oneness here striven for is its consequence. For, those who know that their 'identity' is in God Himself, bear the sign of oneness as a mark of that identity. Therefore oneness is a gift of God! This excludes the possibility of interpreting 'oneness' in terms of human endeavours for solidarity.

The fact that Jesus' oneness with the Father creates conditions for oneness within all humanity (πάντες) and of humanity with the Father reflects the universal dimension of 'oneness.' It is the oneness of total inclusiveness. To be an eschatological sign of God's salvific offer, to be a counter community in the world, the oneness of the community must/can only be universal or else it falls back into a unity based on expulsions and exclusions.[42] Jesus gives the very δόξα that he received from the Father, to be the bearer of δόξα: God's effectual power for bringing salvation and the fullness of divine life (all that God has) is not only a responsibility, but a challenge! If God has given everything, His very δόξα through Jesus, to achieve oneness, and to make oneness perfect (τελειόω) with the humanity He Himself has created, then humanity has no option but to give itself to God in humble worship.

---

42 It has been argued that the oneness/unity talk in the Fourth Gospel resembles that of the Qumran community; a sectarian conscience behind the unity concept is thus indirectly suggested. יחד in the Qumran texts occurs 70 times. להיות ליחד—to be a unity in 1QS V, 2, or בהאספם ליחד—gather together in one community in 1QS V, 7 resemble the Johannine language, but one should notice the gathering of the holy remnant of Israel behind Qumran language and יחד seems to be a community of men living the same way of life. Though the Qumran community had an eschatological dimension to their unity concept, they interpreted it rather in exclusivist terms as יחד that included only those who accepted their particular interpretation of the law. R. E. Brown, *The Gospel according to John*, 2:777–78, and R. Schnackenburg, *The Gospel according to St. John*, 3:193–94.

Only then can it make known and be witness to, and thus lead the world to belief in the God who empties Himself, who offers oneness with Himself, in sending Jesus to whom He has given everything that He has.

6.2.6 Verses 23b–26: The God who loves

Jesus concludes his prayer reminiscing on the love of God that was before the foundation of the world (v. 24), an affirmation that the creation of the world itself was an act of God's love and hence the existence of the possibility of a 'loving relationship' from the beginning.[43] Now in its oneness with God the community will be a sign of God's love (v. 23b). Only 'love' can sustain a network of relationships. The love of God that is recognised and experienced in the oneness of the community is the same love that Jesus enjoys—the love of a father and a son!

The believers do have a share in God's eternal love (v. 26) that is to become the determining power in their lives.[44] The community therefore can now comprehend the Pauline use of the words—the depth, height, length and width of the love of God that is revealed in Jesus. The 'love of God' is to be God Himself. Love is what He is, it consists of His being Creator: God is not God if He exists for Himself. The creation itself that is nothing but His love is God's revelation, as it reflects His readiness to relate. The sending of Jesus and his very presence is the sign of God's salvific love. It reminds them that God is with them, that the love of God is nothing but His constant presence, His being with them, His '*dasein.*'

In affirming through his prayer that God has sent His Son, that God gives identity to human beings, that God protects, sanctifies and that He invites to oneness with Him, the Johannine Jesus in fact delivers an exegesis of the very being of God and His loving acts and sings praise of God's love. Jesus' concluding with the affirmation that the disciples will experience the eternal love of God in them (v. 26) is probably a Johannine way of interpreting the binding of the original creation–Creator relationship. If so, nothing further can be given beyond the gift of the love of God.

---

43 *Pace* R. Bultmann, *Das Evangelium des Johannes,* 400.
44 Ibid., 400–401.

6.3 Summary and Conclusions

a) Chapter 17 of the Fourth Gospel is a well-structured prayer, a strikingly theo-centric text. The Fourth Evangelist brings to climax his theological motifs and concepts as if they are Jesus' own faith affirmation to God who acts in the community and in the world. Chapter 17 presents Jesus' characterisation of God.

b) Linguistically too, the text is God-oriented. All that the community wishes for itself stems out of/originates in God. God gives, sends, protects, sanctifies, unifies and loves. All human orientation, therefore, is naturally directed to God. Word usage such as σύ, σου, παρά σοι, σε, παρὰ σεαυτῷ, ἐν σοί, πρὸς σέ, σός demonstrate this fact.

c) The only true God is a God of relationships, who not only calls humankind into a knowing relationship, but also creates an eschatological model of such a relationship through His Son. In entering such a relationship in obedience one experiences what life really is. Through fulfilling the entrusted mission, Jesus glorifies the Father, renewing and restoring the creational relationship.

d) God, in giving His Name, gives identity. In hearing, accepting and obeying the Word of God humankind is able to interpret their being/relationship to God and to one another, thus rediscovering their identity. The Name gives 'the elect' the assurance of being the people of God.

e) 'Holy Father' combines transcendence, intimacy, awesomeness, distantness and relationship. The assurance of God being their protector fills the disciples with eschatological joy. It is not in seeking safe havens, but in risking one's life for God that one experiences protection.

f) God sanctifies. Sanctification is a discovery of oneself from God's perspective. Sanctifying equips the disciples for mission.

g) God cannot exist for Himself. The very act of creation and sending Jesus to renew creation reflect His love. To be in God's love is to be already in His new creation.

h) 'Oneness' of God is not a dormant attribute, but a creative attitude. It is His power that unites and reconciles those hostile to Him and to each other. Oneness is a network of relationships based on the principle of self-giving of the Father and the Son. Therefore 'oneness' is the soteriological/eschatological existence. It is the Shalom, Peace at the core of being and identity.

Chapter Seven

Incarnate Logos as Historical Theophany
(John 1:1–18)

7.1 Integrity of the Prologue

For a meaningful interpretation of the Prologue one needs to address the question of unity earnestly. Was there a pre-Johannine 'hymn' behind the Prologue? Does the structural unity of the present text seal the question of integrity of the Prologue? These questions are very closely interrelated and puzzling. Here an attempt is made to analyse the research done so far in this direction and to clarify our position.

7.1.1 In Search of a pre-Johannine Hymn

The Prologue's poetic structure, confessional character, and christological focus that is consistent with other New Testament passages which are thought to be based on early Christian hymns (cf. Phil 2:6–11; Col 1:15–20; 1 Tim 3:16; Heb 1:2–5; 1 Pet 3:18–20), have led many Johannine scholars to maintain that the source behind the Prologue could be a Hymn.[1] To detect the pre-Johannine Hymn it is proposed that the following criteria be followed:
a) in accordance with Semitic poetry, one expects short clauses in some form of parallelism,
b) the poetic form,
c) a confessional affirmationist style rather than argumentative or polemical,
d) the absence of specific names, and
e) peculiar vocabulary.[2]

---

1 The research shows that the most revered early Christian hymns such as Phil 2:6–11, Col 1:15–20 and short hymns such as 1 Tim 3:16, Heb 1:2–5 show considerable parallels to the Prologue. See J. M. Robinson, "A Formal Analysis of Col. 1:15-20," *JBL* 76 (1957): 278–80. See also R. E. Brown, *The Gospel according to John*, 1:20–21, and R. Schnackenburg, *The Gospel according to St. John*, 1:227–28.
2 J. H. Bernard, *Commentary on the Gospel according to St. John*, 1:cxiv, and J. Painter, *The Quest for the Messiah: The History, Literature and Theology of the Johannine Community* (2nd ed.; Edinburgh: T&T Clark, 1993), 142–43.

Was the hymn source thus deduced, a Gnostic/Jewish/Christian one, or some combination of the three, is a question that provides theological criteria for the quest, which however has become a very subjective element in the process of analysis, as it differs according to the theological perspectives of a particular scholar.

Rudolf Bultmann, who followed Charles Burney's Aramaic hymn theory,[3] held that the Fourth Evangelist made use of a pre-Christian cultic hymn that was part of an Aramaic poetic discourse whose ultimate source was oriental Gnosticism. This, the Evangelist took as the basis for the Prologue and developed it with his own comments. Bultmann came to this conclusion while he claimed that the basic hymn (*Die Vorlage*) had originally celebrated the 'preexistent Logos incarnate' in John the Baptist who was venerated by a Baptist sect. When the Evangelist was converted from this Baptist sect, he transformed the hymn as a polemic against John the Baptist and applied it instead to Jesus. According to Bultmann the Prologue formed the introduction to the Evangelist's postulated revelatory discourse source (*Offenbarungsreden*).[4] Siegfried Schulz sought the constitutive elements of the Prologue of the Fourth Gospel in the Hellenistic Gnostic use of the term 'Logos' in the Wisdom tradition of late Hellenistic Judaism and in the Old Testament concept of Theophany.[5] He too maintained that this hymn came from a pre-Christian Baptist sect.

---

3   C. F. Burney maintained that a retroversion of the Prologue into Aramaic reveals a hymn-form consisting of eleven couplets interspersed with comments and that the original Logos hymn is preserved in vv. 1–5, 10–11, 14, and 16–17. See C. F. Burney, *The Aramaic Approach to the Fourth Gospel*, 40–41.

4   The basic hymn was composed in couplets, each made up of two short sentences, sometimes both parts of the couplet expressed one thought (vv. 9, 12, 14b), sometimes the second couplet developed the first thought (vv. 1, 4, 14a, 16); sometimes two parts stood together in parallelism (v. 3) or in antithesis (vv. 5, 10, 11).

VV. 1–5, 9–12ab, 14, 16	*Vorlage*
VV. 6–8, 15	Inserted polemical comments about John the Baptist
VV. 12c–13	Exegetical comment of the author and interpretation of the notion "in His name"
V. 17	An exegetical gloss on v. 16 which mentions the name "Jesus Christ" suppressed until now and introduces the 'Law–Grace' antithesis (Pauline?)
V. 18	A note inserted by the Evangelist to stress the absoluteness of the revelation in the Son.

See R. Bultmann, *Das Evangelium des Johannes*, 1–5.

5   Schulz maintained that, vv. 1–5, 10–12a, b came from the Sophia tradition, vv. 14, 17, 18 from the perspective of the Old Testament concept of Theophany and that

The discussion that the original hymn of Prologue was a Baptist hymn has lost ground, as there is not the slightest evidence that the Baptist sectarians ever referred to John the Baptist as 'the Word.' The passages cited from the *Odes of Solomon* by Bultmann to strengthen his Baptist hymn hypothesis is therefore on slippery ground, as it is held today that the *Odes* may have been dependent on the Fourth Gospel. Moreover, the very strong anti-Gnostic features in the Prologue militate against Bultmann's hypothesis.[6]

The poetic criteria that are set on the basis of a hypothetical Aramaic original are themselves subjective. There are several constructions undoubtedly Greek rather than Semitic in the conception.[7] The Prologue as a whole is written in extremely simple, almost naive Greek. This has been regarded as

---

vv. 1, 14 are the Logos title from the late Hellenistic Judaism. Therefore the original hymn, according to him, contained vv. 1–5, 10–12a, b, 14, 17, 18. See S. Schulz, *Komposition und Herkunft der Johanneischen Reden*, esp. 51–57 and 66–69.

6   W. Schmithals has issued a repudiation of Bultmann's theory in sharpest terms: "Der Logos-Begriff des Hymnus ist hellenistischen Ursprungs und dürfte dem christlichen Verfasser gleichfalls durch jüdische Vermittlung (vgl. Philo) zugekommen sein ... Für den Grundgedanken der zweiten Strophe, die Menschwerdung des Logos, gibt es keine außerchristliche Vorlage; der Gedanke als solcher ist christlichen Ursprungs ... Direkte gnostische Einflüsse verrät der Hymnus nicht ... Die Vorstellung, der Hymnus sei vorchristlich gewesen, ist abenteuerlich. Bultmanns Vermutung, es handele sich um ein ursprüngliches Täuferlied, hat mit Recht keinen Anklang gefunden." W. Schmithals, "Der Prolog des Johannesevangeliums," *ZNW* 70 (1979): 34–35. Also see his *Johannesevangelium und Johannesbriefe*, 260–77.

7   An outstanding example is found in v. 11 that is universally allowed to be part of the Prologue. The Evangelist says that "the Word came to His own" (τὰ ἴδια—neuter plural) "and His own people" (οἱ ἴδιοι—masculine plural) "did not receive Him." This variation in gender cannot be expressed in Aramaic (which can only use דלא in each case. It is worth noting that the Syriac New Testament quite fails to make the Fourth Evangelist's point here. From v. 12, "the Word gave authority to become children of God (ἔδωκεν αὐτοῖς ἐξουσίαν τέκνα θεοῦ γενέσθαι)," Bultmann wished to excise 'authority,' which he thinks spoils the rhythm as a Greek addition to the Semitic idiom. 'He gave to become,' Semitic (נתן – διδόναι) means that he 'caused to become,' 'gave permission' or 'delegated authority.' Others have seen ἐξουσία followed by the infinitive as a Semitic turn of speech. But it is perfectly paralleled by the plain Greek of *Corp. herm.* 1:28 'having authority to partake (ἔχοντες ἐξουσίαν ... μεταλαβεῖν) of immortality.' The use of periphrastic tense and of *casus pendens* is by no means exclusively Semitic; C. K. Barrett, "The Prologue of St. John's Gospel," in *New Testament Essays* (London: S.P.C.K., 1972), 35.

a mark of Semitic origin, but it ought not be the criterion. It is not necessarily Semitic because it is simple.[8]

Hans Heinrich Schaeder following Burney affirmed that the origin of the Prologue was in Aramaic and that it was a hymn to Enosh (the God 'man'). According to him, v. 6a—"Enosh was sent by God"—was not merely part of the original hymn, but the key to its interpretation.[9] Christoph Demke has designated vv. 1, 3–5, 10–12b as a song of the 'heavenly ones' recited in a worship service in the community, the confession of the 'earthly ones' of the congregation as its response (vv. 14, 16), and consequently as the Evangelist's source, without making any mention of who the 'heavenly ones' are and we learn only that the heavenly ones are not the Logos or God.[10] J. Rendel Harris has shown exclusive parallels to the Prologue, especially vv. 1–14 that could be found in Wisdom literature.[11] It is argued that the original Jewish hymn praised Wisdom/Torah as God's agent in creation, in whom was Light and Life, but who was rejected by the world and even by Israel as a whole. However, Wisdom/Torah was received by a few wise and holy among whom Wisdom came to dwell revealing her glory. Thus the hymn manifests Jewish piety.

John Painter in agreement with Harris argues that in the conflict with the Synagogue, the Evangelist made use of a sectarian Jewish hymn in praise of Wisdom/Torah as the basis for the Prologue, whereby a Sophia hymn became a Logos hymn. Prior to being used by the Evangelist, the hymn had

---

8   Greek is capable of utmost refinement and complication, but can also be very simple. The Fourth Gospel as a whole is written in a comparatively simple Greek, and moreover the solemn religious hieratic Greek to be found in some inscriptions in religious and magical papyri and in literature such as the Hermetica is very simple Greek. See C. K. Barrett, "The Prologue of St. John's Gospel," 36.

9   But this is the fatal weakness of this hypothesis, quite apart from the questionableness of the retranslation back to Aramaic. The statements in v. 6ff. can be understood of John the Baptist without any difficulty and the secondary nature of vv. 6–8 can hardly be doubted. H. H. Schaeder, "Der Mensch im Prolog des vierten Evangeliums," in *Studien zum Antiken Synkretismus aus Iran und Griechenland* (Leipzig: Teubner, 1926), 306–50, esp. 339ff.

10 C. Demke, "Der sogenannte Logoshymnus im johanneischen Prolog," *ZNW* 58 (1967): 45–68, esp. 61, n. III and 64.

11 J. R. Harris, *The Origin of the Prologue to St. John* (Cambridge: Cambridge University Press, 1917), 4ff., 10–19 & esp. 43. See also for a detailed list of parallels: C. H. Dodd, *Interpretation of the Fourth Gospel*, 274–75, and J. Painter, *The Quest for the Messiah*, 146–47.

been edited and used by a Hellenistic Christian community that was familiar with the Pauline identification of Christ with Wisdom and the antithesis of Law and Grace. This is reflected in the editing of the hymn that then proclaims that not the old Law of Moses, but the new Law of Christ is the Wisdom of God. Painter suggests that, taking this Hellenistic Christian reworking of the Sophia hymn, the Evangelist made his own modification so it became a suitable introduction to the Gospel.[12]

One should be careful in making an automatic leap from Sophia to Logos. The parallels from Wisdom literature do not stem from a single hymn, or from one thematic exposition, but are scattered ideas. Moreover, Wisdom of Solomon 10 begins by attributing the acts of God recorded in Genesis to Sophia as distinct from God (cf. 10:9–10: σοφία . . . ἔδειξεν αὐτῷ βασιλείαν θεοῦ). From 11:8 onwards, however, such acts are attributed directly to God (addressed in the 2nd person). The transition from the one to the other is almost imperceptible (see 9:1–4). At the same time, though Wisdom is the εἰκών of God, the ἀπαύγασμα of eternal light and so forth, a statement such as θεὸς ἦν ἡ σοφία is unthinkable.

Ernst Käsemann,[13] Rudolf Schnackenburg, Raymond Brown, Hans Conzelmann, Andreas Lindemann,[14] Walter Schmithals and many others today believe that the hymn behind the Prologue was a pre-Johannine Christian hymn. The following table gives an overview of eighteen scholars' attempt to reconstruct the original Logos hymn.[15]

Bernard	1–5	10–11	14		18[16]
Burney	1–5	10–11	14	16–17	
Bultmann	1, 3–5	9–12b	14	16	

---

12 J. Painter, "Christology and the History of the Johannine Community in the Prologue of the Fourth Gospel," *NTS* 30 (1984): 460–74. He extends his thesis in *The Quest for the Messiah*, 145–62.
13 E. Käsemann, "Aufbau und Anliegen des Johanneischen Prologs," *Exegetische Versuche und Besinnungen*, vol. 2 (Göttingen: Vandenhoeck & Ruprecht, 1964), 155–80, also came to accept that the original hymn was a Christian hymn almost certainly in Greek. So also J. Jeremias, *The Central Message of the New Testament* (London: S.C.M. Press, 1965), 74.
14 H. Conzelmann & A. Lindemann, *Arbeitsbuch zum Neuen Testament* (14th ed.; Tübingen: Mohr Siebeck], 2004), 141–42.
15 I follow the scheme presented by R. E. Brown in his commentary with additions wherever necessary.
16 J. H. Bernard, *Commentary on the Gospel according to St. John*, 1:1ff.

Schulz	1–5	10–12b	14	17	18
Becker	1, 3–5	11–12ab	14abce	16[17]	
Gächter	1–5	10–13	14	16	18[18]
Green	1–3, 5	10–11	14a–d		18[19]
Demke	1, 3–5	10–12b	14	16	
Haenchen	1–5	9–11	14	16–17	
Käsemann	1, (2?), 3–5	10–12			
Schnackenburg	1, 3–4	9–11	14	16	
Brown	1–5	10–12b	14	16[20]	
Schmithals	1–5	12ab	14abce	17[21]	
Sanders	1–5	9–11			
Painter	1–3ac, 4–5	10–12b	14abce	(16),(17)[22]	
Hofius	1–5	9–12	14	16[23]	
Lindemann	1, 3–5	9, 11	14abce	16[24]	

---

17 J. Becker speaks of a *Vorlage* with three *Strophen*:
    Strophe I   vv. 1, 3, 4   *Die Schöpfungsmittlerschaft des Logos*
    Strophe II   vv. 5, 11, 12ab   *Die Vermittlerschaft des Logos*
    Strophe III   vv. 14abce, 16   *Die Fleischwerdung des Logos*
    According to Becker the original hymn was made up of *Strophen* I & II, while the Evangelist added the church's faith affirmation as the *Strophe* III, see J. Becker, *Das Evangelium nach Johannes*, 79–104, esp. 85–86.
18 P. Gächter, "Strophen im Johannesevangelium," *ZTK* 60 (1936): 99ff.
19 H. C. Green, "The Composition of St. John's Prologue," *ExpTim* 66 (1954–55): 291ff.
20 Brown sees vv. 12c–13 and 17–18 as later, clarifying additions. The final redactor added vv. 6–9 and 15.
21 W. Schmithals reconstructs his '*Vorlage*' comprising three *Strophen*. The first two with six lines and the third with seven lines (in 1970) and then all three with six lines each (in 1992, see his *Johannesevangelium und Johannesbriefe*, 260–77):
    VV. 1a, 1b, 1c, 2, 3a, 3b   }
    VV. 4a, 4b, 5a, 5b, 12a 12b   } Logos asarkos
    VV. 14a, 14b, 14c (14d–1970), 14e, 17a, 17b – Logos ensarkos
    See also his "Prolog des Johannesevangeliums," *ZNW* 70 (1979): 31–32. Here Schmithals takes the first *Strophe* with two parts of six lines each and the second *Strophe* with seven lines and says: "das Bedeutungsvolle dieser Zahlen liegt am Tage!"
22 J. Painter, *The Quest for the Messiah*, 139.
23 O. Hofius has recently proposed a four *Strophen Vorlage* with vv. 1–3, 4+5+9, 10–12c, 14+16. The first and second speak of *Logos asarkos*, while the third and fourth speak of *Logos ensarkos*. The first and second *Strophen* have a 4/3 and the third and fourth have a 5/3 meter construction; O. Hofius, "Struktur und Gedankengang des Logos-Hymnus," *ZNW* 78 (1987): 1–25.
24 Lindemann ascribes verses 2, 6–8, 10, 12ab, 14d, 15 and 18 to the Evangelist. And he thinks that verses 12c, 13 and 17 are the work of the ecclesiastical redactor.

It is evident that to deduce the original hymn, the poetic nature of the lines is the principal criterion, but the discussion on the rhythm, metrical feet, *Einzeiler, Zweizeiler, Dreizeiler, Sechszeiler* (?) differs from scholar to scholar. To minimise the embarrassment, Ernst Haenchen speaks of "free-rhythm." Joseph Sanders calls the Prologue a rhythmical prose. It is observed that the scholars form their set of propositions about the original import of the poem and eliminate those lines that do not agree with their hypothesis. If we analyse the positions of the eighteen scholars, there is a consensus that vv. 6–8 and 15 were added by the Evangelist. Many would identify vv. 12c, 13, 17–18 as additions by the Evangelist or by a later redactor. And those who consider vv. 2 and 14d as later additions give strong theological reasons for a possible redaction. Many also exclude vv. 17 and 18 for the lack of poetic form.

Thus, an exegesis that depends upon a precisely accurate reconstruction of the source hymn is open to suspicion and is virtually unattainable. This however does not mean that such a reconstruction is unhelpful and does not negate the possibility of a *Vorlage/Vorlagen* behind the Prologue. The very consensus on vv. 6–8, 15, 12c–13 as secondary and the near agreement on vv. 17 and 18 as prose which do not belong to the original source seems to tell us that there were traditions (written/oral) responsible for the final form of the Prologue.

7.1.2 The Prologue is a Unity

A group of scholars who have been content to take the Prologue as it stands and not concern themselves with the sources indeed maintain that the Prologue is so closely woven that it is impossible to detect seams and joints in its texture. Edwyn Hoskyns, Robert Lightfoot, C. H. Dodd, and John Marsh fall into this category. It seems that they have overlooked a useful tool by refusing a critical analysis. After quoting Bultmann, that exegesis has to explain the complete text and that critical analysis exists in order to serve this explanation, C. K. Barrett finally also ends up with his British counterparts. True, he does pay attention to all the possible reconstruction theories, pits them one against the other and rejects them coming to a conclusion that the Prologue is not a jigsaw puzzle, but one piece of solid theological writing. The Evangelist wrote it all, recalling as he did so, who knows what pieces of Wisdom and Logos speculation and it sums up the meaning he had seen into the story of Jesus.[25]

Instead of embarking on a quest for a reconstruction of the *Vorlage*, Matthias Rissi tried to explain how the present form of the Prologue came to be. He has argued that the Prologue is made up of two hymns, one underlying vv. 1–13 and the other as the basis of vv. 14–18. Both were hymns from the Evangelist's community. Rissi observes that

a) the form/style of the two sections differ,
b) the Baptist is introduced twice, once in each section in v. 6ff and v. 15,
c) and the incarnation is mentioned in each section, v. 11 and v. 14.

The theory that the Evangelist used and edited two hymns treating them consecutively to form the basis of his Prologue could explain the data. According to Rissi, together the two hymns provide a history of the revelation of the Word. While the first one concentrates on the creative Word reaching a climax with the incarnation, the second focuses on the salvation event in the incarnation.[26]

Klaus Berger suggests that the Prologue is a literary unit, made up of three blocks:

Block I: vv. 1–8   *Gegensatz zwischen dem göttlichen Logos und dem menschlichen Täufer (leitendes Stichwort ist φῶς).*

Block II: vv. 9–13   *Die Opposition von Jesus und Kosmos bestimmend, welche eine Zweiteilung der Menschengruppen zur Folge hat (leitendes Stichwort ist φῶς).*

Block III: vv. 14–18 *Gegensatz zwischen Jesus und Moses (Schlüsselbegriff ist δόξα).*[27]

Eugen Ruckstuhl compiled a list of not less than fifty carefully selected peculiarities of the Johannine style and demonstrated that these are scattered over the whole Gospel with such a frequency and evenness, that in general the literary unity of the Fourth Gospel can no longer be brought into question. Following these criteria, he also investigated the Prologue and

---

25 C. K. Barrett, "The Prologue of St. John's Gospel," in *New Testament Essays*, 48.
26 See M. Rissi, "Die Logos-Lieder im Prolog des vierten Evangeliums," *ThZ* 31 (1975): 321–36, and his "John 1:1–18 (The Eternal Word)," *Int* 31 (1977): 394–401.
27 K. Berger, *Exegese des Neuen Testaments: Neue Wege vom Text zur Auslegung* (Wiesbaden/Heidelberg: Quelle & Meyer, 1977), 27–28.

strongly vouches for its original unity against its evolution from a Logos hymn.[28]

Walther Eltester completely rejected the hypothesis of a reworked hymn. He maintains that John 1:1–18 is a single entity and that the Gospel narrative begins at John 1:1. According to him, each section tells an epoch in salvation history. He rejects a distinction between poetry and prose in the Prologue.[29] In his work, the statement on John the Baptist has central function, but he does not give a satisfactory explanation as to why the statements about John the Baptist appear as early as vv. 6–8 and not just before the incarnation (v. 14), since he does not interpret vv. 9–11 as referring to the incarnation. And his salvation history epoch seems over-schematically forced into the Prologue.

Peder Borgen suggests that the basic structure of the Prologue is not primarily dependant on whether the style is prose or poetry, but argues in a manner comparable to the Jerusalem Targum on Genesis, that the Prologue contains a Targumic exposition of Gen 1:1–5. He regards the Prologue as a unit composed by the Evangelist and tries to show that vv. 1–5 are a basic exposition of Gen 1:1–5 and vv. 6–18 elaborate upon the first five verses.[30]

---

28 E. Ruckstuhl, "Johannine Language and Style: The Question of their Unity," in *L'Évangile de Jean* (ed. M. de Jonge; BETL 44; Leuven: University Press, 1977), 125–48, and his *Die literarische Einheit des Johannesevangeliums: Der gegenwärtige Stand der einschlägigen Forschungen* (Freiburg/Schweiz: Paulusverlag, 1951).

29 W. Eltester, "Der Logos und sein Prophet," in *Apophoreta: Festschrift für Ernst Haenchen* (BZNW 30; Berlin: Alfred Töpelmann, 1964), 109–34, esp. 124.

    VV. 1–5   *Das 'Wort' als Schöpfungsmittler und als Offenbarer*

    VV. 6–8   *Johannes als Gottgesandter und als Zeuge des Offenbarers*

    VV. 9–11   *Der Offenbarer und seine Ablehnung durch Heiden und Juden*

    VV. 12–13   *Die alttestamentlichen Gotteskinder*

    VV. 14–17   *Die Fleischwerdung des 'Wortes' und der Lobpreis seiner Gemeinde, mit Johannes als Zeugen seiner Präexistenz und seiner Gnadengaben im Alten Testament und in Jesus*

    V. 18   *Der eingeborene Sohn als alleiniger Künder Gottes*

30 For a more thorough and clear understanding, Borgen suggests that the Prologue should be interpreted in the following scheme:

    a) VV. 1–2 & vv. 14–18   Logos and God before the creation and the epiphany with the coming of Jesus.

    b) V. 3 & vv. 10–13   Logos which creates in primordial times and which claims its possession by the coming of Jesus.

    c) VV. 4–5 and vv. 6–9   Light and nightfall in primordial time and the coming of the light with Jesus' coming with John the Baptist as a witness.

His discussions on the Prologue and Gen 1:1–5 do constructively augment previous research on the subject, but at the same time borders on the danger of interpreting the Prologue exclusively in terms of creation Theology which is surely a part of interpretation but not the whole of it.

Following N. W. Lund who proposed that the Prologue is an elaborate chiastic structure with v. 13 as its centre,[31] are the other French scholars P. Lamarche,[32] Marie-Émile Boismard and A. Feuillet, though each fix the centre of the structure differently (Lamarche—vv. 10–13; Feuillet—no centre: vv. 10–11 balance vv. 12–13; Boismard—vv. 12–13) to stress the structural unity of the Fourth Gospel.[33] Boismard argues that the Prologue is one unit with a chiastic structure balancing two major theological patterns of Judaism, with vv. 12–13 providing the pivot. He suggests that for vv. 1–11, the author of the Prologue drew his inspiration for the Logos hymn from the Wisdom tradition and for the event of incarnation to which Wisdom literature does not offer a clear analogy, the Evangelist used another theological category, namely the Sinai myth—the dwelling of Yahweh among His people in the holy tent, the revelation He gave to Moses and the bestowal of grace by the God of the covenant.[34]

See P. Borgen, "Observations on the Targumic Character of the Prologue of John," *NTS* 16 (1969–70): 288–95. And also his "Logos was the True Light: Contributions to the Interpretation of the Prologue of John," *NovT* 14 (1972): 115–30.

31 I could not consult N. W. Lund's "The Influence of Chiasmus upon the Structure of the Gospels," *AThR* 13 (1931): 42–46, but could read a summary of the same in R. A. Culpepper, "The Pivot of John's Prologue," *NTS* 27 (1981): 1–31, esp. 2–3.

32 Lamarche sees the Prologue as a unit made up of two major sections:
    I VV. 1–9   addressed to the Gentiles and
    II VV. 14–18   to the Jews
       VV. 10–13   describe the rejection of the Logos by both, Jews and Gentiles, while the community of the Faithful despite their diverse origins accepts the Logos.

See P. Lamarche, "The Prologue of John," in *The Interpretation of John* (ed. J. Ashton; Philadelphia: Fortress, 1986), 36–52. Original: "Le Prologue de Jean," *RSR* 52 (1964): 497–537.

33 For a detailed summary see R. A. Culpepper, "The Pivot of John's Prologue," esp. 3–9.

34 M.-É. Boismard, *St. John's Prologue* (trans. C. Dominicans; London: Blackfriars Publications, 1957), 79–80.

Morna D. Hooker writing on John the Baptist and the Prologue[35] tries to argue that the two pericopes containing the witness of John the Baptist are not mere interpolations into the Prologue, and divides the Prologue into two sections,
a) vv. 1–13 and
b) vv. 14–18,
claiming that both sections independently show a chiastic structure with the testimony of John the Baptist (vv. 6–8 in a and v. 15 in b) forming the pivot on both occasions.

In his very meticulously argued research article "The Pivot of John's Prologue,"[36] R. Alan Culpepper reasoned that the Prologue is a chiastic structure that pivots on v. 12b: "and he gave them the authority to become children of God." He says, neither the incarnation nor the witness of the community—"we beheld his glory"—would have meaning, were it not for the result of the confession of the incarnation—'formation of a covenant community.'

7.1.3 Analysis

Structural/stylistic unity (Ruckstuhl) is not a conclusive evidence for the unity of the Prologue. Even the literary analyst who searches for the 'pre-Johannine hymn' behind the Prologue knows that the Prologue is a tight-knit structural unit. Those in quest of a source go miles beyond what structural analysts think of as the end of the road. They in fact take the structural unity of the Prologue for granted. Literarily, the Prologue in its finished form is a masterpiece; the Evangelist is not a scissors and paste editor. He represents the genial theological faculty of the community, which integrated different layers of traditions into a seemingly single literary unit.

If the quest for the Source has become very subjective business, structural analysis is not an exception. The very chiastic structure is built upon the very subjective theological perspective of the respective researcher. Yet, structural analysis and chiastic proposals are helpful in that they show that the tradition of John the Baptist was not polemically and haphazardly interpolated into the Prologue, but carefully structured into the composition

---

35   In "John the Baptist and the Prologue," NTS 16 (1969/70): 357.
36   R. A. Culpepper, "The Pivot of John's Prologue," NTS 27 (1981): 1–31.

(though a few questions remain). VV. 12b–13 so commonly regarded as a secondary insertion could be the pivot of the entire Prologue, and draws our attention as to how the covenant community theme so much neglected in the discussions related to the Prologue could play a decisive role in its interpretation.

Through both the literary and structural analysis, few things stand out and are due urgent consideration:

a) Literary analysts consider vv. 6–8 and 15 as secondary insertions/interpolations. In the structural analysts' chiastic proposal, vv. 6–8 and v. 15 balance each other on either side of the chiastic and even if they were removed, the chiastic structure would remain unharmed, theologically too.

b) VV. 12b–13 is for literary analysts again a secondary insertion. In the chiastic proposal these verses either become pivots on which the whole Prologue rotates or they balance each other on either side of the chiastic structure. Again, even if these verses were pulled out from the structure, still that which can be interpreted does not differ much.

c) Both literary critics and structural analysts acknowledge that vv. 1–13 and vv. 14–18 have some fundamental stylistic thematic differences (that is that they belong to opposite sides in the chiastic proposal).

This analysis surely points towards the enigmatic problems in this seemingly one unit, the Prologue. If the above observations are right, then one wonders not about reconstructing a "pre-Johannine hymn," or turning a blind eye to the challenges of the Prologue, but to steer our research in order to find out how the Logos tradition, the theophany tradition/the Exodus-Sinai myth, traditions concerning John the Baptist and the theological motif on the covenant community merged together to form one block. What is the motif behind, and the motive of the Evangelist in composing the Prologue as it stands today?

There are several attempts to ascertain individual traditions, but what lacks today is a comprehensive approach to probe, clarify and reflect on how in the early Christian circles these different traditions interacted and integrated into one theological pattern. Did the context force early Christianity into such integration, or was it a gradual climax of a theological discussion within the community? Was it necessitated by the fact that a clarification of the community's theological standpoint was sought on different theological questions and issues raised by the contemporary context?

7.1.4 A Possible Solution

In the Johannine Prologue we may recognise a basic Logos tradition as preserved in vv. 1, 3–5, 9, 11, 14a, b, c, e, and 16. This tradition seems to be Logos-centric in nature. The Evangelist by adding vv. 2 and 14d gives the basic Logos tradition a theological twist and makes it theocentric in nature. Another addition at v. 10 drives in the universality of God's action by portraying Logos already active in the world. The 'elect people' is God's attempt to work in the world through a chosen instrument.

The addition of v. 18 with a primary task of bridging the Prologue and the Gospel meaningfully in fact adds the theological imagery—Theophany—to understand God's relationship with His world. V. 14 now becomes the pivot of two theological imageries: Logos and theophany giving new insights into, and adding new dimensions to the Johannine revelation Theology.

Now the next two block additions:
a) vv. 6–8 and 15—John the Baptist tradition
b) vv. 12, 13, 17—Covenantal theme probably added by a later ecclesiastical redactor, in the wake of the Synagogue crisis are significant and interesting, both in terms of content and in the way they are amalgamated into the Prologue structure.

To the Prologue which has two theological and mythological imageries to explain revelation: Logos vv. 1–5, 9–11, 14, 16 and Theophany vv. 14, 16, 18, the Evangelist by adding the John the Baptist tradition in vv. 6–8 places him in the heritage of God's human agents who interpreted God's relational acts in the world by way of witness. At v. 15 the same Baptist becomes the interpreter and witness for the incarnational theophany. The ecclesiastical redactor also brings in the covenantal theme to the fore once in relation to the Logos concept/imagery in vv. 12–13 and then in v. 17 in relation to theophany concept/imagery.

Thus the Johannine Prologue as it stands today interprets the Jesus event as an exegesis of God using the two mythological, theological imageries of Logos and Theophany. Along with God's witness John the Baptist, God's covenantal community bears witness to God's historical acts in the past and to the incarnational theophany.

7.2 The Logos—A Search for a Mythological Context

Going by the literature produced on the subject, the discussion over the probable background of the Johannine Logos concept is one that has aroused the maximum interest. In fact, the inquisitive genius in Bultmann stirred the discussions to new levels to include Gnostic probabilities with very elaborate research into the Old Testament and Hellenistic-Jewish backgrounds. With the publication of the Nag Hammadi Library, the discussion over the probable Gnostic influence is once again intensively reopened.

7.2.1 The Origin

In the Greek philosophical tradition, the Logos is first encountered as a cosmic divine potency in Heraclitus. The Logos is that which explains the continuity amid all the flux that is visible in the universe. Logos according to Heraclitus is the eternal 'principle' of order in the universe that makes the world a cosmos. For the Stoics, Logos was a concept that explains and controls the regularity of what happens in the cosmos. It is the mind of God—a pantheistic idea, which penetrates all things, guiding, controlling and directing individuals whose Logos is identical with the world of Logos and the cosmos itself.

7.2.2 Old Testament Wisdom Tradition?

Despite the total absence of the Logos concept in the Old Testament and in Jewish Theology, it has been argued that the Old Testament, Pseudepigrapha and related Jewish Wisdom tradition provide the key to the interpretation of the Johannine Logos (Sir 24; Job 28; Prov 8:21, 31; Bar 3:9–4:4; Wis 6:12–11:1; *1 Enoch* 42; also Ps 35 (36):10; 105 (106):24–25; 118 (119):89, 107; Isa 45:7; Ezek 43:7; *Jub.* 2:1).[37]

---

37 So argue J. D. G. Dunn, *Christology in the Making: A New Testament Inquiry into the Origins of the Doctrine of the Incarnation* (London: S.C.M. Press, 1980), 163–212; E. J. Epp, "Wisdom, Torah, Word: The Johannine Prologue and the Purpose of the Fourth Gospel," in *Current Issues in Biblical and Patristic Interpretation: Studies in Honor of Merrill C. Tenney* (ed. G. F. Hawthorne; Grand Rapids: Eerdmans, 1975), 128–46; E. D. Freed, "Theological Prelude to the Prologue of John's Gospel," *SJT* 32 (1979): 257–69; M. Theobald, *Im Anfang war das Wort: Textlinguistische Studie zum Johannesprolog* (SBS 106; Stuttgart: Katholisches Bibelwerk, 1983); B. Lindars, "Traditions Behind the Fourth Gospel," in *L'Évangile de Jean* (ed. M. de Jonge; BETL 44; Leuven: University Press, 1977), 107–24; T. E. Pollard, *Johannine Christology and the Early Church*, 9–15; M. Rissi, "Die Logos-Lieder im Prolog des vierten Evangeliums," *ThZ* 31 (1975): 321–36; J. Ashton, "The Transformation of Wisdom: A Study of the Prologue of John's Gospel," *NTS* 32 (1986): 161–86; J. Painter, "Christology

A contextual exegesis of the above cited passages reveals a few interesting insights:

a) The poetic nature of the writings should be taken seriously and the personification/first person ('I') usage should not be taken literally.
b) The language of seeming hypostasis, or a seemingly independent personality would certainly have had a different connotation in a monotheistic religion.
c) Seen from the worship context, these passages significantly remain very much theo-centric. There is no worship of Wisdom envisaged, but through a language of vivid personification, the Lord God is praised and worshipped.
d) The kaleidoscopic imagery found in these passages should not be pressed too hard into isolation from the context. By ascribing allegoric, picturesque language to Wisdom, the author uses it alongside Jewish monotheistic affirmation, and in order to reinforce Jewish monotheistic belief.
e) These passages if put in a chronological order show a development of thought and this is probably because of the influence of the religious cults and philosophies of the time, and this Wisdom speculation was at the same time a polemic both against polytheism and an explanation and reinforcement of monotheism using the contextual language and philosophy.
f) It is unlikely that Judaism saw Wisdom as independent from God, but it was used to meditate and proclaim the Creator, the Redeemer and the revealing God, who is transcendent but always with His people and His creation.
g) "Wisdom" could probably be called a 'mythological configuration' used to speak of the 'God-self.'

---

and the Fourth Gospel: A Study of the Prologue," *AusBR* 31 (1983): 45–62; idem, "Christology and the History of the Johannine Community in the Prologue of the Fourth Gospel," *NTS* 30 (1984): 460–74; C. H. Dodd, *Interpretation of the Fourth Gospel*, 274–77; P. Schoonenberg, "A Sapiential Reading of John's Prologue," *TD* 33 (1986): 403–21; M. Scott, *Sophia and the Johannine Jesus* (JSNTSup 71; Sheffield: JSOT Press, 1992); C. A. Evans, *Word and Glory: On the Exegetical and Theological Background of John's Prologue* (JSNTSup 89; Sheffield: JSOT Press, 1993), 77–99.

If these observations are true, then the Hellenistic-Jewish Wisdom speculation (along with the philological Logos speculation) does not really help us to find the exact meaning of 'Logos' in the Fourth Gospel, but provides the theological context and the speculative possibilities open to the Fourth Evangelist in order to react to and proclaim the Jesus event, which he thought to be the self-revelation of God for the redemption of His creation!

7.2.3 Philonic Exegesis of the Old Testament?

To bridge the undeniable gap between the Prologue and the Biblical material, scholars have always pointed towards the exegetical and speculative traditions. Philo of Alexandria used the 'Logos' concept in his Hellenistic exegesis of Jewish Biblical interpretation. According to Philo, with his notion of a Platonic conception of a world of ideas, the Logos bridges the gulf between God and creation (*Migr.* 35; *Spec. Leg.* 1.48, 323; 3.1–2; *Opif.* 16–44, esp. 18–19; 139; *Sac.* 80–83; *Ebr.* 132–133, 157; *Somn.* 1.102–114; 2.45; *Her.* 230–231; *Qu. Gen.* 1.4; *Qu. Ex.* 2.122). Though Philo envisages the Logos as a wholly independent being (*Her.* 2–4; *Immut.* 138; *Cher.* 36; *Sac.* 119; *Leg. All.* 1.21; *Conf.* 146; *Qu. Gen.* 2.62; *Qu. Ex.* 2.13, 94), he still remains within the Jewish monotheistic framework clarifying that he has still no thought of Logos with particular functions distinct from God. He claimed that the Logos is what is knowable of God (cf. *Abr.* 119–122; *Qu. Gen.* 4.2, 4; *Somn.* 1.239; *Ebr.* 44; *Praem.* 45; *Qu. Ex.* 2.67).[38]

If we observe the Philonic Logos in the totality of its thought, we envisage two clear directions that may help us to explain the context and philosophical atmosphere in which the Johannine Logos came into being:
a) The direction in which Hellenistic-Jewish Wisdom speculation and the Greek notion of Logos developed together to begin what we may call a

---

38 C. H. Dodd, *Interpretation of the Fourth Gospel*, 54–73; H. Kleinknecht, in *TDNT* 4:77–91; R. L. Duncan, "The Logos: From Sophocles to the Gospel of John," *Christian Scholars Review* 9 (1979): 121–30; T. H. Tobin, "The Prologue of John and Hellenistic Jewish Speculation: A Comparative Study," *CBQ* 52 (1990): 252–69; D. A. Hagner, "The Vision of God in Philo and John," *JETS* 14 (1971): 81–93; B. L. Mack, *Logos und Sophia: Untersuchungen zur Weisheitstheologie im hellenistischen Judentum* (SUNT 10; Göttingen: Vandenhoeck & Ruprecht, 1973); P. Borgen, "Philo of Alexandria," in *Jewish Writings of the Second Temple Period* (ed. M. E. Stone; CRINT 2.2; Assen: Van Gorcum, 1984), 233–82.

"new mythological configuration of language category" to explain the relationship between God and His creation.

b) It points towards a Hellenistic-Jewish exegetical context where Jewish monotheism tried to explain itself by using Greek philosophical ideas, signalling a theological contextualization in Diaspora Judaism.

7.2.4 Targumic Traditions?

It has been argued that the Johannine Prologue stands in the Targum tradition. The Targumic traditions of interpreting Gen 1:1, and the Targumic Memra may provide the analogue for interpreting the Johannine Logos. The external evidence that some of the interpretive traditions preserved in the Targum and Midrashim date back to the 1st century suggest that the New Testament and the Targum share essentially the same interpretive milieu.[39]

7.2.5 Gnosticism?

Bultmann's attempt to interpret the Johannine Logos in terms of the Gnostic Redeemer myth especially seen in the *Odes of Solomon* and some of the Mandaean writings have been considered speculative and no longer held plausible. The publication of Coptic Gnostic codices discovered at Nag Hammadi sparks new interests in the problem and has led a few to think that Bultmann's theory to the extent that, in order to interpret the Johannine

---

[39] P. Borgen, "Observations on the Targumic Character of the Prologue of John," *NTS* 16 (1969–70): 288–95; idem, "Logos was the True Light: Contributions to the Interpretation of the Prologue of John," *NovT* 14 (1972): 115–30; idem, "The Prologue of John—As Exposition of the Old Testament" and "John's Use of the Old Testament and the Problem of Sources and Traditions," both in *Philo, John and Paul: New Perspectives on Judaism and Early Christianity* (BJS 131; Atlanta: Scholars Press, 1987), 75–102 & 145–58, resp.; G. F. Moore, "Intermediaries in Jewish Theology," *HTR* 15 (1922): 41–85; C. T. R. Hayward, "The Holy Name of the God of Moses and the Prologue of St. John's Gospel," *NTS* 25 (1978–79): 16–32; idem, "Memra and Shekhina: A Short Note," *JJS* 31 (1980): 110–18; J. H. Charlesworth, "Jewish Roots of Christology: The Discovery of the Hypostatic Voice," *SJT* 39 (1986): 19–41; B. D. Chilton, "Recent and Prospective Discussion of Memra," in *From Ancient Israel to Modern Judaism: Intellect in Quest of Understanding* (ed. J. Neusner, et al.; Atlanta: Scholars Press, 1989), 119–37; G. Anderson, "The Interpretation of Genesis 1:1 in the Targums," *CBQ* 52 (1990): 21–29; C. A. Evans, *Word and Glory*, 114–45; O. Hofius, "Struktur und Gedankengang des Logos-Hymnus," *ZNW* 78 (1987): 1–25.

Logos we should search in Gnostic milieu must have been right, but had suffered from the lack of adequate documentation.[40] Today Adolf von Harnack's theory of viewing Gnosticism as an acute hellenization of Christianity, the assumption that Gnosticism was a Christian heresy looks naive, rather a fallacy after the study of the Nag Hammadi Library. One should today recognise Gnosticism as a phenomenon broader than Christianity, quite probably prior to Christian origins, implicitly pointing towards probable Jewish Gnosticism.[41] At the same time the Nag Hammadi codices have warned us against underevaluating Hellenistic elements in Gnosticism.[42]

---

40   R. Bultmann, "The History-of-Religions Background of the Prologue to the Gospel of John," in *The Interpretation of John* (ed. J. Ashton; Philadelphia: Fortress, 1986), 18–35, and his "Die Bedeutung der neuerschlossenen mandäischen und manichäischen Quellen für das Verständnis des Johannesevangeliums," ZNW 24 (1925): 100–46; H. A. Fischel, "Jewish Gnosticism in the Fourth Gospel," *JBL* 65 (1946): 157–74; D. Deeks, "The Prologue of St. John's Gospel," *BTB* 6 (1976): 62–78; J. D. G. Dunn, *Christology in the Making*, 239–44; C. Demke, "Der sogenannte Logoshymnus im johanneischen Prolog," *ZNW* 58 (1967): 45–68; E. Fascher, "Christologie und Gnosis im vierten Evangelium," *TLZ* 93 (1968): 721–30; K. Rudolph, "Problems of a History of the Development of Mandaean Religion," *HR* 8 (1969): 210–35; C. H. Talbert, "The Myth of a Descending-Ascending Redeemer in Mediterranean Antiquity," *NTS* 22 (1976): 418–40; R. McL. Wilson, "The Trimorphic Protennoia," in *Gnosis and Gnosticism* (ed. M. Krause; NHS 17; Leiden: E. J. Brill, 1977), 50–54; J. H. Charlesworth & R. A. Culpepper, "The Odes of Solomon and the Gospel of John," *CBQ* 35 (1973): 298–322; E. M. Yamauchi, "Jewish Gnosticism? The Prologue of John, Mandaean Parallels and the Trimorphic Protennoia," in *Studies in Gnosticism and Hellenistic Religions: Presented to Gilles Quispel on the Occasion of his 65th Birthday* (ed. R. B. van den Broek and M. J. Vermaseren; EPRO 91; Leiden: E. J. Brill, 1981), 467–97; C. A. Evans, "On the Prologue of John and the Trimorphic Protennoia," *NTS* 27 (1981): 395–401; H. Koester, "The History-of-Religions School, Gnosis and the Gospel of John," *ST* 40 (1986): 115–36; J. H. Charlesworth, "Qumran, John and the Odes of Solomon," in *John and Qumran* (ed. J. H. Charlesworth; London: Geoffrey Chapman Publishers, 1972), 107–36; G. Robinson, "The Trimorphic Protennoia and the Prologue of the Fourth Gospel," in *Gnosticism & the Early Christian World: In Honor of James M. Robinson* (ed. J. E. Goehring, et al.; Sonoma, Calif.: Polebridge Press, 1990), 37–50; J. M. Robinson, "Gnosticism and the New Testament," in *Gnosis: Festschrift für Hans Jonas* (ed. B. Aland; Göttingen: Vandenhoeck & Ruprecht, 1978), 125–43; idem, "Sethians and Johannine Thought, the Trimorphic Protennoia and the Prologue of the Gospel of John," in *The Rediscovery of Gnosticism.* Vol. 2: *Sethian Gnosticism* (ed. B. Layton; Leiden: E. J. Brill, 1981), 143–62.

41   J. M. Robinson has claimed that the Nag Hammadi codices which open up the prehistory of Jewish mystical traditions showing consistency though it seems that Gnostic trends have continued to carry on a clandestine existence within the

If one can speak of Jewish Gnosticism, Christian Gnosticism and non-Christian Gnosticism in and around the 1st and 2nd century A.D. then, the question as to whether there was an original Gnostic religion with its original pre-Christian myth is significantly incorrect. Rather, the question should be: Was there a Gnostic phenomenon pervading all the religious cults of the 1st century? To speak of a syncretistic phenomenon like Gnosticism, one needs to adopt the polyphyletic rather than the monophyletic model,[43] one should contend with the gnosticising interpretations of religious traditions and mythical materials: Jewish, pre-Christian, Christian and Pagan. They may have been committed to different cults and they developed different myths because each instance of the formation of such a myth is the result of the interpretation of quite different materials, traditions, writings and rituals. Therefore, one should speak of the "phenomenon of Gnosis" in the large number of religions with their distinct cults, rituals and traditions.[44]

---

context of normative Judaism (J. M. Robinson & R. Smith, *The Nag Hammadi Library in English*, 7–8). There have been serious objections to this by Yamauchi, Jonas, Drijvers and Gruenwald; see Yamauchi, "Jewish Gnosticism?" 488–89. Yet, Yamauchi at the end of his article says Yes to Jewish Gnosticism and only disputes its time as late 2nd or 3rd century A.D.; see "Jewish Gnosticism?," 497.

It has been observed that certain tractates in the Nag Hammadi Library were only secondarily christianised. *The Sophia of Jesus Christ* (NHC III, 4) is a christianised form of *Eugnostos the Blessed* (III, 3 and IV), yet they are placed alongside in the same codex. The other tractates appear to be entirely non-Christian (with at best superficial secondary Christianisation) but contain a revealer myth which possibly points to a first/second century Jewish Gnostic apocalyptic milieu, for example the *Apocalypse of Adam* (V, 5), the *Paraphrase of Shem* (VII, 1) and perhaps the *Gospel of the Egyptians* (III, 2 and IV, 2); C. A. Evans, "On the Prologue of John and the Trimorphic Protennoia," *NTS* 27 (1981): 395–96. See also J. M. Robinson, "The Coptic Gnostic Library Today," *NTS* 12 (1968): 372–80.

42 The *Plato's Republic—588A–589B* (VI, 5), the *Three Steles of Seth* (VII, 5), *Zostrianos* (VIII, 1), *Marsanes* (X, 1), *Allogenes* (XI, 3) do not show any confluences/influences of Christianity and are quite clearly non-Christian, though probably not pre-Christian.

43 It is not to suggest that the 2nd century's well-developed Gnosticism took its cosmological myth from Judaism, its anthropology from Hellenistic philosophy and astrology and its soteriology from Christianity.

44 H. Koester, "The History-of-Religions School, Gnosis and the Gospel of John," *ST* 40 (1986): 115–36, esp. 135–36.

If so, then Bultmann might have been wrong in pressing hard the pre-Christian "Redeemer myth" theory[45] as the explanatory category for the Johannine Logos. However, he has made a very valuable contribution in recognising the existent Gnostic tendency/phenomenon in the 1st century and thereby stirred up a provocative debate on the possible background of the Johannine Logos. To locate a tendency towards Gnosticism in the Fourth Gospel is not to be understood as the Fourth Evangelist gnosticising Christianity, but rather to emphasise that he made his proclamation contextual. It is the sensitivity of the Fourth Evangelist to his context, wherein he also sought to answer the question 'the Gnostics' grappled with, although he understood its significance differently. What is crucially significant then, is that while he adopted concepts that Gnostics also adopted, the "historical Jesus" in whom he saw God's revelation became the criterion in answering these questions. The contextual Theology in a Gnostic atmosphere should sound Gnostic if at all to make sense and be effective. Sounding a Gnostic tendency is far from being Gnostic.[46]

7.2.6 Analysis

Where then does our discussion as to the background of the Logos lead us?
a) If we think that in order to explain the Johannine Logos, the Old Testament concepts of Word of God, Wisdom and the Law are sufficient, then we comprehend only the Logos' one strand of meaning and the whole in parts. It really denotes a narrow parochialism. By limiting ourselves to 'biblical traditions,' we forget the very radicality of the Gospel, its capacity and its challenge to create traditions. In fact, the early church

---

45 R. Bultmann listed twenty-eight parallels in the Fourth Gospel and various Gnostic sources to argue for a Gnostic redeemer myth as the background of the Johannine Logos in "Die Bedeutung der neuerschlossenen mandäischen und manichäischen Quellen für das Verständnis des Johannesevangeliums," ZNW 24 (1925): 100–46. Also in his *Theology of the New Testament* (trans. K. Grobel; 2 vols.; New York: Charles Scribner's Sons, 1955), 1:166ff.; 2:12ff., and in *Das Evangelium des Johannes*, 38ff.
46 The Fourth Evangelist's "classic work" in later years was perhaps misunderstood to a great extent. The Gnostic interpreters only took a partial insight and misinterpreted him, while the church in trying to balance these misinterpreting tendencies, went to the other extreme in making 'the Fourth Evangelist' look conservative, as it attempted to reconcile him with the traditional teachings. Both approaches thereby rendered the Gospel congenial to those concerned, and his real geniality did not come to light, as it ought to have.

through its writings created a 'new Biblical tradition,' not against the existing (Jewish) Biblical tradition, but along with it, often giving radical contextual reinterpretations to both 'the Christ event' and the existing Jewish Biblical traditions. Therefore, the new Biblical traditions represent a continuation, an enrichment and a breakaway from the existing Biblical tradition after the radicality of Jesus himself.

b) If we consider that the Fourth Evangelist only took the Greek word 'Logos' from his context (to avoid a feminine Sophia), and filled its contents with the Old Testament and later the Jewish concept of Wisdom, we undermine the creative genius of the Evangelist, and are attempting to make a liberal-radical Fourth Evangelist a 'conservative' at heart with a radical look. The scholarly 'undecidedness' over the background of his Prologue could be seen as a very positive openness. It shows the Evangelist's (the community's) serious effort to make himself understood contextually. In the wake of parting from the Synagogue and losing its identity, the community's search for a 'new identity' was an existential necessity given the situation. If the Fourth Evangelist had only changed the old label, and presented the Gospel with an attractive, new look then he would have become a hypocrite! The Jewish concepts in a Greek language would have become a gross miscalculation and a cause for suspicion and a drastic failure at a time when 'asserting oneself' and fighting for self-identity were the need of the hour. (A new cover with old concepts does not necessarily create a new identity!)

c) The contentious question was: Who is Jesus in relation to God? Is the community ditheistic? The other christological titles such as Son of God, Son of Man and Messiah, instead of Logos would not have helped the Evangelist's cause. Instead of clarifying theological issues, they would have attracted more questions and would have meant nothing but would rather have offended. The other christological titles would not have had any appeal to the Gentiles at a time when they ought to have been convinced of the community's teaching. When the synagogue discredits the community of its identity, then the Gentiles are naturally the ones who help the community to get a new identity even though by passive recognition, since identity comes from being identified by others. Therefore, the Johannine community now portrays its reflection of the Jesus tradition in the form of a Gospel (body of the Gospel) and challenges its context through a Logos concept, which clarifies its Theology. The major themes—God, creation, revelation (God's relationship with His creation), liberation, covenantal children of God, prophetic traditions—are treated in the Prologue, thereby placing the community's proclamation of the Jesus tradition in perspective.

d) The challenge to formulate his Logos Theology arose out of the methodological precedence in the Jewish theological process to personify, hypostasise mythologically 'the Word of God,' 'Wisdom' and 'the Law' in order to speak of "God" and His relationship with His creation within the monotheistic framework. The Hellenistic speculative environment, the Hellenistic Jewish exegetical tradition, the Jewish readiness to explain itself by Hellenistic ideals provided the Evangelist the impetus to use his creativity in the inculturation of the Jesus tradition.

e) The 'Logos' which knits various themes of the Prologue together proves to be a new "reflective mythological category" which is not a living myth, but rather a form of Theology appropriating mythical language, material and patterns from different myths and using these patterns, motifs and configurations for its own theological concerns. Such a Theology is not interested in reproducing the myth itself or the mythical materials as they stand, but rather in taking up and adopting the various mythical elements to its own theoretical concerns and theological goal.[47]

f) 'Logos' provides for the author of the Fourth Gospel a contextual, reflective mythological category (the expression in story form of a deeply held religious conviction concerning God–human relation) that transcends racial and religious boundaries. 'Logos' was understood in his context by everyone in their own different ways. The different understandings proved to be the key to begin a creative dialogue with his context and explain the Jesus tradition through this dialogue. Thus, the Johannine 'Logos' denotes a theological process of demythologising and remythologising in a contextual dialogue. It speaks of the necessity of "creating and recreating new myths or new reflective mythological categories" in order to make the Gospel effective, contextual and meaningful.

---

47 E. Schuessler Fiorenza uses this definition for the term "reflective mythology" in her "Wisdom, Mythology and Christological Hymns of the New Testament," in *Aspects of Wisdom in Judaism and Early Christianity* (ed. R. L. Wilken; Notre Dame: Notre Dame Press, 1975), 17–41, esp. 29.

7.3 Exegesis

7.3.1 Verses 1–2: The Logos and God

Verse 1: Ἐν ἀρχῇ ἦν ὁ λόγος

Since the Septuagint begins with the expression Ἐν ἀρχῇ rendering בְּרֵאשִׁית, it seems likely that the Evangelist alludes to Gen 1:1. In Genesis the creation of the universe is contemporaneous with, or marks, 'the beginning.' But ἐν ἀρχῇ in the Evangelist's opinion means in effect before creation! In the beginning is a designation more qualitative than temporal. In Prov 8:23 (LXX) ἐν ἀρχῇ clearly means 'before time was and before God made the earth.' Therefore, ἐν ἀρχῇ is not said of an act done but of a state of existing in supra/pre-temporality. It speaks not of a beginning, but of something without a beginning. Here eternity is implied. Thus ἐν ἀρχῇ itself evidently presupposes God Himself—who else could be spoken of as supra/pre-temporal?

This pre-temporality is further strengthened by the use of ἦν. The imperfect tense here denotes continuous existence. ἦν is to be carefully distinguished from ἔστι which would have stressed His timelessness at the expense of any emphasis on His manifestation historically (cf. 1:14) and from ἐγένετο which would have implied either that He was a created being (He came into existence) or that by the time of writing He had ceased to exist.[48]

But the Fourth Evangelist, instead of saying 'God was in the beginning' formulates it as Ἐν ἀρχῇ ἦν ὁ λόγος, then the Logos shares what God Himself is! Logos is pre-temporal. Haenchen says that the Prologue does not begin with God and His creation, but with the Logos and is therefore offensive.[49] I do not think so. If we substitute λόγος with σοφία or דבר, then Logos becomes a technique to speak of God without offending Jewish monotheism! For the Greeks λόγος is the eternal principle—"God."[50]

---

48 M. J. Harris, *Jesus as God*, 54.
49 E. Haenchen, *John*, 1:109.
50 Only when one equates Logos with the man Jesus of Nazareth, does it become offensive. Does the Fourth Evangelist draw such a drastic equation? The only peep of Jesus in the Prologue is carefully formulated by Ἰησοῦ Χριστοῦ . . . (v. 17). The Evangelist in my opinion has clarity in his language. The man from Nazareth is addressed as Ἰησοῦς. Ἰησοῦς Χριστός is used only twice in the Fourth Gospel, in v. 17 here and in John 17:3 (and only Χριστός in 20:31) undoubtedly as a

Verse 1b—καὶ ὁ λόγος ἦν πρὸς τὸν θεόν,

It is argued that ὁ θεός automatically designates the Father (John 1:18), but one should be very careful in making such a generalisation.[51] The Fourth Evangelist uses the Father–Son metaphor to explain the relationship of the man Jesus of Nazareth with God. The Father is not a person; it is a title denoting the nature of God. ὁ θεός in the Prologue means God—the universal appeal of this word should be noted.

There has been considerable dispute over the meaning of πρός:

a) Following the term ὁ λόγος the expression ἦν πρός could possibly mean 'spoke to.' Since a word is spoken to a person one might expect an answer to the question 'to whom was the word spoken?' (πρός + accusative ἦν πρὸς τὸν θεόν) rather than 'where was the word?' (παρά + dative ἦν παρὰ τῷ θεῷ). Thus the translation: *The Word spoke to God.*[52] It is argued that this translation shows the dynamic nature of God and the Word. Thus

---

christological title. Does the Fourth Evangelist make a distinction between the historical Jesus and the Christ of faith?

In my opinion "Logos" or "Christ" was defined in, but not confined to Jesus of Nazareth. I do not believe that the Evangelist ever said that the Logos/Christ are completely and exhaustively found in Jesus of Nazareth so that Jesus–Logos–Christ are simply interchangeable. True, in John 1:14 the pre-existent, impersonal Logos becomes personified and personalised in Jesus. Until v. 14 we are still dealing with Jewish wisdom sort of mythology where Logos is not a personal being but a mythological personification. Only v. 14 marks the transition from an impersonal personification to the actual historical person (see J. D. G. Dunn, *Christology in the Making*, 242–43). Jesus then is not the Logos *per se*, he is the Logos become flesh. We may quite properly say that the personified Logos (the mythological personification) first became person in the incarnation. In Jesus we see λόγος ἄσαρκος becoming λόγος ἔνσαρκος. Then, the man Jesus is the key to understand Logos. Thus when the Evangelist says, in the beginning was the Logos, does it mean that Jesus is pre-existent? Does the Evangelist say divine Jesus was in heaven before he came down to earth? These are very crucial questions to the exegesis of the Prologue, especially in vv. 9–13 where αὐτόν is traditionally argued as: only those who believe in the name of "the historical Jesus" have the authority to become the children of God. In my opinion an interpretive clarity and tension between two levels of narrative presentation, the historical Jesus on the one level, and the belief that in the historical Jesus we encounter the Logos, Christ, the Son on the other, should be maintained for a reasonably good exegesis of the Fourth Gospel.

51 This generalisation stems from the Trinitarian understanding that one should by all means restrain from at this point.
52 C. Masson quoted in "πρός," in *NIDNT* 3:1204–1205.

"in the beginning" here is not an unknown, unknowable God or some nameless being enveloped in silence. It denotes that the God who speaks in time, in creation and in redemption is the eternal Word. But one can be scarcely justified in filling out the meaning of ἦν πρός on the basis of an accompanying substantive (ὁ λόγος) that functions as a proper noun.[53] Moreover it is reasonable to think that 1:1b also answers the question as to what the relationship of ὁ λόγος was to God in the beginning.

b) Edwin Abbott understands the phrase πρὸς τὸν θεόν as 'having regard to God,' 'looking towards God,' 'devoted to God.'[54] He however suggests that the phrase has a secondary meaning of 'in converse with God.' Though all these meanings are feasible the combination of εἶναι+ πρός renders at least the first three proposals of Abbott inappropriate.[55]

c) It is suggested that the preposition πρός does not imply any movement or/and action, and therefore is to be viewed as equivalent to παρά denoting position, meaning 'with.' The New Testament parallels where πρός + accusative often follows the verb εἶναι denote not linear motion but punctilinear rest.[56] Bultmann says εἶναι πρός + accusative answers the question 'where?'[57] Burney suggests that the translator of an Aramaic original finding לְ rendered it πρός rather than παρά under the influence of the more common use of this Aramaic preposition to express 'motion towards.'[58] But in v. 14 of the Prologue the Evangelist uses παρά to express the proximity of one person to another or the nearness of the Son to the Father.[59]

---

53 M. J. Harris, *Jesus as God*, 56.
54 Following classical Greek phrase πρὸς ταῦτα 'having regard to these things' and ζῆν πρός τινα 'to live in absolute devotion to anyone,' see his *Johannine Grammar*, § 2366, cf. §§ 2308, 2365.
55 See M. J. Harris, op. cit., 56.
56 Mark 6:3 = Matt 13:56; Matt 9:19 = Luke 9:41; Mark 14:49; 1 Cor 16:6–7; 2 Cor 5:8; 11:9; Gal 1:18; 4:18, 20; Phil 1:26; 1 Thess 3:4; 2 Thess 2:5; 3:10; Phil 1:3; Heb 4:13; 1 John 1:2.
57 R. Bultmann, *Das Evangelium des Johannes*, 16; G. R. Beasley-Murray, *John*, 10; BDF, § 239 (1), and C. F. D. Moule, *An Idiom Book of New Testament Greek*, 52–53.
58 C. F. Burney, *The Aramaic Approach to the Fourth Gospel*, 29.
59 Is the Evangelist speaking here about two divine persons? Does he envisage two persons in the godhead and their communion or oneness by using πρός? These are not at all the issues to be discussed here. The whole discussion about this is forced into the Johannine Prologue after the Niceno-Constantinopolitan formulations of the Christian faith. It is not to say that the Niceno-Constantinopolitan creed is a

d) It is suggested that the basic sense of πρός + accusative is not just movement, but relation or direction.[60] It does not merely just describe spatial juxtaposition or being beside, but maintaining communion and intercourse with.[61] Thus it is an active relationship and a dynamic fellowship that involves peculiar intimacy.[62] Therefore the translation should probably be: the Logos was in dynamic relationship with God.

Thus πρὸς τὸν θεόν excludes all speculations about an archetypal generation in the divine sphere. It excludes every conception of an unfolding of the deity or of an emanation or every idea of the archetypal deity becoming objective to itself.[63] At the same time it speaks of a God of relationship as against the wholly other, the principle or the absolute being. The Fourth Evangelist here broadens the Jewish Wisdom myth that speaks of God's relationship only after "the creation." It is here that I see a major difference in theological emphasis. It is not because God created that He enters into a relationship with His creation but, because He is in Himself "a relation." He creates — what He is in Himself is shown in His act of creation!

Verse 1c: καὶ θεὸς ἦν ὁ λόγος

Joseph Sanders has proposed that a full stop be placed after καὶ θεὸς ἦν and that the second verse should begin at ὁ λόγος οὗτος (this word. . .).[64] No grammatical objections may be raised against this proposal, but the resulting meaning does not differ substantially from the sense the words convey with the traditional punctuation. I follow the tradition for a change. An anarthrous state of θεός poses a tricky problem.[65] Grammatically an anarthrous θεός may indicate that,

---

wrong formulation but only to say that for him it was not an issue. His 'Word'– 'Son' should not be literally understood. Johannine symbolic/anthropological/linguistic techniques should be carefully recognised.

60 Cf. *BDF*, § 239; W. Bauer et al., *A Greek-English Lexicon*, §§ III: 4b and III:7. Cf. 2 John 1:2 — the idea is "face to face with God"; E. L. Miller, "The Logos was God," *EvQ* 53 (1981): 75.
61 Cf. Mark 6:3; 1 John 1:2; 2:1; see also J. H. Moulton & G. Milligan, *The Vocabulary of the Greek Testament*, 4.
62 D. A. Carson, *The Gospel According to John* (Leicester: InterVarsity Press, 1991), 116, and M. Zerwick & J. Smith, *Biblical Greek*, §§ 102–103.
63 R. Bultmann, *Das Evangelium des Johannes*, 17.
64 J. N. Sanders, *A Commentary on the Gospel According to St. John*, 69–70.
65 See, M. J. Harris, *Jesus as God*, 56ff.

a) θεός is indefinite: The non-occurrence of the article may point to the non-particularity and the indefiniteness of the concept. Then the translation of καὶ θεὸς ἦν ὁ λόγος should be: 'the Word was a God.' But the theological context of Jewish monotheism makes this rendering impossible. In the Johannine context θεός could apply only to the supreme being, not to an inferior divine being or emanation, as simply generic θεός.

b) θεός is predicative given the general interchangeability of ὁ θεός and θεός in the Fourth Gospel.[66] It would not be impossible from the point of view of grammar alone to translate 1:1c as 'God was the Word' especially since the word order with θεός pre-placed could indicate the subject.[67] But what is grammatically admissible is contextually inadmissible. If θεός were taken as subject and as equivalent to ὁ θεός the clause would contradict what precedes. But as the text stands all real antiquity is removed. That θεός and not ὁ λόγος is predicative is shown by the anarthrous state of the noun.[68] But is it that the sole or even the main reason for the need to use the anarthrous state of θεός is in order to distinguish the predicate from subject, when the articular ὁ λόγος and the context clearly pointed to the subject thereby isolating the predicate?

c) It was given an adjectival significance. It is suggested that here the anarthrous θεός gets the significance of an adjective and the translation could be 'the word was deity' or 'the word was divine/God like.'[69] But a noun without an article does not virtually convert itself into an adjective; especially θεός which is a very common adjective corresponding to the substantive readily available to the Fourth Evangelist. The anarthrous noun cannot be deemed adjectival.

---

66 The term θεός appears in some form 83 times. Of these 63 are articular and 20 anarthrous. Still, it is highly improbable that the Fourth Evangelist intends any consistent distinction to be drawn between θεός and ὁ θεός. In prepositional phrases θεός occurs 22 times, 12 times with and 10 times without an article. When it is used with the preposition παρά (+ genitive) and ἐκ θεοῦ it sometimes has the article (παρά, 5:44; 6:46; 8:40; 16:26; ἐκ, 7:17; 8:42, 47) and sometimes lacks it (παρά, 1:6; 9:16, 33; ἐκ, 1:13).
67 The Luther translation is of course: "und Gott war das Wort!"
68 R. Bultmann, *Das Evangelium des Johannes*, 17, and J. N. Sanders, *A Commentary on the Gospel According to St. John*, 70.
69 M. Zerwick & J. Smith, *Biblical Greek*, § 285, E. Haenchen, *John*, 1:110, and D. A. Fennema, *Jesus and God according to John: An Analysis of the Fourth Gospel's Father/Son Christology*, 135 n. 58.

d) That it is qualitative in meaning. Moulton in his most frequently quoted dicta asserts that for exegesis there are few of the finer points of Greek which need more constant attention than this omission of the article, when the writer would wish to lay stress on the quality or character of the object.[70] Applied to John 1:1c this principle suggests that being anarthrous θεός describes the nature of the Logos. It attributes the Godhead to the Logos so that the Logos is as truly as He with whom he exists in the closest union of being and life.[71] Therefore the translation (rather paraphrase) should be "what God was the Word also was."[72]

The best possible translation 'and the Word was God' does not really convey that which the Fourth Evangelist intended through the anarthrous θεός. Does the absence of the article avoid a complete equation of λόγος and θεός? Does he wish to say λόγος was θεός while still maintaining that the Logos does not exhaust θεός? It is possible for the following reasons:

a) The Johannine ἐν ἀρχῇ, the pre-existence of Logos, is grounded on ὁ λόγος ἦν πρὸς τὸν θεόν, and θεὸς ἦν ὁ λόγος that Logos being in dynamic relationship with God and Logos was God.[73]

b) If one sums up the discussion on the Logos concept in a phrase probably one may say: 'Logos is the relational face of God.' V. 2ff. in the Prologue confirm this notion.[74]

c) John 1:1b—the dynamic relationship envisages a relative distinction between θεός and λόγος. 1:1c speaks of a commonality between θεός and λόγος still maintaining the relative distinction (note καί joins 1:1b & 1c).

---

70 J. H. Moulton, *A Grammar of New Testament Greek*. Vol. 1: *Prolegomena*, 83.
71 R. Schnackenburg, *The Gospel According to St. John*, 1:234–35, and A. Wikenhauser, *Das Evangelium nach Johannes*, 41.
72 C. H. Dodd, "New Testament Translation Problems II," *BT* 28 (1977): 101–16. Also W. Loader, *The Christology of the Fourth Gospel: Structure and Issues* (BBET 23; Frankfurt am Main: Peter Lang, 1989), 161; R. H. Fuller, *The Foundations of New Testament Christology* (New York: Charles Scribner's Sons, 1965), 33—a personal reality sharing the being of God. NEB, REB, TEV also have translations!
73 Cf. O. Hofius, "Struktur und Gedankengang des Logos-Hymnus," *ZNW* 78 (1987): 16. "Der Stichos v. 1c erklärt zunächst, daß das ἐν ἀρχῇ-sein und das präexistente Bei-Gott-sein des Logos in seinem Gott-sein gründen."
74 R. Bultmann is right in saying, ". . . zwischen jenen Sätzen auch, daß keine einfache Identifikation beabsichtigt ist. Ein paradoxer Sachverhalt soll Ausdruck finden, der mit dem Offenbarungsgedanken gegebene und im folgenden entwickelte Sachverhalt nämlich, daß im Offenbarer wirklich Gott begegnet, und daß Gott doch nicht direkt, sondern nur im Offenbarer begegnet . . ." (*Das Evangelium des Johannes*, 17).

Therefore the very carefully formulated first verse of the Prologue speaks of Logos as the dynamic relational face of God that still does not exhaust ὁ θεός!

d) As we have seen in our discussion on the Logos concept, there was a place for theological personification/hypostatisation within Jewish monotheism. In order to speak of God and His relation with His creation, Judaism speaks of the Word of God, Wisdom and the Law as personified and as though personalised. The Hellenistic speculative environment, the Hellenistic Jewish exegetical tradition and the Jewish readiness to explain itself by Hellenistic ideas gave the Evangelist the impetus to use his creativity. In my opinion the Evangelist here attempts such a 'mythological personification' when he speaks of καὶ θεὸς ἦν ὁ λόγος to maintain a clear balance between the mystery of God and the revelation of God! Of course our idea of God is determined by the idea of revelation, to speak of God means as Bultmann says, to speak of His revelation: however, ὁ θεός is beyond the idea of revelation.

Verse 2: οὗτος ἦν ἐν ἀρχῇ πρὸς τὸν θεόν.

Since v. 2 repeats v. 1, it can be perceived as a purposeful correction of the Evangelist with a distinct theological motif in editing the hymn. Bultmann is probably correct when he insists that the repetition is far from otiose.[75] It guards against the Prologue being incorrectly interpreted Logos-centrically and thus polytheistically.

Logos was with God (πρὸς τὸν θεόν) and that the Logos was God could have led any Hellenistic community to think of the communion of two divine persons polytheistically. But by repeating with οὗτος what he said in v. 1, the Evangelist protects and guards against such misconceptions! In v. 2 οὗτος is stressed—This one of whom it has been just said that he was θεός, ἐν ἀρχῇ πρὸς τὸν θεόν, this brings us to the equation θεός was with ὁ θεός from the beginning. The idea of God in the Prologue is determined at the

---

[75] R. Bultmann, *Das Evangelium des Johannes*, 17; E. Käsemann, "Aufbau und Anliegen des Johanneischen Prologs"; R. Schnackenburg, *The Gospel according to St. John*, 1:227, and H. Thyen, "Aus der Literatur zum Johannesevangelium," *TRu* 39 (1974): 58.

outset by the idea of Logos, the relational face of God, that is the revelation of God is to speak of God.[76]

The repetition of ἐν ἀρχῇ is to emphasise that the Logos is not an act of revelation limited to the temporal order but is pre-existent. But how can one speak of the relational face of God—the revelation while there was yet no creation? Bultmann probably gives the right interpretation: "Welt und Zeit sind nicht aus ihnen selbst zu verstehen, aber aus dem in der Offenbarung redenden Gott... wie es zu Welt und Zeit kam; ihr Dasein ward durch göttliche Tat Ereignis."[77] God's revelation gives substance, meaning and significance to creation!

7.3.2 Verses 3–5: The Logos and the World

Verse 3: πάντα δι' αὐτοῦ ἐγένετο, καὶ χωρὶς αὐτοῦ ἐγένετο οὐδὲ ἕν. ὃ γέγονεν[78]

The preposition διά leaves open several interpretive possibilities. Logos could have been charged as helper by God and equipped with his creative power, a demiurge or the cause, the prototype according to which the actual

---

76 The relational face of God, the revelation of God stands beside/with/in dynamic relationship with God, is analogous to the שׁם of God in the Old Testament tradition. In Exod 23:21; Isa 30:27; Ps 8:2, 10; 20:2 etc. the name of God stands alongside God as a separate power without in fact being anything separate. Rather it describes God in so far as His acts reveal Himself.
77 R. Bultmann, *Das Evangelium des Johannes*, 18–19.
78 Should the word ὃ γέγονεν be joined with what goes before or with what follows? The oldest manusripts P[66], P[75], ℵ* A B have no punctuation here. The scholarly discussions take note of the Arian controversy as the possible explanation for the confusion prevailing on the issue. It is argued that ante-Nicene writers took ὃ γέγονεν with what follows. However, Orthodox writers preferred to take ὃ γέγονεν with the preceding sentence. Therefore, it is suggested that ὃ γέγονεν be taken with what follows, which could also take care of the rhythmical balance of the opening verses in the Prologue. Despite valiant attempts by commentators such as Bultmann, Brown, Aland, Miller to bring out the sense of taking ὃ γέγονεν with what follows the passage remains intolerably awkward and opaque.
  The Fourth Evangelist has a fondness for beginning a sentence or clause with ἐν and a demonstrative pronoun (John 13:35; 15:8; 16:26; cf. 1 John 2:3, 4, 5; 3:10, 16, 19, 24; 4:2). Metzger rightly points out that one of the difficulties that stand in the way of ranging the clause with ἐν αὐτῷ ζωὴ ἦν is that the perfect tense of γέγονεν would require ἐστίν instead of ἦν (B. M. Metzger, *Textual Commentary on the Greek New Testament*, 193) which has been seen in the copyists' attempt to change the tense of the verb from imperfect to present in ℵ D, VL, Syr[c] Cop (sa fay); the presence of the second ἦν in the clause ἡ ζωὴ ἦν τὸ φῶς seems to require the first.

world was created in its multiplicity or finally the creator Himself through whose action all things came to be.[79]

In the Old Testament Wisdom is described as sharing in the creation as spectator and master workman (Prov 8:27–30; Wis 9:9), as counsellor (Wis 8:4), as artisan (Wis 8:6) and even as creator (Wis 7:12, cf. Prov 3:19). In the creation story God creates the world by His Word, which is emphatically confessed in the Old Testament poetic literature (Ps 33:6, 9; 14:7, 15–18; 148:5; Isa 40:26; 48:3; Wis 9:1). Philo uses the preposition διά for the activity of Logos as demiurge and understands the Logos as the instrumental cause used by God to fashion the world.[80] The Logos is in Philo's thinking the pre-existent prototype of the visible world and the instrument in the creation of the world.[81]

Thus, Old Testament and Hellenistic Judaism each had its doctrine of the universal agent of creation. The Fourth Evangelist probably remoulds here the early Christian understanding of the relationship between God and Christ to creation. Paul's formula in 1 Cor 8:6 makes a distinction between God the Father from whom are all things (ἐξ οὗ τὰ πάντα) and the one Lord Jesus Christ through whom all things are and we exist (δι' οὗ τὰ πάντα καὶ ἡμεῖς δι' αὐτοῦ). Col 1:16 uses the prepositions διά and εἰς referring to Christ as cause and consummation of all things, while ἐκ is reserved for God the Father, the origin of all. Through the use of different prepositions the early church attempted to explain the different relationships in which the world stands with God and with Christ. But it is not always consistent; as Rom 11:36 uses them together in the praise of God (ἐξ αὐτοῦ καὶ δι' αὐτοῦ καὶ εἰς αὐτὸν τὰ πάντα), Heb 1:2 also speaks of God creating all things through (δι' οὗ) His Son.

The Evangelist's confession "all things were made through him" here is an attempt to see a role for the pre-existing Logos in the creation activity while still safeguarding the truth that God is Creator. Logos is not just an intermediary between God and the world, he is not just the creative power of God or the form according to which God created the world. Here the Evangelist through the use of διά not only emphatically pronounces that the

---

79 R. Schnackenburg, *The Gospel According to St. John*, 1:236.
80 Philo, *Spec. Leg.* 1.81; *Leg. All.* 3.96; cf. *Opif.* 20, 24, 139; *Sacr.* 83; *Somn.* 1.75.
81 Philo, *Cher.* 125ff. God is the first cause of the world (ὑφ' οὗ) the matter from which it was produced (ἐξ ὧν) are the four elements; the instrument by which they were formed (δι' οὗ) is the Logos. See *Sacr.* 8; *Immut.* 57; *Fug.* 95; *Somn.* 1.241–242.

creative activity of Logos is the activity of God through him but also affirms that God Himself stands behind the creation activity. At the same time Logos is not envisaged just as an instrument but also as the one who is co-operating with God.

Πάντα is carefully used instead of κόσμος to denote the universal significance of the Logos and to denote not just the humanity but that "all" that has been created owes its existence to him; nothing is outside his activity. πάντα also arouses a feeling for the fullness of that which has its origin in God.[82] πάντα is counterbalanced with οὐδὲ ἕν, 'not even one' is stronger than οὐδέν, 'nothing' (P[66] οὐδέν).

Ἐγένετο describes the idea of creation. It rejects the notion of emanation, the concept of an original duality of light and darkness according to which the world was formed by a collision of both powers, and the Greek view of creation as a correlation of form and matter, an arrangement of a chaotic stuff, with Logos as principle. ἐγένετο does not speculate how "all things" came to be, but just states "all things came through him," which is probably the Johannine way of confessing what we today call creation *ex nihilo*.[83] The aorist ἐγένετο and the perfect γέγονεν describe the act of creation and the state of creation. ἐγένετο regards creation in its totality as one act, and the perfect γέγονεν conveys the thought of the continuing existence of created things. The Logos that gave existence to creation continues to be the ground of existence for all created ones.

Verse 4—ἐν αὐτῷ ζωὴ ἦν, καὶ ἡ ζωὴ ἦν τὸ φῶς τῶν ἀνθρώπων·

Logos was not just the agent of God in creation, but also in its continuance. The Logos as the basis for life sustains creation. Here ζωή is used as spiritual life in contrast to natural life. ζωή is the very meaning of existence, it denotes the dynamic vitality basis and quality of existence. ζωή is always spoken of as God's precious, divine gift to the creation lying beyond creation's reach. It is only if God gives, that the creation can receive and this gift of God to the creation is seen as 'in' the Logos. In the Old Testament, Wisdom is portrayed as leading humankind to life (Prov 4:13; 8:32–35; Sir 4:12; Bar 4:1; cf. Wis 6:18–19). The Fourth Evangelist here presents "Logos" as the One in whom God endowed Creation with life.

---

82 R. Bultmann, *Das Evangelium des Johannes*, 19.
83 Cf. John 17:24; R. Bultmann, op. cit., 20.

Commentators draw our attention to John 5:26 where it is affirmed that "as the Father has life in Himself, so He has granted the Son to have life in himself." In the Fourth Gospel one should be very careful in equating "the Word" with "the Son," but one can conveniently say that the relationship of God and the Word in the Prologue and the Father–Son relationship in the rest of the Gospel are parallel and described in identical words. Both the Word and the Son share the self-existing life of God.[84]

And this *life* in Logos is affirmed as the light. The light often comes to mean a divine power, the essential nature of divinity is seen as φῶς. Naturally the sphere of the divine, which is an experience of an undisturbed life of happiness and joy, is conceived as the sphere of light (Ps 104:2; Isa 60:19–20, also cf. Exod 3:6). In the Old Testament and especially in Judaism law is praised as the light (Ps 119:105; Isa 26:9; Bar 4:2 LXX; Prov 6:23; Wis 18:4). The Rabbis viewed the law as the light of the world, a lamp for Israel but also a light-giver for the individual.[85]

"The Light" is also used to describe salvation itself in its ultimate sense, light is taken as the symbol of God's final eschatological gift — the eschatological ζωή.[86] Light makes it possible to see, makes everything perceptible, offers freedom. It illuminates, helps to understand, helps in orienting oneself. Thus it symbolises a kind of existence where one feels secure. In formulating the 'life' of Logos as the light of men, the Fourth Gospel speaks of the Logos as that which offers a secure, meaningful, dynamic, illumined and enlightened state of existence. Then life in Logos is in the first place the life-creating force that calls creation into existence, but also that which carries within itself the necessity and the possibility of illumined existence.

Verse 5—καὶ τὸ φῶς ἐν τῇ σκοτίᾳ φαίνει, καὶ ἡ σκοτία αὐτὸ οὐ κατέλαβεν.

The imperfect tense that had been used till now changes into the present φαίνει. What does this present tense suggest? Does it suggest a timeless truth? φαίνει probably is a point in transition from the eternity of God to the

---

84 Later on, the Johannine Jesus claims that he is the life (John 11:25; 14:6). Interestingly both Wisdom and Torah are commonly associated with life and light in Jewish sources. The Fourth Evangelist ties them in with Logos and Christ.
85 Cf. H. L. Strack & P. Billerbeck, *Kommentar zum Neuen Testament aus Talmud und Midrasch*, 2:357ff.
86 Isa 9:1; 60:1–3, 19–20; Zech 14:17; Dan 13:3; Ps 27:1. For Rabbinic literature see, H. L. Strack & P. Billerbeck, op. cit, 2:248.

history that followed creation. The light shone in the primal darkness at creation and continues to shine. It portrays light in continuous action. It embraces past, history and present. True, it reminds one of the creation story and the story of the fall, but echoes the faithfulness of God who continues to present to His creation the life and the light, the creative, dynamic, illuminating existence in the Logos. It may be the Evangelist's way of remembering the salvation history as he speaks in the following verse of the witness to the light—John the Baptist.

The verse emphatically portrays the tension between the light and darkness. Opposition of darkness and light were used in fully dualistic systems deriving ultimately from Zoroastrianism, to describe two opposing and equally real principles of good and evil. But Jewish monotheism was strong enough to resist the idea of ultimate dualism just as the Jewish linear view of history resisted the associated notion of an endless cycle of conflicts. The monotheistic belief strongly emphasised the affirmation that God is in ultimate control and will triumph in the end. The Qumran community cultivated a moral dualism, as if the cosmic dualism is reflected in the inner life of the individuals who were torn between the competing claims of light and darkness.[87]

In Jewish literature the *Testaments of the Twelve Patriarchs* often speak of the contrast of light and darkness, but they do not go beyond ethical exhortations and can hardly think in terms of cosmic principles.[88] There are some striking parallels in the Texts from Qumran where there is a sort of cosmic dualism,[89] but the conflict takes place on the moral level. In so far as the elect sin, their misdeeds belong likewise to the darkness, but God sends them help and light.[90] But there are fundamental differences from the Fourth Gospel. For the Qumran community there is no conversion of the children of darkness who are to be annihilated in the eschatological war (1QM). It is only the spiritual trend, the dualistic but theocentric thought, the hope of

---

87 B. Lindars, *The Gospel of John*, 87.
88 *T. Levi* 19:1: "Chose therefore, for yourselves either the light or darkness, either the law of the Lord or the works of Beliar"; *T. Benj.* 5:3: "Where there is reverence for good works and light in mind, even the darkness fleeth away from him"; *T. Gad* 5:7: "For true repentance after godly sort (destroyeth ignorance and) driveth away the darkness and enlighteneth the eyes, giveth knowledge to the soul and leadeth the mind to salvation." Cf. also *T. Levi* 18:3–4 and 4:3.
89 For a detailed discussion see, R. Schnackenburg, *The Gospel according to St. John*, 1:248ff.
90 1QS III, 20–21, 25; IV, 2–12; VII, 25; IX, 26; XI, 3–4, 5–6 and 9–10.

divine light in the darkness of this world and in the thankful acceptance of God's gracious revelation and help that brings the texts of Qumran to some extent into line with the thought of the Fourth Evangelist.[91]

In the Fourth Gospel the contrast between the light and darkness which appears in John 3:19; 8:12; 12:35, 46 (cf. 9:4; 11:9–10; 1 John 1:6–7; 2:8, 9–11) is metaphorical. They present the divine realm of light as fundamentally opposed to darkness. It has been a way of looking into the dynamic movement of salvation history and a dualism that calls for decision. It does not judge or condemn, instead Johannine dualism is a way of presenting possibilities, making it plain which possibility should be chosen for a meaningful, dynamic, creative existence. Seen from this perspective σκοτία is not an autonomous existence alongside φῶς. It is neither substance nor the sheer power of fate, it is pseudo-existence. It is the result of being against the light, not accepting the possibility of a meaningful, creative, illuminative existence. It is the negation and misuse of the "freedom" given through the gift of life and light. Darkness is all that robs, negates and deprives the possibility of a meaningful existence.

The verb καταλαμβάνω is difficult to translate. It may mean 'to master,' 'to absorb,' 'to overwhelm' or 'to overcome.' It also denotes intellectual comprehension, grasping/embracing with mind and will. The use of the aorist κατέλαβεν is very difficult to interpret. Is it the complexive aorist that denotes an action that is regarded as complete and whole,[92] or the gnomic and futuristic aorist denoting an act that is valid for all time and still to a certain extent futuristic or a timeless event?[93] "The darkness has not overcome it" may in the context be a word of exhortation/assurance/hope, or it may denote a particular event. If the dualism in the Fourth Gospel is an anamnesis of various stages of the history of salvation describing how God over and over again offers the possibility of new beginnings, it does not denote a particular event as some scholars indicate the fall after creation or the moment of incarnation. Καταλαμβάνω is a word of assurance to humanity, it is a way of reminding oneself of the fact that God's offer of a meaningful existence of life and light is still valid and a challenge to overcome the darkness.

On the other hand it speaks of the Evangelist's reflection on the life of Jesus of Nazareth. It is a confession that in the life of Jesus he has seen the

---

91 R. Schnackenburg, *The Gospel according to St. John*, 1:249.
92 So R. E. Brown, *The Gospel According to John*, 1:171ff.
93 So *BDF*, § 333.

light shining and the passion and resurrection as the failure of the powers to overcome the light. It may also reflect the precarious, yet victorious context of the Johannine community. The conviction and the certainty of the Evangelist points towards the courage with which the Johannine community withstood the Synagogue's attack on it. Thus 'the light shines in the darkness and the darkness overcame it not' holds together the historical experience of God's victorious acts both in the past, present and the future and bears witness to it.

7.3.3 Verses 6–8: Witness to and Interpreter of God's Acts in the World — God's Human Instrument 'the Man' John

These verses (along with v. 15) are considered to be later additions.[94] The additions are considered as polemic and a rebuttal against a group of Baptists who were claiming that John, not Jesus was the light or as a systematic correction of a Baptist Christology by the Johannine community in favour of its own christological safeguard to preserve the uniqueness of Jesus. These are surely possibilities. It is true that the Fourth Evangelist actually annihilates the possible claims made for John, but one should note that the Evangelist achieves this without depreciating the man Jesus. It is a marvellous piece of writing where the Evangelist debases and exalts John throughout the Gospel.

Superficially v. 6 seems to be a crude intrusion of a 'man' John into the supra-historical realm of vv. 1–5, thereby carelessly dropping John into eternity. The construction ἐγένετο ἄνθρωπος reminds us of a normal opening of a historical narrative. ἐγένετο implies an appearance at a given moment of history (cf. Judg 13:2, 19:1; 1 Sam 1:1; Mark 1:4; Luke 1:5). Anthropology here may not be alien intrusion. After affirming faith in a cosmic God who created the cosmos and remains in close relationship with the created cosmos, the Evangelist invites our attention to a certain ἄνθρωπος. It affirms that God always maintained relationship with His cosmos through 'human agents.' ἄνθρωπος Ἰωάννης thus becomes a symbol of God's activity in the past and the present through His "human instruments." Ἀπεσταλμένος παρὰ θεοῦ emphasises God's initiative and suggests that the activity of the person sent can be understood only in terms of God's purposes. ἀποστέλλειν

---

94 R. Bultmann, *Das Evangelium des Johannes*, 29; R. E. Brown, *The Gospel According to John*, 1:28; R. Schnackenburg, *The Gospel According to St. John*, 1:249ff.

denotes a specific mission, and the Evangelist affirms that the activity of John should be seen inside the realm of God.

John is not 'chosen or called' as in the Old Testament prophetic tradition (cf. Exod 3:10ff.; 1 Sam 12:8; Isa 6:8; Jer 14:14; 19:14; 23:21; Ezek 2:4; 13:6; Zech 2:13, 15; 6:15; Mal 4:5) but has been 'sent.' He is God's messenger; his authenticity and authority lie in his being "sent." He has a God-given role to play. God is the programmer! John's mission is to be a witness to the light, to the liberating acts of God. For the Fourth Evangelist God not only acts, but also helps His people to identify and recognise His acts through the "witnesses." Even in the Theology of Israel the prophets were God's instruments who called people's attention to God's doing mighty acts. Here μαρτυρία is a matter of providing perspectives to understand the phenomena of happenings and interpreting them for the people. A witness is the one who identifies God's signs and interprets them, making them plain to the people—a prophetic task indeed.

The aim of John's witness in the Fourth Evangelist's view is that 'all might believe through him.' John invites people's attention to the liberative possibilities of human existence. He helps them to identify the light, supernatural acts of God breaking into history, he interprets for the people happenings around them so that people may identify them as God's acts and respond! John thus actually leads them to God! The δι' αὐτοῦ in v. 7 and the whole of v. 8, emphatically stress John's instrumentality, and warn us against making God's instruments gods or ascribing God's acts to His instruments.

Thus seen from this theological perspective vv. 6–8 do not sound polemic against John the Baptist or his movement. Instead we see a 'theological inclusiveness' that affirms John as an authentic, authoritative human witness to the acts of God! In placing John before the incarnation of Logos in the Prologue, the Evangelist makes 'the man John' a theological symbol for such witness who called people to God!

7.3.4 Verses 9–13: God's A-historical Presence and Covenant with the World through the Logos

Verse 9: Ἦν τὸ φῶς τὸ ἀληθινόν, ὃ φωτίζει πάντα ἄνθρωπον, ἐρχόμενον εἰς τὸν κόσμον.

There is disagreement about the ἐρχόμενον at the end of the verse. Is it joined with ἦν as a periphrastic conjugation, or is it accusative masculine agreeing

with ἄνθρωπον? The statement is ambiguous. Schnackenburg suggests that this remark is a rather awkward and incorrect addition to the hymn,[95] the "coming into the world" as it can relate to the light and to every person. The verse may be translated as:
a) the true light that gives light to every man was coming into the world,
b) *or*, this was the true light that gives light to every man who comes into the world.

Does ἐρχόμενον envisage a distinct action on the part of the Logos distinct from creation? Does it prepare the way to the incarnation—the historical coming of the Logos? The Logos who is the basis of existence for the whole creation "coming into the world" is an absurd idea. The verb that the Evangelist uses for incarnation is γίνομαι, not ἔρχομαι. The Fourth Evangelist conveys incarnation as not the coming, but the historical becoming of the eternal Logos. Therefore we understand the phrase ἐρχόμενον as masculine attached to ἄνθρωπον and prefer the second translation which envisages the universal function of the Logos.

The attribute ἀληθινός indicates that only the Logos gives genuineness, fullness and reality, the qualitative uniqueness in its incomparable excellence, the proper and the authentic existence to the human beings only. Only in the "illumination/enlightenment" does each person get an opportunity to "see what he/she is" and get the knowledge and choice of good conduct to live as "he/she should be" according to the will of the Creator. Thus φωτίζειν which indicates the universal salvific mission of the Logos, introduces the "covenant" theme in the Prologue, gives it a larger basis and perspective. Instead of seeing God's act through the chosen ones in the world (an important issue in Jewish Theology), the Fourth Gospel begins with God's direct salvific act in the world.

Verse 10: ἐν τῷ κόσμῳ ἦν, καὶ ὁ κόσμος δι' αὐτοῦ ἐγένετο, καὶ ὁ κόσμος αὐτὸν οὐκ ἔγνω.

Does this verse speak of the historical existence of Logos? Is it to be interpreted as the activity of God in the Old Testament period as Israel spoke of the presence of the wisdom of God in the world and in Israel? Or does it make logic as Schnackenburg sees it—v. 10 as standing for the time of Adam and Moses, v. 11 for the Sinai covenant and v. 12 as the faithful remnant of

---

95 R. Schnackenburg, *The Gospel According to St. John*, 1:255.

Israel?⁹⁶ It seems to me that the Fourth Evangelist who in his pluralistic context already ventured into picking up a Hellenistic concept—Logos—to speak of the relation of God to creation now creates a new horizon where he sees God's acts in the past, not only in the Old Testament community but also outside it.

"He was in the world" indicates the a-historical presence of God through Logos in the world. Logos was so close to humankind that they could reach out to him for their salvation. κόσμος here means humankind that made itself independent of God as it refused to see itself in relation to God as Creator.⁹⁷ But as Logos dwells in the world it is also the object of God's love (cf. John 3:16) in spite of its rebellious nature. "The world knew him not" speaks of the world's ignorance. Here too the Johannine tradition probably remoulds the Wisdom traditions of Israel. *1 En.* 42:2: "Wisdom came to make her dwelling place among the children of men and found no dwelling place," Bar 3:20–21: "They did not know the way of wisdom or understand her paths and their children did not reach her, they strayed far away from her way" (cf. Bar 3:31, 37; Prov 1:20–30; Wis 9:9–18). "Not knowing" implies missing the opportunity and offer of God to have a meaningful existence. "To know" speaks of personal recognition that not only implies intellectual apprehension of the revelation but also personal response. The Hebrew connotation brings in the notion of relationship. "The world knew him not" speaks of the world's failure to relate to its Creator, its rejection of the offer of an illumined/enlightened existence.⁹⁸ It is a disastrous act of one's own chosen false self-understanding and this is the basis of moral dualism in the Fourth Gospel. When humankind chose false existence and clung to it as though it was the existence, the dualism of light and darkness, truth and falsehood came into play.⁹⁹ The world missed the opportunity of a creative/dynamic relationship with the Creator by not recognising the presence of Logos in the world.

Verse 11: εἰς τὰ ἴδια ἦλθεν, καὶ οἱ ἴδιοι αὐτὸν οὐ παρέλαβον.

Does v. 11 represent some kind of advance upon the thought of v. 10? Or do we just have a case of Johannine repetition? For Bultmann v. 11 is exactly

---

96 R. Schnackenburg, *The Gospel According to St. John*, 1:255ff.
97 R. Bultmann, *Das Evangelium des Johannes*, 34.
98 B. Lindars, *The Gospel According to John*, 90.
99 R. Bultmann, op. cit., 33–34.

parallel to v. 10 and each verse explains the other—εἰς τὰ ἴδια ἦλθεν corresponds to ἐν τῷ κόσμῳ ἦν as οἱ ἴδιοι αὐτὸν οὐ παρέλαβον corresponds to ὁ κόσμος αὐτὸν οὐκ ἔγνω.[100] But in Brown's opinion, v. 11 particularises God's activities in the world to His acts in the midst of Israel.[101] To settle the contention over the relationship of vv. 10 and 11 one needs to first settle the meaning of the two words τὰ ἴδια and οἱ ἴδιοι (cf. John 16:32; 19:27; Acts 21:6).

Τὰ ἴδια can mean either home/homeland or can refer to possessions, property, substance, characteristics (cf. John 8:44; 15:19; Luke 18:28; 1 Thess 4:11). In the Septuagint, τὰ ἴδια occurs substantively fifteen times mostly carrying the meaning home/homeland. More significant is the fact that εἰς τὰ ἴδια never means anything but "to one's home" (Esd 5:10; 6:12; 3 Macc 6:27, 37; 7:8). In the Gnostic writings τὰ ἴδια has a technical sense of conveying the characteristics/property of the heavenly kingdom to which τὰ ἴδια is that which shares in a common nature.[102]

What then is the meaning of εἰς τὰ ἴδια ἦλθεν? Should one interpret Logos' own possession in terms of the world as a whole, or limited to Israel as a unique possession? In the Prologue, though the Evangelist speaks about the relationship of God to His creation, though he sounds universal, one should not lose sight of the fact that the Evangelist here tries to give his community legitimacy over against the Israel which proclaimed itself the chosen/covenant people of God. In the context of the synagogue excommunication, the Johannine community now tries to remould its Theology in such a way that it sounds universal as against Jewish particularism with regard to itself. Vv. 1–11 are surely intended as a prelude to vv. 12–18 where the polemic of the Johannine community against Judaism to install itself as the chosen community may rest on sound theological grounds. Therefore the universality in v. 10 is in v. 11 very deliberately narrowed down to curtail the universal significance of Judaism. τὰ ἴδια/οἱ ἴδιοι do not therefore refer to the Cosmos and to the wider world community, but to Israel and her people. The translation may therefore, be "He came to his home and his people did not receive him."

---

100 R. Bultmann, *Das Evangelium des Johannes*, 56; S. Schulz, *Das Evangelium nach Johannes*, 24–45.
101 R. E. Brown, *The Gospel according to John*, 1:30.
102 *Acts Thom.* 124; *Mandaean Literature* 114:4–5, cited by R. Bultmann, *Das Evangelium des Johannes*, 34–35, n. 7.

Subsequently οἱ ἴδιοι refers to Israel as God's chosen people.¹⁰³ Probably the Fourth Evangelist uses again the Wisdom tradition to point to God's acts in the history of Israel and its unfaithfulness. The acts of God are seen and interpreted as His coming to it—the Evangelist interprets it as the coming of Logos—His relational/revelational face. Thus the Evangelist draws two important stages:
a) the universal acts in Logos not recognised by the world and
b) God's acts through His chosen people for the universe, not recognised by the very people He chose to be His own.

Verse 12a: ὅσοι δὲ ἔλαβον αὐτόν, ἔδωκεν αὐτοῖς ἐξουσίαν

Here λαμβάνω etymologically means to grasp, to seize, to welcome (active), to receive (passive).¹⁰⁴ Here ἔλαβον seems to imply an active sense as it forms an antithetical parallel to οὐ παρέλαβον of v. 11. Thus v. 12a refers to the active, definite acceptance of God's offer of a meaningful, dynamic existence in Logos. To those who took the definite action of accepting God's offer of life and light in Logos, He gave the power. Two aorists ἔλαβον and ἔδωκεν mark the simultaneous character of the reception of Logos and the giving of power.

The term ἐξουσία admits various interpretations—freedom or right to do something, power of might, authority. Etymologically ἐξουσία comes from ἔξεστιν and implies a freedom to dispose of something and the ability to do it.¹⁰⁵ It implies a meaning in contradistinction to δύναμις, ἰσχύς and κράτος which all indicate an in-dwelling objective physical or spiritual power.¹⁰⁶ In the Fourth Gospel ἐξουσία is always a power that is given by God (5:27; 10:18; 17:2; 19:10–11 Father and 1:12) and always accompanied by the verb δίδωμι. The emphasis seems to be on the aspect of ability, not one's own but *given* by God.

---

103 Commentators point to the Septuagint use of λαός περιούσιος in reference to Israel as God's people in Exod 19:5; Deut 7:6; 14:2; 26:18; cf. Ps 135:4; Mal 3:17, see also J. W. Pryor, "Jesus and Israel in the Fourth Gospel—John 1:11," *NovT* 32 (1990): 217–18, who argues that this verse refers to the rejection of Jesus by his own people where οἱ ἴδιοι must mean: Jesus' own people according to the flesh, the people of his homeland. But does v. 11 refer to the historic ministry of Jesus?
104 G. Delling, in *TDNT* 4:5.
105 W. Bauer et al., *A Greek-English Lexicon*, 227.
106 W. Foerster, in *TDNT* 2:566.

The combination of ἐξουσία and δίδωμι in v. 12b implies that to become children of God is not a right, on account of one's racial birth, a claim therefore to call God as Father without responding to the offer of life and light through the Logos (cf. 8:41). It is only through the gracious gift of God that one has the ability to become the child of God. It is in reinforcing the basics of the Jewish covenantal Theology that God enters into a covenant with His people not because they are able, but because they are unable on their own. The Fourth Evangelist excludes the racial claim of Israel as the chosen people. He does it exactly by keeping "Logos" as his subject and reinterprets the whole history of Israel as decisions for or against the offer of new existence in Logos. Only those who responded to the acts of God, not all Israel are the children of God and conversely those outside Israel's fold who responded positively could also be recognised as children of God.

Verse 12b: τέκνα θεοῦ γενέσθαι,

γενέσθαι is significant in the understanding of the specific character of the divine sonship affirmed here. γίνομαι in its original, ordinary sense means "to come into being," "to become" or "to originate."[107] It is used of persons and things which change their nature to indicate their entering into a new condition.[108] In the Fourth Gospel γίνομαι seems to keep the original meaning specially when used with a noun or adjective as a complement of the predicate.[109] Here in v. 12 the aorist infinitive which may often be similar to future indicative is used. The Fourth Evangelist here uses γενέσθαι in contradistinction to εἶναι (cf. 5:6; 8:58; 9:27). These make the intention of the Fourth Evangelist clear: the becoming of children of God is not a static event that takes place once and for all at a definite moment in history, but as something that gradually takes places and remains dynamic, moving towards final perfection. τέκνα θεοῦ is a designation and identity of those who accept the Logos of God.[110] The Fourth Evangelist actually modifies the

---

107 J. H. Moulton & G. Milligan, *The Vocabulary of the Greek Testament*, 126.
108 W. Bauer, et al., *A Greek-English Lexicon*, 158.
109 Cf. John 1:12, 14; 2:9; 4:14; 5:4, 6, 9, 14; 9:22, 27, 39; 10:16; 12:36–42; 15:8; 16:20 — out of fifty occurrences of γίνομαι in the Fourth Gospel, seventeen are with such complements of nouns or adjectives and all of them signify a change from one condition to another. See M. Vellanickal, *The Divine Sonship of Christians in the Johannine Writings* (AnBib 72; Rome: Biblical Institute Press, 1977), 139–40.

election/obligation concept that makes the idea of the children of God in Israel a universal possibility that is to be accepted and authorised. This can help the community in achieving two important purposes:
a) While it can claim the designation, it can as well include those who were not from the Jewish fold and this could increase the validity of the community's universal appeal in a sound theological basis.
b) Israel's failures not only that of rejecting Jesus as Christ but its very failures, in its history in being unfaithful to God result in the disqualification of Israel as the race bearing the designation "children of God." It questions the very understanding of racial security as the chosen ones and calls their attention to emphasise the "unqualified grace of God and unqualified faithfulness of the people as major criteria for being children of God."

Verse 12c—τοῖς πιστεύουσιν εἰς τὸ ὄνομα αὐτοῦ,

πιστεύειν is characteristically a Johannine word.[111] The Johannine preference for the verb rather than the noun πίστις is to be noticed.[112] The participial expression ὁ πιστεύων is almost proper to the Fourth Gospel.[113] The use of the verb form shows that the Fourth Evangelist expresses faith not as a static disposition but as an active commitment[114] and the predilection for participial expression shows that the active commitment is a continual life of commitment.[115]

τοῖς πιστεύουσιν εἰς τὸ ὄνομα αὐτοῦ means not only those who believe in the person of, considering the name for the person in a Semitic way, but also accepting fully what that name expresses and adhering to this person as formally signified by the name. Here the question is: in whose name? If in the context our interpretation of v. 11 is correct, then ὄνομα should stand for God's Logos—God who encounters and relates to His creation through His Logos. Then the clauses v. 12a ὅσοι δὲ ἔλαβον αὐτόν and v. 12c τοῖς

---

110 For a very detailed background study of this concept see, R. A. Culpepper, "The Pivot of John's Prologue," NTS 27 (1981): 17–31, and M. Vellanickal, op. cit., 9–103.
111 Out of the 241 occurrences in the New Testament, 107 are in the Johannine writings, whereas in the Synoptics it is found only 34 times.
112 πίστις does not occur in the Gospel.
113 The only exception we find in the New Testament is in Acts 13:39 while the Fourth Evangelist uses it 23 times.
114 R. E. Brown, *The Gospel According to John*, 1:512.
115 See M. Vellanickal, *The Divine Sonship of Christians in the Johannine Writings*, 141.

πιστεύουσιν εἰς τὸ ὄνομα αὐτοῦ are mutually related and explain each other. While v. 12a expresses an active acceptance or welcome of the Logos based on a new existence, v. 12c expresses an active, dynamic, life-long self-commitment to him who gives this existence.

It is however also probable that the early Christian baptismal formula "believing in his name" is a later ecclesiastical redaction along with v. 17 against the synagogue which binds its identity to the Law to proclaim that it is not the law, but "belief in his name" that decides the identity of God's community.

Verse 13: οἳ οὐκ ἐξ αἱμάτων οὐδὲ ἐκ θελήματος σαρκὸς οὐδὲ ἐκ θελήματος ἀνδρὸς ἀλλ' ἐκ θεοῦ ἐγεννήθησαν.

Here the Fourth Evangelist emphatically states that to become children of God is a work wholly of God's operation. The phrases contrast birth from God with human begetting and reiterate the inability of human beings to reproduce it. The plural αἵματα, the will of the flesh, will of a male, all denote human initiatives in begetting. The possibility of v. 13 relating to the birth of Jesus, and suggesting the virgin birth should be questioned.[116] The redactor might have cleverly and deliberately employed the language suggestive of the virgin birth when describing the new birth of the believers, which is patterned on and determined by the miracle of incarnation.[117] The community's massive polemic against synagogue's understanding of its racial chosenness and soteriological exclusivism as in v. 12c should be noticed.

7.3.5 Verses 14–18: The Incarnation and the Exegesis of God— a Historical Theophany

Verse 14a: Καὶ ὁ λόγος σὰρξ ἐγένετο

This clause at first glance scarcely allows a wide variety of interpretation: it simply asserts that the Word which was God and with God, became human.

---

[116] All Greek manuscripts, virtually all of the early versions and most of the Patristic witnesses read in v. 13 οἳ οὐκ ἐξ αἱμάτων οὐδὲ ἐκ θελήματος σαρκὸς οὐδὲ ἐκ θελήματος ἀνδρὸς ἀλλ' ἐκ θεοῦ ἐγεννήθησαν as agreeing with the τοῖς πιστεύουσιν εἰς τὸ ὄνομα αὐτοῦ of v. 12. The Old Latin manuscript b reads singular but the external evidence for plural is overwhelming and most commentators adopt it without hesitation.

[117] E. C. Hoskyns, *The Fourth Gospel*, 164–65.

The issue here is about the Fourth Evangelist's understanding of incarnation. Recent exegetical discussion has sharpened the forms of the question casting a critical eye on the exact connotations of the word σάρξ and resultant implication for interpreting ὁ λόγος σὰρξ ἐγένετο. What was σάρξ intended to mean? Does the use of σάρξ emphasise the assertion that God had revealed Himself in transitory/fleshy sphere? Does the σάρξ demand an incarnation that entitles Jesus' unquestioned humanity? That is to say does it represent an antidocetic insistence on Jesus' corporeality against a denial of its reality? Or is it merely a way of asserting that the Word entered into this world yet only in the guise of σάρξ, simply disguised as a human being?

Indeed it is startling to see the use of σάρξ especially after its occurrence in the previous verse where it is one of the three elements set over against God. The very context emphatically suggests that σάρξ is not used in the usual dualistic sense as that which is against the divine God.[118] It is not easy to define the exact meaning of σάρξ in this context. According to Schweizer, σάρξ here means more or less the same as ἄνθρωπος.[119] Then why did the Evangelist not use ἄνθρωπος? It is therefore clear that σάρξ intends to state more than the fact that Logos became man. In contrast to σῶμα (which had other connotations in contemporary religious thought) which indicated only the body σάρξ designates the human nature in totality.[120] σάρξ denotes a typical earthly existence with all its frailty, brokenness, defectiveness, transitoriness and helplessness,[121] that which is visible and audible within

---

118 Logos that which is with God, was God, cannot now suddenly become against God! The logic of the Logos hymn does not permit such an interpretation. Moreover one of the distinctive features of the Fourth Gospel is the employment of a single word in more than one sense such as κόσμος which is used of humankind, as both the object of God's love (3:16) and as the world system in revolt against Him (14:30). The double use of 'lifted up' (12:32) is more subtle. R. E. Brown in his *The Gospel According to John*, 1:30–32, states that the stress on flesh in v. 14a differs from the attitude taken towards flesh in v. 13. G. Richter, "Die Fleischwerdung des Logos im Johannesevangelium," *NovT* 13 (1971): 94ff., and H. Thyen, "Aus der Literatur zum Johannesevangelium," *TRu* 39 (1974): 58ff., think that vv. 13 and 14 were not written by the same person and find a definite antidocetic polemic in v. 14 which suggests that σάρξ has a different connotation than it does in v. 13.
119 See E. Schweizer, "σάρξ," in *TDNT* 7:140.
120 R. E. Brown, op. cit., 13, suggests the 'whole man' indicating almost the same concept/idea.
121 See R. Bultmann, *Das Evangelium des Johannes*, 39.

the limitations of space and time. It points to creatureliness, weakness and susceptibility to suffering and to the created world.[122]

The word σάρξ seems to have been associated with the incarnation from the earliest days. Rom 8:3 speaks of God sending His own Son in the likeness of sinful flesh. 1 Tim 3:16 contrasts manifestation in the flesh with vindication in the spirit. Does the mention of σάρξ represent a kenotic element comparable to what we find in the hymn of Phil 2:7: ἀλλὰ ἑαυτὸν ἐκένωσεν μορφὴν δούλου λαβών, ἐν ὁμοιώματι ἀνθρώπων γενόμενος καὶ σχήματι εὑρεθεὶς ὡς ἄνθρωπος? One should note that there are *christological* assertions! These do not speak of God's Kenosis, instead the Kenosis of Christ or the Son of God or pre-existent Jesus! In my opinion, the Fourth Evangelist in his Prologue goes one step further. He risks and stretches his theological language to speak of a 'phenomenon of God's Kenosis.'

If our articulation and the meaning of σάρξ is plausible, then it marked a contemporary revolution in the understanding of God. It spoke of God risking Himself to be a human! It added a new dimension to the contemporary understanding of revelation. The very element σάρξ which was seen as at odds with God,[123] as sinful or sin-creating power,[124] now not only becomes the vehicle/instrument for the relational/revelatory face of God/Logos to present itself, but itself becomes the relational/revelatory face of God! No more should one speak of Logos in transcendental/supra-historical language; God risked Himself (the Fourth Evangelist risked!) so that one could speak of his relational/revelatory Logos in visible, tangible, audible, time-bound and historical terms.

To the Greeks, who revered the Logos as formulating the orderliness of the world and aspired to be joined with God in His universe,[125] the Fourth Evangelist suggests, that the ultimate encounter with the 'Logos' could only be when the Logos became flesh. The Prologue does not say that the Logos entered into flesh or abided in flesh, but that the Logos became flesh. Therefore, instead of supplying the liberation from the material world that the Greek mind yearned for, the Logos was now inextricably bound to human history.

---

122 See E. Käsemann's "Aufbau und Anliegen des johanneischen Prologs," 171.
123 The Old Testament understanding, see Jer 17:5; Ps 78:39; Job 10:41.
124 For the Pauline understanding of σάρξ see, E. Schweizer, "σάρξ," in *TDNT* 7:139.
125 Hindus also have a similar "Advaitha" philosophy.

Verse 14b: καὶ ἐσκήνωσεν ἐν ἡμῖν,

The verb σκηνόω will remind Hellenistic Jews and the other Septuagint readers of the σκηνή, the tabernacle, where God met with Israel before the temple was built (cf. Exod 25:8ff. and 33:7). The Tabernacle/Tent became a site of God's localised presence on earth for pilgrim Israel, in their wilderness wandering on their way to the promised land.[126] It may also allude to Sir 24:8, where Wisdom says "the one who created me assigned a place for my tent (σκηνή)" and he said "Make your dwelling (κατασκηνόω) in Jacob." Thus Wisdom finds a home with the chosen people (also cf. Sir 24:10). Does the Evangelist draw parallels between the Word and Wisdom, to say that the Word is acting in the manner of Wisdom?

The prophets prophesied the eschatological tent-pitching of God among His people: Joel 4:17, "You will know that I am the Lord your God who makes His dwelling (κατασκηνόω) in Zion." Ezekiel had prophesied to the exiles deprived of the Tabernacle and the comfort of God's presence: "They will live under the shelter of my dwelling, I shall be their God and they will be My people" (Ezek 37:7) and "God will make His dwelling in the midst of His people forever" (Ezek 43:7). At the time of the return from the Babylonian exile Zechariah proclaims, "Sing and rejoice, O daughter of Zion, for look, I come and will make my dwelling (κατασκηνῶν) in your midst" (Zech 9:9).

σκηνόω might also have been chosen for its similarity to שכינה of post-Biblical Mishnaic times. It is a circumlocution for God, an ultimate visible manifestation of the presence of God among men. Thus Logos pitting his Tabernacle/Tent among us may mean the eschatological fulfilment of God's promise to be present among His people. It must have been a very special kind of comfort for a community that was seeking a new identity, and was deprived of Temple/Synagogue worship (cf. John 4:24). It interprets the Christ event as that localising God's very presence among men—the first statement of realised Eschatology in the Fourth Gospel. God is no more just a transcendental reality; He resides as one among His pilgrim people. As the

---

126 The language in vv. 14–18 is seen as evocative of the revelation of God's glory in Exodus by the Red Sea, on Mount Sinai and at the Tent of Meeting in Israel's camp. See A. T. Hanson, "John 1:14–18 and Exodus 34," *NTS* 23 (1977): 90–101; H. Mowvley, "John 1:14–18 in the Light of Exodus 33:7–34:35," *ExpTim* 95 (1983–84): 135–37. Also see J. C. Meagher, "John 1:14 and the New Temple," *JBL* 8 (1969): 57–68.

Tabernacle gave a cultic identity to wandering Israel, the enfleshed Logos gives identity to the community.

Verse 14c: καὶ ἐθεασάμεθα τὴν δόξαν αὐτοῦ,

The "we" group which forms the subject of ἐθεασάμεθα primarily designates those belonging to the community. Whether they were eyewitnesses could not be deduced from the text.[127] "Seeing" here should not be narrowed down to the seeing signs performed by Jesus (cf. 2:11; 11:4, 40). It means more than just the vision of the eye. It includes comprehension and knowing. It is a faith affirmation. It is the ethos that the community shares; it reflects a community's consciousness of its spirituality and experience.

"Glory" originally implied the idea of weight or mass, determined an object's importance, the respect it inspired. The real value and worth were estimated by its weight. The basis for glory could be found in riches/possessions (Gen 33:2), power (Isa 8:7; 16:14), that which always implied brilliance, dazing splendour (Isa 8:7). The glory of a king rested on his wealth, power and grandeur (1 Chr 29:28). The glory of God is in His revelation of resplendent majesty, effulgence of light, magnificence, His power, His radiant holiness, the dynamism of His being, in His awe-inspiring interventious judgements and signs (Num 14:22; Isa 6:1–2), in His acts of liberation (Exod 16:7; Isa 35:1–4; 44:23) and redemption. Often the imagery is derived from the triumph of the victor or from the power of natural phenomena like storm, cloud and light (e.g. Exod 15:1, 6, 11, 21; Ps 24:8) God manifests His glory in saving Israel from suffering (Isa 52:13, cf. 4:2). It is in participating in the suffering of His people, in order to help them to overcome it that God's glory is revealed.

In the Fourth Gospel the statement following, "beholding His glory" tends to create all sorts of associations of power and splendour. The impression seems to be confirmed by the Evangelist's comment at the end of the first sign: "this is the first of the signs Jesus did in Cana and manifested His glory." Käsemann in fact has strongly argued that in spite of the fleshy

---

127 Contra H. N. Ridderbos, "The Structure and Scope of the Prologue to the Gospel of John," *NovT* 8 (1966): 180–201; R. Schnackenburg, *The Gospel According to St. John*, 1:270; O. Cullmann, *Early Christian Worship*, 42. However, E. Haenchen, "Probleme des johanneischen Prologs," *ZTK* 60 (1963): 323, interprets "we" as a designation of the whole Christian community.

appearance the splendour and power of God was not completely veiled. Jesus in fact was God walking on earth.[128]

In the Fourth Gospel the glory of Jesus is his death on the cross, his being lifted up (cf. John 7:39; 12:16, 23, 28, 31ff.; 13:31; 17:1, 5), and the Evangelist explains this through Jesus' prophetic action of washing the disciples' feet (13:1ff.)—the nature of glorification in terms of love and service (13:12–17).[129] Glory is expressed in terms of selfless love/unmerited generosity. They are not to be understood as acts of power, but as acts of love, as an expression of God's generosity (cf. 3:16).[130] It should be noted that the allegory of death and fruit-bearing (seed dying to live and multiply) emphatically expresses the power of such acts of love. Therefore Glory in the Fourth Evangelist's understanding is God in love transcending even His transcendence. It is His real presence in time and space! It is God's coming in love and condescension. In glory God is, and can be met.

Verse 14d—δόξαν ὡς μονογενοῦς παρὰ πατρός,

The quest for the meaning and an effective translation of μονογενής has engaged Johannine scholars in a lively and fierce debate. Disagreements seem to be the result of such a pursuit, for on this unique Johannine christological word rests the theological exegesis of the whole gospel. For a text-based interpretation, a thorough word study is necessary to explore and unlock the Theology that lies embedded, rather than allow the exegesis to be dictated by later theological developments.

Etymologically the element μόνος is a simple adjective defined by the lexicons as 'alone,' 'unique,' 'solitary,' 'bereft of' or 'without.' And the second component γένος is a primarily verbal substantive with the stem γεν- denoting 'offspring,' 'race,' 'kind,' 'genus,' 'stock,' 'species,' 'family.' But they combine to form a descriptive, determinative adjective which literally means one of a kind, only, unique.[131] μονογενής thus expresses basically

---

128 E. Käsemann, *The Testament of Jesus*, 8ff.
129 M. Pamment, "The Meaning of *Doxa* in the Fourth Gospel," ZNW 74 (1983): 13.
130 *Ibid.*
131 H. G. Liddell & R. Scott, *A Greek English Lexicon*, s.v. μονογενής; W. Bauer, et al., *A Greek-English Lexicon*, 529: "In the Johannine literature μονογενής is used only of Jesus. The meaning only, unique, may be quite adequate for all its occurrences here." J. H. Moulton & G. Milligan, *The Vocabulary of the Greek New Testament*, 416, say that the only begotten is γεννητός from γεννάω, which literally means beget (of

uniqueness of being, rather than any remarkableness of the manner of coming into being or the uniqueness resulting thereof.

The uniqueness of being can be interpreted in two ways:
a) emphasising the special/unique relationship or kinship;[132]
b) the peerlessness, the matchlessness of its own or its own singular excellence and uniqueness.[133]

The Hebrew equivalent of μονογενής is יָחִיד meaning only, the only one, individual, privy member or singular or lonesome. In the Psalms יָחִיד is used in a more general way to mean "my only possession" parallel with נַפְשִׁי (Ps 22:21; 35:17; cf. 24:16; 67:7 which has instead μονότροπος in the Septuagint, see also Tob 3:15; 6:14; *Pss. Sol.* 18:4; 2 Esd 6:58). The Septuagint renders יָחִיד as 'beloved,' ἀγαπητός (Gen 22:2, 12, 16; Jer 6:26; Amos 8:10; Zech 12:10; cf. ἀγαπώμενος in Prov 4:3; Judg 11:34). Flavius Josephus uses μονογενής in connection with Isaac's story (*Ant.* 1.13.1). Philo never uses μονογενής, but always uses ἀγαπητός in much the same sense, again in connection with Isaac's story (*Leg. All.* 3.209; *Migr.* 140; *Abr.* 168, 194). Isaac being proclaimed as μονογενής of Abraham in the Septuagint (Gen 22:2, 12, 16), also in Heb 11:17 is surely not because he was the only son, but he was in a special relationship to his father, he was the only bearer of the promise of God. Therefore he was the *"unique"* son, or the specially beloved.[134] Abraham's readiness to sacrifice even this *"unique son"* enhances the quality of faith and fidelity and the cost of following the true God (cf. Rom 3:25; 8:32).

In all these texts of the New Testament[135] μονογενής means 'only child.' Luke is responsible for the motif of the "only child" through the use of μονογενής which is absent from the Synoptic parallels in Matthew and Mark.

---

the father), give birth (of the mother) or be born (child). B. Lindars, *The Gospel of John*, 96, states, however, that "of the father" is decisive for 'only begotten.' See also J. V. Dahms, "The Johannine Use of Monogenes reconsidered," *NTS* 29 (1983): 222–32. M. Theobald, *Die Fleischwerdung des Logos: Studien zum Verhältnis des Johannesprologs zum Corpus des Evangeliums und zu 1Joh* (NTA NF 20; Münster: Aschendorff, 1988), 250–54.

132 F. Büchsel, in *TDNT* 4:737–41, cites as parallels διογενής, ἐγγενής, συγγενής.
133 T. C. de Kruijf, "The Glory of the Only Son (Jn. 1:14)," in *Studies in John: Presented to J. N. Sevenster* (ed. M. C. Rientsma, et al.; NovTSup 24; Leiden: E. J. Brill, 1970), 112. It is not *"einzig"* but *"einzigartig"* — several persons can be μονογενής each in one's own manner.
134 G. Pendrick, "μονογενής," *NTS* 41 (1995): 593; D. Moody, "God's Only Son: The Translation of John 3:16 in the Revised Standard Version," *JBL* 72 (1953): 217.
135 Luke 7:12; 8:42; 9:38.

Obviously the fact that there are 'only children' increases the pathos of the parents' situation, as they are especially beloved as well as the 'saving' significance of Jesus' miracles. Thus both the 'Isaac typology' and the Lukan 'only child motif' in fact portray the soteriological greatness involved. "God sending His Son in order that . . ." is an ancient soteriological formula which is also referred to in Gal 4:4; Rom 8:3 and in the parable of the vineyard and tenants (Mark 12:1–9 and Synoptic parallels). This formula does not speak of the Son's eternal generation, instead it is written of as proof *par excellence* of the unlimited depth of God's salvific love for the world.

In the Fourth Gospel μονογενής appears four times (John 1:14, 18; 3:16, 18), and all of them portray the relationship of Jesus to God in a pictorial metaphor of a relationship between a uniquely loved son to the father. It is of immense soteriological significance that a metaphysical relationship in 3:16, 18 is spoken of in picturesque language of the extent of God's self-emptying to save the cosmos. In John 1:18 it speaks of the revelation that Jesus brings through his unique relationship to God as Son.

In v. 14 the clause is probably added to the original "we beheld his glory" as an explanation and correction to say it is not His (God's) glory directly (cf. v. 18) but the glory of God's salvific nearness the community experienced in and through Jesus. Again the soteriological motif is made explicit. Therefore one may conclude that the Evangelist is not speaking about the eternal generation of the son or the Father's only begotten even before creation. There is no reference to Jesus as "begotten" in the Fourth Gospel. Rather it characterises Christians/believers as "begotten by God" and speaks of spiritual birth of believers (John 1:13; 3:3–5).[136] It emphatically proclaims the soteriological significance of Jesus in his relationship to God.

Verse 14e—πλήρης χάριτος καὶ ἀληθείας.

What does this adjective modify? The nominative masculine singular form would have been in agreement with the Logos of v. 14a. Then it would strengthen the argument for considering v. 14d as an addition by the

---

[136] For a detailed discussion of how the interpretation of Johannine μονογενής as 'only begotten' originates in and is the result of the developments in Christology which do not antedate the 2nd century A.D., see G. Pendrick, "μονογενής," *NTS* 41 (1995): 597–600.

Evangelist.[137] Latin translations have πλήρης with Logos. Bultmann says that πλήρης is clearly not predicated by δόξα and is either related to the dominating term ὁ λόγος which is especially likely if vv. 14e and 16 are read together or taken with αὐτοῦ and used without inflection.[138]

That Philo has used πλήρης to characterise God (used absolutely in *Sac.* 9; *Det.* 54; *Her.* 187; *Leg. All.* 1.44; *Mut.* 27; *Spec. Leg.* 2.53) and the Logos (*Somn.* 1.75; 2.223, 245) should be noticed. The word pair ἡ χάρις καὶ ἡ ἀλήθεια brings immediately to mind the Hebrew word pair וְרַב־חֶסֶד וֶאֱמֶת. The passage cited to be of primary importance is Exod 34:6.[139] חֶסֶד may mean 'genuine faithfulness,' 'mercy,' 'goodness,' 'loving kindness,' 'mutual reciprocacy,' 'steadfast love,' 'goodwill,' 'favour' showed even when it is undeserved. חֶסֶד is to demonstrate faithfulness and loyalty towards members of the family (Gen 47:29–30; 20:43; 24:49; Ruth 3:10; 2:15). It is the profound regard for the established relationship and fellowship covenant (Gen 19:19; Josh 2:12–14; 1 Sam 20:8, 14–15; 2 Sam 9:1, 3, 7). When one speaks of God's חֶסֶד in the Old Testament it always means the steadfastness of God to the covenant relationship established with His people, His readiness to forgive

---

137 If it is indeclinable, then it can agree with μονογενής or with πατρός. Also grammars such as J. H. Moulton & N. Turner, *A Grammar of New Testament Greek.* Vol. 3: *Syntax,* 315 and *BDF,* § 137 inform that πλήρης in Hellenistic Greek is generally indeclinable only when followed by a dependent genitive and when it is not followed by a genitive it is declinable.

138 Bultmann, *Das Evangelium des Johannes,* 49, and J. N. Sanders, *A Commentary on the Gospel According to St. John,* 82.

139 See for the argument that vv. 14–18 are written after the language of Exod 33–34, A. T. Hanson, "John 1:14–18 and Exodus 34," *NTS* 23 (1977): 90–101; H. Mowvley, "John 1:14–18 in the Light of Exodus 33:7–34:35," 135–37, and M. D. Hooker, "The Johannine Prologue and the Messianic Secret," *NTS* 21 (1975): 50–58.There are five important points of convergence between Exodus 33–34 and vv. 14–18:
  a) the general character between Moses and Jesus presupposes the giving of the law at Sinai at v. 17: "the law was given through Moses, grace and truth came through Jesus Christ";
  b) Moses' request to God "show me your glory" (Exod 33:18, cf. 40:31) and the Prologue's declaration "we beheld his glory";
  c) the Prologue's assertion that no one has ever seen God (v. 18) echoes God's response to Moses: "you cannot see my face" (Exod 33:20, cf. v. 23);
  d) the Prologue's assertion that the unique son existed in the bosom of the Father (v. 18) contrasts with Moses' fleeting glimpse of God's back (Exod 33:23);
  e) the Prologue's "full of grace and truth" (v. 14) echoed in v. 17 has very lively allusions to Exod 34:6: "abounding in steadfast love and faithfulness."

Exegesis 203

His people, and His unlimited favours to the chosen Israel (Deut 7:9, 12; 2 Kgs 8:23; 2 Chr 6:14; Neh 1:5; 9:32; Psalm 89; 2 Sam 7:14). One should note that this is the language of Paul when he speaks of the grace of God.

In the Old Testament God's אֱמֶת could not be understood apart from his חֶסֶד, truth for the Old Testament community did not denote an idea or a concept. It describes action (Gen 24:4, 9; 47:29; Josh 2:14; Hos 4:1; Prov 20:28). It gives content for the חֶסֶד of God. It expresses the idea of fix, confirm, establish, the qualities of firmness and stability as an attribute of God the One who is absolutely trustworthy. Bultmann objects to interpreting χάρις and ἀλήθεια from the conceptual framework of וְרַב־חֶסֶד וֶאֱמֶת. He draws out that the Septuagint regularly translates the Hebrew word חֶסֶד with ἔλεος not χάρις.[140]

In contrast to Bultmann, Dodd recognises the connection between grace and truth in the Fourth Gospel and וְרַב־חֶסֶד וֶאֱמֶת in the Old Testament noting that in the course of time χάρις was employed more frequently as the translation of חֶסֶד. He draws attention to the fact that in Hellenistic Judaism after the Septuagint period χάρις came to be preferred to ἔλεος as the rendering of חֶסֶד and cites Est 2:9; cf. 2:17; Sir 7:33; 40:17.[141] Given the polemical/antithetical tone in the verses against the law that was seen as the sign of God's grace and truth by the Jews, it is difficult to neglect the וְרַב־חֶסֶד וֶאֱמֶת background. It is true that the Hellenistic influence must have added new dimensions of meaning to χάρις and ἀλήθεια as Bultmann contends that in Hellenism, χάρις is the act or conduct or gift which brings joy and happiness and the demonstration of goodness, and ἀλήθεια is the truth, reality, the meaning of divine reality and the content of the gift.[142]

In the Johannine usage this paired ἡ χάρις καὶ ἡ ἀλήθεια (cf. v. 17) stand for characterising God's gift, God's revelation. They refer to God's reliability, dependability and goodness (righteousness and justice). They portray His love and tenderness in forgiving His people, as He in His revelation confronts them 'as they are.' They characterise God as the One who manifests in acts of kindness and protective faithfulness, who creates and sustains a

---

140 R. Bultmann, *Das Evangelium des Johannes*, 49–50.
141 See C. H. Dodd, *Interpretation of the Fourth Gospel*, 82, 175, also R. Schnackenburg, *The Gospel According to St. John*, 1:272.
142 R. Bultmann, op. cit., 49–50.

fellowship that extends the momentary grace into a continuous 'reality.'[143] They describe God's being not in itself, but as he relates Himself to and His activity towards humankind. Probably the Evangelist in adding the adjective πλήρης speaks of the fullness of God's revelation that the incarnation has enabled and made possible.

Verse 15: Ἰωάννης μαρτυρεῖ περὶ αὐτοῦ καὶ κέκραγεν λέγων· οὗτος ἦν ὃν εἶπον· ὁ ὀπίσω μου ἐρχόμενος ἔμπροσθέν μου γέγονεν, ὅτι πρῶτός μου ἦν.

John who has been sent to witness to the light, to the liberating and mighty acts of God, now identifies the incarnation and bears witness! The God-sent authentic, authoritative witness pronounces a solemn "amen" to the Johannine community's experience of the incarnate Logos. Only a God-sent witness can identify, interpret and authoritatively declare "the only one" from God. If the interpretation of the Baptist concurs with the experience of the Johannine community, then it should be true.

The Evangelist in listing John as a witness to the incarnation is probably cashing in on the contemporary popular opinion that John the Baptist was a righteous man, who commanded respect.[144] The Baptist's witness given by crying out (κράζειν) is used in the Fourth Gospel with a special sense for inspired speech (7:28; 12:44). The Baptist's witness, therefore, should be understood as a proclamation by divine command. The mixture of tenses μαρτυρεῖ (in present) and κέκραγεν (perfect) perhaps reflect its frequent citation. The perfect tense probably represents what the Baptist used to say and the present μαρτυρεῖ indicates that his testimony continues to ring out in the Christian kerygma.[145]

---

143 So Beasley-Murray, *John*, 14–15; C. H. Dodd, *Interpretation of the Fourth Gospel*, 177, and R. Bultmann, *Das Evangelium des Johannes*, 49–50.
144 See Josephus, *Ant.* 18.116–119, who pictures John the Baptist as a non-political, religious reformer who, stirred by the sinfulness of the people, exhorts them to lead virtuous lives and to practice justice towards their fellows and piety towards God! So high indeed was John held in the eyes of the people that they explained the defeat of Herod's army as a vindication of the Baptist's virtue and righteousness—this account of Josephus on the Baptist is revealing with all his presumed Roman bias.
145 But one should also note that the perfect κέκραγεν could be used in the sense of a present, so J. H. Moulton in his *A Grammar of New Testament Greek*. Vol. 1: *Prolegomena*, 147; BDF, §§ 321, 341. It is not historical present but points at the events where the narrator imagines himself to be present. R. Schnackenburg opinions that

It was commonly assumed that the Baptist sect claimed superiority of John the Baptist over Jesus, as their master came first and the priority in time involved priority in dignity.[146] In the Prologue the Evangelist by pointing to the πρῶτος of the Logos negates the priority in dignity of the Baptist. It also negates the Synoptic notion of John the Baptist as forerunner/*praeparatio evangelii*. As the Logos is already πρῶτος he can have no forerunner.

The relationship of v. 15 to v. 30 helps us to understand the significance the Evangelist ascribes to Baptist's witness to the incarnation of Logos and also his insistence that the Baptist is only 'the witness,' a human instrument in God's hands. In spite of the christological interpretations given, the Synoptic episode of John the Baptist baptising Jesus indirectly suggests Jesus as the Baptist's disciple, and John the Baptist as his teacher and master. This was probably used in argument by the Baptist group to vouch for the Baptist's priority in dignity. V. 30 comes in the context of the Baptist recognising one whom he himself had never so far seen! For a full-fledged recognition, neither does the Baptist need to send his disciples as in the Synoptic tradition (Matt 11:2ff.; Luke 7:18ff.), nor do Jesus and John converse as John restrains himself from ministering to Jesus. The Fourth Evangelist sees no need for John's ministrations. Instead God gives him a sign (John 1:31–34) that John promptly recognises, interprets and makes plain by witnessing to 'the Jesus event.'

Thus by shifting v. 30 with a minimum alteration to the Prologue, the Evangelist emphasises that John "the witness" could recognise "the sign of God," thus the incarnation of the Logos. In the Fourth Evangelist's opinion John becomes a 'prototype for witness,' the one who only as a mere

---

the Evangelist makes the voice of the precursor audible in the present time, in his *The Gospel According to St. John*, 1:273.

146 ἔμπροσθεν is commonly used in time and rank. The basis of the use here according to Bultmann, probably the rabbinical, to precede is to have the greater dignity. See also H. L. Strack & P. Billerbeck, *Kommentar zum Neuen Testament aus Talmud und Midrasch*, 3:256. Also cf. Gen 48:20 that stresses that Jacob put Ephraim before (ἔμπροσθεν) Manasseh. Robinson has made a case for the thesis that John the Baptist thought of the one to come as pre-existing, not in any Christian sense of the pre-existing Son of God or in the Johannine sense of pre-existence of the Word, but in terms of pre-existence of Elijah as he had existed nine hundred years before John the Baptist. Of Elijah, John could say, "he ranks ahead of me because he existed before me." Though it seems fantastic, it is not plausible. See J. A. T. Robinson, "Elijah, John and Jesus: An Essay in Detection," *NTS* 4 (1957–58): 263–81.

instrument of God recognises, interprets and leads others to God, in the process himself getting transparent and decreased (John 3:30). The Fourth Evangelist does not consider the Baptist movement as a parallel challenge to the Jesus movement. Instead he sees John the Baptist as the one who points towards and leads people towards God's movement and acts as revealed in the Jesus movement.

Verse 16: ὅτι ἐκ τοῦ πληρώματος αὐτοῦ ἡμεῖς πάντες ἐλάβομεν καὶ χάριν ἀντὶ χάριτος·

This verse confirms the affirmation of v. 14e and grounds it (ὅτι) on the community experience.[147] πλήρωμα takes up πλήρης χάριτος καὶ ἀληθείας, the fullness of revelation that the community witnessed in the incarnate Logos. The interpretation of the phrase χάριν ἀντὶ χάριτος is a notorious crux. The nub of the problem is the meaning of the preposition ἀντί. It may mean:

a) 'in front of,' 'opposite' in a strictly local sense;[148]
b) 'instead of,' 'in the place of';[149]
c) 'in return for';[150]
d) 'corresponding to as effect corresponds to cause';[151]
e) 'upon,' 'in addition to' referring to the inexhaustible bounty of gifts resulting in a constant stream of grace.[152]

Of these five possibilities the two 'in return for,' 'corresponding to,' do not stand the first scrutiny, since God's grace being given 'in return' for human

---

147 καὶ is read by many manuscripts: A W Θ lat sy; but ὅτι is to be preferred as in the main Alexandrian witnesses and as the *lectio difficilior* P[66, 75] B C* D L 33 sa bo al.
148 There are traces of this meaning in classical Greek in some Hellenistic papyri, see H. G. Liddell & R. Scott, *A Greek-English Lexicon*, s.v. ἀντί; J. H. Moulton & G. Milligan, *The Vocabulary of the Greek Testament*, s.v. ἀντί.
149 In the Septuagint corresponding to Hebrew תחת cf. Gen 22:13, also cf. Matt 2:22; Luke 11:11. Moulton & Milligan cite *P. Tebt.* II 343.24 to argue that 'instead of' is most common in Hellenistic papyri.
150 It occurs most notably in Biblical references: Exod 21:22–23; cf. Matt 5:38; Rom 12:17; 1 Thess 5:15; 1 Pet 3:9.
151 See J. M. Bover, "χάριν ἀντὶ χάριτος (Joh 1:16)," *Bib.* 6 (1925): 454–60, esp. 458; also J. H. Bernard, *Commentary on the Gospel according to St. John*, 1:29.
152 Bultmann, Schnackenburg, Lindars, Barrett, Gnilka and Bruce support this meaning in their commentaries and find parallels, e.g., Sir 26:15: χάρις ἐπὶ χάριτι. . ., in Philo's *Post.* 145 where God is said to give constantly new graces in addition to the earlier ones, cf. *Leg. All.* 3.82. W. Bauer, et al. cite Theognis 344 in their *Lexicon* in support of this meaning.

gratitude is totally un-Johannine and the idea that grace which a Christian receives in some sense corresponds to the grace of Christ, has no contextual support and in fact obscures the meaning instead of simplifying and enlightening it. The Johannine community and the Evangelist in the Gospel do not argue for "the Jesus movement" instead of "Judaism." It does not claim a revelation instead of that which has been already given. It is not attempting to lay side-by-side two forms of revelation and asking its readers to choose the better one.

It in fact claims its share in the salvation history heritage. It does not negate the earlier revelation, rather it claims share in its spiritual heritage yet claims that the "fuller revelation" in Logos is the additional grace bestowed upon by God. "We all have received . . ." — a jubilant affirmation of thankfulness by the community.

Verse 17: ὅτι ὁ νόμος διὰ Μωϋσέως ἐδόθη, ἡ χάρις καὶ ἡ ἀλήθεια διὰ Ἰησοῦ Χριστοῦ ἐγένετο.

This verse must have been a later ecclesiastical addition as it tries to proclaim the greatness of the revelation that has come through Jesus. The mention of two historical persons, Moses and Jesus, is the peculiarity of this verse and also it is worth noting that Ἰησοῦ Χριστοῦ are paired together again only in 17:3 in the Gospel. It is widely assumed that the author is referring to a Pauline contrast or even an opposition between the Gospel and the Law.[153]

It is important to note that the redaction possibly in the wake of synagogue conflict/excommunication in the Fourth Gospel does not negate the revelation given to the Jews, instead makes an attempt to claim a share in the theological heritage of Judaism, and at the same time proclaims the superiority of the revelation through Jesus. It is a constructive parallelism, however not necessary to see a synthetic solution while a continuity is seen

---

153 W. Zimmerli writes, "Paul's antithesis of grace and law is adopted," in *TDNT* 9:399. J. Gnilka describes v. 17 as "ein polemisch und paulinisch klingender Satz" in his *Johannesevangelium* (NEchtB 4; Würzburg: Echter, 1983), 16. E. Haenchen sees it as setting grace and truth "im Gegensatz" to the law in his *John*, 1:210, and in "Probleme des johanneischen Prologs," *ZTK* 60 (1963): 305–34. See also H. H. Essar, in *NIDNTT* 2:119; A. Richardson, *An Introduction to the Theology of the New Testament* (London: SCM Press, 1958), 283–84; S. Pancaro, *The Law in the Fourth Gospel: Moses and Jesus, Judaism and Christianity According to John* (NovTSup 42; Leiden: E. J. Brill, 1975), 541.

between Moses and Jesus in that it is the grace and truth already found in the Law that is fully found in Jesus Christ.[154]

The Fourth Evangelist in fact uses Mosaic traditions positively in constructing his Christology. Moses traditions offer an adequate background for the prophet-king Christology of the Evangelist, where the reader who is well informed with the Mosaic traditions will recognise that Jesus fulfils for the believer what elsewhere is attributed to Moses in a superior and exclusive way and that Moses is made a witness to Jesus. In fact in doing so he has not deserted Moses, but true belief in Moses led to belief in Jesus.[155]

Moreover, the Law was given *through* (διά) Moses. The Law-giver is God, Moses is only the medium.[156] But through Jesus ἡ χάρις καὶ ἡ ἀλήθεια, the fullness of revelation (see exegesis of John 1:14e) ἐγένετο, came into being. In Jesus revelation is not just a 'written idea' to be grasped or followed, it has become 'living,' thus experienced in relationship, seen and historicized. Therefore the redactor with this highly abbreviated statement in v. 17 on the one hand does not conceal the conflict between the community and the synagogue, and on the other leaves room open for a vital element of Judaism to be claimed by his community as their own, as the rightfully chosen people of the true God.

Verse 18a: Θεὸν οὐδεὶς ἑώρακεν

What does the Fourth Evangelist convey here—no one has ever seen God or ever will? Sanders suggests that the Fourth Evangelist added πώποτε after οὐδείς "no one ... ever yet" to leave open the possibility of some future direct vision of God when the faithful have been united with God in Christ. But it goes against the theological perspective of the Fourth Evangelist (the realised and open Eschatology of the Evangelist, see also 14:9). Moreover it is doubtful whether πώποτε (at any time in the past or future) may bear the

---

154 R. E. Brown, *The Gospel According to John*, 1:16; J. Jeremias, "Μωϋσῆς," in *TDNT* 4:872–73.
155 Cf. John 1:45; 5:46, 47. For a fascinating account of Mosaic traditions in the Fourth Gospel see, W. A. Meeks, *The Prophet-King*, esp. 286–318; also J. Jeremias, in *TDNT* 4:877; M.-É. Boismard, *Moses or Jesus*, and A. Lindemann, "Mose und Jesus Christus. Zum Verständnis des Gesetzes im Johannesevangelium," in *Das Urchristentum in seiner literarischen Geschichte. Festschrift Jürgen Becker* (ed. U. Mell and U. B. Müller; BZNW 100; Berlin/New York: Walter de Gruyter, 1999), 309–34.
156 Cf. John 7:19a if formulated as a statement: "Moses did not give you the Law" paralleled "Moses did not give you the bread from heaven," 6:32.

sense of οὔπω or οὐδέπω (not yet).¹⁵⁷ The implication of ἑώρακεν which is used with πώποτε is possibly a present perfect of broken continuity.¹⁵⁸

God as He is, in Himself¹⁵⁹ to the physical or even to the spiritual eye¹⁶⁰ was axiomatic in Judaism.¹⁶¹ At the same time the Jews could not have denied, that on occasion through self-disclosure, God permitted Himself to be seen in some form either indirectly or partially.¹⁶² For me the statement strongly expresses God's invisibility, incomprehensibility, inaccessibility and hiddenness. But this idea of the direct inaccessibility of God is neither founded on a concept of God as a being of a particular kind nor on the notion of the adequacy of the human faculties to perceive Him. There is no attempt to raise ontological and epistemological questions about God. The Evangelist rejects any concept of God by which He can be thought of as the object of human knowledge. God ceases to be God if He is thought of as an object! To attempt to make God an object of vision is to loose the true idea of God. That God is inaccessible means that he is beyond human control. We have here a radical form of the oriental and the Old Testament idea of sovereignty and absoluteness of God.¹⁶³

Verse 18bi: πώποτε μονογενὴς υἱός

First of all we face a tricky textual problem. Four variant readings call for consideration:

a) ὁ μονογενής,

b) μονογενὴς υἱός,

c) ὁ μονογενὴς θεός,

d) μονογενὴς θεός.

---

157 οὐδεὶς οὔπω in Luke 23:53 and οὐδέπω οὐδεὶς in John 19:41 both of which mean "no one ... ever yet."
158 J. H. Moulton, *A Grammar of New Testament Greek*. Vol. 1: *Prolegomena*, 144.
159 Anarthrous θεός has been rendered 'God in His being,' God as God, the divine nature, the Godhead etc. I think these renderings read the later theological developments back into the text.
160 Bultmann rightly observes that the Johannine usage of ὁράω should not be restricted to visual perception (*Das Evangelium des Johannes*, 54–55). Cf. Abbott in his *Johannine Vocabulary*, §§ 1597–1611.
161 See for example Exod 33:20–23; Deut 4:12; Ps 97:2; Sir 43:31. See also H. L. Strack & P. Billerbeck, *Kommentar zum Neuen Testament aus Talmud und Midrasch*, 4:939–40.
162 See for example Gen 32:30; Exod 24:9–10; Num 12:6–8; Deut 34:10; Isa 6:1, 5. On the prophetic or theophanic vision of God see, W. Michaelis, in *TDNT* 5:329–34.
163 See Bultmann's *Das Evangelium des Johannes*, 55.

Though the first reading ὁ μονογενής is to be preferred on the principle *"lectio brevior potior"* it has a very weak attestation.[164] ὁ μονογενὴς θεός is the most difficult of the four major variants which has both proto-Alexandrian P[75] and later Alexandrian support. Naturally μονογενὴς θεός, has again both proto-Alexandrian (P[66] B) and later Alexandrian (C*, L) support with α* being the only manuscript representing the western text type. (These two readings have close relationship, probably the latter corrects the first to reserve precisely the distinction that the Fourth Evangelist had made at the outset of the Prologue between ὁ θεός and Logos as θεός).[165]

I prefer ὁ μονογενὴς υἱός for the following reasons:[166]
a) Witnesses supporting this variant are geographically widespread—later Alexandrian (892, 1241), Western (W supp, it, vg, Syr^c, Irenaeus^{lat} Tertullian), pre-Caesarean (f¹, f¹³, 28), Caesarean proper (Θ, 565, 700, arm, geo, Eusebius) and Byzantine (A, K, Π, most minuscules).
b) The reading accords with Johannine usage (John 3:16, 18; 1 John 4:9) whereas μονογενὴς θεός is unparalleled.
c) The clause that follows—ὁ ὢν εἰς τὸν κόλπον τοῦ πατρός—seems to demand an antecedent, referring to υἱός.[167]
d) At least three explanations of the origin of the other principal variant μονογενὴς θεός have been given: 1) it arose as an accidental misreading

---

164 M.-É. Boismard, *St. John's Prologue*, 91–92, and J. N. Sanders, *A Commentary on the Gospel According to St. John*, 85 n. 1, support ὁ μονογενής.
165 Supported by: UBS Text 4th edition, Nestle-Aland 27th edition; T. Zahn, *Das Evangelium des Johannes* (6th ed.; Leipzig: Werner Scholl, 1921), 94–95; J. H. Bernard, *Commentary on the Gospel according to St. John*, 1:31; C. K. Barrett, *The Gospel According to St. John*, 169 (in the first edition μονογενὴς υἱός); R. E. Brown, *The Gospel According to John*, 1:17 and 36; L. Morris, *The Gospel according to John*, 113; B. Lindars, *The Gospel of John*, 98–99; F. F. Bruce, *The Gospel of John*, 44–45; O. Hofius, "Der in des Vaters Schoß ist: Joh 1,18," *ZNW* 80 (1989): 163; D. A. Fennema, "John 1.18: God the only Son," *NTS* 31 (1985): 124–35; O. Cullmann, *The Christology of the New Testament*, 309; T. E. Pollard, *Johannine Christology and the Early Church*, 14; NIV and NRSV translations.
166 Supported by E. C. Hoskyns, *The Fourth Gospel*, 151–52; R. Bultmann, *Das Evangelium des Johannes*, 55–56; R. H. Lightfoot, *St. John's Gospel*, 90; S. Schulz, *Das Evangelium nach Johannes*, 34; R. Schnackenburg, *The Gospel According to St. John*, 1:279–80; B. D. Ehrman, *The Orthodox Corruption of Scripture: The Effect of Early Christological Controversies on the Text of the New Testament* (New York/Oxford: Oxford University Press, 1993), 78–82; Büchsel, in *TDNT* 4:740, n. 14; Luther, RSV, NEB translations.
167 See E. C. Hoskyns, *The Fourth Gospel*, 152, and R. V. G. Tasker, *The Gospel According to St. John* (London: Tyndale Press, 1960), 425.

of abbreviations (ΘΣ for ΥΣ),[168] 2) as an error of dictation or as an assimilation to John 1:1c,[169] and 3) the other two variants would therefore presumably be the results of deliberate omission (ὁ μονογενής an article being added in order to avoid having an articular participle phrase—ὁ ὤν ... dependent on an anarthrous noun) or deliberate addition for doctrinal reasons.

e) If our supposition that vv. 2 and 14d were added by the Evangelist to the basic Logos tradition in order to theocentricise it, is true, then the same Evangelist at v. 18 (another addition by him) could not have proclaimed a μονογενὴς θεός, but must have written ὁ μονογενὴς υἱός.

f) Most importantly Johannine theological scheme does not equate λόγος = μονογενής = υἱός. The Fourth Evangelist uses the Logos metaphor to describe God's relationship with the world whereas the Father–Son metaphor to describe Jesus' relationship with God. Here in v. 18 the Fourth Evangelist is not out to prove that Jesus is the θεός, instead he articulates and defines his mission as the unique Son!

g) Given that Alexandria was one of the later theological centres that developed the two-nature Theology and subsequently Trinitarian teaching, the Alexandrian manuscripts' unanimity for μονογενὴς θεός may reflect an ecclesiastical theological decision.

h) [ὁ] μονογενὴς θεός then embodies exclusivity, as it means Jesus is the unique God. The μονογενὴς θεός is found not only in predominantly Alexandrian Greek manuscripts, but among a variety of Alexandrian writings, both Orthodox and Gnostic. The key point is that, all those who support the text attest a 'high' Christology: Alexandrians, Clement, Origen, Ptolemy, and Heracleon all affirm that μονογενής was God! The origin of the variant does not lie in the Orthodox–Gnostic controversy, but in their combined attack against adoptionists. If the Alexandrian reading was derived from an anti-adoptionist context, then it represents an Orthodox corruption to ascertain that Christ was not merely a man adopted by God, He himself is God, unique God who is to be differentiated from the Father in whose bosom he resides. An answer to the question as to why only this particular occurrence of μονογενὴς υἱός was

---

168 B. M. Metzger, *A Textual Commentary on the Greek New Testament*, 198.
169 R. Bultmann, *Das Evangelium des Johannes*, 54–55.

changed, may lie in its strategic/central position within the Prologue, as well as it setting the stage for the interpretation of the Gospel.[170]

Verse 18bii: ὁ ὢν εἰς τὸν κόλπον τοῦ πατρὸς ἐκεῖνος ἐξηγήσατο.

What does ὁ ὢν mean? At least five different views have been expressed,

a) ὁ ὢν as a title that is, 'He that is,' rendering it as a third person equivalent of the ἐγώ εἰμι,[171]

b) 'who is' to express the simultaneous presence of Jesus in heaven and earth during his earthly ministry[172] or, his un-interpreted fellowship with the Father while on earth,[173]

c) ὁ ὢν alludes to the position of Christ after his ascension, the Evangelist expressing himself from his own stand-point in time,[174]

d) standing for the non-existent past participle of εἶναι, ὁ ὢν has an imperfect sense, that is (ὃς ἦν) "the one who was." Before his incarnation the son dwelt with the Father,[175]

e) ὁ ὢν as the atemporal present of characterisation meaning "to what has always been and always is."[176]

The meaning of ὁ ὢν is thus intrinsically connected with the issue as to whether it refers to the pre-existing one/post-existing one (the ascended) or to the human Jesus. The unique Son ὁ ὢν εἰς τὸν κόλπον of the Father is the subject of ἐξηγήσατο. The state described by ὢν is closely related to the principal verb. The one who made God known *is also* the one who is in the

---

[170] In 1 John 3:23 Codex Alexandrinus lacks the word τοῦ υἱοῦ A 1846 Vg^mss; in John 10:33 P^66 adds an article to θεόν (originally ποιεῖς σεαυτὸν θεόν) and the trend is to be seen in Alexandrian manuscripts. P^72 in 2 Pet 1:1 omits καί leading to the identification of Jesus as God. Also in Jude 5 it stands alone saying that Saviour of the people from Egypt was "the God Christ" (θεὸς χριστός); in Gal 2:20 the Alexandrian text P^46 τῇ τοῦ υἱοῦ τοῦ θεοῦ is changed to τῇ τοῦ θεοῦ καὶ Χριστοῦ. See B. D. Ehrman, *The Orthodox Corruption of Scripture*, 78–82.

[171] E. A. Abbott, *Johannine Grammar*, §§ 1938, 1964.

[172] L. Morris, *The Gospel according to John*, 224.

[173] C. H. Dodd, *Interpretation of the Fourth Gospel*, 258–59; R. E. Brown, *The Gospel According to John*, 1:133.

[174] T. Zahn, *Das Evangelium des Johannes*, 96; R. Bultmann, *Das Evangelium des Johannes*, 56; W. Loader, *The Christology of the Fourth Gospel*, 152.

[175] E. Haenchen, *John*, 1:121; M. J. Harris, *Jesus as God*, 96.

[176] M. Zerwick & J. Smith, *Biblical Greek*, § 372; G. Schrenk, in *TDNT* 5:998.

Father's bosom. He revealed God in his human existence and thus his being in the bosom of the Father also refers to his human life.

What does the preposition εἰς mean in this phrase? εἰς τὸν κόλπον is generally translated as "in the heart/bosom" etc. We have two uses of the word κόλπος in the Fourth Gospel and they are governed by two different prepositions: 13:23 ἐν τῷ κόλπῳ; 1:18 εἰς τὸν κόλπον. It is argued that in Hellenistic Greek the difference between ἐν + dative and εἰς + accusative has been lost.[177] Therefore, εἰς is interpreted as static and means location—"in." De la Potterie points out that the Fourth Evangelist seems to maintain a careful distinction between εἰς and ἐν and pleads to allow him to be consistent with his use of εἰς + accusative.[178] He suggests that it denotes not simply orientation or direction, but 'movement towards or into,' be it literal or metaphorical. He renders the phrase "turned towards the Father's bosom."[179] But there is another possibility: if εἰς τὸν κόλπον τοῦ πατρός is construed with ἐκεῖνος ἐξηγήσατο that follows, rather than with ὁ ὤν that

---

177 John 1:18 and 13:23 are cited as evidence for the Fourth Evangelist's oscillation from εἰς to ἐν in conformity with his predilections for stylistic variations. R. Schnackenburg, *The Gospel According to St. John*, 1:281, states that as so often in Koine, εἰς + accusative is certainly the equivalent of ἐν with dative. Also see J. H. Moulton, *A Grammar of New Testament Greek*. Vol. 1: *Prolegomena*, 234–35; BDF, § 205; M. Zerwick & J. Smith, *Biblical Greek*, §§ 102–104; also A. Oepke, in *TDNT* 2:433; W. Bauer, *Das Johannesevangelium*, 18; E. C. Hoskyns, *The Fourth Gospel*, 151; C. K. Barrett, *The Gospel According to St. John*, 169–70, and L. Morris, *The Gospel according to John*, 114. F. J. Moloney, "John 18: In the Bosom of or Turned Towards the Father," *AusBR* 31 (1983): 63–71.

178 He points to the dilemma of the grammarians who maintain in Turner's words: "there is therefore, nothing very profound here concerning mutual motion between Father and Son." Nevertheless the Fourth Evangelist does not usually blur the distinction between εἰς and ἐν and except for Matthew he has fewer examples of εἰς = ἐν than any other. J. H. Moulton & N. Turner, *A Grammar of New Testament Greek*. Vol. 3: *Syntax*, 254. See C. F. D. Moule, *An Idiom Book of New Testament Greek*, 69, and BDF, § 111.

179 For him it expresses two theological truths:
   a) a personal distinction between the Father and the Son and
   b) the constant orientation of the Son towards the bosom of the Father as towards his origin (εἰς), as towards the source of his own life (εἰς τὸν κόλπον). This seems to be influenced by later theological reflections.

De la Potterie is quoted by F. J. Moloney, "John 18: In the Bosom of or Turned Towards the Father," 63–65. Moloney adds that Jesus turned towards the Father's bosom in love and obedience throughout the whole of his historical presence among humankind, see *ibid.*, 68; M. J. Harris, *Jesus as God*, 97.

precedes, εἰς may bear its regular sense of "into," thus the rendering "who has led the way to the Father's bosom has made Him known."

κόλπος is generally translated in English as 'bosom'/'heart.' Such a translation shows the influence of the classical understanding of the passage. The Greek fathers interpreted the passage as an indication of the consubstantiality of the Father and the Son. For Augustine it showed intimacy created by perfect communion.[180]

κόλπος refers only to the external part of the body, be it man (chest) or woman (chest–breast). There is no reference to some sort of inner space within which something or someone may dwell, be kept or held. But the imagery behind the word as used in the Biblical tradition could be "festal" (of reclining at a meal, position of closeness/friendship accorded, cf. John 13:23), "familial" (used to speak of infant nourishment upon the breast of its mother, of the child on a parental lap or embrace, cf. 1 Sam 3:20; Ruth 4:11; Isa 49:22) or "conjugal" (of the embrace of husband and wife, cf. Deut 13:7; 28:54, 56; 2 Kgs 12:8; Sir 9:1).

Therefore at the level of the word itself, there is no idea of some sort of divine in-dwelling, but the imagery's significance points towards the exclusive and privileged intimacy of a deeply affectionate interpersonal relationship. Probably we should interpret εἰς τὸν κόλπον as an imagery that speaks of a wonderful blossoming relationship. One cannot be on one's bosom unless one feels and interacts. Thus 'being in the bosom' cannot be a static or passive location! (Surely this has nothing to do with discretion on eternal generation/consubstantiality.) "Being in the bosom" speaks of an intimate relationship where one loses oneself to find the other. It is very much in line with our interpretation of the "Father–Son" metaphor in the discourse material of the Gospel, especially in interpreting the oneness motif as a "oneness of self-emptying." Then the one who is in the bosom of the Father emphatically describes and reflects the intimate relationship of the historical Jesus with God, a relationship that can only be described in terms of "a very intimate Father–Son imagery."

ἐξηγέομαι which stands without an object is a technical term designating the communication of divine secrets or divine knowledge.[181] It was also

---

180 F. J. Moloney, "John 18: In the Bosom of or Turned Towards the Father," 64.
181 See J. H. Moulton and G. Milligan, *The Vocabulary of the Greek Testament*, s.v. and W. Bauer, in *TDNT*, s.v.

referred to the mystagogue in the mystery cults whose business it was to interpret the ritual to the initiates, in the sense of 'to lead' or 'show the way.' ἐξηγέομαι is held to be the vocation of the prophets.[182] In the Septuagint ἐξηγέομαι stands for actions of interpretive or informative nature (Judg 7:13; 1 Kgs 8:5; Job 12:8; 28:27; Prov 28:13; cf. *1 Clement* 49:2), it is also used for the actions of perceptive nature (Lev 14:57). Among the New Testament writers Luke uses it to mean 'to relate,' 'to narrate' or 'to give an account of' (Luke 2:35) or 'to make plain,' 'explain' (Acts 10:8; 15:12, 14; 21:19). Thus ἐξηγέομαι conveys a verbal action of communication, information or interpretation!

In the Fourth Gospel ἐξηγέομαι is used only here but elsewhere Jesus is seen as "revealer" (17:6, φανερόω), "teacher" (13:13, διδάσκαλος). He is also spoken of as the one who gives the vision of the Father (14:7, ὁράω). Thus we may conveniently conclude that in v. 18 the Evangelist speaks of Jesus' 'historic life' as one that teaches, reveals and gives visions of God with necessary interpretations! Moreover, ἐξηγήσατο is a constative/aorist denoting a historical event rather than an abstract idea encompassing in a single glance the whole of Jesus' life,[183] thus bridging the Prologue's theological witness to the phenomenon of God's relationship with the world through Logos to the life and mission of Jesus of Nazareth as lived in intimate fellowship with God!

7.4 Summary and Conclusions

a) The basic Logos tradition behind the Prologue seems to be Logos/Christocentric. Through his explanatory/clarifying additions the Evangelist makes it Theocentric.
b) To explain the revelation of God he uses two theological/mythological conceptual imageries, "Logos" and Theophany.
c) In developing his God-language the Evangelist enters into a methodological and theological dialogue with his religious environment. He seems to symbolise the critical contextual faculty of the community in inculturating Theology even risking himself being syncretistic. He takes

---

182 R. Bultmann, *Das Evangelium des Johannes*, 56. Also see Philo's *Leg. All.* 3.207 who calls Logos ἑρμηνεύς, προφήτης, ὑποφήτης.
183 See T. C. de Kruijf, "The Glory of the Only Son (John 1:14)," 121.

the Hellenistic theological concept of "Logos" with all the risks involved, of being exposed even to the Gnostic tendencies, of being understood differently in different theological situations, transforms and enriches it through his theological ethos and merges it with his Jewish theophany tradition to present a "new Logos," a mythological/theological conceptual category.

d) Logos is the relational face of God. The mythological personification helps the Evangelist to maintain a clear balance between the mystery of God and the revelation of God.

e) The Logos — the relational/revelational face of God — is not that which came into being, it was from the beginning, being pre-existent. The relationality is what God is in essence.

f) Creation which comes into being through the Logos affirms what God is in Himself. Only in its relation to God does creation have its existence, for Logos calls creation into existence and gives it substance and meaning.

g) Logos, the relational face of God, is to the creation the light which makes everything perceptible and offers freedom, is the life, the source of security, dynamic meaning and the illumined state (as it ought to be).

h) That the forces which deprive creation the possibility of light and life could not overwhelm Logos is an assurance, hope and exhortation to the creation.

i) Only Logos gives genuine and authentic existence to human existence. When one encounters Logos, the relational face of God, one understands what he/she is and what he/she ought to be.

j) Through the thought of the ahistorical presence of Logos in the cosmos, the Fourth Evangelist could envisage that God's acts of liberation are not only confined to the Old Testament community, and thereby witnessed in its traditions, but intervene into and overwhelm the whole cosmos. God chose a particular community, so that it may be a historical metaphor for his relationality to the whole cosmos. The chosen community could not understand it and became exclusive. But God gives the possibility for all human beings in spite of their inability, to become the children of God through an act of active, unqualified, dynamic, life-long commitment to the Logos.

k) John the Baptist is a theological sign for the fact that God acts in His world through human instruments. The witness of God's human agents to the liberating acts of God aid humankind to recognise and identify God the Light who stands behind every act of liberation.

l) The Logos becoming flesh is the Evangelist's theological language to speak of a phenomenon of God's kenosis. God risks Himself to be human. The transcendental God thus becomes visible, tangible, time-bound and inextricably interwoven into human history. The ultimate encounter with the Logos was possible for human beings only in the Logos that became flesh.

m) The tabernacling of the Logos is the fulfilment of God's eschatological promise to be present among His people.

n) The incarnation of the Logos manifests the protective faithfulness of God in creating and sustaining a relationship which extends the momentary grace into a continuous reality, thus the fullness of the revelation of God.

o) The glory of God for the Fourth Evangelist is God's love transcending even His transcendence; it is His real presence in time and space; it is God's coming in love and condescension. In glory, God is and can be met.

p) God's salvific nearness, God's reliability and dependability, His love and tenderness in forgiving His people is experienced through Jesus Christ by the community which now calls itself a covenant community that gives witness to the incarnation of Logos.

q) Through incarnational Theophany, the relationality of God which was from the beginning, now reveals itself in the historical Jesus–God relationship which is discussed by the Evangelist through the Father–Son imagery in the whole Gospel. In understanding this unique relationship, we understand the Logos, the relational/revelational face of God. Thus the unique Son-Jesus through his historical existence gives us an exegesis of God.

Chapter 8

Theology in Dialogue — Dialogue with the Considerate Jews

(John 3:1–21)

8.1 Introduction

The dialogue between Nicodemus and Jesus is usually interpreted as a pep talk of a person who was genuinely interested in Jesus but failed to understand him. However, the 'text' if read with proper attention points to a 'symbolic communal figure' — and therefore to a representative figure, because Nicodemus speaks to Jesus in the plural and is addressed likewise in return. Nicodemus says "we know that. . ." (οἴδαμεν, v. 2), and subsequently Jesus replies, "you people. . ." (ὑμᾶς, v. 7). Indeed Jesus applies the plural both to himself and to Nicodemus in vv. 11–12: λαλοῦμεν (we speak), οἴδαμεν (we know), ἑωράκαμεν (we have seen), μαρτυροῦμεν (we testify), ἡμῶν (our), οὐ λαμβάνετε (you people do not receive), οὐ πιστεύετε (you people do not believe). Since the interview is reported as between two persons, these plurals are both surprising and significant. Nicodemus does not stand for himself alone, but for some specific group which is portrayed rather negatively. In the same manner "Jesus" undoubtedly speaks for the Johannine Christians and stands against the group represented by Nicodemus.[1]

Nicodemus is introduced as a Pharisee, a ruler of the Jews (3:1). The second appearance of Nicodemus (7:42–52) makes it clear that he was in a position of authority. J. Louis Martyn suggests that these ἄρχοντες may be the secret believers among the Jewish authority in contrast to the hostile Pharisees (cf. 12:43ff.).[2] These may be the group who were the "teachers of Israel" (cf. 3:10) who were ready to accept and acknowledge Jesus as one of the teachers (3:2) highly gifted by God. Probably this was the group who

---

1 Cf. C. K. Barrett, *The Gospel according to St. John*, 111.
2 J. L. Martyn, *History and Theology in the Fourth Gospel*, 87–88.

apparently hoped to be disciples of the "teacher" Jesus, but also remain within the framework of synagogue Judaism. Thus the readiness also, to give a very fair hearing to Jesus within the realm of Pharisaic legal debate (cf. 7:45–52). Their high regard for Jesus is symbolised in Nicodemus' coming to pay his last homage to Jesus with myrrh (19:39).[3] This 'high esteem' was termed (rightly) by the Johannine group as inadequate faith and fearfulness, since the group fancied their position of authority and dreaded a synagogue excommunication.[4]

The dialogue between Nicodemus and Jesus is often interpreted as the Johannine community's attempt to correct the low Christology of the above-mentioned group to their higher Christology.[5] But when we look closely at 3:1–21, it becomes clear that it is a chapter in the history of the Johannine community, a narrative protocol of a dialogue between the above mentioned Nicodemus' group and the Johannine community, in a quasi historical manner retrospectively projected to the history of Jesus, where the attempt is made not to give primarily christological reasons but predominant

---

3   Nicodemus' contribution in bringing spices is often seen as one of true and open devotion, even confession, see R. E. Brown, *The Gospel according to John*, 2:959–60; R. Schnackenburg, *The Gospel according to St. John*, 3:296–97, and B. Lindars, *The Gospel of John*, 592. But it is more likely an act of disbelief. Nicodemus shows himself capable only of burying Jesus with a kind of absurd finality. So Nicodemus loading down Jesus' body is to make clear that he does not expect a resurrection more than he expects a second birth. Cf. W. A. Meeks, "The Man from Heaven in Johannine Sectarianism," 155; M. de Jonge, *Jesus: Stranger from Heaven and Son of God*, 33–34, and P. D. Duke, *Irony in the Fourth Gospel: The Shape and Function of a Literary Device* (Atlanta: John Knox Press, 1985), 110.

4   This group fits the description of that of J. L. Martyn's "secret Christian Jews" (J. L. Martyn, *The Gospel of John in Christian History: Essays for Interpreters* [New York: Paulist Press, 1978], 109–15). He does not, however, make explicit reference to Nicodemus here, but cf. his *History and Theology in the Fourth Gospel*, 87–88. See also R. E. Brown's description of the "crypto Christians," in his *The Community of the Beloved Disciple*, 71–73, although he does not regard Nicodemus as a representative of this group.

5   M. de Jonge, *Jesus: Stranger from Heaven and Son of God*, 30–32, 37–42; see also J. Becker, "Joh 3:1–21 als Reflex johanneischer Schuldiskussion," in *Das Wort und die Wörter: Festschrift Gerhard Friedrich* (ed. H. Balz and S. Schulz; Stuttgart: Kohlhammer, 1973), 86–88, who finds that Nicodemus represents a group of quasi Jewish Christian teachers with a false Christology, opposed to the group represented by Jesus.

8.2 Exegesis

8.2.1 Verses 3–6: God Creates a New Eschatological Community

On his arrival for a dialogue through the way of polite greetings, Nicodemus does not negate the presence of God with Jesus (the Jesus community). However he gives sufficing indications through clever rhetoric that he still has doubts to clarify. This was sufficient to provoke the community's pride as the Johannine Jesus declares the real condition to enter the kingdom of God. βασιλεία τοῦ θεοῦ according to the Fourth Evangelist is the rule of God, God's realm. This expression is used by him only here in vv. 3 and 5. In other places he replaces it with his specific ζωὴ αἰώνιος. In fact these are two synonyms used in the Fourth Gospel, the Kingdom of God is eternal life, salvation. ἰδεῖν (v. 3)/εἰσελθεῖν (v. 5) mean 'to see,' 'to enter,' 'to participate,' 'to come to know,' 'to experience by possession.' In the Fourth Gospel 'to see' or 'to enter' the kingdom of God is to participate in, and to experience God's life. This is possible by γεννηθῇ ἄνωθεν or by γεννηθῇ ἐξ ὕδατος καὶ πνεύματος. γεννάω suggests to be born or to be begotten. γεννηθῇ the aorist subjunctive passive refers to the act of begetting. The imagery of begetting, divine seed and regeneration are a very important part of Johannine tradition (cf. 1 John 2:29; 3:9; 4:7; 5:1, 4, 18, cf. John 1:12, perhaps 11:52 also). The crude realism of being begotten to eternal life is even more brutal in 1 John 3:9 where it is said that one begotten by God has God's seed abiding in him. The Pastorals (cf. Tit 3:5 and 1 Peter) too share this imagery. Paul prefers the metaphors of death and resurrection and new creation to supernatural begetting. Though he uses the metaphor of divine adoption (Gal 4:5; Rom 8:23) it has a different connotation.

In the early stages of Old Testament Theology the holy people of God, Israel, was treated as God's first-born child (Exod 4:22; Deut 32:6; Hos 9:1). However, this sonship was the result of covenant choice, there is no clear idea of begetting by God. With the establishment of the Davidic monarchy, the anointed King of God's people was hailed as the son of God (2 Sam 7:14; Ps 2:7; 89:27). It is important to note that the term begetting appears in

Psalm 2 to describe the anointing.[6] In the post-exilic period we find only pious individual Israelites designated as sons of God. Certainly it was considered a future reward in the eschaton when the just will be acclaimed as sons of God (Wis 5:5; *Pss. Sol.* 17:30; cf. Sir 4:10; 23:1, 4; Wis 2:13, 16, 18).

Why does the Fourth Evangelist particularly use this birth/begetting imagery? I see three major reasons:

a) According to him a person becoming like a child, a simple transformation is not enough to enter/see the kingdom of God. One needs an entirely 'new beginning.' This even radicalises Paul's imagery of new creation, which too has in its background the idea of transition.

b) It is a protest against the moralistic/praxiological Pharisaic scheme that took on a pompous appearance. A moment of discontinuity comparable to physical birth is essential. The Evangelist prefers an imagery that holds the understanding/experience of pain, suffering and joy very close together.

c) This imagery brings out the Johannine open eschatological understanding very clearly and forcefully—now and not yet (waiting) aspects held together with a bundle of immense possibilities. (Just waiting even when someone is being born.)

ἄνωθεν means 'anew,' 'afresh,' 'again from the beginning or start,' 'completely/utterly different,' 'from above' or 'from the sphere of God.' Here in v. 3 as it is in 3:31; 19:11, 23 it means 'from above.' The Fourth Evangelist does not concern himself with human conversion. If we compare the parallel texts in the Synoptic Gospels which seem to define who will enter the kingdom of God, we see 'turning,' 'conversion' and 'becoming like children' in Matthew, 'repentance,' 'receiving the kingdom of God like a child' in Mark and Luke (Matt 18:3; Mark 10:15; Luke 18:17; cf. Matt 3:2; Mark 1:12).

If in the Synoptics the change over is described from the point of view of man, the Fourth Evangelist considers it from that of God without whose action such a change would be impossible. ἄνωθεν is a notion/an event that originates and is brought about by God, outside human control. Thus the Evangelist right at the beginning uncompromisingly states that as he is, a person is excluded from salvation from the sphere of God, for a person as he

---

6   This imagery of the 'king' as the "Son of God" may have had its roots in pagan Egyptian parallels where it was thought that a god sexually begat the king of a human mother. The specific Israelite concept associated sonship with the anointing which made a person king.

is, there is no possibility of it.⁷ But one is still a bundle of possibilities, not just a process to be played out.⁸ ἄνωθεν gives a chance to vertical intervention of newness. Thus prior to any human efforts, God must create the basis of a new beginning in a person, which makes new life possible.⁹

Nicodemus' question now is to know how this could happen which is interpreted as misunderstanding ἄνωθεν as δεύτερον. If we take the Pharisaic-Johannine community dialogue situation seriously, he is challenging the very validity of the self-understanding of the Johannine community as "that from above." How can your pluralistic/mixed community comprising of Jews, Samaritans and Gentiles be from above? Are not the Jews the only 'from above' community? It shows Nicodemus' narrow parochial perspective of limiting 'birth from above' to one community. The Johannine Jesus answers the challenge in affirming the action of God as the basis of an elect community! — the kingdom of God. ἐὰν μή τις γεννηθῇ ἐξ ὕδατος καὶ πνεύματος, οὐ δύναται εἰσελθεῖν εἰς τὴν βασιλείαν τοῦ θεοῦ.

In the near eastern literature, ὕδωρ (water) was used as a well known technical term, circumlocution for matters involving procreation (semen and amniotic fluid), for the act and process of giving birth (from the breaking of water to the actual delivery).¹⁰ Thus 'water' should signify the natural course of birth. ὕδωρ is also connected with ritual purification. Jewish religion had an eschatological expectation that God Himself will cleanse His people with the sprinkling of water (Ezek 36:25–36). Judaism developed the importance of ritual washing in which the external rite pointed to the yet unfulfilled future and symbolic present.¹¹ Pharisaic Judaism developed liturgical washing, foremost among these being the proselyte baptism. And in apocalyptic Judaism this cleansing and transformation were a prerequisite for entry into the coming kingdom. Baptismal cleansing was required for the Qumran initiates too.¹² Thus, water should signify 'the birth' from purification rituals and proselyte baptism. In a dialogue situation with the considerate Pharisaic

---

7   R. Bultmann, *Das Evangelium des Johannes*, 95.
8   E. Haenchen, *John*, 1:200.
9   R. Schnackenburg, *The Gospel according to St. John*, 1: 368; J. Frey, *Die johanneische Eschatologie*, 3:250.
10 B. Witherington, "The Water of Birth: John 3:5," *NTS* 35 (1989): 156.
11 G. M. Burge, *The Anointed Community: The Holy Spirit in the Johannine Tradition* (Grand Rapids: Eerdmans, 1987), 162.
12 *Ibid.*

Jews, it may mean the natural birth into the Jewish or chosen people, or a ritual purification into the chosen people.

πνεῦμα in the human sphere means 'breeze,' 'breath' or 'wind,' then consequently in super-human spheres, the divine power. 'Spirit' is used as the self-portrayal of human presence, to the epiphany of God. Spirit in the Old Testament primarily means the active agent of divine work in nature, energy or power of God (Judg 6:34; 13:25; 14:6; 1 Kgs 10:6, 10; 11:16; 16:13; 18:12; Isa 31:3; 63:7–14; Ps 62:11; 66:5ff.; 78:104–107 etc.). Begetting of the Spirit also has its derived meaning from the Old Testament. The pouring out of the Spirit is an important feature of Old Testament prophecy on eschaton (Joel 2:28–29; Ezek 36:25–26). The Spirit was to bring about at the end of time an onward change of heart that would make the perfect fulfilment of a new covenant possible (Ezek 11:19; 36:25ff.; Isa 44:3; Jer 31:31). The imagery of the resurrection of the dry bones, through the Spirit (breath) of God is probably another imagery lying behind the "πνεῦμα" of the Fourth Gospel. The Spirit is that which gives life—the creative power of God.

The connection between the gift of the Spirit and becoming children of God is found in the 2nd century B.C. in *Jub.* 1:23–25: "I will create in them a holy spirit and I will cleanse them. I will be their Father and they shall be my children." The Qumran community also looked forward to the day of divine visitation when God would root out the spirit of falsehood from man through the pouring of the Holy Spirit (1QS IV, 19–21; cf. 1QH III, 21; XI, 10–14, also VII, 6–7; IX, 32; XII, 12; XVI, 12; XVII, 26). In the Rabbinic circle, the Midrashic instructions expected the outpouring of Spirit and new creation in the future eschatological time.[13]

The concept of "Spirit" could then portray the manner in which God encounters people, with the power that makes new birth, new creation possible. It speaks both of the "miraculous act" which lies beyond human control and sphere and an active guarantee, which brings the act of new birth into fulfilment.[14] ἐκ, 'out of' or 'from,' a birth which comes forth, out of water and spirit. Perhaps in this case water and spirit are seen as mediums or agencies through which or out of which birth comes. The two

---

13 Midrash on Ezek 36:26; Joel 3:1 in Midrash Ps 14, see H. L. Strack & P. Billerbeck, *Kommentar zum Neuen Testament aus Talmud und Midrasch*, 2:615–16; 4:482–83, 847–48, 913–14, also *Ex. Rab.* 41 (48a), m. *Yoma* VIII:9; cf. R. Schnackenburg, *The Gospel according to St. John*, 1:370–71.

14 Cf. R. Bultmann, *Das Evangelium des Johannes*, 98–99.

nouns water and spirit are anarthrous and governed by one preposition ἐκ. This leads to some interesting observations. Do water and spirit belong together? Or is it a case of typical Johannine idiom of pairs intention?[15] Its context suggests here that the significance of the one fills (spills) over into the other, the second absorbs the first and completely overwhelms it. Human birth into the chosen race Israel is of no use until and unless overwhelmed by the Spirit.

Verse 6 makes this new understanding of "people of God" explicitly clear: τὸ γεγεννημένον ἐκ τῆς σαρκὸς σάρξ ἐστιν, καὶ τὸ γεγεννημένον ἐκ τοῦ πνεύματος πνεῦμά ἐστιν (Flesh gives birth to flesh, but the Spirit gives birth to spirit). In Johannine thinking nature is determined by its origin. 'To be from' expresses both the origin and the type of being. The contrast between σάρξ and πνεῦμα has nothing to do with the Greek anthropological dualism of body and soul. It is not the contrast between the material and the spiritual. The contrast refers to two possibilities of life, man as he is and man as God can make him. Therefore, those born of the Spirit, which is the life giving and quickening power of God can see the rule of God, can enjoy, experience and share God's life even if they do not belong to the chosen race![16]

Note the perfect tense used in v. 6 (γεγεννημένον) that refers to a continued state of begetting. This new birth is a process, which God continues to strengthen habitually by His Spirit. The life imparted is not developed in a separate independent existence, but it is dependent in its sustenance and growth upon the continuous influx of life from the parent source. The divine begetting once carried out is a germ that still goes on to flower forth and develop.

8.2.2 Verses 7–8: A New Community—The Sign of God's Freedom to Act

Nicodemus is advised not to refuse evidence of a new beginning (constitution of the new community) and not to be astonished at it, given the fact that it betrays the provisions of the law. Through a simile of the wind he is

---

15 G. R. Beasley-Murray, *John*, 48.
16 In Jewish Theology in order to enter the kingdom of God one needed to be born/regenerated into the 'race.' Human lineage for them is as important as God's act. God's act just gave a preference to their particular human race.

reminded of the fact that the miraculous operation of the Spirit is bound by no discoverable law, not even by the Torah! The incomprehensibility of the wind is used as a simile more than once in the Old Testament and Jewish literature, to provide a comparison for the incomprehensibility of God's way (Eccl 11:5; Prov 30:4; Eccl 16:21; 2 Esd 4:5–11). The wind is a "mystery" as to its origin and goal, but still remains a reality perceptible by means of its sound and recognisable through its effects. The wind blows to its own power and according to its own law.[17]

All that comes from God has an element of mystery—the spontaneity and inscrutability of His ways. The mystery remains impenetrable yet. But it cannot take away the reality of action that is revealed by its effects. In the dialogue the Evangelist seems to suggest that the 'very birth of a new community' is the effect of the freedom of God in election and to call people to grace and salvation. 'Life' is impossible for the community if considered as a human possibility, but it is possible through πνεῦμα, the decisive divine action.

8.2.3 Verses 9–15: Jesus—The Normative Determinant to Understand God's Action

The plural in vv. 11 and 12 makes it very obvious now that the Johannine Jesus speaks for the community. He exhorts Nicodemus to recognise the earthly experiences like 'being born' and 'hearing the wind blow' only as those pointing beyond themselves to the acts of God. The Creation points to the Creator. But Nicodemus remained puzzled and unable to associate in spite of being encouraged to go beyond the superficial understanding of life. In fact Nicodemus here is being asked by the community to rise above the narrow, rigid realm of legality to see the acts of God in a larger perspective. "How can this be?" (v. 9) is to be understood as Nicodemus' plea for the new normative determinant to understand God's act of freedom, the Johannine interpretation of which he now finds difficult to accept on the basis of the "Law."

The community points to the one and only normative determinant that is necessary to understand God and His actions—Jesus. It presents and

---

17 C. H. Dodd compares this to the metaphor of seed in Mark 4:26–29: "the seed sprouts and grows without the mass who planted it knowing how" (*Historical Tradition in the Fourth Gospel*, 364–65).

portrays the Son of Man, the eschatological figure who is expected to bring fuller revelation of God (see John 1:51; cf. Dan 7:14) by using the literary metaphors κατάβασις and ἀνάβασις. It explains how a new eschatological relationship has been created.[18] In the κατάβασις of the Son of Man we have a metaphorical expression for God's graciousness reaching out to humankind (cf. Numbers 11; Ps 78:21; Wis 16:20). The coming down has been complemented by the going up.[19] Thus the heavenly and earthly spheres now stand in a new relationship in and through Jesus. Thus the title "Son of Man" reflects both the community's conviction that eschaton has already come, and its faith in the new eschatological relationship of God and humankind in Jesus.

Using the metaphor of the Bronze Serpent the community now declares the normative determinant necessary to understand God's act of freedom. As God used the Bronze Serpent on a pole to give new life to the suffering children of Israel (Num 21:4–9), the lifting up[20] of the Son of Man is the sign, the normative determinant to understand God's act of freedom. Note the passive ὑψωθῆναι which indicates that it is God who lifted up the Son of Man. δεῖ emphasises the necessity, ἵνα suggests its goal. As those who "gazed on the Bronze Serpent" received life, one should gaze on the 'hanging,' 'suffering,' 'humiliated' Son of Man, Jesus, to receive life. The 'passion,' the 'self-emptying' on the cross and the cross itself is the ultimate key to understand God's acts in our midst. Those who gaze on the humiliated Son of Man on the cross will see God, God acting in His eternal freedom.

8.2.4 Verses 16–17: Jesus—The Metaphor of the Self-emptying God

οὕτως γὰρ ἠγάπησεν ὁ θεὸς τὸν κόσμον, speaks of a love as a historical happening (note the aorist ἠγάπησεν) which embraces the whole world. The

---

18 See M. Davies, *Rhetoric and Reference in the Fourth Gospel*, 170–81, esp. 178–79.
19 Note the perfect tense ἀναβέβηκεν—the community speaks from a post resurrection perspective. Here the coming down of the Son of Man does not portray the idea of the heavenly pre-existent Son of Man. See J. W. Pryor, "The Johannine Son of Man and the Descent-Ascent Motif," *JETS* 34 (1991): 341–51, esp. 348, and D. Burkett, *The Son of Man in the Gospel of John*, 76–119.
20 For the various meanings of ὑψόω see, G. Bertram, in *TDNT* 8:606–13, and H. Hollis, "The Root of the Johannine Pun ὑψωθῆναι," *NTS* 35 (1989): 475–78. Cf. Lindemann, "Mose und Jesus Christus," 312–13, and J. Frey, *Die johanneische Eschatologie*, 3:277–78.

Jews were ready enough to think that God loved Israel, but no passage appears to be cited in which any Jewish writer maintains that God loved the world.[21] Here the Johannine community articulates its faith, saying that the God it believes in embraces the whole world. "κόσμος" in the Fourth Gospel is sinful humankind that has turned away from God, and is therefore used pejoratively. Here the world is a perverted creation, which took temporary for the ultimate, the spurious for genuine, death for life,[22] and was therefore unlovable.[23] Such a "world" became the object of God's love. This love, ἀγάπη, is not just of sentimental feeling or passive caring, it is an outgoing, effect-producing, life-giving, infinite and boundless love in action in human history.

"God so loved that He gave. . . ." The Fourth Evangelist uses the indicative ὥστε . . . ἔδωκεν (not the infinitive ὥστε . . . δοῦναι which might have been expected). His use is rather unusual and probably emphatic.[24] 'Giving' is programmatic for the Fourth Gospel. God as the gift-giver is a very important belief in the Old Testament. God gives land, progeny, wealth (Gen 17:8; 16, 20; 24:7; Josh 24:3–4; Job 1:21), ability to work signs, to speak (Exod 4:11, 21; Isa 7:14; Jer 1:9; 5:14), wisdom, providence and understanding (Wis 9:4; 7:7, 9). God gives food (Exodus 16; Psalm 78; Num 11:18) and God gave the Sabbath rest (Exod 16:29). All these are intimations of the salvation He gives (Ps 18:35), the renewal of the covenant with Israel (Ezek 36:26–28), and in Isaiah, the servant is given as a covenant to the people, a light to the nations (Isa 42:6; 49:6).

The Fourth Gospel radicalises God's gift-giving. It is no more through the elect, it is to the world, it is grounded in His love for the 'world.' It is not from His bounty that He gives, it costs Him. He gives what is μονογενής (see the exegesis of 1:14, 18), unique and incomparable, all that He has as of worth, as the only son to a parent.[25] He gave all that He could; His gift is His

---

21   See H. Odeberg, *The Fourth Gospel*, 116.
22   R. Bultmann, *Theology of the New Testament*, 2:27.
23   See for a detailed discussion, TDNT 3:871ff.; L. Morris, *The Gospel according to John*, 126ff., and R. E. Brown, *The Gospel according to John*, 1:508ff.
24   See L. Morris, op. cit., 229. This is the Fourth Evangelist's only use of ὥστε, but ὥστε is found 84 times in the New Testament of which only 21 times have the indicative (15 times in Paul). Thus outside Pauline epistles it is infrequent.
25   The story of Abraham's sacrifice of Isaac in Genesis 22 (cf. Heb 11:17) might have played a parabolic significance behind this imagery.

self-sacrifice, His self-emptying. The idea of 'giving' is developed so that everything Jesus achieves is to be understood as God's gift. This makes Jesus a metaphor of God in human history—a metaphor of self-emptying. It is in God's self-emptying that the "world" gets filled, becomes a "new creation." Thus when God empties Himself, He fills humankind with life, humankind partakes in God's life, that is what the Evangelist means with the term eternal life.

Here the Fourth Evangelist introduces the theme "belief" (πιστεύειν). It is the response to the self-emptying love of God. It is nothing but: self-emptying. In Jesus who is portrayed in the Fourth Gospel as "the Son to the Father" we have the model for our belief in God. As God self-emptied, Jesus emptied himself, therefore the disciples too. It picturesquely explains v. 16—God loves the world so much that He empties Himself. Humankind in response to His all-giving love should believe, which means, it ought to empty itself, in order to be filled with life. Only in self-emptying there is eternal life.

8.2.5 Verses 18–21: Only a Self-emptying Community Can Represent a Self-emptying God

The community's monologic recommendation to the "Nicodemus group" is clear and precise. V. 18: "He who believes in Him is not condemned, he who does not believe is condemned already." It is a call to the Jews who wanted to believe secretly to give up false security, identity and authority and to empty themselves. The decision whether to empty to God's loving, self-giving or not, constitutes judgement. Only a self-emptying community can represent a self-emptying God—in losing an identity, a new identity is received.

The light is the 'self-emptying model given by Jesus.' Those who do not come to the light (see 3:2: Nicodemus comes in the night) remain in the darkness; such cannot understand the mighty acts of God's freedom. The Johannine community gives a theological basis to its excommunication and loss of social identity. The sociological predicaments were seen as a way to represent God whom they believed. V. 21 refers to the community's resurrection faith that God will fill it with His self-giving love and life.

8.3 Summary and Conclusions

a) In John 3 we have a peep into a part of the Johannine community's history. We re-read a narrative protocol of a dialogue between the secret/"crypto"-Christian groups of considerate Jews (Nicodemus) and the Johannine community (Jesus).
b) Racial identity or ritual purification cannot build an eschatological community. God Himself creates an eschatological community, which owes its entirely new beginning to the Spirit who is both the guarantor to and the consummator of the newness. A community owing its identity to racial/ritual initiations is rendered superfluous by God's eschatological community.
c) God is utterly free in His act of creating a new community. This freedom is a mystery. The presence of the new community is both the effect and the sign of God's freedom to act.
d) The normative determinative factor to understand God's movement and actions is Jesus. While the literary metaphor of the association "coming down" indicates God's gracious reaching out to His creation, "going up" binds the new relationship between Creator and the creation that was long foreseen through the image of the Son of Man. A gaze on the "lifted up" is the ultimate key to understand God and His actions.
e) God's self-emptying is the sign of His universal love to make the "cosmos" again His Creation. Jesus who is the metaphor for the self-emptying God invites the cosmos to believe in God, that is, to empty itself in order to be filled with life eternal.
f) The Johannine community exhorts the crypto-Christian groups to shed their false security and identity. Only a believing and self-emptying community can represent a self-emptying God. Decision for or against self-emptying constitutes judgement.
g) The Community's theological thought and its relevant sociological context are dialectical.

Chapter Nine

Theology in Dialogue—Dialogue with the Samaritans

(John 4:1–42)

9.1 Introduction

Chapter 4 has always been the centre of discussions over the Samaritan influence on the Fourth Gospel. Contemporary scholarly opinion aims in three directions:
a) the Gospel being possibly influenced by Samaritan traditions,
b) the possibility of the Evangelist writing it partly to win Samaritan converts, and
c) the Gospel stemming from a Samaritan-Christian community, the Evangelist himself being a Samaritan.

At the same time, the tendency to give Samaritan traditions a fair hearing is bitterly challenged on two counts:
a) the possible similarities found only in the later Samaritan texts—thus open to the interpretation that Samaritanism was influenced by Christianity, especially by the Fourth Gospel.
b) The Synoptics speak of the opposite, that Jesus forbade mission in Samaria (Matt 10:6) or the Samaritans did not accept him (Luke 9:51–56).[1]

---

1   See M. Pamment, "Is there Convincing Evidence of Samaritan Influence on the Fourth Gospel?" *ZNW* 73 (1982): 221–23; C. H. H. Scobie, "The Origins and Development of Samaritan Christianity," *NTS* 19 (1973): 390–414; G. W. Buchanan, "The Samaritan Origin of the Gospel of John," in *Religions in Antiquity* (ed. J. Neusner; Leiden: E. J. Brill, 1968), 149–75; O. Cullmann, *The Johannine Circle: Its place in Judaism, among the Disciples of Jesus and in Early Christianity* (trans. J. Bowden; NTL; London: SCM Press, 1976), 46–69; E. D. Freed, "Samaritan Influence in the Gospel of John," *CBQ* 30 (1968): 580–87; W. A. Meeks, "Moses as God and King," in *Religions in Antiquity* (ed. J. Neusner; Leiden: E. J. Brill, 1968), 354–71; idem, *The Prophet-King*.

Andreas Lindemann has suggested that John 4 is an attempt by the Evangelist to certify the Samaritan Christianity as that founded by Jesus himself: Samaritan mission was not only a commission of the resurrected Jesus to his disciples, the historical Jesus himself did missionary work in Samaria.[2] Given the quasi-historical nature of the Fourth Gospel (even if one goes by the Synoptic Gospels' assertion that the historical Jesus did not carry out missionary work in Samaria), Lindemann's observations should be taken seriously. The community, in order to legitimise its own experience with the Samaritans, now projects its experience to the historical Jesus.

Taking J. Louis Martyn's hypothesis that the Fourth Gospel is a two-level drama, the minute work of literary critics who see chapter 4 as composed of many bits of traditions and sayings,[3] and the work of those who practice 'new criticism' that is, text linguistic analysts, discourse analysts, structural critics and narrative critics who together see in Chapter 4 a tight-knit literary unit,[4] it is possible that the dialogue between the Samaritan

---

2   A. Lindemann, "Samaria und Samaritaner im Neuen Testament," *WuD* 1993: 51–76, esp. 67–70.

3   The literary critics vary in their judgements. Their major suggestions are as follows:

	Pre-Johannine source Sign material?	Johannine addition	Post Johannine
Bultmann	5 (4)–7, 9 (10), 16–26, 28–30, 40	8 (10), 11–15, 20, 27, 31–38, 39, 41–42	1–3 (4)
Wilkens	5–7, 9–26, 28–30, 40	4, 8, 27, 31–38, 39, 42	
Schenke	5–7, 9ab, 16–22 (23), 28–30, 20–23–Urform–35–36a, 40	(1) 3–4, 8, 10–15, (23) 24–27, 31–34, 36b, 39, 41–42	(1) 2, 9c, 37–38
Fortna	4–7, 9, 16–19, 25, 26, 28, 30, 40	1–3 (4), 8–9c, 10–15, 20–24, 27, 31–39, 41 (42)	
Nicol	5–7, 9, 16, 29, 40	1–3, 10–15, 20–26, 31–39, 41 (42)	
Schulz	5–7, 9, 16–19, 29, 40	1–4, 10–15, 20–27, 31–39, 41 (42)	
Von Wahlde	5–9, 16–19, 25–30, 39	10–15, 20–24, 31–38, 40–42	

The work of the literary critics proves that the episode was not a historical unit. The traditions/editions enlighten us of the creative literary device of the Evangelist. The traditions/editions may also probably indicate how traditional material was used in the inter-community situations, but it is not our primary task here.

4   Through text linguistic analysis: B. Olsson, *Structure and Meaning in the Fourth Gospel: A Text-Linguistic Analysis of John 2:1–11 and 4:1–42* (trans. J. Gray; ConBNT

woman and Jesus actually forms a chapter in the history of the Johannine community. It portrays probably a narrative protocol of a very successful dialogue between the two communities. The following exegesis should clarify this assumption and bring out the central theme of the dialogue into light.

9.2 Exegesis

9.2.1 Verses 5–6: The Place of the Dialogue

The events narrated take place at the Samaritans' holy centre—at Sychar, in Joseph's field, at Jacob's well. The text gives a surprising amount of information both explicitly and implicitly. The Samaritans called Jacob their father. Jacob and Joseph in particular held a prominent position in the Samaritan sources. They proudly and defiantly asserted that they were Joseph's sons.[5] The description of the site here brings to the fore the Samaritans' claim to have been descendants of Jacob, the Patriarch, who has a special relationship to the people of Israel.[6]

According to the Samaritan belief he is the actual progenitor of the elect.[7] Therefore, the description of the site here not only gives a geographic placement of the events, but points to central religious traditions among the Samaritans. For them Joseph's field (a gift of Jacob to Joseph), the land there, and its vicinity became an equivalent to the Jews' Memre at Hebron. It became their religious centre. (This probably indicates that which is told in Josh 24:33—Joseph's bones were buried on the piece of land which Jacob

---

6; Lund: C. W. K. Gleerup, 1974); through speech act reading: J. E. Botha, *Jesus and the Samaritan Woman: A Speech Act Reading of John 4:1–42* (NovTSup 65; Leiden: E. J. Brill, 1991), and through narrative criticism: G. R. O'Day, *Revelation in the Fourth Gospel*. All come to the same conclusion that John 4 is a literary unit!

5   See J. Macdonald, *The Theology of the Samaritans* (NTL; London: SCM Press, 1964), 227, 448, and W. A. Meeks, *The Prophet-King*, 227ff.

6   Jacob is presented as the true heir of Abraham. The "children of Jacob" is a parallel expression to Israel, Jacob and his seed are to be sanctified by God as a nation of his inheritance. God will cleanse them and renew the covenant with them. See *Jub.* 1:28; 19:15ff.; 22:10ff., 14ff., 29ff.; 25:4ff.; 33:21ff. and 36:1ff.

7   J. Macdonald, *The Theology of the Samaritans*, 448.

brought according to Gen 33:19. In the later times Joseph's grave at Shechem became a cult site.[8])

Jacob's well (incidentally inherited along with the field Joseph received from Jacob) is generally identified as the one at the foot of Mount Gerizim.[9] The mountain was assumed to be so well known that it is not named at all. Mount Gerizim's all-overshadowing place in the Samaritan belief is emphatically indicated.[10] Then the description of the place and allusions to it in introducing the site of the event, direct our attention to Samaritan centres, Samaritan beliefs and traditions and thus to the Samaritans.

On the other hand, one needs to identify the "well" symbolism too. A well was regarded as a gift of God (like Manna, the Quails, the pillar of cloud or the pillar of fire) especially for the 'wanderers,' a place of rest, to recuperate and refresh themselves (cf. Genesis 21, 24, 29 and Exod 2:15).[11] In Genesis wells also provided backdrops for betrothal-type scenes.[12] Now one should not dilute 'the well' and the 'wooing women situation' to Jesus' and the Samaritan woman's personal levels. Here the 'Samaritan woman' is a representative of the 'Samaritan community' and Jesus represents the Johannine community. It depicts possibly a life scenario in the social context of Johannine community. The excommunicated and wandering community now seeks 'water'—a place of rest in the Samaritan community among

---

8   See also B. Olsson, *Structure and Meaning in the Fourth Gospel*, 140ff., and H.-M. Schenke, "Jakobs Brunnen – Josephs Grab – Sychar. Topographische Untersuchungen und Erwägungen in der Perspektive von Joh 4,5–6," *ZDPV* 84 (1968): 158–84. Also Stephen's speech in Acts implies that all the Patriarchs were buried at Shechem (Acts 7:15ff.). This has been taken as an indication of Samaritan background of Stephen's speech—and this indicates the belief that Jacob was also buried at Shechem. On the contrary, the Old Testament, Josephus and other Rabbinic sources state Jacob's tomb as being at Hebron; see, H. L. Strack & P. Billerbeck, *Kommentar zum Neuen Testament aus Talmud und Midrasch*, 2:676.
9   This is implied by the words ἐν τῷ ὄρει τούτῳ in vv. 20ff. See R. J. Bull, "An Archaeological Context for Understanding John 4:20," *BA* 38 (1975): 54–59; R. Schnackenburg, *The Gospel according to St. John*, 1:422–23; also B. Olsson, op. cit., 140.
10 For Gerizim's role in Samaritan belief see, J. Macdonald, *The Theology of the Samaritans*, 327ff.
11 For a detailed excurse on "well symbolism" see, B. Olsson, op. cit., 42–172.
12 See Genesis 21, 24, 29, cf. Exod 2:15. Also see Lyle Eslinger, "The Wooing of the Woman at the Well: Jesus, the Reader and Reader-Response Criticism," *Journal of Literature and Theology* 1/2 (1987): 167–83. He sees in vv. 31–34 a Johannine reworking of the betrothal meal typology.

changing/shifting social structures. It requests to be identified and woes the Samaritan community to enter a betrothal covenant.

9.2.2 Verses 7–15: Dialogue on God's Gift which Transcends all Traditions

Jesus asks for water: δός μοι πεῖν. The woman who has come to draw water and Jesus both share in the common human experience of thirst and the quenching thereof. Here comes the Johannine double meaning into play. It is said that the Fourth Evangelist used the double meaning in such a way that the concepts and statements that at first sight refer to earthly matters, provokingly refer to the divine.[13] One should pose here a question as to whether this double meaning refers symbolically to the human sociological experience of both the Samaritans and the Johannine community in the sight of Jews. Do both communities here share the human experience of thirst for social identity?[14]

Δός μοι πεῖν has two parallels in its Old Testament usage: Exod 17:2: Δὸς ἡμῖν ὕδωρ, ἵνα πίωμεν, and Num 21:16: καὶ δώσω αὐτοῖς ὕδωρ πιεῖν, the request not only describes the situation, but brings into play the "well" theme. It is then an invitation to begin a relationship. But the woman refuses to oblige—the reason (the Evangelist says) is the οὐ συγχρῶνται between the Jews and the Samaritans.[15] The polarity between the Jews and the Samaritans was so great that it gave sociological expression to their hostility in that they did not co-use with one another. It points towards a social context of reciprocal contempt and separation. In the woman's words "you are a Jew, I am a Samaritan," the emphasis is on the Jewishness of Jesus and her Samaritan identity. She is surprised by Jesus' invitation to violate the religious/ethnic barrier.

Jesus strikingly does not debate on the issue of national antagonism between the Samaritans and the Jews; rather he transfers the discussion to

---

13 See R. Bultmann's *Das Evangelium des Johannes*, 135, n. 1.
14 D. W. Wead, *The Literary Devices in John's Gospel* (Basel: Friedrich Reinhart Kommissionsverlag, 1970), 71–94, regards this double meaning technique as a metaphor, though he does not interpret "give me water" in this way!
15 For the meaning of συγχράομαι see R. Bultmann, *Das Evangelium des Johannes*, 130; D. Daube, "Jesus and the Samaritan Woman: The Meaning of συγχράομαι," *JBL* 69 (1950): 137–47, and D. R. Hall, "The Meaning of συγχράομαι in John 4:9," *ExpTim* 83 (1971–72): 56–57.

the sphere of God's relationship and God's dealing with human beings. Jesus speaks of God's gift/the self-giving God that is a central theme of the Fourth Gospel. Verse 10 reminds one of John 3:16 (see exegesis there). The governing principle of God's relationship with people is His generous/free gift. The word δωρεά is a noun—the root meaning of the term bears the notion 'free'/for nothing.[16] God is the one who freely gives the gift of living. Without Him living is impossible. God's gift/giving surpasses religious/ethnic identity. It is not primarily the ethnicity/religions that give us identity; it is God's gift of 'living' that gives us an identity. According to the Evangelist, here Jesus is the One who from God gave us this knowledge, thus he brings us the gift itself.[17]

But the woman understands the 'living water' as natural spring water. She draws Jesus' attention to the predicament of his own situation (v. 11). Given the prevalent conditions, the fact that Jesus himself is thirsty having just asked for a drink now offers her 'spring water,' must, to say the least, appear ridiculous. Thus "You with nothing to draw, how can you give me to drink?" is a legitimate question. She also focuses on the depth of the well, its revered traditional associations and that it was a semi-eternal well for her. Is the Evangelist here making the Samaritans ask the same question to the community? You who just asked us to "recognise you," now tell us that you give us the real identity of living—how can you?

From the primary stand-point of 'spring of water' the woman understands, reacts and compares him with Jacob (v. 12) the giver of the well, whose water in her view Jesus seems to slight. Her reply in v. 11 is in fact a defence of their ancestral traditions. Note carefully how the Evangelist who compares Jesus to Moses whenever he has a Jewish audience in mind elsewhere in the Gospel, now compares Jesus with Jacob. Jacob's well, his place of worship gave the Samaritans a cultic/ethnic identity they claim of over against the Jewish nation. How can this 'new living water' that Jesus gives be better than the one she already has? Only if Jesus is greater than Jacob can he provide living water. Her question prefaced by μή however implies that Jesus cannot possibly be greater than Jacob, or can he? The

---

16 Cf. Büchsel, "δωρεά," in *TDNT* 2:167.
17 The overtones of the wisdom motif seem to be echoing here, cf. Prov 8:35. See also M. Theobald, *Im Anfang war das Wort*, 98–109, and E. D. Freed, *Old Testament Quotations in the Gospel of John*, 21–38.

possibility is thus left open for thought, the μή question expects a negative answer; but it does not necessarily rule out a positive one.

Jesus again does not dispute any of the issues raised by her—his lack of a utensil to draw water, the depth of the well, the revered traditions associated with it and the Jacob greatness proved by the gift of semi-eternal well. Still the partakers of the dialogue are not on the same wave-length. They speak what they think important from their point of view. The woman disputes what Jesus says, Jesus, however, does not. Instead he goes on to describe and expand the meaning of living water, the gift of God still further (vv. 13 & 14)—what he speaks of is not drinking water but "living water." Drinking from Jacob's well is expressed by the present participle ὁ πίνων thus indicating that the action is indeed one that is repeated, while drinking of the living water, that is God's gift, is aorist subjective πίῃ, indicating a completed, self-contained act.[18] Living water is located in individuals. It is not only accessible, but is very personal and intimate, being the unique possession of the drinker. The verbs γίνομαι and ἄλλομαι aptly describe both conceptionally and visually the living and life-giving quality of water. This water wells up from within of its own accord, energising and giving new life where there was previously none—"leaping up" symbolises sustained abundance and joy.[19] Thus the "gift of God" quenches in a radical way the thirst for life that makes it felt in the physical thirst. It achieves what no earthy sustenance can achieve, not even the highest and most indispensable of all—water.[20] Thus Jesus explains the "gift of God" using the imagery of water and the task of water-fetching, both of which are familiar to the woman.

The woman slowly begins to comprehend Jesus' words little by little. Though she has not fully grasped the concept of the gift of God she asks Jesus for the water, she thinks it can slake thirst forever and further trips to the well be spared (v. 15). This shows her inability to cross from the material symbol that it symbolises. There is an implied willingness to abandon Jacob's well to which she was previously loyal. She was ready to risk her ethnic/religious identity in order to get a better and securer identity.

---

18 B. Lindars, *The Gospel of John*, 182ff., and G. R. O'Day, *Revelation in the Fourth Gospel*, 63.
19 See T. Okure, *The Johannine Approach to Mission: A Contextual Study of John 4:1–42* (WUNT 2.31; Tübingen: J. C. B. Mohr [Paul Siebeck], 1988), 103.
20 See R. Bultmann, *Das Evangelium des Johannes*, 132–33.

9.2.3 Verses 16–26: Dialogue on God's Worship, the Centre of a New Tradition

Verse 16: λέγει αὐτῇ· ὕπαγε φώνησον τὸν ἄνδρα σου καὶ ἐλθὲ ἐνθάδε.

Jesus perceives both her readiness for a new relationship and also her miscomprehension. He changes the topic, or rather he gives it a turn so as to speak to her of something she ought to understand very easily: "Go and call your husband" (v. 16). What is Jesus' motive in asking the woman to call her husband, which has no apparent connection with what has just preceded? Is it to provide her an opportunity to realise her true position, so that she may understand that Jesus can satisfy needs of which she is as yet not conscious? Or is it to drive in hard the importance of the gift of God (living water) that should not merely be enjoyed for selfish ends, but must always be shared? Did then Jesus tell the woman to call the person with whom she would have naturally shared the past?

The verb φωνέω usually has a sense of 'call,' 'summon,' 'call by name' and when used with God as object may mean 'summon/invoke God.'[21] If we allow a Semitic usage and biblical concept of God as "husband" (Hos 2:2, 7, 16) since the Hebrew word husband (בעל, 'master,' 'Lord') was used also as a name for a pagan deity, the passage in the Fourth Gospel is interpreted as a play on words. Is Jesus asking her to go and invoke her God?

Verses 17–18: ἀπεκρίθη ἡ γυνὴ καὶ εἶπεν αὐτῷ· οὐκ ἔχω ἄνδρα. λέγει αὐτῇ ὁ Ἰησοῦς· καλῶς εἶπας ὅτι ἄνδρα οὐκ ἔχω· πέντε γὰρ ἄνδρας ἔσχες καὶ νῦν ὃν ἔχεις οὐκ ἔστιν σου ἀνήρ· τοῦτο ἀληθὲς εἴρηκας.

The woman says, "I have no man," which seems to be misleading.[22] We notice that the woman's seemingly evading answer is being appreciated by Jesus: "You are right in saying: I have no man." But in the same breath (in characteristic Johannine irony) he adds that she had five husbands and that the man with whom she now lived was not her husband. Is it a literary technique of the Evangelist intended to convey to his readers that Jesus had

---

21   O. Betz, in *TWNT* 9:295, gives the meaning "rufen, beim Namen rufen," when a person is the object (cf. *TDNT* 9:278–309). See also B. Olsson, *Structure and Meaning in the Fourth Gospel*, 184.

22   Most scholars interpret it as an attempt of the woman to evade the issue; see R. E. Brown, *The Gospel according to John*, 1:171, 177; L. Morris, *The Gospel according to John*, 264, and B. Lindars, *The Gospel of John*, 184.

a supernatural, divine insight into every person? Or, does it have a function of revealing Jesus' omniscience?[23]

Or did Jesus expose the sin of the woman? Did he awaken the moral conscience in her? Bultmann says, "revelation is for a person the disclosure of one's own life." Jesus shows the woman the truth of her own situation. Only by a person becoming aware of her/his true nature can the revealer be recognised.[24] But Jesus reveals to the woman nothing new that she did not already know about herself. Her moral life seems not to be the issue here. The Samaritan woman's report to the villagers that a man had told her all– *everything*, and she and the villagers taking her invitation at face value to see the "one" to whom she bears witness give it sufficient credibility, and militate against the consideration that she had a very questionable morality. Would the villagers have listened to her if her reputation were as sullied as it is commonly portrayed?[25]

According to the Pentateuch, it was technically not forbidden for a woman to be married five times, but the Jewish teachers forbade a woman to be married more than twice, or at the most three times.[26] Moreover, there is no indication in the passage that the Evangelist intends to present Jesus as confronting the woman with her sinful life. For, nowhere in the entire Gospel tradition does Jesus set out to confront individuals with their sinfulness.[27]

Teresa Okure suggests that the woman's five husbands should be taken literally, and adds that the Evangelist's portrait of the woman five times married living with a man not her husband places her in the same category as other "hopeless cases" which serve as the material for Jesus' signs in the

---

23 So R. Bultmann, *Das Evangelium des Johannes*, 139; A. Wikenhauser, *Das Evangelium nach Johannes*, 107, and R. Schnackenburg, *The Gospel according to St. John*, 1:48.
24 R. Bultmann, op. cit, 139; see also T. Zahn, *Das Evangelium des Johannes*, 242; E. C. Hoskyns, *The Fourth Gospel*, 243; R. Schnackenburg, *The Gospel according to St. John*, 1:468, and B. Lindars, *The Gospel of John*, 185, tend to highlight Jesus laying bare the woman's sins.
25 See E. Haenchen, *John*, 1:243, and W. Bauer, *Das Johannesevangelium*, 45.
26 H. L. Strack & P. Billerbeck, *Kommentar zum Neuen Testament aus Talmud und Midrasch*, 2:437.
27 In the Fourth Gospel there is an appeal to faith and a warning of the consequence of unbelief (8:21, 24; 9:41; 15:22, 24) and against sinning in the future (5:14, cf. 8:11), but never a confrontation of the individuals with their sinful life. Indeed it is by coming to Jesus 'the light,' 'the saviour of the world,' that individuals are enabled to change from their sinful life to a life "lived in God."

Gospel,[28] but here Jesus did not perform any sign. It has been observed, 'the husband/husbands' are not important to the Evangelist's story as his tendency to present women independent shows, the mother of Jesus, the Samaritan woman, Mary, Martha, Mary Magdalene (cf. 11:1–53; 12:1–18; 19:25; 20:1–2, 11–18).[29] Then the talk of husband/man or husbands/men must point towards a symbolical interpretation.

If, as we suggested earlier in v. 16, "man" be interpreted as "God," then the woman's answer should be understood as: "She now has no God." Then Jesus' appreciation of her confession and his ironical "five husbands" should refer to the earlier Samaritan cult and the contemporary religious conditions in Samaria. The 'five husbands' then should be taken as symbolic of the gods worshipped by the five nations settled in Samaria by the Assyrians.[30] The sixth man then should mean either the God of Israel whom the Samaritans did not worship properly, or some deity whose cult had recently been introduced to the Samaritans, for instance by Simon Magus (Acts 8:9ff.).

The temporal comparison aorist ἔσχες and νῦν should also be noted here—you "had" and "but now." The distinction between then and now becomes a key factor and bridge between the interpretation we preferred and the interpretation of the next verse.

---

28 T. Okure, *The Johannine Approach to Mission*, 112. Her understanding and interpretation that the material objects of Jesus' signs prove to be extraordinarily inadequate—the water of purification, 38 years crippled, the man born blind, Lazarus dead for four days, the hopeless situation as suggested by Philip before the feeding miracle—are partially true. According to her their adequacy throws greater relief into their sign value.

29 Cf. S. M. Schneiders, "Woman in the Fourth Gospel and the Role of the Women in the Contemporary Church," *BTB* 12 (1982): 44–45. The women in the Fourth Gospel do not appear to be dependent on husbands or other male legitimates, nor as seeking permission for their activities from male officials. They envisage remarkable originality in their relationship within the community. They are privileged recipients of Jesus' most important self-revelation.

30 Cf. 2 Kgs 17:24ff.—it speaks of seven gods, but in his history Josephus (*Ant.* 11.288) mentions five gods: ἕκαστοι κατὰ ἔθνος ἴδιον θεὸν εἰς τὴν Σαμάρειαν κομίσαντες (πέντε δ' ἦσαν). The following commentators do not agree to this interpretation: R. Bultmann, *Das Evangelium des Johannes*, 138–44; R. Schnackenburg, *The Gospel according to St. John*, 1:468; G. R. Beasley-Murray, *John*, 61; C. K. Barrett, *The Gospel according to St. John*, 235; E. Haenchen, *John*, 242, and J. N. Sanders, *A Commentary on the Gospel according to St. John*, 144. B. Olsson, *Structure and Meaning in the Fourth Gospel*, 186, and R. E. Brown, *The Gospel according to John*, 1:171, however, say this interpretation is possible.

Verse 19: λέγει αὐτῷ ἡ γυνή· κύριε, θεωρῶ ὅτι προφήτης εἶ σύ.

The woman formulates her understanding of Jesus as προφήτης εἶ σύ. She 'perceives' that he is a prophet. θεωρέω probably denotes an intellectual perception of a fact, not a spiritual insight into the meaning. In the Fourth Gospel though θεωρεῖν is close to πιστεύειν (cf. John 12:44ff.), the Evangelist usually uses the perfect of ὁράω (John 1:34; 3:11, 32; 19:35: ἑωρακώς) to signify a kind of 'having seen' which produces a permanent result enabling the person who has seen to bear witness.[31]

προφήτης here is anarthrous, therefore probably to be understood in a generic way. The image of the prophet is as one having a spiritual understanding of the people and an ability to reveal the will of God and as the one sent by God to speak the words that God has put in his mouth. But it is well known that the Samaritans rejected the prophetic books and the only prophet they recognised was the prophet who was to return—a prophet like Moses.[32] How should we then interpret 'prophet'—in the Jewish or in the Samaritan sense? In v. 19 we may well assume she means it from the Jewish perspective—a seer. Verse 20 supports this, as she goes on to compare 'our fathers' and 'you'—here "you" clearly is a pointer to Jesus' Jewish background!

Verse 20: οἱ πατέρες ἡμῶν ἐν τῷ ὄρει τούτῳ προσεκύνησαν· καὶ ὑμεῖς λέγετε ὅτι ἐν Ἱεροσολύμοις ἐστὶν ὁ τόπος ὅπου προσκυνεῖν δεῖ.

The man who simply made plain her/the Samaritans' most treasured cultic/ethnic identity sounds like a prophet, very straightforward and authoritative in speech. Now the woman would like to test whether this seemingly Jewish prophet is the prophet who is to come (Samaritan?). Therefore, she places before him the question that seeks his opinion on the most central dispute over their religious/ethnic identity with the Jews: "Our fathers worshipped on this mountain, but you Jews say that the place where God must be worshipped is in Jerusalem." "What is your opinion over the long standing issue of Gerizim[33] versus Jerusalem?" The ploy is simple: if he takes on the

---

31 E. A. Abbott, *Johannine Vocabulary*, §§ 1579–1611, esp. 1605.
32 See J. Macdonald, *The Theology of the Samaritans*, 204–11, also see W. A. Meeks, *The Prophet-King*, 32ff., and M. de Jonge, *Jesus: Stranger from Heaven and Son of God*, 170.
33 The Samaritans held the sanctity of Gerizim at least as much as the Jews held that of Jerusalem as the place of worship. Belief in Gerizim formed the fourth article of

side of the Yahweh cult of Jerusalem then he is a Jewish prophet, if he speaks of Gerizim then the prophet to come, Taheb. Is she looking for the priest who will teach Samaritans the right form of worship (2 Kgs 17:34)? The woman proves to be in remarkably good touch with the dispute between the two nations.

ὁ τόπος refers to the Temple (cf. John 11:48). This expression is regarded as specifically Samaritan.[34] The verb προσκυνεῖν is a technical term on cultic worship and is also used (cf. 12:20) in reference to the pilgrimages to Jerusalem.[35] Where is the true temple of God on earth? Note the neutrality in the woman's formulation of the question, as if she has no identity of her own, yet the attachment to ancestral practices/traditions as "collective reassurance" against the contempt of the Jews.

Another important issue is, whether the Samaritan woman places her tradition as against that of the Jewish tradition, or whether she contrasts hers with that of the community's which was perceived to be predominantly Jerusalem-centred? Bultmann rightly interprets the "you" as indicating the Johannine community.[36] It is clear that the early church "saw" Jerusalem as the departure point (Acts 2) and as the eschatological "centre"/capital! It not only took over the Hebrew Bible into its tradition and proclaimed a Jerusalem-centred Eschatology, but also looked forward to a "new Jerusalem." Therefore, in a dialogue situation, that the Samaritans wished to know whether the Johannine community insisted on a 'Jerusalem'-centred Eschatology is but natural and logical!

Note again the question formulation, our fathers worshipped (not we worshipped). The temporal feature of the question should also be taken note

---

the Samaritan creed and it is well known that the Samaritan Pentateuch reads Gerizim in place of "Ebal" in Deut 27:4. Therefore, not only was Gerizim the place of sacrifice of Isaac, but next to Sinai, it was the mount of revelation of the eternal will, the point of entry into the invisible, the new Eden of the end time; see, J. Macdonald, *The Theology of the Samaritans*, 406. Cf. also R. E. Brown, *The Gospel according to John*, 1:171–72.

34   A. Spiro, "Stephen's Samaritan Background," in J. Munck, *The Acts of the Apostles* (AB 31; New York: Doubleday, 1967), 285–300.
35   R. Bultmann, *Das Evangelium des Johannes*, 139. See also H. Greeven, in *TDNT* 6:758ff.
36   See his *Das Evangelium des Johannes*, 120. The opposite view is presented by R. E. Brown, *The Gospel according to John*, 1:172, who considers this will betray the historic (!) setting of the episode.

of, προσεκύνησαν aorist is used here. The woman avoids references to the present/contemporary state of Samaritan worship by speaking only of the earlier religious practice at Gerizim.[37] Should this point towards a possible state of confusion regarding the contemporary cultic practices in Samaria that they themselves regarded as legitimate (cf. v. 17)? Also the discussion is not about the contemporary cultic practice of the Samaritans, as against the Jerusalem-centred worship. It speaks of "our fathers." It has been suggested that it refers to the recent history of the Samaritans, to the period of the temple from the end of the fourth century to the year 129/28 B.C., when John Hyrcanus destroyed the Gerizim temple,[38] but it seems to me that the question is addressed to the Johannine community. It should be paraphrased as: 'which cultic centre do you prefer'? Do you prefer the tradition of "our fathers," that goes back to the time of Abraham who performed his greatest act of faith and worship in the sacrifice of Isaac on Mount Gerizim? Or do you give preference to the contemporary Jewish dogma that one ought to worship at Jerusalem that only dates from the Davidic era?

Verse 21: λέγει αὐτῇ ὁ Ἰησοῦς· πίστευέ μοι, γύναι, ὅτι ἔρχεται ὥρα ὅτε οὔτε ἐν τῷ ὄρει τούτῳ οὔτε ἐν Ἱεροσολύμοις προσκυνήσετε τῷ πατρί.

Jesus bids her to trust him. Here πιστεύειν + dative is not used in the usual Johannine terms (to believe in order to witness). It comes as a consoling promise. Instead of contradicting, Jesus transposes this issue of worship to a completely different level, namely, that of Eschatology. He speaks of a time when both Jerusalem and Gerizim become irrelevant and lose their significance. Old shrines will not matter.

The Evangelist speaks of worship of God that transcends ethnic traditions. "Our Father" is no more an ethnic, ancestral figure, but God Himself. A time will come when we can look above our cultic patterns and ethnic traditions to God's own traditions who is our Father, and God's traditions are not confined to any cultic places or shrines, or are of a specific, particular ethnicity/pattern. It transforms and transcends every particular ethnic/cultic

---

37 This temporal reference is what Jesus uses to speak of five men in v. 18. Thus ἔσχες and προσεκύνησαν may be regarded as the connecting link in interpreting vv. 18 and 20. Cf. B. Olsson, *Structure and Meaning in the Fourth Gospel*, 201.
38 H. G. Kippenberg, *Garizim und Synagoge: Traditionsgeschichtliche Untersuchungen zur samaritanischen Religion der aramäischen Periode* (RGVV 30; Berlin: de Gruyter, 1971), 48ff.

identity into a "universal tradition"! A time will come when people will worship God in a God-given pattern. God our Father will define and provide a universal worship pattern.

Verse 22—ὑμεῖς προσκυνεῖτε ὃ οὐκ οἴδατε· ἡμεῖς προσκυνοῦμεν ὃ οἴδαμεν, ὅτι ἡ σωτηρία ἐκ τῶν Ἰουδαίων ἐστίν.

It is suggested that the knowing-not of the Samaritans could be explained with 2 Kgs 17:34 as its background, as it attests the continued ignorance of the Samaritans over the true form of worship: "To this day they do according to the former practice. They do not fear the Lord and they do not follow the statutes or the ordinances or the law or the commandments which the Lord commanded the children of Jacob whom He named Israel!" Attention is also drawn to Sir 50:25–26 according to which "the foolish people live in Shechem" and *T. Levi* 7, where Shechem is mentioned as "the city of the ignorant." These Jewish polemics against the Samaritans seem to also be the opinion of Josephus (*Ant.* 12.258–264) as he reports the message sent to Antiochus Epiphanes by the Samaritans.[39]

To think that the Johannine community in dialogue with the Samaritans speaks out these Jewish wits is unbelievable. Likewise the interpretation that the Jews knew about God's promise of salvation to others, especially Samaritans does not hold good for, the Samaritans too are the sons of Abraham and have like the Jews Jacob as their father. Even 2 Kings 17 speaks of God's covenant with these people although it speaks of Samaritans' unfaithfulness to it. And most importantly here we do not have a 'Jews against Samaritans' situation, but a dialogic situation between the Samaritans and the Johannine community (cf. v. 20).

It should be noted that while the woman tends to hide defensively behind the tradition of the fathers ("our fathers/you" in v. 20), Jesus addresses the present generation ("you/we" in v. 22). The contemporary generation should assume full responsibility for its current religious practices and needs to do this not only in the light of what "the fathers" did long ago or the dogmatic assertions and traditions of the recent past, but in response to what 'the Father' wants now. The community tells the Samaritans they do

---

39 See O. Betz, "To Worship God in Spirit and in Truth: Reflections on John 4, 20–26," in *Standing before God: Studies on Prayer in Scriptures and in Tradition* (ed. A. Finkel and L. Frizzell; New York: Ktav Publishing House, 1981), 56.

not know (which may indicate the contemporary uncertainty regarding their cultic practices) how to respond to 'the Father' who creates new universal worship traditions. "We know" here speaks of the confidence of the community, which has come to grasp the "gift of God" through Jesus.

ὅτι ἡ σωτηρία ἐκ τῶν Ἰουδαίων ἐστίν (it is from Jews that salvation comes, v. 22b). Do the Jews have a precedence in the history of salvation? This very dogmatic sounding statement has been the point of heated scholarly discussion. Bultmann reduces this to gloss, Bauer and Odeberg too. Brown tries to explain out this "hard" statement, saying the Fourth Gospel does not reject the spiritual heritage of Judaism.[40] Probably the exegetical basis lies in Gen 49:10 where, according to the blessing given by Jacob, the tribe of Judah assumes the key role for Israel's salvation[41] and the Messiah tradition connected with this verse also proclaimed that one from the tribe of Judah would bring salvation not only to the Jews, but also to the nations. "To him shall be the obedience of the people" (Gen 49:10) should be understood as the universal nature of salvation. In the Johannine context ἡ σωτηρία is to be understood primarily as the gift of God as announced in v. 10. The Johannine implied meaning of this "gift of God"—salvation—is to have eternal life, life in its fullness, to be free from bondage, and as natural opposite to judgement.[42]

Rhetorically, the Fourth Evangelist writes that salvation has its earthly departure (ἐκ), not its origin (παρά) from the Jews.[43] Again the emphasis is on the universality of salvation. "Judah" is here the channel, salvation is God's gift, He is the giver, 'Jews' are the medium (a passive role indeed!). It must also be understood as the community's way of coming to terms with its Jewish origin. Instead of being 'cocooned' by the fact, it tries to explain out its being above Judaism and forms its eschatological conceptions accordingly.

---

40 R. E. Brown, *The Gospel according to John*, 1:172.
41 See O. Betz, "To Worship God in Spirit and in Truth," 56, 67.
42 Cf. John 3:15, 16; 5:24, 29; 8:24, 34–36; 10:10; 11:25–26. Cf. also σώζειν, in *TDNT* 7:997; T. Okure, *The Johannine Approach to Mission*, 119.
43 παρά is the preposition most frequently used in the Fourth Gospel for origin or source (1:6; 8:40 from God) other than the reference to the places of origin (for example, Beth-sa'ida, cf. 1:44; 7:42; 11:1; 12:21; 19:38). The Gospel uses ἀπό to imply causality/ originator (3:2; 6:38; 13:3; 16:30).

Verses 23–24: —ἀλλὰ ἔρχεται ὥρα καὶ νῦν ἐστιν, ὅτε οἱ ἀληθινοὶ προσκυνηταὶ προσκυνήσουσιν τῷ πατρὶ ἐν πνεύματι καὶ ἀληθείᾳ· καὶ γὰρ ὁ πατὴρ τοιούτους ζητεῖ τοὺς προσκυνοῦντας αὐτόν. πνεῦμα ὁ θεός, καὶ τοὺς προσκυνοῦντας αὐτὸν ἐν πνεύματι καὶ ἀληθείᾳ δεῖ προσκυνεῖν.

It has been proposed that at least four possible biblical traditions and that of Qumran stand behind these verses, thus providing an exegetical key:

A) In 2 Kgs 17:34–41 the Samaritans' obligations for proper worship is shown explicitly. It has been noted that v. 35 ". . . you shall bow down (προσκυνεῖν)" corresponds to true worship spoken of in John 4:23–24. This text also binds together the related concepts of 'fear of God' and 'worship of God.'

B) The covenant at Shechem (Josh 24) is the second tradition suggested. The proposed points of contact between Josh 24 and John 4 are five:
   a) The place—Shechem (or the vicinity).
   b) The similarity of persons—Joshua and Jesus (Jehoshua) are both representatives of God.
   c) The decision to worship the true God in contrast to the gods of their fathers, which has to be made "now."[44]
   d) In Josh 24:14 and John 4:23–24 the dual characterisation of proper worship, namely "in sincerity and truth," is emphasised. The emphasis in Shechem is on the true worship in correspondence, reaction and answer to the revelation of God. It is the grateful acceptance of God who revealed Himself to His people as Helper and Redeemer.
   e) It is also very significant that the covenant at Shechem united the now separated tribes of Jews and Samaritans into one covenant-worshipping community.

C) The third Old Testament passage that may shed light on vv. 23–24 are Psalms 42 and 43 which form a unit. Here the desired goal is divine worship in the temple. The physical distance makes a pilgrimage impossible, but God's light and truth are called powers that diminish the dividing might of space and, as it were, allow for a spiritual divine worship. The prayer from afar finds its way to God and the divine worship in light and truth consists of praise of God whom one trusts as Saviour (Ps 43:4; 42:12).

---

44 Cf. Josh 24:15, "Your ancestors served God," with John 4:20, "Our fathers worshipped," also Josh 24:14, "now," with Josh 24:15, "today," with John 4:23, "and now."

D) The Qumran texts provide exegetical help not only because the cult of that community was separated from that of the temple in Jerusalem, but also because in them one finds close association of spirit and truth.
   a) 1QS VIII, 5–6; IX, 6–7 speaks of the community's self-understanding as a living spiritual sanctuary in whose life the Holy Spirit and truth are embodied. It replaces the defiled, malfunctioning temple in Jerusalem.
   b) For the community, foundation of the spirit of holiness for eternal truth means also that God Himself is the builder of His spiritual house and fills it with His power (1QH VI, 25). Thus it is founded in truth (1QS VIII, 4) and its living stones become witnesses of truth at judgement (1QS VIII, 6).
   c) The Qumran community stands in the tradition of the covenant on the Mount Sinai and also in that of Shechem, since it strives for a perfect and true divine worship. It is a house of perfection and truth in Israel, wherein one brings an offering of pleasant fragrance and where the covenant is established according to the eternal precepts (1QS VIII, 9–10).
   d) God is defined as truth (1QH IV, 40; XV, 25) where it is clear that this expression wishes to emphasise the character of God's historical deeds in relation to human beings. His mouth (1QH XI, 7), His actions are truth (1QH XIV, 12; I, 30; 1QS X, 17). God's truth provides itself in His loving action towards people and He judges with great pity and forgiveness (1QH XI, 8–9). Thus it becomes possible for the actions of a purified person to be in truth (1QH VI, 8–9).
   e) In the *Temple Scroll* from Cave 11, God Himself announces: "I will sanctify my temple through my glory because I will let my glory dwell upon it until the day of blessing when I will create my temple in order to establish it myself forever according to the covenant which I made with Jacob at Bethel" (columns XXIX, 8–10).

Being aided from the above passages which provide exegetical help, the Johannine imperative—πνεῦμα ὁ θεός, καὶ τοὺς προσκυνοῦντας αὐτὸν ἐν πνεύματι καὶ ἀληθείᾳ δεῖ προσκυνεῖν ("God is Spirit and those who worship Him must worship Him in spirit and truth")—clears all the confusions on the central issue of discussion—'the worship.' God is no more a God of (or bound to) a place, or a race. God is a Spirit. πνεῦμα is a definition of God (cf.

parallel Johannine definitions—God is light in 1 John 1:5; God is love in 1 John 4:8). It is a reminder that God is different from all that is earthly and human. It is not a definition of God's essence, but it portrays God's mode of operation/action (see the exegesis of 3:3–8). It speaks of His nearness, His creative, regenerative, life-giving acts which the human world experiences, His omnipresence and His spontaneity in dealing with humankind. It speaks of His "otherness," His invisibility, His incomprehensibleness, His transcendence. It speaks of His freedom to penetrate and hold everything together and to bring everything to wholeness, as He will make His will known, in convincing the world of sin and of righteousness, of judgement, and will lead it to all truth (cf. 16:8, 13).

The fitting response to such a God is worship, δεῖ a necessity. And the worship must be in spirit and in truth, as we worship Him for what He is and as He is. Only those who are overwhelmed by the Spirit (according to 3:5ff. only those who are born of the Spirit) can understand Him and worship Him authentically with a new proper perspective. ". . . for such the Father seeks to worship Him" (v. 23b) means, only God can enable us to worship Him rightly through His working in such: an act of grace (cf. Psalms 42, 43).

The Spirit makes possible the worship that transcends all barriers, such as nationality, ethnicity and religious backgrounds. "Truth" here assures the reality of encounters with Him, as one experiences liberation (8:32), sanctification and consecration (cf. 17:17–19). It also emphasises human trustworthiness, as God Himself is truthful. Thus the worship in spirit and in truth has the transcendental power to build an eschatological (now!), ecumenical (Samaritan-Johannine community) unity. This eschatological community will in its worship in spirit and in truth understand what/who God is in relation to human beings and encounter, experience God's mighty act—the gift of salvation—and pledge itself "true" to God who is Spirit. The Evangelist in the dialogue context foresaw a new tradition that God would create an eschatological community that would be given the true knowledge of true worship of God Himself.

Verse 25: λέγει αὐτῷ ἡ γυνή· οἶδα ὅτι Μεσσίας ἔρχεται ὁ λεγόμενος χριστός· ὅταν ἔλθῃ ἐκεῖνος, ἀναγγελεῖ ἡμῖν ἅπαντα.

As far as we know the title Μεσσίας was not used by the Samaritans. Accordingly, it was placed in the woman's mouth. The second half of the verse: "when he comes he will proclaim all things to us" actually gives content to the title Μεσσίας here. After understanding the talk of 'true worship' rightly, she expresses her Samaritan belief in the prophet who will speak the words of God and reveal all things.⁴⁵ The prophet mentioned here was seen as 'the one and only' Teacher, Interpreter of the law, he gives insight into all things.⁴⁶ Now the question arises whether she is referring here to the Samaritan Taheb (the one who is to return), or is this knowledge based on Gen 49:10, whereby the woman understands the coming of Shiloh? Could it be the sent one from the tribe of Judah?⁴⁷ Since the Samaritan woman is most patriotic (vv. 9b, 11–12, 20) one would naturally expect her Messiah to be the same as that expected by her nation. But the crux of the problem is determining the nature of this "one who is to return." Was he a 'Moses redivivus', a 'Joshua redivivus', or 'Henoch redivivus'? Is he a restorer? a restorer of the cultus? A revealer of the truth? A converter of the nations? A gatherer of the scattered?⁴⁸ Or a political figure in religious garb as is described by Josephus? (*Ant.* 18.85–86)

Though we cannot decide on the exact meaning of the woman's confession, we should neither interpret it as her confession of the Jewish Messiah nor as a usual Jewish title which she anyhow confessed without actually meaning it! It should rather be interpreted as her sincere longing to be part of such a worshipping community.⁴⁹ Probably she brings in two very important features of Samaritan Eschatology into the dialogue, one being her confession of the coming one as discussed above, and the other, his being closely related to the Taheb. The Samaritans' held a belief that God's habitation (Miskan) had been set upon Gerizim by Moses, but had later been

---

45 Here the woman confesses her Samaritan faith not her belief in Jesus, which was based on Deut 18:18; LXX–Deut 18:18: προφήτην ἀναστήσω αὐτοῖς ἐκ τῶν ἀδελφῶν αὐτῶν ὥσπερ σὲ καὶ δώσω τὸ ῥῆμά μου ἐντ ᾧ στόματι αὐτοῦ, καὶ λαλήσει αὐτοῖς καθότι ἂν ἐντείλωμαι αὐτῷ.
46 See H. G. Kippenberg, *Garizim und Synagoge*, 326.
47 See O. Betz, "To Worship God in Spirit and in Truth," 64.
48 For the detailed discussion on 'Taheb' in Samaritan sources see, J. Macdonald, *The Theology of the Samaritans*, 262–71; W. A. Meeks, *The Prophet-King*, 250–57, H. G. Kippenberg, *Garizim und Synagoge*, 276–327; E. D. Freed, "Samaritan Influence in the Gospel of John," *CBQ* 30 (1968): 580–87; H. Odeberg, *The Fourth Gospel*, 181–87; F. Dexinger, "Samaritan Eschatology," in *The Samaritans* (ed. A. D. Crown; Tübingen: J. C. B. Mohr [Paul Siebeck], 1989), 267–76.
49 In a dialogic situation in a pluralistic society, such basic confessional longings of people of our neighbours of faith are sometimes interpreted as their confession of their Christian faith—absurd as it is!

hidden there at the beginning of the era of divine disfavour. Since the Gerizim temple was destroyed in 129/28 B.C., they expected that Miskan would be there once more in the future in the period of divine favour. The Samaritans seem to have expected their eschatological manifestation on the mountain.[50]

Verse 26: λέγει αὐτῇ ὁ Ἰησοῦς· ἐγώ εἰμι, ὁ λαλῶν σοι.

When the woman confesses her faith in a revealer to come, Jesus says to her: "I am he, I who am speaking to you." Does Jesus identify himself with the Samaritans' Taheb? Do we see a levelling of terminologies, Christ and Taheb?[51] Or is it the Evangelist's way of leading the woman from her belief that Jesus is a prophet, to make her confess that he is the Messiah? A closer examination of the texts compels us to say an emphatic No. Jesus does not say he is the Messiah. He just says ἐγώ εἰμι. He presents himself as the one who now fulfils the basic longings and faith of the woman.[52] Jesus is not just the Jewish Messiah or the Samaritan Taheb, he is the ἐγώ εἰμι, he is the one who speaks.

λαλέω is a technical word in the Fourth Gospel for proclamation, for the salvation, the gift of God it embodies. For the Fourth Evangelist, Jesus is the gift of God, symbolising God's own self-giving for the world and this gift cannot be defined or explained by one particular community's language, expectations, longings, and concepts. Jesus as God's gift, as the 'Sent One' who transcends the religious/ethnic traditions, he can be nothing but 'the cosmic' "I am."

If seen from the perspective of the Johannine community's dialogue with the Samaritans, this should become clear. The community presents Jesus as the one who fulfils the Samaritans' basic expectations and beliefs. The Samaritans do not accept Jesus as the Messiah, but as the Saviour of the world. Therefore, in presenting Jesus to the non-Jewish world especially to those to whom Jesus was anathema, we see the Johannine community's

---

50 H. G. Kippenberg, *Garizim und Synagoge*, chapter 9, esp. p. 253; also B. Olsson, *Structure and Meaning in the Fourth Gospel*, 190–91.
51 W. A. Meeks, *The Prophet-King*, 318; M. L. Appold, *The Oneness Motif in the Fourth Gospel*, 70.
52 See absolute ἐγώ εἰμι as a presentation formula. For a detailed excursus see R. E. Brown, *The Gospel according to John*, 1:535ff.; R. Schnackenburg, *The Gospel according to St. John*, 2:79–89.

eagerness to evolve new terminologies, which of course had direct bearing on the community's understanding of God. For only those who can identify God's working in the so-called 'others' who were not from the so-called 'elected,' may also identify the longings and expectations of the other people as genuine, authentic and as that stemming from God Himself.

9.2.4 Verses 27–38: Dialogue on God's Will—The Basis of New Traditions

These verses make clear four important issues, if one reads them from the perspective of a Samaritan-Johannine community dialogue. The narrative hides behind the story the actual situation and tensions within the community.

a) The disciples are amazed, but they do not make it known. It has been suggested that their behaviour should be interpreted as their awe and reverence for their master.[53] Their behaviour should be seen in contrast to that of the Samaritan woman who was ready to ask when anything was startling and incongruous. In fact, the unvoiced questions in v. 27 in reality mirror the disciples' ignorance and disengagement, their lack of understanding of Jesus. The disciples wish to disregard and ignore the strange behaviour of Jesus.

b) Instead of reacting sensitively, as to the demands of the situation, the disciples try to change the subject. They ask him to "eat" (vv. 31–32) — notice the imperative here! But when Jesus refused to tread their path, they again instead of asking Jesus enquire of one another, with the full knowledge that they cannot enlighten each other as they were not present. Their question formed with μή (vv. 33–34) speaks of their having an answer already in their minds (preconceived ideas). This suggests tension between Jesus and the disciples, a situation where the disciples were not inclined to a sincere dialogue with their master. Does this also mirror a contemporary situation of the Johannine community where the leaders (see the exegesis of the Paraclete passages—the leader of the community as Paraclete is a possible interpretation) and the members of the community were not always in agreement. Some kept quiet,

---

53 R. Schnackenburg, *The Gospel according to St. John*, 1:443, and L. Morris, *The Gospel according to John*, 1:274.

some discussed among themselves without venturing an open dialogue with those responsible for a creative dialogue with the Samaritans.

c) The woman leaving behind the jar must mean the negation of the need for drinking water (in so far as it represents the means of satisfying that need). The woman understood what Jesus said.[54] This act also indicates that she will return.[55] "Come and see" is her invitation to her people to try to understand who Jesus is (cf. 1:39, 46). Here ὁ χριστός should be understood not as a title but simply as the anointed one. The woman is inviting her people to scrutinise the claims of Jesus (vv. 28–30). In the Johannine community's history this may have been a stage in the dialogue process between the two communities. The primary understandings and findings were put forth for communal scrutiny.

d) The Evangelist now gives a theological basis for the dialogue situation. Jesus: "My food is to do the will of Him who sent me and accomplish His work." On the primary level this clearly suggests the theocentricity of Jesus. He himself interprets his dialogue with the Samaritan woman as God's will and his doing nothing but God's work. On the secondary level the community sees its engagement in the dialogue with the Samaritans not as a struggle to obtain social recognition and identity but as obeying God's will and it has no choice, but to comply to His will as Jesus is theocentric, the community is also bound to be theocentric.

e) Then Jesus uses the image of the harvest (vv. 35–37). He exhorts his disciples to "lift up their eyes and see," they are asked to read the signs of the times. One can understand God's will through the happenings around. It is in being sensitive to the needs of the time and in right reactions to the situations that God's will is obeyed. Those who read the signs and work accordingly will gather the crop, receive the reward and rejoice. Thus the community is here asked to see what is happening around it and to work (instead of keeping quiet or discussing among themselves). The community is reminded that what it now 'sees,' 'gathers' and witnesses is a completion of a process where 'others'[56] also

---

54 See H. Boers, *Neither on this Mountain nor in Jerusalem: A Study of John 4* (SBLMS 35; Atlanta: Scholars Press, 1988), 183.
55 B. Lindars, *The Gospel of John*, 198.
56 This may suggest concrete conditions at Samaritan mission of the early church — probably beginning from the mission of Philip (Acts 8). Cf. Luke 9:52–56; 10:33–37; 17:11, 19; Acts 1:8; 9:31. Cf. also O. Cullmann, *Early Christian Worship*, 186.

have put in their strength and laboured (v. 38). The community is thus asked to work in obedience to the will of God in order to rejoice.

9.2.5 Verses 39–42: The Dialogue's Ultimate Goal—Recognising the God-sent Saviour and Confessing the Saviour-hood of God

The dialogue comes to a very fruitful completion: the communal scrutiny of the woman's invitation "come and see," her sharing of primary findings so completely and successfully, and the community coming to a "confession" that Jesus is the 'Saviour of the world.' Note carefully that the Jews did not apply the term Saviour to the Messiah: the title σωτήρ, that in the Old Testament (representing some derivative from the root ישע) was given sometimes to humans, who delivered Israel from its enemies, was mostly reserved for God Himself.[57] As a divine title it is frequent in the later chapters of Isaiah.[58] In the Synoptics, it is confined to Luke. "God my Saviour" (Luke 1:47) echoes the very expression of the Old Testament and again in Luke 2:11 Christ is called σωτήρ. It would suggest naturally the very etymology of the name of Jesus. Christians, therefore, freely applied the title Saviour to Jesus for they saw him as the representative of God the Saviour, who brings God's gift of salvation.[59]

The Evangelist writing at a time when the title 'Saviour of the world' was applied to the emperor of Rome and to certain deities, was affirming that Jesus fulfils the hopes of the Samaritans, Jews and the world of nations. The Evangelist may have thought of a dramatic propriety in putting it in the mouth of the Samaritans, who in the Gospel represent some sort of Gentile world over against the Jews! No explanation of the title is offered, but for a clue at v. 34 where Jesus is portrayed to be the representative of God. Then this title actually is a confession of 'God' as the Saviour of the world.

---

57 G. R. Beasley-Murray, *John*, 64; C. H. Dodd, *Interpretation of the Fourth Gospel*, 238.
58 For example, Isa 43:3, 11; 63:8–9—Isa 45:21–22 sets forth the concept of God as Saviour of the world without using the expression.
59 Cf. Acts 5:31; 13:23; Phil 3:20 and the Pastoral epistles.

9.3 Summary and Conclusions

a) Chapter 4 speaks of a successful dialogue between the Samaritan and the Johannine community that unfolds at different levels—consultations, community scrutiny, inner-Johannine community ripples and a fruitful ecumenism.

b) The dialogue takes place in the setting of the Samaritan traditional heritage and cult site, Jacob's well at Gerizim.

c) Discussing on the living water, the Johannine community emphasises its conviction that salvation—the gift of God—transcends all traditions. It transforms and fulfils the sociological longings of the two communities and their respective traditional heritages are each brought into dialogue in order to build a new tradition.

d) The dialogue on the centrality of worship in the new tradition openly confronts the confusion in the existing Samaritan worship. The traditions of the fathers and the traditions related to the temple in Jerusalem are here regarded with respect only to affirm that God creates new traditions which destroy religious, ethnic and ritual barriers.

e) God creates an eschatological-ecumenical-worshipping community that is sustained by the parental care of God-the Father. God is defined as Spirit, the mode of His action that holds the nearness, the otherness and the freedom of God together to bring wholeness.

f) In confessing Jesus as cosmic "I am"-'Saviour of the world' who fulfils the particular expectations and longings of the universal community, the Saviour-hood of God is affirmed.

g) The dialogue is seen as God's will and His work.

h) Though the Johannine Community probably tried to make the Samaritan converts confess Jesus as Messiah, a particularly Jewish expectation and belief, fact is that the Samaritans find 'Saviour of the world' as most suitable to express their faith. This reflects how creative dialogue can enrich and unearth new theological perspectives.

Chapter Ten

Revelation Continued—the Authentic Theology
The Paraclete and the Understanding of God

10.1 Composition of the Farewell Discourses

The Paraclete passages confront us within the context of the famous Johannine Farewell Discourses, and provide us with the context in which the Paraclete passages should be interpreted and understood. Jesus' call to move out of the upper room in 14:31 finds its natural continuation in 18:1ff. Apparent breaks and dislocations detected within the seemingly monolithic discourse in 13:31–16:33 have led to various theories about the composition and order of the Farewell discourses. Traditionalist attempts which explain the break at 14:31—"ἐγείρεσθε, ἄγωμεν ἐντεῦθεν"—considering 15:1ff. as spoken on the way as Jesus walked with his disciples to Gethsemane, do not hold ground for there is no indication at 15:1ff. that they are on the way and it is difficult to imagine chapter 17 as a prayer on the way.

Bultmann's reconstruction which suggested a reading of the Farewell discourse in the following order: 13:1–31a; 17:1–26; 13:31b–35; 15:1–27; 16:1–33; 13:36–14:31 and 18:1ff. certainly overcomes the problem of dislocation, but at the expense of the structure and development of the discourses as a whole.

The scholarly world is unanimous today in recognising 13:31–14:31 as the first (original) farewell discourse, but its relationship to chapters 15–16, and the problem of explaining contextual differences within 15–16 have led to great debates. They however do agree that 15:1–17; 15:18–16:4a; 16:4b–33 when considered as three sections within chapters 15–16 make sense for a reasonably good interpretation. However, whether these three sections form three separate discourses (15:1–17; 15:18–16:4a; 16:4b–33) or comprise two (15:1–16:4a; 16:4b–33) later interpretive editions to the first farewell discourse is the issue of a fascinating debate.[1]

---

1   C. K. Barrett, *The Gospel according to St. John*, 455; R. E. Brown, *The Gospel according to John*, 2:587–88, and G. R. Beasley-Murray, *John*, 223, see chapters 15–16 as one later addition. J. Gnilka, *Johannesevangelium*, 120–22; S. Schulz, *Das Evangelium nach*

To study the Paraclete passages however, we suggest that they be interpreted within the context of the three farewell discourses: 13:31–14:31; 15:1–16:4a; 16:4b–33. These provide three distinctive contexts to the Paraclete passages. The first two occur in the context of the first farewell discourse in 13:31–14:31, where we see Jesus authorising his disciples for mission after his departure promising them his presence with them to motivate and to overcome fear.[2] The third passage occurs in the second discourse which points towards the context of witnessing in a situation of persecution and expulsion, where the community feels the heat of the world.[3] The fourth and fifth Paraclete passages confront us in the third farewell discourse in 16:4b–33, where the context points towards the community which asks no more questions, but rather attempts to interpret its being in the light of the gift of the Paraclete.[4]

10.2 The Paraclete—God's Comforting and Challenging Presence

John 14:16–17: κἀγὼ ἐρωτήσω τὸν πατέρα καὶ ἄλλον παράκλητον δώσει ὑμῖν, ἵνα μεθ' ὑμῶν εἰς τὸν αἰῶνα ᾖ, τὸ πνεῦμα τῆς ἀληθείας, ὃ ὁ κόσμος οὐ δύναται λαβεῖν, ὅτι οὐ θεωρεῖ αὐτὸ οὐδὲ γινώσκει· ὑμεῖς γινώσκετε αὐτό, ὅτι παρ' ὑμῖν μένει καὶ ἐν ὑμῖν ἔσται.

The Paraclete is the gift of God. The coming of the Paraclete is explained through the Father's giving, which reminds us of the whole theological

---

Johannes, 200–201; R. Schnackenburg, *The Gospel according to St. John*, 3:89–96; A. Dettwiler, *Die Gegenwart des Erhöhten: Eine exegetische Studie zu den johanneischen Abschiedsreden (Joh 13,31–16,33) unter besonderer Berücksichtigung ihres Relecture-Charakters* (FRLANT 169; Göttingen: Vandenhoeck & Ruprecht, 1995), 53–55, see two separate discourses in 15–16: 15:1–16:4a; 16:4a–33. Among others, M. Winter, *Das Vermächtnis Jesu und die Abschiedsworte der Väter*, 260–84; F. F. Segovia, *The Farewell of the Word: The Johannine Call to Abide* (Minneapolis: Fortress, 1991), 62–64, 170–74; J. Painter, *The Quest for the Messiah*, 417–21, and F. F. Segovia, "John 15:18–16:4a: A First Addition to the Original Farewell Discourse?" *CBQ* 45 (1983): 210–30, interpret 15:1–17; 15:18–16:4a; 16:4b–33 as three separate later additions. Becker too suggests three separate discourse additions: 15:1–17; 15:18–16:15; 16:16–33 (J. Becker, *Das Evangelium nach Johannes*, 2:477–506).

2   M. Winter, *Das Vermächtnis Jesu und die Abschiedsworte der Väter*, 273–74.
3   Ibid., 277–78.
4   Ibid., 279–81.

spectrum that the Fourth Evangelist conveys through the act of 'giving' (δίδωμι) the Word. But God giving the Paraclete is a response to Jesus' praying (ἐρωτάω).

The first Paraclete passage introduces and presents the Paraclete describing him by two attributes: ἄλλος παράκλητος and τὸ πνεῦμα τῆς ἀληθείας. How is ἄλλος παράκλητος to be understood? Does it imply that Jesus himself has been the first Paraclete to his disciples? Attention has been drawn to Deut 18:15 where Moses promises "a prophet like me," though Moses himself was never described in the Pentateuch as a prophet. In both instances the designation comes at the announcement of a successor! Did the Fourth Evangelist conceive Jesus to be the unmentioned Paraclete to whom the first Paraclete passage refers?[5] Indeed the Johannine community described Jesus indirectly as Paraclete in 1 John 2:1: καὶ ἐάν τις ἁμάρτῃ, παράκλητον ἔχομεν πρὸς τὸν πατέρα Ἰησοῦν Χριστὸν δίκαιον. Here Jesus is portrayed as the heavenly Paraclete, the mediating intercessor! The Paraclete as ἄλλος παράκλητος is then for the community as though he were another Jesus![6]

The first two Paraclete passages found in the first farewell discourse portray the Paraclete and Jesus as parallel figures and the following table shows Johannine theocentricity in picturising both Jesus and the Paraclete.[7]

---

5 E. Franck, *Revelation Taught: The Paraclete in the Gospel of John* (ConBNT 14; Uppsala: Gleerup, 1985), 38.
6 R. E. Brown, "The Paraclete in the Fourth Gospel," NTS 13 (1967): 128; J. Frey, *Die johanneische Eschatologie*, 3:159ff.
7 See for a detailed discussion R. E. Brown, *The Gospel according to John*, 2:1140–41, and G. M. Burge, *The Anointed Community*, 140–42. But both obscure the distinction and relativise them through using the Paraclete passages in the later farewell discourse additions, which present the Paraclete from the Christocentric perspective. However, if one for a while would ignore the Christocentric interpretation of the Paraclete concept in the next three passages—Paraclete as a gift of Jesus, sent by Jesus—, then we have an astonishing picture emerging.

Paraclete		Jesus
15:26; 16:7, 13	Comes	5:43; 16:28; 18:37
15:26	Gives testimony	5:31ff.; 8:13ff.; 7:7
16:8	Convicts the world	3:19–20; 9:41; 15:22
16:13	Speaks not of self but what is heard	7:17; 8:26ff.; 14:10
16:14	Glorifies the Sender	12:28; 17:1, 4
16:13ff.	Reveals, discloses, proclaims	4:25; 16:25
16:13	Leads into the fullness of Truth	18:37; 14:6
16:13	Spirit of Truth	14:6

Then Jesus could be conveniently called the Other Paraclete!

Paraclete		Jesus
14:16	Given by the Father	3:16
14:16–17	With in/by the disciples	3:22; 13:33; 14:20
14:17	Not received by the world	1:11; 5:53 (12:48)
14:17	Not known by the world; Only believers know him	16:3; 8:19; 10:14
14:7	Not seen by the world; Only believers see him	14:19; 16:16–17
14:26	Sent by the Father	cf. Chapters 5, 7, 8, 12
14:26	Teaches	3:2; 7:14–15; 8:20; 18:19
14:17	The Spirit of Truth	14:6

If seen from the first farewell discourse context, the Paraclete is indeed portrayed to be 'another' separate entity who replaces Jesus after his death. His link with Jesus is only secondary, because Jesus can only pray to God to send him. Brown's famous "the presence of Jesus when Jesus is absent"[8] should therefore indeed be corrected as "the presence of God when Jesus is absent." The ἄλλος in fact sees the 'limitation' of the 'historical theophany' (see our Chapter Seven on Jesus as the historical theophany) in Jesus, and thus as Barrett correctly mentions the Paraclete is the 'eschatological continuum' in which God's work in Jesus, awaiting its termination at his return, is continued.[9]

The second attribute of the Paraclete used in the passage τὸ πνεῦμα τῆς ἀληθείας strengthens the idea of comparison to Jesus. We encounter the Spirit of Truth just after Jesus himself proclaiming ἐγώ εἰμι ἡ ὁδὸς καὶ ἡ ἀλήθεια καὶ ἡ ζωή in 14:6. The narrative structure of the first Farewell Discourse clearly points to the 'truth' that is revealed in Jesus and that will be revealed through the Paraclete!

The genitive construction may be understood both as a subjective genitive, or as an objective genitive. The 'Spirit that is dependent on Truth,' or 'Spirit which communicates Truth,' would be the interpretation.[10] If one interprets 'Truth' as 'the ultimate reality,' as God's liberative power which gives creational realities meaning and existence (see Truth in our exegesis

---

8   R. E. Brown, *The Gospel according to John*, 2:1139.
9   See C. K. Barrett, *The Gospel according to St. John*, 90; also G. M. Burge, *The Anointed Community*, 37ff.
10 R. E. Brown, op. cit., 639; C. K. Barrett, op. cit., 463; both prefer objective genitive.

of 8:31–32), then the Spirit is God's instrument to bring it about in the community. The Paraclete is then 'God's salvific sign' filling the lacuna created by Jesus' departure in the community. As a sign of truth, the Paraclete is part of it and can communicate the truth.

The two attributes of the Paraclete in the 14:16–17 saying correspond to the two most important intentions of the Farewell Discourse genre, to preserve the continuity in performance of tasks and to legitimise the succession.[11] The world οὐ θεωρεῖ αὐτὸ οὐδὲ γινώσκει is expected here. Given the special Johannine theological overtones that we encounter in θεωρεῖν and γινώσκειν, one cannot 'see' or know without having the faith perspective. The Paraclete is not something which one can first get to know and then 'see,' or first see and then get to know. Seeing and getting to know coincide. The gift of the Paraclete is the 'how' of a believing existence.[12] The world cannot 'know' the Paraclete, the Spirit of Truth because it does not know the 'Truth'—'God Himself.' Does then the Fourth Evangelist at this point exclude the κόσμος from God's actions? Does he thereby also withhold His salvific grace of giving the Paraclete as an eschatological continuum of what He has already offered in Jesus to the κόσμος to renew the creational relationship?

Three prepositions used in the passage suggest the relationship of the Paraclete to the disciples. Μετά with genitive suggests 'to be with,' it conceptualises fellowship,[13] presence and communion. παρά suggests 'standing by,' 'beside,' it conceptualises nearness. ἐν suggests 'in,' indicating indwelling. The Paraclete then is the 'sign' of God being with the disciples, He standing by at the hour of need and at every minute through His dwelling in them.[14] It speaks metaphorically of God making His home in the disciples (cf. 1:14). It assures God's nearness especially when the world sees them as those abandoned[15] and orphaned. The Johannine articulation of the Paraclete concept therefore is their reflection of experiencing God's nearness, fellowship, and the joy of God making His home among them. And placing

---

11 E. Franck, *Revelation Taught*, 39, and M. Winter, *Das Vermächtnis Jesu und die Abschiedsworte der Väter*, 270ff.
12 R. Bultmann, *Das Evangelium des Johannes*, 476.
13 R. Schnackenburg, *The Gospel according to St. John*, 3:75.
14 F. W. Beare, "Spirit of Life and Truth: The Doctrine of the Holy Spirit in the Fourth Gospel," *TJT* 3 (1987): 116.
15 J. Painter, *The Quest for the Messiah*, 424.

this affirmation in Jesus' Farewell context it draws strength in the assurance that God is the Creator and Sustainer of the community through his double gift of the 'gift of His Son' and the 'gift of another Paraclete.'

The attempt to imply an allusion to the Old Testament thought that God is with His people and will come closer to them and be with them in the new covenant as stated in Jer 31:33–34 is not completely out of place.[16] In Jeremiah the promise is connected with the accomplishment of the Law, obedience to the commandments and the true knowledge of God. The introductory presentation of the Paraclete saying makes believers keeping commandments (v. 15) as the pre-condition for the gift of the Paraclete, the Paraclete therefore is God's seal on the community (cf. Eph 1:13).

In the first Paraclete passage the Paraclete sent by God is God's gift to the community through Jesus' request, who is another Paraclete. He is the eschatological continuum of Jesus, the Spirit of Truth, who is both God's comforting sign through His nearness, fellowship and in-dwelling, and God's challenge to the community to be a visible sign of the invisible God to the world.

10.3 The Paraclete—Re-enactor of God's Revelation in Teaching and Remembering

John 14:26: ὁ δὲ παράκλητος, τὸ πνεῦμα τὸ ἅγιον, ὃ πέμψει ὁ πατὴρ ἐν τῷ ὀνόματί μου, ἐκεῖνος ὑμᾶς διδάξει πάντα καὶ ὑπομνήσει ὑμᾶς πάντα ἃ εἶπον ὑμῖν [ἐγώ].

When Jesus leaves his disciples and the world, he will be succeeded by the Paraclete who will carry out his function. The Father will send ἐν τῷ ὀνόματί μου—Brown translates 'in my place,' 'as a replacement.'[17] The Fourth Evangelist here emphatically features through πέμπειν the Paraclete as the envoy, agent or apostle of God. ἐν τῷ ὀνόματί μου, is mentioned to confirm that he is not sent to reveal some other Saviour or to supplant the historical mission of Jesus, but to continue, give full effect and bring to completion the

---

16 E. Franck, *Revelation Taught*, 40.
17 R. E. Brown, *The Gospel according to John*, 2:653, and C. K. Barrett, *The Gospel according to St. John*, 2:467.

revelation that Jesus has brought.[18] And the Paraclete is now identified as τὸ πνεῦμα τὸ ἅγιον, to imply he is the power given to the community, the power in which the eschatological event continues to be carried through.[19] The nature of this work of the Paraclete is two-fold:

a) to teach (διδάσκειν),
b) to remind (ὑπομιμνήσκειν).

The Paraclete's judicial background and the office of teaching at first seem contradictory. But an advocate must be a good teacher, he needs to prepare his witnesses, he needs to teach. Teaching is communication, and formed part of the authentic exposition of Scripture in Judaism. The Teacher of Righteousness in Qumran was entitled to interpret the present and future prophetically. According to Otto Betz the Teacher of Righteousness was a prophetic interpreter who, as an exegete of the Torah was able to point to God's will and as a revealer of prophetic words preached the approach of the last judgement.[20] Philo usually associates teaching with exegetising, explaining. Interpreting the Word of God, Scriptures, the Law (*Mut.* 18; *Her.* 207; *Post.* 132) is in Philo's thought διδάσκειν. Only he who is the source of all knowledge is able to give knowledge and guidance to others (*Migr.* 42). Real teaching is not in the knowledge of the teacher, but in the needs of those who are taught (*Post.* 140–142). In two passages of Philo, teaching is combined with the motif of remembering to gain knowledge (*Post.* 148; *Spec. Leg.* 4.107). Philo considered teaching as revelatory, and as supported by remembering!

In the Fourth Gospel teaching is an event of revelation. Jesus is the teacher (3:2), and the revelatory activity of Jesus is described as teaching (7:16–17, 28; 8:28). In 1 John 2:27 διδάσκειν is regarded as a function of τὸ χρῖσμα—by this it is shown in the epistles that the Spirit does not speak in new revelation loosened from the ties of history, but in continuity of the office of proclamation.[21]

The Paraclete teaching is not just the continuation of revelation—it is interpreting, contextualising. His teaching activity is to make the disciples

---

18   F. W. Beare, "Spirit of Life and Truth," 116.
19   R. Bultmann, *Das Evangelium des Johannes*, 484.
20   O. Betz, *Der Paraklet: Fürsprecher im häretischen Spätjudentum, im Johannes-Evangelium und in neu gefundenen gnostischen Schriften* (AGSU 2; Leiden: E. J. Brill, 1963), 130–33.
21   R. Bultmann, op. cit., 484.

understand and imbibe the Jesus event. It brings out to light the things that were hidden to knowledge, it illuminates that which was/is understood in parts and misunderstood. The Paraclete interprets Jesus in the post-resurrection perspective. The second Paraclete passage's significance lies in its definite attempt to historicise the work of the Spirit. Even then the Paraclete is not just a conservative, preserving voice in revelation.[22]

The teaching function relativises the revelation brought by Jesus in his historical mission. He spoke *"these things"* (ταῦτα, v. 25) and the Paraclete will lead them from ταῦτα to πάντα—he will teach them everything! It brings out the limitations of the historical theophany in Jesus and the all-embracing revelatory significance of the Paraclete's teaching activity. Through his revelatory teaching he will lead the community in new avenues, bringing new understandings of God. The Paraclete's teaching is revelation, the authoritative knowledge originating from the Father.

This revelatory radicality of the Paraclete consists in his office of 'reminding and making one remember.' The explicit role of causing to remember to the Spirit is not ascribed to the Paraclete elsewhere in the New Testament.[23] 'Remembering' in the Fourth Evangelist's mind cannot be just a recollection and historical reconstruction, for his attempt to witness is not just a historical report. In the Old Testament tradition, remembrance forms an important aspect in the relationship between God and His people. Religiosity of Israel is centred on 'remembering,' God remembers His covenant with His people (e.g., Exod 2:24; 6:5; Lev 26:42; Ps 105:8; 106:45; Ezek 16:60). Inversely, Israel remembers 'liberation' in particular and God's gift to them (Num 15:39–40; Deut 8:2)—the Pascal celebration is a feast of 'remembering.' And the Deuteronomy through its farewell discourse presents a remembrance Theology. In New Testament writings remembering, interpreting and reflecting the meaning of that which is remembered to the present is primarily a prophetic task (1 Cor 11:24–25; 2 Pet 1:12–13; Jude 5; cf. *Barn.* 12:2).[24]

In the Fourth Gospel the remembering motif occurs three times, twice in the account of cleansing the temple (2:17, 22) and again in the narrative of triumphal entry (12:16). In these sections the Fourth Evangelist does not

---

22 See for the opposite opinion, G. M. Burge, *The Anointed Community*, 213.
23 U. B. Müller, "Die Parakletenvorstellung im Johannesevangelium," *ZTK* 71 (1974): 46.
24 See U. B. Müller, "Die Parakletenvorstellung im Johannesevangelium," 57.

explicitly quote from the Scripture, instead he makes the disciples 'remember' the Scripture. It suggests that remembering is the act of re-interpretation of Scripture, in order to acquire a new memory of the Scripture in the light of the disciples' post-resurrection experience.[25] Remembering is an attempt to determine what happened in what 'seems' to have happened and to perceive the real authentic meaning of the event.[26] It is an attempt to use new insights and new understandings about the Christ event, to know the significance of the event in its totality and wholeness.

But the Paraclete passage does not speak of human attempts to remember. It emphatically speaks of the Paraclete bringing into remembrance all that Jesus has said to the disciples. He will not just stimulate the disciples' minds by merely recalling the data, or just intensify the disciples' capacity to recall Jesus' words in their entirety,[27] rather he will direct, guide the process of 'remembering,' he will make the 'words' so effectual as to determine the disciples' thought and action! Revelation is not mechanistic, so as to reprocess the historical data in advance for present contextual interpretation! The remembrance is to relive and re-enact the Christ event, to bring about new eschatological decision in time and space. Therefore the Paraclete passage affirms through sending the Paraclete, that God Himself teaches the community. The Paraclete 'bringing into remembrance' God's historical theophany means God Himself authenticating the community's Theology—the community's understanding of God. He gives new direction, new perspectives, new insights so that the community may encounter God anew. In His act of reminding through the Paraclete, God continues to reveal as He has revealed in Jesus. In making the community remember He will challenge it and transform it to relive and to re-enact the Christ event anew in order to call the world to a faith decision.

---

25 B. Woll, *Johannine Christianity in Conflict: Authority, Rank and Succession in the First Farewell Discourse* (SBLDS 60; Chico, Calif.: Scholars Press, 1981), 100.
26 E. Franck, *Revelation Taught*, 47.
27 F. R. Harm, "Distinctive Titles of the Holy Spirit in the Writings of John," *Concordia Journal* 13 (1987): 123.

10.4 God Creates the Possibility of 'Authentic Witness' in the Face of the World's Vicious Contempt through Paraclete

John 15:26: "Ὅταν ἔλθῃ ὁ παράκλητος ὃν ἐγὼ πέμψω ὑμῖν παρὰ τοῦ πατρός, τὸ πνεῦμα τῆς ἀληθείας ὃ παρὰ τοῦ πατρὸς ἐκπορεύεται, ἐκεῖνος μαρτυρήσει περὶ ἐμοῦ·

The context of 15:25 seems to be the community's bitter conflict with the Synagogue, as reference to 16:1–4a, especially 16:2: ἀποσυναγώγους ποιήσουσιν ὑμᾶς.[28] The Synagogue must have rejected and cast out those belonging to the Jesus movement or was in the process of doing so. 15:18–25 relating to the theme of the world's hostility towards the community is recorded, and the community wants to take courage in the fact that the hatred and persecution it is facing is only the continuation of what Jesus himself had to experience. "A servant is not greater than his master" is the key for the community to interpret its suffering at the hands of the world and the Synagogue. The context in which the Paraclete saying should now be interpreted is therefore not that of the impending departure of Jesus, but the crisis that has developed thereafter—the trial situation.

The context of the passage brings to memory the description of the Spirit's role when the disciples were accused in the courts in the Q source (Luke 12:11–12). The 'Q' saying records the Spirit's action in terms akin to that of a 'Prompter'—the Holy Spirit will teach you in that very hour what to say, whereas the Fourth Gospel defines the Paraclete as a direct witness.

And rightly the Paraclete is called a 'witness' here (15:26), the forensic meaning of Paraclete as advocate suits the context perfectly! The Paraclete's task therefore is that of an advocate speaking in defence of the disciples in the trial. The Paraclete will himself become the prosecuting attorney![29] μαρτυρεῖν here means valid testimony imparting the knowledge, the revelation to awaken and strengthen the faith. It is through *enabling* the

---

[28] The terms for excommunication from the Synagogue are used only in John 9:22, 12:42 and 16:2 in the whole of the New Testament. This probably reflects the particular Johannine situation. See J. L. Martyn, *History and Theology in the Fourth Gospel*, 17ff.; C. K. Barrett, *The Gospel according to St. John*, 361–62, and J. Painter, *The Quest for the Messiah*, 425–26.

[29] G. R. Beasley-Murray, *John*, 277.

disciples to stand firm and in protecting them from being shaken in their faith,[30] that he becomes the power of proclamation in the community.[31]

Though the Johannine text makes a subtle distinction between the witness of the Paraclete and that of the disciples, the Paraclete is not a phenomenon apart from the disciples. In the absence of Jesus, the Paraclete's task is to illuminate, reveal to the disciples and together with them be an actual living and authoritative knowledge of Jesus.[32]

And this 'witness' of the Paraclete creates κρίσις in the world. The world is challenged to make a choice either of reception or of rejection of witness. Reception creates faith, rejection brings judgement. The authentic witness comes therefore from the Paraclete, from God Himself. As the Paraclete comes from the Father, the disciples provide a concrete means of assistance to the Paraclete to further the mission of God even in the midst of hatred and persecution.

Before we conclude our exposition of the third Paraclete saying, we should observe the clause in the theological perspective, in which the community interprets its Paraclete construct. The Paraclete has been said to be sent by the Father in the first two Paraclete passages. He is now said to be sent by Jesus. The Paraclete construct now changes its theocentrical interpretation and becomes christocentric. The Evangelist in his redaction allows the christological interpretation to stand as it is, along with the theocentrical original Paraclete construct. Does this reflect the co-existence of theocentric/christocentric interpretive modes within the community? By noting that the Paraclete is now sent by Jesus, the saying makes the Paraclete Jesus' apostle on the one hand, but adds that the Paraclete comes from the Father! Do we detect herein the first steps in the history of the community, which now stand in 'isolation,' of a tendency to allow 'Christology' to engulf 'Theology'? Or is it due to the community's situation of conflict and its struggle to evolve an own identity that the community lost sight of the perspective and was unaware of keeping its Christology within the framework of Theology?

---

30 Evidences from Philo's understanding of the notion of μαρτυρεῖν reflect primarily a didactic, and the forensic aspects. Witness is for him prophetic, expressing the notion of inspiration and is therefore revelatory (*Abr.* 262; *Conf.* 44; *Somn.* 2.172; *Mos.* 2.263).
31 R. Bultmann, *Das Evangelium des Johannes*, 484–85.
32 E. Franck, *Revelation Taught*, 56.

'The witness' of the Paraclete is directed to the world, even though the world hates and rejects. The witness of the community becomes the symbol of 'concern'—the love of God to relate, where building relationships is not at all possible! Therefore 'witness' is not 'self-defence' but also an invitation to 'embrace' God and His acts, to be God-centred instead of being self-centred.[33]

10.5 The Paraclete Creates a 'Mirror Model' of God's World

John 16:7b–8: ἐὰν γὰρ μὴ ἀπέλθω, ὁ παράκλητος οὐκ ἐλεύσεται πρὸς ὑμᾶς· ἐὰν δὲ πορευθῶ, πέμψω αὐτὸν πρὸς ὑμᾶς. καὶ ἐλθὼν ἐκεῖνος ἐλέγξει τὸν κόσμον περὶ ἁμαρτίας καὶ περὶ δικαιοσύνης καὶ περὶ κρίσεως·

D. A. Carson in his detailed article on the "Function of the Paraclete in John 16:7–11" surveys the hub of the exegetical problems and points out but two dominant assertions that should help the interpreter to grasp the third Paraclete saying.[34] On the one hand, how do we understand ἐλέγχειν περί in 16:8? Does the Paraclete convince, convict or prove the world wrong? In whom does this work transpire: in the disciples or among their opponents? On the other, how are we to understand the three ὅτι clauses? Are they explicative, explaining the nature of sin, righteousness and judgement? Or are they causal, providing the basis of this conviction, and hence modifying the verb ἐλέγχειν?

In the Septuagint ἐλέγχειν is connected with education, and especially God teaching and educating His people (LXX Ps 93:10; Sir 18:13; 19:14; Prov 15:12; Hab 1:12; Wis 12:2). In Isa 11:3a–4 LXX, ἐλέγχειν is used of God 'deciding' for the poor. In the New Testament, in the church discipline logion in Matt 18:15, ἐλέγχειν is used to denote the act of winning back one who has sinned. In 1 Cor 14:24 ἐλέγχειν is seen as the result of the prophetic activity, by a preaching of a searching and judging kind.[35] In 2 Tim 4:2

---

33 See A. Lindemann, "Gemeinde und Welt im Johannesevangelium," in *Kirche: Festschrift für Günther Bornkamm* (ed. D. Lührmann and G. Strecker; Tübingen: J. C. B. Mohr [Paul Siebeck], 1980), 152–53.
34 D. A. Carson, "The Function of the Paraclete in John 16:7–11," *JBL* 98 (1979): 547–66.
35 U. B. Müller, "Die Parakletenvorstellung im Johannesevangelium," 70.

ἐλέγχειν is used with ἐπιτιμεῖν and παρακαλεῖν, the purpose here is to preserve them who remain in the faith. ἐλέγχειν is also used to represent internal exhortation, or exhortatory preaching in *Did.* 15:3; 4:3 and *Barn.* 19:4.

The function of the Paraclete is ἐλέγχειν. Bultmann visualises the image of a cosmic lawsuit taking place before the court of God (reminds me of Micah 6), with the world as accused and the Paraclete as the prosecutor.[36] ἐλέγχειν could be interpreted in John 16:8 as 'to prove wrong about' and ὅτι as an explicative to interpret that the Paraclete in the community constitutes the right perspective regarding the matters of sin, judgement and righteousness.[37] ἐλέγχειν is not condemnation, conviction to scratch the world from the salvific plan of God. It is not just bringing the world to self-conscious convictions or self-conscious recognition.[38] It is rather that "Der Paraklet »konfrontiert« sie [die Welt] mit dem, was Sünde, Gerechtigkeit und Gericht ist."[39] ἐλέγχειν is therefore 'creating a model'/ 'setting standards.' It is presenting the world with a choice, an option. A prophetic, didactic role for the Paraclete binds the present passage to 15:26 where his office is explained in terms of creating a witness.

Verse 9: περὶ ἁμαρτίας μέν, ὅτι οὐ πιστεύουσιν εἰς ἐμέ, denotes that remaining self-centred is sin! Sin is not moral failure or any ghastly action, such as crucifying Jesus, but unbelief in Jesus, and therefore apartness from God (see exegesis of John 8). Such unbelief entails rejection of the possibility given, not ignorance. The possibility offered for life through the work of the Paraclete in the community 'living in faith' uncovers the unbelief—the sin of the world.[40] Therefore sin is the attitude of the world towards God who reveals and offers relationship. The Paraclete through his working in the community, works up a living model of love that gives itself to the utmost; in the community the world has the example what love and life is, excuse of

---

36 R. Bultmann, *Das Evangelium des Johannes*, 433.
37 W. Bauer, *Das Johannesevangelium*, 149; J. Blank, *Krisis*, 335–39; R. Bultmann, *Das Evangelium des Johannes*, 433; R. E. Brown, *The Gospel according to John*, 2:704–14. Some scholars take ἐλέγχειν to mean 'to convict' and ὅτι clauses as causal, see C. K. Barrett, *The Gospel according to St. John*, 488–89; E. C. Hoskyns, *The Fourth Gospel*, 484–85; R. V. G. Tasker, *The Gospel according to St. John*, 179–80, and J. Frey, *Die johanneische Eschatologie*, 3:183–84.
38 G. Johnston, *The Spirit-Paraclete in the Gospel of John* (SNTSMS 12; Cambridge: Cambridge University Press, 1970), 35–36.
39 A. Lindemann, "Gemeinde und Welt im Johannesevangelium," 152.
40 See *ibid*.

ignorance is now taken away; to remain out of the community is therefore to reject God's initiative. Thus the condemnation lies in the not-loving and not-willing-to-live-out-of-love, or becoming unable to love.[41]

John 16:10–11: περὶ δικαιοσύνης δέ, ὅτι πρὸς τὸν πατέρα ὑπάγω καὶ οὐκέτι θεωρεῖτέ με· περὶ δὲ κρίσεως, ὅτι ὁ ἄρχων τοῦ κόσμου τούτου κέκριται.

The interpretation of δικαιοσύνη is considered to be a problem of the exegesis of this verse. δικαιοσύνη does not mean innocence,[42] not even moral uprightness; the observation that δικαιοσύνη is used as the opposite to ἁμαρτία is right.[43] But in what sense is righteousness intended here? Is the Paraclete pointing to Jesus' righteousness? Righteousness is defined through Jesus' going to the Father and the community seeing him no more. Then we do have a relationship between this act of the Paraclete with that of his act in interpreting the Jesus event for the community. In his interpretation the community will be challenged to be 'a living model of righteousness.'

Jesus' complete obedience to the Father—a life of self-giving after the self-emptying of God—is righteousness as whatever falls short of it is 'sin'—refusal to be obedient to God, refusal of His offer of salvation. Righteousness is the victory of God, the meaning and significance of the departure of Jesus is now interpreted through the Paraclete. The world is ruled by norms and standards that are not of God. The world is captive to these powers, to whom it never belonged. The standard ideals and securities that the world has established for its well-being in reality bind the captivity of the world. God's Sent One, Jesus, in his coming into the world and in his departure, has not only overcome the world's standards, but shattered it precisely by entering it and then departing without obeying the powers controlling the world, but to 'God' to whom the world actually belongs.

Thus in the mission of Jesus 'the ruler of this world' is defeated,[44] not the world, but the 'ruler of the world' is judged. The world is the creation brought under its original owner! The phrase addressed to the disciples:

---

41 J. Blank, *Krisis*, 336.
42 As B. Lindars argues in "ΔΙΚΑΙΟΣΥΝΗ in Jn 16.8 and 10," in *Mélanges Bibliques: En Hommage au R. P. Béda Rigaux* (ed. A. Descamps and A. de Halleux; Gembloux: Duculot, 1970), 275–85.
43 R. Bultmann, *Das Evangelium des Johannes*, 436, and R. Schnackenburg, *The Gospel according to St. John*, 3:131.
44 See A. Lindemann, "Gemeinde und Welt im Johannesevangelium," 152–53, n. 113.

"you will see me no more" is surprising. One would have expected: "the world will see me no more" (cf. 14:19; 7:34; 8:21; 12:36b). Betz points out: "no longer seeing a righteous man may be evidence of the fact that his ascent has taken place."[45] Thus the departure of Jesus, now as interpreted by the Paraclete is for the community "a sign that God is demonstrating his justice to him."[46] The departure of Jesus is God's victory over the ruler of this world. The world sees victory in what is visible—but the significance of the victory lies precisely in the overcoming of the visible by the invisible,[47] which is why the world does not recognise God's victory in Jesus defeating the ruler of the world: the Paraclete will show the world the victory of the righteousness of God.

Now the 'world' still has a possibility, a choice either to obey 'God' which is righteousness, or to obey the ruler of the world which is sin! The world is liberated from its captivity in the hands of the false 'rulers.' The Paraclete creates, therefore, through his work for the community, 'a mirror model of God's world' through which the world can see for itself and decide, either to be for or against God. Through the Paraclete in the community, God gives the world the possibility of knowing what sin is, what righteousness is, and therefore what judgement is!

10.6 The Paraclete—the Sign of God's Revelation Continued

John 16:12-13: Ἔτι πολλὰ ἔχω ὑμῖν λέγειν, ἀλλ' οὐ δύνασθε βαστάζειν ἄρτι· ὅταν δὲ ἔλθῃ ἐκεῖνος, τὸ πνεῦμα τῆς ἀληθείας, ὁδηγήσει ὑμᾶς ἐν τῇ ἀληθείᾳ πάσῃ· οὐ γὰρ λαλήσει ἀφ' ἑαυτοῦ, ἀλλ' ὅσα ἀκούσει λαλήσει καὶ τὰ ἐρχόμενα ἀναγγελεῖ ὑμῖν.

Jesus who already told his disciples (15:15) that he has made known to them everything (πάντα) he has heard, now in 16:12, 13 indicates that he has much to share with his own, but the disciples cannot bear it now. βαστάζειν is an interesting word as it is used for raising stone (10:31) and carrying the cross (19:17), it prepares the way for the christological interpretation of the original Paraclete saying in 14:26: "The Paraclete will teach all things." The

---

45 O. Betz, *Der Paraklet*, 201.
46 R. Schnackenburg, *The Gospel according to St. John*, 3:131.
47 R. Bultmann, *Das Evangelium des Johannes*, 436.

limitation of the historical theophany is being interpreted in terms of the disciples' limited ability to perceive and comprehend.

Verse 13 as such follows and expands 14:26 ἐκεῖνος ὑμᾶς διδάξει πάντα. "The Spirit of Truth will lead the disciples to grasp all the truth" has been interpreted taking the reading εἰς τὴν ἀλήθειαν πᾶσαν to mean: the Spirit leading to the very heart of truth[48] or on the basis of ἐν τῇ ἀληθείᾳ πάσῃ to mean Spirit leading along the way of truth.[49] In the Old Testament the Psalter records prayers such as "O Lord teach me your path, guide me in your truth" (Ps 25:4–5), "Your good spirit will guide me along a level path" (Ps 143:10). In one of the servant songs of Isa 42:1–9, we read of God placing His Spirit upon His servant (42:6: "God takes the hand of the servant who is to lead those who are bound out of prison;" 42:9: "God promises that He will proclaim [ἀναγγέλλειν] new things that have not come to pass.").

The Paraclete's guidance along the way of all truth involves a way of life in conformity with Jesus' teaching. Barrett expresses it as guidance in the whole sphere of truth, which keeps the disciples safe from deviation.[50] This mission of the Paraclete does not seem to be the recounting of the words of Jesus, but his leading the disciples beyond the point that they have been brought, unfolding new dimensions, depths of significance of the ultimate reality of the truth—God.

The mission of the Paraclete is not only translating the 'words of Jesus' in every situation which challenges a new interpretation. It is not even having an interpretive relationship to the 'figurative' (ἐν παροιμίαις), but to perfectly clarify it, speaking openly (ἐν παρρησίᾳ).[51] The Paraclete in order to lead to all truth needs to indigenise, contextualise and inculturate the revelation! It is in enabling the disciples to see each and every experience from God's perspective, thereby having a new outlook in their life-philosophy, that the Paraclete leads to all truth. Even so the revelation continued in the Paraclete's mission is not something entirely different from that of the historical mission of Jesus "οὐ γὰρ λαλήσει ἀφ' ἑαυτοῦ, ἀλλ' ὅσα ἀκούσει λαλήσει." Bultmann thinks it is irrelevant from whom he hears, whether from Jesus or from God, for in his opinion as in v. 15a they are the same! The new revelatory work of the Paraclete is not without limitations.

---

48 G. R. Beasley-Murray, *John*, 283.
49 R. E. Brown, *The Gospel according to John*, 2:703.
50 C. K. Barrett, *The Gospel according to St. John*, 489.
51 G. M. Burge, *The Anointed Community*, 214.

For the Paraclete is completely dependent for the revelations he mediates to the One who sent him. The authority of his revelation lies in his being sent, on the One who has sent him. He will speak only what he will hear (ἀκούσει—Barrett rightly calls ἀκούει a dogmatic improvement of ἀκούσει)— notice the tense of the verb. The Fourth Evangelist does not say that the Spirit will only 'repeat' the 'prompts,' but 'reiterate' that which has already been said. Hearing is the process that should move one, there will be future progressive revelation, the historical revelation that took place in Jesus will continue in the community and the Paraclete will be its authoritative channel.

Does τὰ ἐρχόμενα ἀναγγελεῖ ὑμῖν in v. 13b refer to the Paraclete's prophetic ministry? In fact the Evangelist himself and the Johannine Jesus too show little or no interest in predicting future events either eschatological or historical (see exegesis at 5:27).[52] Thüsing remarks that 'the things that are to come' should be understood from the stand-point of the company in the upper room, most naturally referring to the hour that is coming of which Jesus in the Gospel often speaks.[53]

Boring makes a cogitate observation, as he describes the Paraclete in John 14–16 as the 'pneumatic Christian charisma.' Verbs such as διδάσκειν, ὑπομιμνῄσκειν (in 14:26), μαρτυρεῖν (15:26), ἐλέγχειν (16:8), ἀναγγέλλειν (16:13), and δοξάζειν (16:14), lead to the conclusion that the Johannine community was not unaware of a prophetic charisma.[54] Bernard however remarks that this is the only place in the Fourth Gospel where any of the Pauline χαρίσματα of the Spirit are mentioned (cf. 1 Cor 12:29–30).[55] Brown attempts to correct this perspective. In his study of ἀναγγέλλειν he claims that in the Fourth Gospel the prefix ἀνά- preserves its force of reiterative announcement, as in classical and Septuagint Greek, then the Spirit will re-announce the things to come.[56]

---

52 M. E. Boring, "The Influence of Christian Prophecy on the Johannine Portrayal of the Paraclete and Jesus," NTS 25 (1979): 119.
53 W. Thüsing, Die Erhöhung und Verherrlichung Jesu im Johannesevangelium (3rd ed.; NTA 21/1–2; Münster: Aschendorff, 1979), 149–53.
54 M. E. Boring, "The Influence of Christian Prophecy," 113.
55 J. H. Bernard, Commentary on the Gospel according to St. John, 2:511; also see A. Wikenhauser, Das Evangelium nach Johannes, 295; G. Johnston, The Spirit-Paraclete in the Gospel of John, 38–39, and O. Betz, Der Paraklet, 191–92.
56 R. E. Brown, The Gospel according to John, 2:708.

Hoskyns suggests that the broader application may include the significance of the departure of Jesus.⁵⁷ Bultmann simply views it as the essential significance of the Word, it illuminates the future! If the Paraclete is disclosing that which he heard (from God/Jesus), then the Word interprets the past, discloses the will of God for the present, and reveals the purpose of God that determines future.⁵⁸ Then the prophetic ministry of the Paraclete is indeed to illuminate the understanding of the disciples to discern the 'sign of the time' in specific, concrete historical hours, in the light of the historical revelation of Jesus especially of its eschatological significance.

ἐκεῖνος ἐμὲ δοξάσει suggests that the revelatory work of the Paraclete has a special relationship to the redemptive work of Jesus—the lifting up, the death of Jesus (cf. 12:23, 27, 28; 13:31–32; 17:1–5). In the unfolding of that revelation Jesus' glorification continues, for the revelation of God consists supremely in the self-emptying of the Father in the Son which finds its apex in Jesus' death on the cross, the self-emptying of the Son.

10.7 Summary and Conclusions

a) Of the five Paraclete passages, two passages in the original farewell discourse formulate the Paraclete theocentrically. Three other passages found in the additional farewell discourses are however christocentric. The Evangelist in his final redaction allows the christological interpretation of the Paraclete to stand along with the theocentrical original Paraclete construct.

b) Paraclete is a gift of God. He is for the community as though he were another Jesus. He is the presence of God when Jesus is absent, the eschatological continuum of God's salvific purpose revealed in Jesus.

c) Paraclete is God's comforting sign of nearness, fellowship, presence and in-dwelling. As sustainer and strength of the community he is God's challenge to the community to be the visible sign of the invisible God.

d) He is the master teacher, expositor and prophetic interpreter of the Jesus tradition. He is the source of creativity in the community. In authenticating the community's theology through reminding the community of

---

57 E. C. Hoskyns, *The Fourth Gospel*, 487.
58 G. R. Beasley-Murray, *John*, 284; J. Frey, *Die johanneische Eschatologie*, 3:190–91.

Jesus, he helps it to re-interpret, contextualise, re-live and re-enact the Christ event.

e) Paraclete is a witness to God, an enabler in the community, the power of proclamation which strengthens and awakens faith and creates κρίσις in the world. His witness is not a self-defence, but a call to embrace God.

f) He creates in the community a mirror-model of God's world and places before it a choice, a decision and a possibility of knowing what sin is, righteousness is and judgement is.

g) The Paraclete will lead the community beyond what they could understand through the historical theophany of God in Jesus, unfolding new dimensions. He will indigenise, contextualise and inculturise the revelation. The revelation of God that was historicized in Jesus will now continue in the community, and the Paraclete will be the authentic channel.

Chapter Eleven

Conclusion: Johannine Exegesis of God

11.1 The Characterisation of God in the Fourth Gospel

"God is Spirit" (4:24) is the Fourth Evangelist's explicit characterisation of God. Thereby he emphasises the invisibility, unknowability, the mystery and freedom of God's being, and affirms that no one has seen God (1:18), heard His voice, or seen His form (6:46; 5:37). God belongs to the above/ heavenly realm (3:13, 31; 8:23) which is described as that of light, life and truth. He is the only true God (3:33; 17:3). He is a reality whether one acknowledges it or not. He is the creator, originator of all that has come into being (1:3–4), the unceasing Worker (5:17). He loves His creation, the world (3:16).

The very affirmation that God is the Creator proclaims His intention 'to relate.' He is God *in relation* to His creation. God's readiness and eagerness to relate Himself to the below world, to His creation is characterised through the categories of light, truth, revelation, liberation and freedom. The imagery of the Father in the Fourth Gospel holds these categories together to exegetise the relationality of God. The Fatherhood of God in the Fourth Gospel primarily relates to Jesus the 'Son,'[1] and in a secondary and derivative sense, to the community of believers (compare 'my Father, your Father,' 'my God, your God' in 20:17c).[2] The Father of Jesus is also the Father

---

1 The Johannine Jesus uses 'my Father' 25 times, and especially in the Father–Son passages we find the absolute use of the Father 74 times.
2 G. Schneider, "Auf Gott bezogenes «mein Vater» und «euer Vater» in den Jesus-Worten der Evangelien, zugleich ein Beitrag zum Problem Johannes und die Synoptiker," in *The Four Gospels, 1992: Festschrift Frans Neirynck* (ed. F. van Segbroeck, et al.; 3 vols.; BETL 100; Leuven: University Press, 1992), 3:1771–82; D. Juel and P. Keifert, "I Believe in God: A Johannine Perspective," *HBT* 12 (1990): 50. This, of course, follows the Old Testament model of the understanding of the Fatherhood of God, and the logical development from the God of the fathers, the God of Moses. Even there the Fatherhood of God extended in a derivative sense

of his friends (John 15:14). In the risen Lord, the Johannine community has been called into the same relationship that Jesus, the Son had with God, the Father.

The Fatherhood of God is defined and presented in the relationship of the Father and the Son in the Fourth Gospel, denoting intimacy and accessibility of the Almighty. It assures that God is not distant, aloof or withdrawn, God draws very near, God is with us. The purpose of the 'Father' image here, is not to give the community an opportunity to build a sentimental, anthropomorphic image of the eternal, distant, dominating and tremendous Creator, but to emphasise primarily the nearness and approachableness of God. The image of the Father in the Fourth Gospel evokes in the reader a notion of a family.[3]

The Evangelist reinterprets the divine Fatherhood of God, radically demythologising it from all projections of patriarchal constructions of power, and from its association with one particular race/tribe.[4] Using the traditional God-language, the Fourth Gospel attempts to turn over the imagery, though the Evangelist does affirm that the Fatherhood of God did reveal itself in God's historical relationship with Israel. God as the Father of Israel is understood in the context of the unique act of liberation that Israel experienced in history.[5] But the idea of divine Fatherhood of God in the Fourth Gospel moves definitely away from God being Father of a chosen people, chosen family defined in racial terms, to a universal Fatherhood, making God a loving, affectionate protector of the individual and the world family. The Father of Israel now becomes the Father of the whole of creation as reflected in the Father of a new community, a community without barriers and boundaries.

---

to the patriarchal family and to Israel. See R. Hamerton-Kelly, *God the Father: Theology and Patriarchy in the Teaching of Jesus* (OBT; Philadelphia: Fortress, 1979), 21–34.

3 See also D. A. Lee, "Beyond Suspicion? The Fatherhood of God in the Fourth Gospel," *Pacifica* 8 (1995): 151–52.
4 See R. Hamerton-Kelly, *God the Father*, 21–34.
5 In prophetic tradition (Hosea, Jeremiah, Third-Isaiah), the Fatherhood of God symbolised a new creation, a new covenant with Israel. He is the Father who prevents His people from being irresponsible and unfaithful. See also C. Geffré, "'Father' as the Proper Name of God," in *God as Father?* (ed. J.-B. Metz and E. Schillebeeckx; Edinburgh: T&T Clark, 1981), 44.

Normally patriarchy is not only defined by exclusive and elitist relationships, but also keeps members at a distance from the power-centre and 'others' on an inferior level. However, in the Fourth Gospel those who are considered to be at a distance and on an inferior level than that of God's chosen family (4:1–42; 12:20–26) are drawn into the intimacy of the Father and His family. The boundaries that are to be seen as dividing the community of the Father and the world are not those that God erected, but that arise out of humankind's decision against God's invitation! In affirming the universality of God, the Fourth Evangelist fights against the attempts to 'particularise' the Fatherhood of God only to the community using exclusive language and considers it as human sin which arises out of misunderstanding and misappropriating the universal Fatherhood of God (see exegesis of John 8).

The Father in the Fourth Gospel does not scheme to retain, increase and exercise power, on the contrary it is not held on to, but is given up again and again to the point of self-emptying (see exegesis of John 5). The Father image in the Fourth Gospel shows a two way dynamic.[6] It consists of:

a) *giving and drawing*. The Fatherhood of God reveals itself by the giving of power in its self-emptying love. The pivot of the Father's relationality is His self-emptying, which consequentially reflects God's universal Fatherhood. The opposite dynamic of giving is the Father's drawing of everyone to His loving relationship (6:43; cf. 12:32). This is also reflected in God's longing for 'relationship' which is affirmed with the concept of '*sending*' which is motivated by the immeasurable love for the world (3:16), and His zeal for building relationship with His own creation which has neglected the relationship and fallen away, costs the Father all that He has, even His 'Son' who represents His invaluable gift to the world. The Son represents God's own self. In a costly and vulnerable sending, in which the Father risks His Son, exposing him to hurt, rejection (1:11; 3:14–17; 12:27) and finally even to death, the Sent One is given a mission, the authority and identity of the Sender[7] (cf. 5:23b; 6:38; 8:26;

---

6   See also D. A. Lee, "Beyond Suspicion?" 151–52.
7   W. Loader, *The Christology of the Fourth Gospel*, 30–32; P. Borgen, "God's Agent in the Fourth Gospel," in *The Interpretation of John* (ed. J. Ashton; Philadelphia: Fortress, 1986), 68–69; cf. J. Becker, *Johanneisches Christentum: Seine Geschichte und Theologie im Überblick* (Tübingen: Mohr Siebeck, 2004), 165–69. Although Becker characterizes God as the Father of the Sent-One and describes the Christology of

12:44; 13:20; 14:24; 17:8), and the assurance that He will continually abide in him (10:38; 16:32).

b) *delegating power and obedience*. The Father in the Fourth Gospel delegates all power and sends ambassadors entrusted with a responsible mission. The power of God is contrasted with that of religious and secular authorities of the Evangelist's time. When the world power harasses and destroys those powerless (15:18–19; 19:6–7, 15a), and makes them succumb to political expediency (11:47–50; 19:8, 13–16a), God's power as seen in His agent/Son Jesus enables the meek to resist the forces of darkness. It creates healing and wholeness and empowers those who are weak as they stand up for the truth (16:33). Therefore the Father's power that He delegates to His Son has the function not of life-threatening, but of life-giving, not of judging to condemnation, but judging to save.

In the Fourth Gospel authority is not given for self-aggrandisement, but for self-giving and self-surrender. Thus the delegation of power is balanced by the dynamic of obedience. Obedience in the Fourth Gospel is to keep the will of God, is to be responsible and is a free will obligation. The Evangelist radically transforms the concept of obedience as he does not speak of ὑπακούειν, but of τηρεῖν (8:51, 52, 55; 14:15, 21, 23–24; 15:10, 20; 9:16; 17:11–12, 15). Obeying belongs to the patriarchal residue giving the notion of an unquestioning, uncritical subservience. The fitting response for the delegation of power and self-emptying love of the Father is to recognise the worth of the mission entrusted and act with full responsibility. It is a loving response to an act of loving entrusting! Self-emptying love becomes the pattern of life, rejecting the patriarchal pattern of retaining and making an exclusive relationship. The Father imagery in the Fourth Gospel reveals a fundamentally relational theology.[8]

The Father cares for His family, He works continually to sustain and heal His family (5:17); the people of this world belong to God, they are His. Through His name He gives them *identity*, as they are elected out of the world (17:6), and sent after God's mode of sending His ambassadors (Jesus/

---

the Fourth Gospel using phrases such as "der gesandte Sohn des Vaters," "Weg und Auftrag des Gottessohnes," "der Gesandte als Auferstehung und Leben," he argues that epiphany Christology and not Theology is central to the Fourth Evangelist.

8   See also D. A. Lee, "Beyond Suspicion?" 151–52.

Paraclete) to be in the world (17:17–18). The election is not a privileged position: as His heavenly agent, His earthly agents are to be challenged to understand the Father's ruling philosophy. Instead of seeking safe havens in the family, they are challenged to imitate the Father, in confronting the world, to empty themselves in order to fulfil the entrusted task, to be God's mirror models in the world. The Father as He is holy, sanctifies His earthly agents too. He equips them, makes them 'ready' for the task (17:16). He enlightens and teaches the community through the Spirit (14:26; 16:12–13). Fatherhood denotes God as the source of strength and the faithful companion. His being gives confidence to His people to fulfil the entrusted mission and to command control even in the midst of grave adversity (18:1ff.; 19:30). The Father steers the human world towards a creative future—the relationship between the Creator and creation originally thought of in terms of Master and Slave imagery must now be replaced by the model of love relationship of the Father and Son. The community, who are God's children through the Son are now regarded as friends and given access to divine mysteries (15:15; 16:25, 27).

As He Himself is 'relational', the task of His community is to reflect this all-embracing relationality and build a relational chain. In entering the relationship offered and invited into, one shares in the very life of God, which is eternal. In this relationship one discovers what it means to be human, as one ought to be. God transpires and shapes a new identity. The Fatherhood of God in the Fourth Gospel places all things into that relation to God, which belong to them as God's creatures from the very beginning. It reveals the 'natural' identity of human beings and all that is with an urgency nowhere achieved outside the eschatological event. This relational oneness with God, and with the fellow human beings is not in merging or getting dissolved, but in experiencing and sharing the 'Shalom' at the core of one's identity (17:20ff.). Those who have come to know of their origin and their individual and corporate identity can understand the gift of oneness that the Father offers through the Son. Love is to be the pattern of 'oneness' of the community's life just as it is in the relationship of the Father and the Son. This oneness brings wholeness to the community and awakens to be in the love of God that encompasses the whole creation, which is salvation. The salvation of the world constitutes the Creator–creation relationship being restored and renewed, manifesting the glory of God which is His love transcending even His transcendence (1:14; 17:2).

11.2 Johannine Theo-centric Christology

11.2.1 Agent Christology

The Johannine Jesus is the 'One Sent' by God! The language used of God commissioning and the expression 'God sent' stress God's initiative. Thus the Agent commissioned and sent can be understood only in terms of God's purpose. The Johannine Jesus does not only the will of God, he manifests absolute dependence on God and he reveals and exegetises God. Then the Johannine Christology must be a divine Agent Christology.[9]

The Johannine Jesus understands his mission as God's commissary; his 'sent-ness' gives Jesus' mission both the purpose and authority. Jesus represents 'the Father who sent me' (4:34; 5:23, 24, 30, 37) and thus disowns/ disclaims any authority of his own. The mission that is entrusted is God's salvific purpose for the world (3:17) that has to be completed in a restricted time (9:4). The Father determines what he says and does, but also enables him to carry out his mission (7:26, 28; 12:49; 14:24). As the Sent One, Jesus experiences God's fidelity and assuring presence with him (7:28; 8:26). Therefore the one believing in Jesus, believes in God, recognising Jesus, recognises God (14:9), receiving Jesus, receives God (13:20), hating Jesus, hates God (15:23), rejecting Jesus, rejects God (15:21), honouring Jesus, honours God (5:23; 17:18), in knowing Jesus, knows God (17:3, 25).

Therefore the Johannine Jesus rightly proclaims: "the Father is greater than I" (14:28). Jesus is dependent on God for his power (5:19), for his authority (17:2). He is dependent on the Father as to know the destiny of his own life, and also that of his disciples (6:37) whom he appoints as earthly agents to extend the mission of God in time and space (17:17). Jesus as Agent is accountable to God for the performance/fulfilment of his entrusted task (19:30).

---

9 Compare P. Borgen, "God's Agent in the Fourth Gospel," 67–78; J. A. Bühner, *Der Gesandte und sein Weg im 4. Evangelium*; J. P. Miranda, *Der Vater, der mich gesandt hat: Religionsgeschichtliche Untersuchungen zu den johanneischen Sendungsformeln* (Europäische Hochschulschriften, Reihe 23: Theologie, vol. 7; Frankurt am Main: Peter Lang, 1972); G. R. Beasley-Murray, "The Mission of the Logos Son," in *The Four Gospels, 1992*, 3:1855–68, and M. de Jonge, "Christology and Theology in the Context of Early Christian Eschatology, particularly in the Fourth Gospel," in *The Four Gospels, 1992*, 3:1847–50.

The Agent Christology of the Fourth Gospel emphasises both unity between the Agent and his Sender, and subordination of the Agent to the Sender. Therefore we may very well conclude that the Johannine Agent Christology points beyond itself as a witness to Theology in the Fourth Gospel.

We do not venture into a detailed analysis of each christological title once again; it should suffice in this context to indicate that though the Evangelist did remould and reinterpret the traditional christological titles, ultimately they rest upon God the Father. The Son, the Messiah (Christ), the Holy One of God, the Lamb of God, the Son of Man, the King of Israel, all theologically reflect the concept of divine agency embedded in them. Only in relation to God they have meaning, significance and function.

However the Evangelist distinguishes between the sending of a human agent with the message from God to His people (such as the man John—1:6–8), and the sending of the messenger Son to reveal the Father, and recall humanity to creational relationship, for the salvation of the world. The former is a man thrust forth with a commission from God; the latter is 'the Man from heaven.'

11.2.2 Mediator Christology

The dualistic language supplements Agent Christology with 'Mediator Christology'—ἔρχομαι ἀπό (8:42; 16:28); ἔρχομαι παρά (13:3–4; 16:7–8; cf. 17:8); ἐκ τῶν ἄνω (8:23) ἐπάνω/ἄνωθεν (3:31); πορεύομαι (14:2, 3, 12, 28; 16:7, 8); ὑπάγω (7:33; 14:4); μεταβαίνω (13:1); ἀφίημι (16:28); καταβαίνω/ἀναβαίνω (1:51; 3:31). These literary metaphors express the fact that Jesus is from God, commissioned (ἔρχομαι) and sent, that he owes his identity to God, and that he needs to go back to the Father in order to fulfil his mission, as he owes Him accountability. Thus Jesus' mission has its beginning and end in God, in the 'above.' The Johannine Christology using these word metaphors for theological references to Jesus' life, death and resurrection, sees therein God's purpose and plan in sending Jesus as the one 'coming and going.' Jesus mediates between the human world and God. He demolishes the barrier that was established between the two spheres due to human unfaithfulness.

The descent–ascent scheme closely follows the Son of Man title (cf. 1:51; 3:31). To Nathaniel the descending–ascending Son of Man promises that he shall see greater things. But to Nicodemus the question is asked as to how he could believe if told heavenly things. The intention remains enigmatic: Does it mean that the descending–ascending Son of Man is to mediate the 'belief' between the two spheres, the sight and perception to see greater things? In 8:23 we are confronted with an identical situation: "you are from below, I am from above." In the context, Jesus of Nazareth (8:18, 48) knows his origin; others do not. He claims to be able to lead those from below to know the above, God's heavenly realm, and to be part of it. Salvation—the vision of greater things—is only through the change of realm, in faith. Using vertical dualism the Fourth Gospel individualises the universal salvific purpose of God, or rather individual appropriation of the universal salvation, through the belief in the descending–ascending, coming–going Man from heaven.[10]

11.2.3 'I am' Christology

The ἐγώ εἰμι sayings in the Fourth Gospel are often regarded as the Johannine Jesus taking up the divine name of the Old Testament. But as we noticed in our interpretation of "I am the Light of the world," the ἐγώ εἰμι formulas with a predicate relate the mission of Jesus to human life. Jesus is Light to the people, he is the Truth and the Way offering guidance and direction. Jesus is Bread and the Vine that sustains the branches both offering life to those who adhere to him and accept his food (Word). He is the Door through which people may enter securely and he is the Shepherd who gives not just nourishment in pasture, but protection from evil and unites the sheep into one fold. Finally Jesus is the Resurrection that is the real sign of the promise of Eternal Life. These represent the community's deep reflection on 'Jesus' and personify in him the promise of the reign of God. In him the community can encounter the breaking in of the reign— God's just world. Scholars have already noted that it may be the 'I am' with predicate 'images' that probably constitute the Johannine replacement for synoptic parables/allegories.[11] In the divine Agent, the Son, God confronts hearers with the Word. The ἐγώ εἰμι sayings with predicate have particular advantages of making the saving character of Jesus' mission visible in

---

10 W. A. Meeks, "The Man from Heaven in Johannine Sectarianism," in *The Interpretation of John*, 141–73.
11 E. Schweizer, *Ego Eimi*, 112–24.

impressive images and symbols. Jesus' mission is described in what he gives. ἐγώ εἰμι is the Johannine interpretation of the meaning of Jesus.

Moreover, our exegetical investigation revealed that the use of absolute ἐγώ εἰμι could well have been an identification formula rather than the general belief that it proclaims Jesus' divinity. Among the absolute uses of ἐγώ εἰμι in the Fourth Gospel, intriguingly three uses need to be referred to at this point. With regard to 18:5, 8 we concluded that the ἐγώ εἰμι is used in the context as a simple identification formula, meaning 'I am he, Jesus of Nazareth' and that the reaction of the officers who came to arrest Jesus was that they fell back on hearing Jesus' ἐγώ εἰμι, God's affirmation to Jesus that his righteous Agent doing His Will, will be under His protection. The enemies do not have power over him unless Jesus gives himself up as a free will submission to the will of God.

In 4:26 the most one can affirm is that Jesus identifies himself as the Messiah with the prophetic office of the One who reveals everything when he comes. In 13:19, 20 having prophesied what is to come in order that when the prophecy is fulfilled 'you may believe that ἐγώ εἰμι,' the Johannine Jesus in the next verse declares 'he who receives me receives Him who sent me'! If taken as an absolute ἐγώ εἰμι, the Johannine presentation here of ἐγώ εἰμι as Jesus' divinity after the Old Testament God predicate, then it becomes intolerable that Jesus is made to say: 'I am God (of the Old Testament) and I am here because someone sent me'! Even in 8:28 as our exegetical investigation has shown, the absolute ἐγώ εἰμι is included in the same ὅτι clause "and I do nothing of myself, but speak as the Father taught me" and the meaning of ἐγώ εἰμι in 8:24 is determined by that of 8:28.

In 8:58 our observation was that the Fourth Evangelist refers to the 'relational face' of God, God's salvific purpose for the world. The Johannine Jesus says (if we are allowed paraphrasing) that 'the salvific purpose of God which was before Abraham came into being, now encounters you here and now. I as God's Sent One/Son, the relational face of God, the presence and revelation of God here and now.'

To come to a consensus therefore, ἐγώ εἰμι in the Fourth Gospel does not ascribe divinity to Jesus. It would be a misunderstanding of ἐγώ εἰμι if it were interpreted as Jesus' identification with God.[12] However, they proclaim the presence of God that encounters the world in the person of Jesus and

---

12 R. Schnackenburg, *The Gospel according to St. John*, 2:88.

they affirm God's salvific purpose revealed through the historical mission of the Son. Jesus is the Sent One in whom God Himself speaks: ἐγώ εἰμι is an elaboration and intensification of the Christology of mission. ἐγώ εἰμι therefore in other words is an expression of Christology not Theology.[13]

11.2.4 Oneness Christology

The Johannine oneness Christology[14] is presented, depicting the oneness of the Father and the Son through two theological metaphors:

a) *The Apprentice Metaphor:* The Father of the Fourth Gospel is a Worker, a loving owner of a 'workshop' where the Son does his apprenticeship under his own Father. Father and Son both work in their family business, on one and the same task. The Father working continuously shows everything to the Son, no business secret is kept hidden. The Son has the opportunity to watch, imitate and learn. Because of His work, the Father can preserve and care for His family, the Son shares His task. The oneness of the Father and the Son is seen in their work, for the providence and care, and to sustain the life of the community.[15]

b) *The Self-Emptying Metaphor:* The Father giving everything He has (3:16) is the basis of the oneness of the Father and the Son. The oneness therefore is a gift of God. Following his apprenticeship, the Son does what the Father does—he empties himself (10:10). The Father's giving and the Son's reciprocation to fulfil the task entrusted, bring salvation to the world. The mutual reciprocal self-emptying phenomenon leads the Father and the Son to a 'relational' oneness, to the point of mutual in-dwelling! Mutual/reciprocal in-dwelling has often been described as 'mystical.' Actually it is a relational and functional oneness described by means of a linguistic metaphor. Through self-emptying the Father and the Son mutually express the perfect, complete expression of solidarity and representation. This highest level of relationality leads to an interpretation of identities at the core of their being which envisages the deepest level of peace with each other: thus the 'oneness' of the Father and the Son remain 'relational' and 'in-dwelling' at once.

---

13   D. M. Ball, *'I am' in John's Gospel*; P. B. Harner, *The "I am" of the Fourth Gospel*.
14   Cf. M. L. Appold, *The Oneness Motif in the Fourth Gospel*.
15   Cf. D. A. Lee, "Beyond Suspicion?" 140ff.

11.3 Theological Hermeneutic

In our exegetical venture we have observed a creative dialogue between Christology and Theology. We came across the so-called high christological (the phrase 'high Christology' is misleading, what we encounter here is the sapling of a theological adventure) affirmations that could very well be interpreted as ascribing divinity to Jesus. The Evangelist also presents a noticeably sub-ordinate Christology (the phrase 'low Christology' is misleading, what we encounter here is a very well developed Christology) that looks as if belonging to the earlier Christian heritage, but very neatly reworked and reinterpreted. In fact, one can interpret the Johannine 'sub-ordinate' Christology in terms of his divine Christology, deeming it the zenith of Johannine Theology—to be led to behold 'God striding on the earth.' Or, one can even turn the interpretive model upside down to 'behold the Man, the Logos in the flesh'!

The Johannine Christology therefore has been a hotbed for theological disputation. To the question what type of Christology we encounter in the Fourth Gospel, the paradoxes of Glory[16]/Flesh, Divinity/Humanity,[17] Docetic/Anti-docetic are the categories in which theologians have tried to answer the question. In the course of our exegetical exploration, we made the following startling observations:

a) In its finished form, the Prologue is theocentric. But the Logos hymn behind the Prologue is christological. The Prologue represents a theocentrical reworking of the christocentric tradition.

b) The theological affirmations on the pre-existence of Jesus have been made to appear as theological projections, as of liberator to the pre-existent Son in the model of Israel's theological discovery in recognising the liberator God as the Creator Himself. Thus in confessing Jesus as pre-existent, the community in fact affirms faith in the pre-existent universal salvific will of God, sending 'Jesus' being its supreme sign.

c) The editorial bridge between the Prologue and the Gospel proclaims Jesus, the unique Son as the exegesis of God.

---

16 E. Käsemann, *The Testament of Jesus*, esp. 7–13, 21–26, 34–35, and his "Aufbau und Anliegen des Johanneischen Prologs," in *Exegetische Versuche und Besinnungen*, 155–80.

17 M. M. Thompson, *The Humanity of Jesus in the Fourth Gospel*.

d) The Johannine Jesus is made to pray, and his prayer is set to clear the order of the only True God and the Sent One Jesus Christ and to explicitly pronounce his theocentricity.
e) The Jesus proclamation of oneness with the Father—"I and my Father are one"—has been explicitly balanced through "the Father is greater than I."
f) During the conflicting theological discussion with the Jews/Synagogue the Evangelist cleverly raises the christological questions—Is Jesus equal to God? Are Jesus and the Father one? Is Jesus pre-existent?, to answer in the negative, and thereby affirms the community's theocentricity—monotheism.
g) The Thomas pericope and the Betrayal-Arrest Scene must have been christocentric in their origin. The Evangelist sandwiches them in his redaction so effectively, that they be interpreted in the larger theocentric context of the Passion-Resurrection narratives.
h) The Paraclete passages in the original (?) farewell discourse are theocentrically conceptualised, whereas the later additions to the farewell discourses contain christologically interpreted Paraclete passages. Affirming the 'Paraclete,' the community's theological construct, as the sign and authenticator of God's continuing revelation, the Evangelist relativises God's historical theophany in Jesus.

Given our observations, the major challenge that the Evangelist was confronted with in his creative narrative redaction was not Jesus' two natures—divine and/or human—but the difficult task of keeping the community's Christology within the most revered monotheistic framework, in other words to attempt to contain the damages of theological adventure of a creative section of the community, not by disturbing the creative genius of the community's theologians, but by exploring ways to accommodate their theological experience and language within the community's theological framework, and without compromising on its Theo-logy and without allowing Christology to replace Theology. In presenting almost in parallel the christological interpretations of the Jesus tradition as well as the theological interpretation of it, he ventures to find a hermeneutical key.

The Evangelist makes plain to the community the theological consequence of theologising Jesus as God, through presenting the community's protocol of its conflict with the Synagogue. His theological hermeneutics is to offer 'freedom' for theological adventures, and evaluate it in the light of basic Theo-logy! The community's understanding of God in/through Jesus and now in the Paraclete becomes the criterion for evaluation. Along with the theological questions, the community's sociological situation also pressurised it to reinterpret its own social identity, or even theologise its whole struggle for a viable social identity. The social alienation that began with the Synagogue excommunication (John 9) aggravated with the entry of Samaritans (John 4), or Hellenists or like groups (12:20). And this gave rise to a probable geographical shift and a struggle to keep contact with the larger 'church' (probably the travel narrative of Jesus pendling in and out of Jerusalem figuratively narrates the Johannine community's dialogue with the church). This provided the community an opportunity for a theological reflection of its own identity in a five-way conversational context: with the synagogue, with the considerate Jews, with the Samaritans, with the Hellenists, and with the wider church.

Thus one could very well say: the theology of the Johannine community developed a creative dialectic with its sociological context. In its alienation, the community experienced the God of freedom and faithfulness who made people free even when they were unfaithful. In the rock-like dependability of God it understood the faithfulness, loving kindness, and trustworthiness of the only true God. In its suffering identity it experienced God's liberating and transforming power. This experience, as it reflects in the community's theological conversation with the Synagogue, affirms that God liberates from all traditional bonds, is above all human traditions and creates traditions. This firm belief that God is with them is evident in its new-found confidence reflected in its dialogue with those considerate Jews as it challenges them to decide and take sides. Only in deciding/taking sides with God one experiences the liberating power of God.[18] A compassionate by-passer cannot understand the mighty works of God, brought about by his self-emptying. The self-emptying community—a community forced to self-emptying—can understand a self-emptying God, which sees its experience as teaching and re-enacting the Jesus event! It is experiential theologising.

The contextual Christology of the Johannine community thrived while it gained new insights to its agency Christology by incorporating the from above/from below, ascending/descending 'Man from heaven' dualistic

---

18 D. Rensberger, *Johannine Faith and Liberating Community* (Philadelphia: Westminster Press, 1988), 107–34.

metaphoric christologies. It not only brought the community's sociological experience in contact with Theology, but its sociological language was made theological. Logos became the key term to share the community's experience with the relational face of God in Jesus. It helped the community to comprehend the universal salvific heritage, of which it has now become a part and partakes. It encouraged the community to enter into methodological and theological dialogue with its environment with a critical contextual faculty even to risk itself, to transform and enrich the theological ethos, either carried in by its members from Judaism, or other religions, in the light of God's ultimate revelation in Jesus. Thus for the community, Jesus became the historical sign of God. But the community's understanding of God's continual authentic revelation in the Paraclete at once relativised the historical revelation of God in Jesus and placed the community in 'open eschatological present.'

11.4 Whither Theo-logy?

Did the Evangelist succeed in his attempt to give a hermeneutical key to the community for its Christology? Probably the 1st Epistle of John answers the question, but in the negative. In the Epistle we see theological crystallisation as already taken place. The Presbyter who identifies himself with 'we' probably refers to those who saw themselves as faithful tradition carriers whose task it was to see that traditions were handed over faithfully. Then 'we' could correspond to the 'school'[19] within the framework of the wider community. It is from within this 'we' that the Presbyter speaks in the epistles in order to warn the community against attempting to split it from within.

The 'Gospel'—the testimony of the community, with various explosive theological concepts—had already been now interpreted within the community, and a schism had already taken place (1 John 2:9). Probably a larger group (1 John 4:5) went out of the community. It is important to note that the schism occurred not through outside influences. Nowhere in his criticism of them does the Presbyter allude to outside pressures. Rather the clause of the split rests within the community itself, and in the way in which

---

19 R. A. Culpepper, *The Johannine School*.

it was interpreting the Christology as it was recorded and expressed in the Gospel.

The community must have become theocentric[20] as the following collection of references related to the community's Christology and Ethic in the 1st Epistle shows:

Theocentric Christology:

2:15 Do not love the world or the things in the world. The love of the Father is not in those who love the world;

4:1–3 Beloved, do not believe every spirit, but test the spirits to see whether they are from God; for many false prophets have gone out into the world. By this you know the Spirit of God: every spirit that confesses that Jesus Christ has come in the flesh is from God, and every spirit that does not confess Jesus is not from God. And this is the spirit of the antichrist, of which you have heard that it is coming; and now it is already in the world.

4:6 We are from God. Whoever knows God listens to us, and whoever is not from God does not listen to us. From this we know the spirit of truth and the spirit of error.

5:1 Everyone who believes that Jesus is the Christ has been born of God, and everyone who loves the parent loves the child.

5:5–7 Who is it that conquers the world but the one who believes that Jesus is the Son of God? This is the one who came by water and blood, Jesus Christ, not with the water only but with the water and the blood. And the Spirit is the one that testifies, for the Spirit is the truth. There are three that testify:

Theocentric Ethics:

1:6 God is light and in him there is no darkness at all. If we say that we have fellowship with him while we are walking in darkness, we lie and do not do what is true;

1:8 If we say that we have no sin, we deceive ourselves, and the truth is not in us.

1:10 If we say that we have not sinned, we make him a liar, and his word is not in us.

---

20 R. A. Whitacre, *Johannine Polemic: The Role of Tradition and Theology* (SBLDS 67; Chico, Calif.: Scholars Press, 1982), 153–86, esp. 178ff.

3:9		Those who have been born of God do not sin, because God's seed abides in them; they cannot sin, because they have been born of God.
4:8–10		Whoever does not love does not know God, for God is love. God's love was revealed among us in this way: God sent his only Son into the world so that we might live through him. In this is love, not that we loved God but that he loved us and sent his Son to be the atoning sacrifice for our sins.
4:20		Those who say, "I love God," and hate their brothers or sisters, are liars; for those who do not love a brother or sister whom they have seen, cannot love God whom they have not seen.
5:18		We know that those who are born of God do not sin, but the one who was born of God protects them, and the evil one does not touch them.

Based upon his theo-centric Christology and the theo-centric ethics, the Presbyter attacks those who have been responsible for the schism! Who were 'those opponents'?[21] Were they docetics? Or the 2nd century Gnostics? Attempting answers to this question is beyond the scope of this study, however, it becomes clear that one of the reasons for such a schism in the community was that of overstepping the theological hermeneutics of the Fourth Evangelist. Extreme 'christocentric' interpretation of the Jesus tradition seems to be the root cause for the schism. Did these christocentrics become Gnostics?[22] Probably yes. But our intention is not to commend the theocentric wing of the community that held onto its orthodox conservatism, or to regret the demise of extreme christocentric elements into the Gnostic circle.

Rather, the Johannine community provides a canonical example as to how theological hermeutic could become too rigid and curb the creative theological faculty, thereby bringing destruction. The dialogue and discussion with both the opponents, and the friendly harmonious environment where

---

21 R. A. Whitacre, *Johannine Polemic*, 176ff. Also F. Vouga, "The Johannine School: A Gnostic Tradition in Primitive Christianity?" *Bib.* 69 (1988): 371–85, esp. 377–78. See also his commentary, *Die Johannesbriefe*, esp. 46–48. However, J. Becker contends that it was the non-adherence of a section of the Johannine community to epiphany Christology that led to its demise. See his *Johanneisches Christentum*, 223–33.

22 We recall the Nag Hammadi Tractates such as *The Gospel of Truth*, *Trimorphic Protennoia*, *The Gospel of Philip* that show close affinities to Johannine language.

belief is lived in fellowship are two important factors which seem to have come to a standstill during the writing of the 1st Epistle of John. The truth that is revealed in living relationships was encumbered into written dogma. The very traditions that were built breaking the exploiting and death-smelling structures of their Jewish Theology through self-emptying discipleship, become death traps for some of its own members. Radicalism that thrived in breaking new ground, new interpretive expositions of Jesus tradition which enriched the community's theological language through bold theology in dialogue with contemporary philosophical context, and the sociological situation now in the times of the 1st Epistle becomes conservative.

The theological language that flowered forth in the time of the Gospel redaction, its interaction with Christology, now at the time of the 1st Epistle became bland with polemical overtones. God who 'unites' and calls to oneness became God who divides! The very community that risked to be heretical with the new-found theological freedom and structural freedom now become prey to the same structures that once fostered creativity.

Who were right? Who kept to the theological hermeneutics of the Fourth Evangelist? Every community needs to answer this question in its struggle with problems and sufferings, in its dialogues with its neighbours of faith, within its cultural and philosophical environment and in its continuous conversation with its members local and universal. Theology is the language of the people of God, which comes to life in their becoming radicals rather than conservatives, their not dwelling in tradition, but in growing beyond traditions to build dynamic traditions, in believing firmly in the God of liberation and freedom, in risking relationships that bring 'oneness' and in becoming christocentric in order to become theocentric, and in becoming theocentric while still being able to recognise and affirm Christ even beyond Christology can ever dream to venture, for: God is Spirit, and those who worship Him must worship Him in Spirit and in Truth!

Bibliography

1. Tools and References

Abbott, Edwin A. *Johannine Vocabulary: A Comparison of the Words of the Fourth Gospel with those of the Three.* London, 1905. Reprint Farnborough, Hants.: Gregg Press, 1968.

———. *Johannine Grammar.* London: A. and C. Black, 1906.

Aland, Barbara, Kurt Aland, Johannes Karavidopoulos, Carlo Maria Martini and Bruce M. Metzger, eds. *Novum Testamentum Graece.* 27th edition. Stuttgart: Deutsche Bibelgesellschaft, 1993.

Aland, Kurt, ed. *Vollständige Konkordanz zum griechischen Neuen Testament.* 2 vols. Berlin/New York: de Gruyter, 1978–1983.

Aland, Kurt, Matthew Black, Carlo Maria Martini, Bruce M. Metzger and Allen Wikgren, eds. *The Greek New Testament.* 4th edition. Stuttgart: Deutsche Bibelgesellschaft, 1994.

Balz, Horst, and Gerhard Schneider, eds. *Exegetisches Wörterbuch zum Neuen Testament.* 2nd edition. 3 vols. Stuttgart: Kohlhammer, 1992.

Bauer, Walter, William F. Arndt, F. Wilbur Gingrich and Frederick W. Danker. *A Greek-English Lexicon of the New Testament and Other Early Christian Literature.* Chicago, Ill.: University of Chicago Press, 1979.

Blass, Friedrich, and Albert Debrunner. *A Greek Grammar of the New Testament: A Translation and Revision of the 9th–10th German Edition, Incorporating Supplementary Notes of A. Debrunner,* by Robert W. Funk. Chicago, Ill.: Chicago University Press, 1961.

Brown, Colin, ed. *The New International Dictionary of New Testament Theology.* Translated, with additions and revisions, from the German. 3 vols. Exeter: Paternoster, 1978.

Charlesworth, James H., ed. *The Dead Sea Scrolls: Hebrew, Aramaic, and Greek Texts with English Translations.* Tübingen: J. C. B. Mohr (Paul Siebeck); and Louisville, Ky.: Westminster John Knox Press. Vol. I: *Rule of the Community and Related Documents,* 1994; vol. II: *Damascus Document, War Scroll, and Related Documents,* 1995.

Elliger, Karl, and Wilhelm Rudolph, eds. *Biblia Hebraica Stuttgartensia.* Stuttgart: Deutsche Bibelgesellschaft, 1967/1977.

Freedman, David N., ed. *Anchor Bible Dictionary.* 6 vols. New York: Doubleday, 1992.

García Martínez, Florentino, ed. *The Dead Sea Scrolls Translated: The Qumran Texts in English.* Leiden/New York: E. J. Brill, 1994.

Kubo, Sakae. *A Reader's Greek-English Lexicon of the New Testament.* Berrien Springs, Mich.: Andrews University Press, 1973.

Kittel, Gerhard, and Gerhard Friedrich. *Theologisches Wörterbuch zum Neuen Testament.* 10 vols. Stuttgart: Kohlhammer, 1933–1979; English Translation: *Theological Dictionary of the New Testament.* Translated and edited bei Geoffrey W. Bromiley. Grand Rapids: Eerdmans, 1964–1976.

Liddell, Henry George, and Robert Scott. *A Greek-English Lexicon: With a Supplement.* 9th edition. 2 vols. Oxford: Clarendon Press, 1968.

Maier, Johann, ed. *Die Qumran-Essener: Die Texte vom Toten Meer.* 3 vols. Munich/Basel: Reinhardt, 1995–1996.

Malatesta, Edward. *St. John's Gospel 1920–1965: A Cumulative and Classified Bibliography of Books and Periodical Literature on the Fourth Gospel.* Rome: Pontifical Biblical Institute, 1967.

Metzger, Bruce M. *A Textual Commentary on the Greek New Testament.* London: United Bible Society, 1975.

Moule, Charles Francis Digby. *An Idiom Book of New Testament Greek.* Cambridge: Cambridge University Press, 1953.

Moulton, James Hope. *A Grammar of New Testament Greek.* Vol. 1: *Prolegomena.* 2nd edition. Edinburgh: T&T Clark, 1906.

Moulton, James Hope, and George Milligan. *The Vocabulary of the Greek Testament: Illustrated from the Papyri and Other Non-Literary Sources.* London: Hodder and Stoughton, 1930.

Moulton, James Hope, and Nigel Turner. *A Grammar of New Testament Greek.* Vol. 3: *Syntax.* Edinburgh: T&T Clark, 1963.

Moulton, William Fiddiam, Alfred S. Geden and Harold Keeling Moulton. *A Concordance to the Greek Testament: According to the Texts of Westcott and Hort.* 5th edition. Edinburgh: T&T Clark, 1980.

Philo. *Complete Works.* Edited by Francis Henry Colson and Graham H. Whitaker 10+2 vols. Loeb Classical Library. Cambridge, Mass./London: Heinemann, 1929–1962.

Rahlfs, Alfred, ed. *Septuaginta.* Stuttgart: Deutsche Bibelgesellschaft, 1979.

Robinson, James M., and R. Smith, eds. *The Nag Hammadi Library in English.* 3rd edition. San Francisco: Harper & Row, 1988.

van Belle, Gilbert. *Johannine Bibliography 1966–1985.* Bibliotheca Ephemeridum Theologicarum Lovaniensium 82. Leuven: Leuven University Press, 1988.

Wenham, John William. *The Elements of New Testament Greek.* Cambridge: Cambridge University Press, 1965.

Zerwick, Maximilian, and Joseph Smith. *Biblical Greek.* Adapted from the 4th Latin edition by Joseph Smith. Scripta Pontificii Instituti Biblici 114. Rome: s.n., 1963.

2. Commentaries on the Gospel according to John

Barrett, Charles Kingsley. *The Gospel According to St. John: An Introduction with Commentary and Notes on the Greek Text.* 2nd edition. London: S.P.C.K., 1978.

Bauer, Walter. *Das Johannesevangelium.* 3rd edition. Handbuch zum Neuen Testament 6. Tübingen: J. C. B. Mohr (Paul Siebeck), 1933.

Beasley-Murray, George R. *John.* Word Biblical Commentary 36. Waco, Tex.: Word Books, 1987.

Becker, Jürgen. *Das Evangelium nach Johannes.* 2 vols. 3rd edition. Ökumenischer Taschenbuch-Kommentar 4/1–2. Gütersloh: Mohn, 1991.

Bernard, John H. *A Critical and Exegetical Commentary on the Gospel According to St. John.* 2 vols. International Critical Commentary on the New Testament 31. Edinburgh: T&T Clark, 1928.

Blank, Josef. *Das Evangelium nach Johannes.* 3 vols. Geistliche Schriftlesung 4. Düsseldorf: Patmos, 1977–1981.

Boice, James Montgomery. *The Gospel of John: An Expositional Commentary.* Grand Rapids: Zondervan, 1975.

Brodie, Thomas L. *The Gospel according to John: A Literary and Theological Commentary.* Oxford: Oxford University Press, 1993.

Brown, Raymond Edward. *The Gospel according to John.* 2 vols. Anchor Bible 29.29A. Garden City, N. Y.: Doubleday, 1966–1970.

Bruce, Frederick Fyvie. *The Gospel of John: Introduction, Exposition and Notes.* Grand Rapids: Eerdmans, 1983.

Büchsel, Friedrich. *Das Evangelium nach Johannes.* Das Neue Testament Deutsch 4. Göttingen: Vandenhoeck & Ruprecht, 1934.

Bultmann, Rudolf. *Das Evangelium des Johannes.* 21st edition. Kritisch-exegetischer Kommentar über das Neue Testament 2. Göttingen: Vandenhoeck & Ruprecht, 1986.

Carson, Donald A. *The Gospel according to John.* Pillar New Testament Commentary. Leicester: InterVarsity Press, 1991.

de Boor, Werner. *Das Evangelium des Johannes.* 2 vols. Die neue Wuppertaler Studienbibel, Neues Testament 4. Wuppertal: Brockhaus, 1968–1970. Reprint 2000.

Edwards, Rowland A. *The Gospel according to St. John: Its Criticism and Interpretation.* London: Eyre & Spottiswoode, 1954.

Ellis, Peter F. *The Genius of John: A Composition-Critical Commentary on the Fourth Gospel.* Collegeville, Minn.: Liturgical Press, 1984.

Evans, Owen E. *The Gospel according to St. John.* London: Epworth Press, 1965.

Gnilka, Joachim. *Johannesevangelium.* Die Neue Echter-Bibel 4. Würzburg: Echter, 1983.

Gruenler, Royce Gordon. *The Trinity in the Gospel of John: A Thematic Commentary on the Fourth Gospel.* Grand Rapids: Baker, 1986.

Haenchen, Ernst. *John: A Commentary on the Gospel of John.* Translated by Robert Walter Funk. 2 vols. Hermeneia. Philadelphia: Fortress, 1984.

Hendriksen, William. *New Testament Commentary: Exposition of the Gospel according to John.* 2 vols. Grand Rapids: Baker, 1953–1954.

Holtzmann, Heinrich Julius. *Evangelium, Briefe und Offenbarung des Johannes.* 3rd edition. Hand-Commentar zum Neuen Testament 4. Freiburg i.Br.: J. C. B. Mohr (Paul Siebeck), 1908.

Hoskyns, Edwyn Clement. *The Fourth Gospel.* 2 vols. Edited by Francis Noel Davey. London: Faber and Faber, 1940.

Hunter, Archibald Macbride. *The Gospel according to John.* The Cambridge Bible Commentary on the New English Bible. Cambridge: Cambridge University Press, 1965. Reprint 1986.

Jeremias, Johannes. *Das Evangelium nach Johannes: Eine urchristliche Erklärung für die Gegenwart.* Leipzig: Müller, 1931.

Kysar, Robert. *John.* Augsburg Commentary on the New Testament. Minneapolis: Augsburg, 1986.

Lightfoot, Robert Henry. *St. John's Gospel.* Oxford: Clarendon Press, 1956.

Lindars, Barnabas. *The Gospel of John.* New Century Bible. London: Oliphants, 1972.

Macgregor, George Hogarth Carnaby. *The Gospel of John.* Mofatt New Testament Commentary. London: Hodder and Stoughton, 1928.

Maier, Gerhard. *Johannes-Evangelium.* 2 vols. Neuhausen-Stuttgart: Hänssler, 1984–1986.

Marsh, John. *The Gospel of St. John.* Pelican Gospel Commentaries. Harmondsworth: Penguin, 1968.

McPolin, James. *John.* New Testament Message 6. Dublin: Veritas, 1979.

Michaels, J. Ramsey. *John.* Good News Commentary. San Francisco: Harper & Row, 1984.

Morris, Leon. *The Gospel according to John.* New International Commentary on the New Testament 4. London: Morgan & Scott, 1971. Reprint Grand Rapids: Eerdmans, 1987.

Odeberg, Hugo. *The Fourth Gospel Interpreted in its Relation to Contemporaneous Religious Currents in Palestine and the Hellenistic-Oriental World.* Uppsala: Almqvist & Wiksell, 1929.

Perkins, Pheme. *The Gospel according to St. John—A Theological Commentary.* Chicago, Ill.: Franciscan Herald Press, 1978.

Richardson, Alan. *The Gospel according to Saint John.* Torch Bible Commentaries. London: SCM Press, 1959.

Sanders, Joseph N. *A Commentary on the Gospel According to St. John.* Edited and completed by B. A. Mastin. Black's New Testament Commentaries 4. London: Black, 1968.

Sanford, John A. *Mystical Christianity: A Psychological Commentary on the Gospel of John.* New York: Crossroad, 1993.

Schenke, Ludger. *Das Johannesevangelium: Einführung – Text – Dramatische Gestalt.* Stuttgart: Kohlhammer, 1992.

Schnackenburg, Rudolf. *The Gospel according to St. John.* Translated from the German by C. Hastings, et al. 3 vols. London: Burns and Oates, 1968–1980.

Schneider, Johannes. *Das Evangelium nach Johannes.* Theologischer Handkommentar zum Neuen Testament 4, Sonderband. 4th edition. Berlin: Evangelische Verlags-Anstalt, 1988.

Schulz, Siegfried. *Das Evangelium nach Johannes.* 4th edition. Das Neue Testament Deutsch 4. Göttingen: Vandenhoeck & Ruprecht, 1983.
Smith, Dwight Moody. *John.* 2nd edition. Proclamation Commentaries. Philadelphia: Fortress, 1986.
Strathmann, Hermann. *Das Evangelium nach Johannes.* Das Neue Testament Deutsch 4. Göttingen: Vandenhoeck & Ruprecht, 1959.
Tasker, Randolph V. G. *The Gospel According to St. John.* London: Tyndale Press, 1960.
Tenney, Merrill C. *John the Gospel of Belief: An Analytic Study of the Text.* Grand Rapids, Mich.: Eerdmans, 1948. London: Marshall, Morgan & Scott, 1954.
Wikenhauser, Alfred. *Das Evangelium nach Johannes.* 3rd edition. Regensburger Neues Testament 4. Regensburg: Pustet, 1961.
Zahn, Theodor. *Das Evangelium des Johannes.* Kommentar zum Neuen Testament 4. 6th edition. Leipzig: Werner Scholl, 1921.

3. Books and Articles

Abba, R. "God comes to Man." *Expository Times* 91 (1979/80): 51–52.
Ackerman, James S. "The Rabbinic Interpretation of Psalm 82 and the Gospel of John (John 10:34)." *Harvard Theological Review* 59 (1966): 186–91.
Ahn, Byung Mu. "Jesus and People (Minjung)." Pages 163–72 in *Asian Faces of Jesus.* Edited by Rasiah S. Sugirtharajah. London: SCM Press, 1993.
Amaladoss, Michael A. "Ein Inder liest das Evangelium des heiligen Johannes." Pages 19–34 in *Wir werden bei ihm wohnen: Das Johannesevangelium in indischer Deutung.* Edited by George M. Soares-Prabhu. Translated by Ursula Faymonville. Theologie der Dritten Welt 6. Freiburg/Basel: Herder, 1984.
———. "The Pluralism of Religions and the Significance of Christ." Pages 85–103 in *Asian Faces of Jesus.* Edited by Rasiah S. Sugirtharajah. London: SCM Press, 1993.
Anderson, Gary. "The Interpretation of Genesis 1:1 in the Targums." *Catholic Biblical Quarterly* 52 (1990): 21–29.
Appasamy, Aiyadurai Jesudasen. *Christianity as Bhakti Marga: A Study of the Johannine Doctrine of Love.* Madras: Christian Literature Society for India, 1926.
———. *The Johannine Doctrine of Life: A Study of Christian and Indian Thought.* London: S.P.C.K., 1934.
Appold, Mark L. "Christ Alive! Church Alive! Reflections on the Prayer of Jesus in John 17." *Currents in Theology and Mission* 5 (1978): 348–64.
———. *The Oneness Motif in the Fourth Gospel: Motif Analysis and Exegetical Probe into the Theology of John.* Wissenschaftliche Untersuchungen zum Neuen Testament 2.1. Tübingen: J. C. B. Mohr (Paul Siebeck), 1991.
Ashton, John. "The Identity and Function of the Ἰουδαῖοι in the Fourth Gospel." *Novum Testamentum* 27 (1985): 40–75.
———. "The Transformation of Wisdom: A Study of the Prologue of John's Gospel." *New Testament Studies* 32 (1986): 161–86.
———. *Understanding the Fourth Gospel.* Oxford: Clarendon, 1991.

———. *Studying John: Approaches to the Fourth Gospel.* Oxford/New York: Clarendon Press, 1994.

Aune, David E. *The Cultic Setting of Realized Eschatology in Early Christianity.* Novum Testamentum Supplements 28. Leiden: E. J. Brill, 1972.

Aycock, Don M. "John 17 and Jesus' Prayer for Unity." *The Theological Educator* 38 (1988): 132–44.

Bacchiocchi, Samuele. "John 5:17: Negation or Clarification of the Sabbath." *Andrews University Seminary Studies* 19 (1981): 3–19.

Ball, David Mark. *'I am' in John's Gospel: Literary Function, Background and Theological Implications.* Journal for the Study of the New Testament: Supplement Series 124. Sheffield: Sheffield Academic Press, 1996.

Bammel, Caroline P. "The Farewell Discourse in Patristic Exegesis." *Neotestamentica* 25 (1991): 193–208.

Bammel, Ernst. "Jesus und der Paraklet in Johannes 16." Pages 199–217 in *Christ and Spirit in the New Testament: In Honour of Charles Francis Digby Moule.* Edited by Barnabas Lindars and Stephen S. Smalley. Cambridge: Cambridge University Press, 1973.

———. "Die Abschiedsrede des Johannesevangeliums und ihr jüdischer Hintergrund." *Neotestamentica* 26 (1992): 1–12.

Barclay, William. "Great Themes of the New Testament II—John 1:1–14." *Expository Times* 70 (1958/59): 78–82, 114–17.

Barrett, Charles Kingsley. "The Holy Spirit in the Fourth Gospel." *Journal of Theological Studies* 1 (1950): 1–15.

———. "The Dialectical Theology of St. John." Pages 49–69 in *New Testament Essays.* London: S.P.C.K., 1972.

———. "The Prologue of St. John's Gospel." Pages 27–48 in *New Testament Essays.* London: S.P.C.K., 1972.

———. "'The Father is Greater than I' (Jn 14:28): Subordinationist Christology in the New Testament." Pages 144–59 in *Neues Testament und Kirche: Für Rudolf Schnackenburg.* Edited by Joachim Gnilka. Freiburg/Basel: Herder, 1974.

———. "Christocentric or Theocentric? Observations on the Theological Method of the Fourth Gospel." Pages 1–18 in *Essays on John.* Philadelphia: Westminster, 1982.

———. *Essays on John.* Philadelphia: Westminster, 1982.

———. "St. John: Social Historian." *Proceedings of the Irish Biblical Association* 10 (1986): 26–39.

Barrosse, Thomas. "The Johannine Relationship of Love to Faith." Pages 153–76 in *A Companion to John: Readings in Johannine Theology (John's Gospel and Epistles).* Edited by Michael J. Taylor. New York: Alba House, 1977.

Barth, M. "Ultimate Reality and Meaning in the Light of John's Gospel." *Ultimate Reality and Meaning* 12/2 (1989): 84–103.

Beare, Francis Wright. "Spirit of Life and Truth: The Doctrine of the Holy Spirit in the Fourth Gospel." *Toronto Journal of Theology* 3 (1987): 110–25.

Beasley-Murray, George Raymond. "John 13–17: The Community of True Life." *The Community of True Life* 85 (1988): 473–83.

———. *John*. Word Biblical Themes. Dallas, Tex.: Word, 1989.
———. *Gospel of Life: Theology in the Fourth Gospel*. Peabody, Mass.: Hendrickson, 1991.
———. "The Mission of the Logos Son." Pages 1855–68 in vol. 3 of *The Four Gospels, 1992: Festschrift Frans Neirynck*. 3 vols. Edited by Frans van Segbroeck, Christopher M. Tuckett, Gilbert van Belle, and Jozef Verheyden. Bibliotheca Ephemeridum Theologicarum Lovaniensium 100. Leuven: Leuven University Press, 1992.
Beck, David R. "The Narrative Function in Fourth Gospel Characterization." *Semeia* 63 (1993): 143–58.
Becker, Heinz. *Die Reden des Johannesevangeliums und der Stil der gnostischen Offenbarungsrede*. Forschungen zur Religion und Literatur des Alten und Neuen Testaments 68. Göttingen: Vandenhoeck & Ruprecht, 1956.
Becker, Jürgen. "Die Abschiedsreden Jesu im Johannesevangelium." *Zeitschrift für die Neutestamentliche Wissenschaft* 61 (1970): 215–46.
———. "Joh. 3,1–21 als Reflex johanneischer Schuldiskussion." Pages 85–95 in *Das Wort und die Wörter: Festschrift Gerhard Friedrich zum 65. Geburtstag*. Edited by Horst Balz and Siegfried Schulz. Stuttgart: Kohlhammer, 1973.
———. "Aus der Literatur zum Johannesevangelium (1978–80)." *Theologische Rundschau* 47 (1982): 279–301, 305–47.
———. "Das Johannesevangelium im Streit der Methoden (1980–84)." *Theologische Rundschau* 51 (1986): 1–78.
———. "Die Hoffnung auf ewiges Leben im Johannesevangelium." *Zeitschrift für die Neutestamentliche Wissenschaft* 91 (2000): 192–211.
———. *Johanneisches Christentum: Seine Geschichte und Theologie im Überblick*. Tübingen: Mohr Siebeck, 2004.
Berger, Klaus. "Zu «Das Wort ward Fleisch» Joh. I 14a." *Novum Testamentum* 16 (1974): 161–66.
———. *Exegese des Neuen Testaments: Neue Wege vom Text zur Auslegung*. Wiesbaden/Heidelberg: Quelle & Meyer, 1977.
Best, Thomas F. "The Sociological Study of the New Testament: Promise and Peril of a New Discipline." *Scottish Journal of Theology* 36 (1983): 181–94.
Betz, Otto. *Der Paraklet: Fürsprecher im häretischen Spätjudentum, im Johannes-Evangelium und in neu gefundenen gnostischen Schriften*. Arbeiten zur Geschichte des Spätjudentums und Urchristentums 2. Leiden: E. J. Brill, 1963.
———. "To Worship God in Spirit and in Truth: Reflections on John 4,20–26." Pages 53–72 in *Standing before God: Studies on Prayer in Scriptures and in Tradition with Essays. In Honor of John M. Oesterreicher*. Edited by Asher Finkel and Lawrence Frizzell. New York: Ktav Publishing House, 1981.
Beutler, Johannes. *Martyria: Traditionsgeschichtliche Untersuchungen zum Zeugnisthema bei Johannes*. Frankfurter Theologische Studien 10. Frankfurt am Main: Knecht, 1972.
Birdsall, J. Neville. "John X.29." *Journal of Theological Studies* n.s. XI (1960): 342–45.
Bittner, Wolfgang J. *Jesu Zeichen im Johannesevangelium: Die Messias-Erkenntnis im Johannesevangelium vor ihrem jüdischen Hintergrund*. Wissenschaftliche Untersuchungen zum Neuen Testament 2.26. Tübingen: J. C. B. Mohr (Paul Siebeck), 1987.

Black, C. Clifton. "Christian Ministry in Johannine Perspective." *Interpretation* 24 (1990): 29–41.

Black, David A. "On the Style and Significance of John 17." *Criswell Theological Review* 3 (1988): 141–59.

Blank, Josef. *Krisis: Untersuchungen zur johanneischen Christologie und Eschatologie.* Freiburg: Lambertus-Verlag, 1964.

Blomberg, Craig L. "To What Extent is John Historically Reliable?" Pages 27–56 in *Perspectives on John: Method and Interpretation in the Fourth Gospel.* Edited by Robert B. Sloan and Mikeal C. Parsons. Lewiston, N. Y.: Edwin Mellen Press, 1993.

– – –. *The Historical Reliability of John's Gospel: Issues and Commentary.* Leicester: Apollos, 2001.

Boers, Hendrikus. *Neither on this Mountain nor in Jerusalem: A Study of John 4.* Society of Biblical Literature Monograph Series 35. Atlanta: Scholars Press, 1988.

Boice, James Montgomery. *Witness and Revelation in the Gospel of John.* Exeter: Paternoster Press, 1970.

Boismard, Marie-Émile. *St. John's Prologue.* Translated by Carrisbrooke Dominicans. London: Blackfriars Publications, 1957.

– – –. *Moses or Jesus: An Essay in Johannine Christology.* Translated by Benedict T. Viviano. Minneapolis: Fortress; and Leuven: Peeters, 1993.

Bonsack, B. "Syntaktische Überlegungen zu Joh. 1:9–10." Pages 52–79 in *Studies in New Testament Language and Text: Essays in Honour of George D. Kilpatrick.* Edited by James Keith Elliott. Novum Testamentum Supplements 44. Leiden: E. J. Brill, 1976.

Boobyer, George H. "Jesus as 'Theos' in the New Testament." *Bulletin of the John Rylands University Library* 50 (1967/68): 247–61.

Booth, K. N. "The Self Proclamation of Jesus in St. John's Gospel." *Colloquium* 7/2 (1975): 36–47.

Borchert, Gerald L. "The Resurrection Perspective in John: An Evangelical Summons." *Review and Expositor* 85 (1988): 501–13.

– – –. "The Spirit and Salvation." *Criswell Theological Review* 3 (1988): 65–78.

– – –. "The Passover and the Narrative Cycles in John." Pages 303–16 in *Perspectives on John: Method and Interpretation in the Fourth Gospel.* Edited by Robert B. Sloan and Mikeal C. Parsons. Lewiston, N. Y.: Edwin Mellen Press, 1993.

Borgen, Peder. "Observations on the Targumic Character of the Prologue of John." *New Testament Studies* 16 (1969/70): 288–95.

– – –. "Logos was the True Light: Contributions to the Interpretation of the Prologue of John." *Novum Testamentum* 14 (1972): 115–30.

– – –. "Philo of Alexandria." Pages 233–82 in *Jewish Writings of the Second Temple Period.* Edited by Michael E. Stone. Compendia Rerum Iudaicarum ad Novum Testamentum 2.2. Assen: Van Gorcum, 1984.

– – –. "God's Agent in the Fourth Gospel." Pages 67–78 in *The Interpretation of John.* Edited by John Ashton. Philadelphia: Fortress, 1986.

– – –. "Creation, Logos and the Son: Observations on John 1:1–18 and 5:17–18." *Ex Auditu* 3 (1987): 88–97.

———. "John's Use of the Old Testament, and the Problem of Sources and Traditions." Pages 145–58 in *Philo, John and Paul: New Perspectives on Judaism and Early Christianity*. Brown Judaic Studies 131. Atlanta: Scholars Press, 1987.

———. "The Old Testament in the Formation of New Testament Theology." Pages 159–70 in *Philo, John and Paul: New Perspectives on Judaism and Early Christianity*. Brown Judaic Studies 131. Atlanta: Scholars Press, 1987.

———. "The Prologue of John—As Exposition of the Old Testament." Pages 75–102 in *Philo, John and Paul: New Perspectives on Judaism and Early Christianity*. Brown Judaic Studies 131. Atlanta: Scholars Press, 1987.

———. "The Son of Man Saying in John 3:13–14." Pages 103–20 in *Philo, John and Paul: New Perspectives on Judaism and Early Christianity*. Brown Judaic Studies 131. Atlanta: Scholars Press, 1987.

Boring, M. Eugene. "The Influence of Christian Prophecy on the Johannine Portrayal of the Paraclete and Jesus." *New Testament Studies* 25 (1979): 113–23.

———. "Markan Christology: God-Language for Jesus?" *New Testament Studies* 45 (1999): 451–71.

Bornkamm, Günther. "Der Paraklet im Johannes-Evangelium." Pages 68–89 in vol. 1 of *Geschichte und Glaube*. Beiträge zur Evangelischen Theologie 48. Munich: Kaiser, 1968.

———. "Das Vaterbild im Neuen Testament." Pages 136–54 in *Das Vaterbild in Mythos und Geschichte: Ägypten, Griechenland, Altes Testament, Neues Testament*. Edited by Hubertus Tellenbach. Stuttgart: Kohlhammer, 1976.

———. "Towards the Interpretation of John's Gospel: A Discussion of The Testament of Jesus by Ernst Käsemann." Pages 79–98 in *The Interpretation of John*. Edited by John Ashton. Philadelphia: Fortress, 1986.

Bossman, David M. "Images of God in the Letters of Paul." *Biblical Theology Bulletin* 18 (1988): 67–76.

Botha, J. Eugene. "Reader 'Entrapment' as Literary Device in John 4:1–42." *Neotestamentica* 24 (1990): 37–47.

———. *Jesus and the Samaritan Woman: A Speech Act Reading of John 4:1–42*. Novum Testamentum Supplements 65. Leiden: E. J. Brill, 1991.

Bover, José María. "χάριν ἀντὶ χάριτος (Joh 1:16)." *Biblica* 6 (1925): 454–60.

Boyd, Robin H. S. "Indian Christian Thinking in Relation to Christ." *Religion and Society* 11 (1964): 61–71.

———. *Khristadvaita: A Theology for India*. Madras: Christian Literature Society, 1977.

———. *An Introduction to Indian Christian Theology*. 2nd edition. Delhi: Diocesan Press, 1979.

Boyle, John L. "The Last Discourse (Jn 13:31–16:33) and Prayer (Jn 17): Some Observations on their Unity and Development." *Biblica* 56 (1975): 210–22.

Braine, David D. C. "The Inner Jewishness of St. John's Gospel as the Clue to the Inner Jewishness of Jesus." *Studien zum Neuen Testament und seiner Umwelt* A/13 (1988): 101–55.

Breck, John. *Spirit of Truth: The Holy Spirit in Johannine Tradition*. Crestwood, N.Y.: St. Vladimir's Seminary Press, 1991.

Bridges, Linda M. "Flashes of Light in the Night: Reading the Aphorisms of Jesus in the Fourth Gospel." Pages 103–20 in *Perspectives on John: Method and Interpretation in the Fourth Gospel*. Edited by Robert B. Sloan and Mikeal C. Parsons. Lewiston, N. Y.: Edwin Mellen Press, 1993.

Brockington, Leonard H. "The Greek Translator of Isaiah and his Interest in δόξα." *Vetus Testamentum* 1 (1951): 23–32.

Brown, Raymond E. "The Problem of Historicity in John." *The Catholic Biblical Quarterly* 24 (1962): 1–14.

———. "Does the New Testament Call Jesus God?" *Theological Studies* 26 (1965): 545–73.

———. "The Kerygma of the Gospel According to John." *Interpretation* 21 (1967): 387–400.

———. "The Paraclete in the Fourth Gospel." *New Testament Studies* 13 (1967): 113–32.

———. "Johannine Ecclesiology—The Community's Origins." *Interpretation* 31 (1977): 379–93.

———. "Other Sheep not of this Fold: The Johannine Perspective on Christian Diversity in the Late First Century." *Journal of Biblical Literature* 97 (1978): 5–22.

———. *The Community of the Beloved Disciple*. New York: Paulist Press, 1979.

———. *An Introduction to New Testament Christology*. New York: Paulist Press, 1994.

Buchanan, George W. "The Samaritan Origin of the Gospel of John." Pages 149–75 in *Religions in Antiquity*. Edited by John Neusner. Leiden: E. J. Brill, 1968.

Bühler, Pierre. "Ist Johannes ein Kreuzestheologe? Exegetisch-systematische Bemerkungen zu einer noch offenen Debatte." Pages 191–207 in *Johannes-Studien: Interdisziplinäre Zugänge zum Johannes-Evangelium. Freundesgabe der Theologischen Fakultät der Universität Neuchâtel für Jean Zumstein*. Edited by Martin Rose. Publications de la Faculté de Théologie de l'Université de Neuchâtel 6. Neuchâtel: Theologischer Verlag, 1990.

Bühner, Jan-Adolf. *Der Gesandte und sein Weg im 4. Evangelium: Die kultur- und religionsgeschichtlichen Grundlagen der johanneischen Sendungschristologie sowie ihre traditionsgeschichtliche Entwicklung*. Wissenschaftliche Untersuchungen zum Neuen Testament 2.2. Tübingen: J. C. B. Mohr (Paul Siebeck), 1977.

Bull, Robert J. "An Archaeological Context for Understanding John 4:20." *The Biblical Archaeologist* 38 (1975): 54–59.

Bulman, James M. "The Only Begotten Son." *Calvin Theological Journal* 16 (1981): 56–79.

Bultmann, Rudolf. "Die Bedeutung der neuerschlossenen mandäischen und manichäischen Quellen für das Verständnis des Johannesevangeliums." *Zeitschrift für die Neutestamentliche Wissenschaft* 24 (1925): 100–46.

———. *Theology of the New Testament*. Translated by Kendrick Grobel. 2 vols. New York: Charles Scribner's Sons, 1955.

———. "The History-of-Religions Background of the Prologue to the Gospel of John." Pages 18–35 in *The Interpretation of John*. Edited by John Ashton. Philadelphia: Fortress, 1986.

———. "Welchen Sinn hat es, von Gott zu reden?" Pages 26–37 in *Glauben und Verstehen: Gesammelte Aufsätze*. Vol. 1. 9th edition. Tübingen: J. C. B. Mohr (Paul Siebeck), 1993.

Burge, Gary M. *The Anointed Community: The Holy Spirit in the Johannine Tradition*. Grand Rapids: Eerdmans, 1987.

Burkett, Delbert. *The Son of the Man in the Gospel of John*. Journal for the Study of the New Testament: Supplement Series 56. Sheffield: JSOT Press, 1991.

Burnett, Fred W. "Exposing the Anti-Jewish Ideology of Matthew's Implied Author: The Characterization of God as Father." *Semeia* 59 (1992): 155–91.

Burney, Charles Fox. *The Aramaic Approach to the Fourth Gospel*. Oxford: Clarendon Press, 1922.

Cadman, William H. *The Open Heaven: The Revelation of God in the Johannine Sayings of Jesus*. Edited by George B. Caird. Oxford: Blackwell, 1969.

Caird, George B. "The Will of God in the Fourth Gospel." *Expository Times* 72 (1960/61): 115–16.

———. "The Glory of God in the Fourth Gospel. An Exercise in Biblical Semantics." *New Testament Studies* 15 (1968/69): 265–77.

Cameron, Ron. "Seeing Is Not Believing: The History of a Beatitude in the Jesus Tradition." *Forum* 4 (1988): 47–57.

Cantwell, L. "Immortal Longing in Sermone Humili: A Study of John 4.5–26." *Scottish Journal of Theology* 36 (1983): 73–86.

Carl, K. J. "Knowing in St. John: Background of the Theme." *Indian Theological Studies* 21 (1984): 68–82.

Carroll, John T. "Present and Future in Fourth Gospel Eschatology." *Biblical Theology Bulletin* 19 (1989): 63–69.

Carson, Donald A. "Current Source Criticism of the Fourth Gospel: Some Methodological Questions." *Journal of Biblical Literature* 97 (1978): 411–29.

———. "The Function of the Paraclete in John 16:7–11." *Journal of Biblical Literature* 98 (1979): 547–66.

Carson, Donald A., Douglas J. Moo and Leon Morris. *An Introduction to the New Testament*. Grand Rapids: Apollos, 1992.

Carter, Warren. "The Prologue and John's Gospel: Function, Symbol and the Definitive Word." *Journal for the Study of the New Testament* 39 (1990): 35–58.

Casurella, Anthony. *The Johannine Paraclete in the Church Fathers: A Study in the History of Exegesis*. Beiträge zur Geschichte der biblischen Exegese 25. Tübingen: J. C. B. Mohr (Paul Siebeck), 1983.

Charlesworth, James H. "Qumran, John and the Odes of Solomon." Pages 107–36 in *John and Qumran*. Edited by James H. Charlesworth. London: Geoffrey Chapman Publishers, 1972.

———, ed. *John and Qumran*. London: Geoffrey Chapman Publishers, 1972.

———. "Christian and Jewish Self-Definition in the Light of the Christian Additions to the Apocryphal Writings." Pages 27–55 in vol. 2 of *Jewish and Christian Self-Definition*. 3 vols. Edited by Ed P. Sanders. Philadelphia: Fortress, 1981.

———. "Jewish Roots of Christology: The Discovery of the Hypostatic Voice." *Scottish Journal of Theology* 39 (1986): 19–41.
Charlesworth, James H., and R. Alan Culpepper. "The Odes of Solomon and the Gospel of John." *The Catholic Biblical Quarterly* 35 (1973): 298–322.
Chembakaserry, J. "Johannine Concept of Believing and its Relevance in India." *Bible Bhashyam* 11 (1985): 61–67.
Chilton, Bruce D. "Recent and Prospective Discussion of Memra." Pages 119–37 in *From Ancient Israel to Modern Judaism: Intellect in Quest of Understanding. Essays in Honor of Marvin Fox.* 4 vols. Edited by Jacob Neusner, Ernest S. Frerichs and Nahum M. Sarna. Atlanta: Scholars Press, 1989.
Clark, Douglas K. "Signs in Wisdom and John." *The Catholic Biblical Quarterly* 45 (1983): 201–209.
Coetzee, J. C. "Life (Eternal Life) in John's Writings and the Qumran Scrolls." *Neotestamentica* 6 (1972): 48–66.
Cole, R. G. "We beheld His Glory." *Expository Times* 90 (1978/79): 50–51.
Collins, Marilyn F. "The Hidden Vessels in Samaritan Traditions." *Journal for the Study of Judaism* 3 (1972): 97–116.
Collins, Raymond F. "He Came to Dwell Among Us (John 1:14)." *Melita Theological Journal* 28 (1976): 44–59.
———. "The Representative Figures of the Fourth Gospel—I&II." *The Downside Review* 94 (1976): 26–46, 118–32.
———. "Cana (Jn. 2:1–12)—The First of His Signs or The Key to His Signs?" *Irish Theological Quarterly* 47 (1980): 79–95.
Colwell, Ernest C. "A Definite Rule for the Use of the Article in the Greek New Testament." *Journal of Biblical Literature* 52 (1933): 12–21.
Conzelmann, Hans. *Grundriß der Theologie des Neuen Testaments*. 6th edition. Revised by Andreas Lindemann. Tübingen: J. C. B. Mohr (Paul Siebeck), 1997.
Conzelmann, Hans, and Andreas Lindemann. *Arbeitsbuch zum Neuen Testament*. 14th edition. Tübingen: Mohr Siebeck, 2004.
Cook, W. Robert. "The 'Glory' Motif in the Johannine Corpus." *Journal of the Evangelical Theological Society* 27 (1984): 291–97.
———. "Eschatology in John's Gospel." *Criswell Theological Review* 3 (1988): 79–99.
Countryman, Louis William. *The Mystical Way in the Fourth Gospel: Crossing over into God*. Philadelphia: Fortress, 1987.
Cullmann, Oscar. *Early Christian Worship*. Translated by A. Stewart Todd and James B. Torrance. London: SCM Press, 1954.
———. *The Christology of the New Testament*. Translated by Shirley C. Guthrie and Charles A. M. Hall. 2nd edition. London: SCM Press, 1963.
———. "Sabbat und Sonntag nach dem Johannesevangelium, Joh 5:17." Pages 187–91 in *Vorträge und Aufsätze 1925–1962*. Tübingen: J. C. B. Mohr (Paul Siebeck), 1966.
———. *The Johannine Circle: Its place in Judaism, among the Disciples of Jesus and in Early Christianity: A Study in the Origin of the Gospel of John*. Translated by John Bowden. New Testament Library. London: SCM Press, 1976.
———. "The Theological Content of the Prologue to John in its Present Form." Pages 295–98 in *The Conversation Continues: Studies in Paul and John in Honor of J.*

Louis Martyn. Edited by Robert T. Fortna and Beverly R. Gaventa. Nashville: Abingdon, 1990.

Culpepper, Richard Alan. *The Johannine School: An Evaluation of the Johannine-School Hypothesis Based on an Investigation of the Nature of Ancient Schools*. Society of Biblical Literature Dissertation Series 26. Missoula, Mont.: Scholars Press, 1975.

―――. "The Pivot of John's Prologue." *New Testament Studies* 27 (1981): 1–31.

―――. *Anatomy of the Fourth Gospel: A Study in Literary Design*. Philadelphia: Fortress, 1983.

―――. "The AMHN AMHN Sayings in the Gospel of John." Pages 57–102 in *Perspectives on John: Method and Interpretation in the Fourth Gospel*. Edited by Robert B. Sloan and Mikeal C. Parsons. Lewiston, N. Y.: Edwin Mellen Press, 1993.

Cupitt, Don. "Jesus and the Meaning of God." Pages 31–42 in *Incarnation and Myth: The Debate Continued*. Edited by Michael Goulder. London: SCM Press, 1979.

Dahl, Nils Alstrup. *The Crucified Messiah, and Other Essays*. Minneapolis: Augsburg, 1974.

―――. "The Neglected Factor in New Testament Theology." *Reflection* 73/1 (1975): 5–8.

―――. "The Johannine Church and History." Pages 122–40 in *The Interpretation of John*. Edited by John Ashton. Philadelphia: Fortress, 1986.

―――. "'Do Not Wonder!': John 5:28–29 and Johannine Eschatology Once More." Pages 322–36 in *The Conversation Continues: Studies in Paul and John in Honor of J. Louis Martyn*. Edited by Robert T. Fortna and Beverly R. Gaventa. Nashville: Abingdon, 1990.

―――. *Jesus the Christ: The Historical Origins of Christological Doctrine*. Minneapolis: Fortress, 1991.

Dahms, John V. "The Johannine Use of Monogenes Reconsidered." *New Testament Studies* 29 (1983): 222–32.

Daube, David. "Jesus and the Samaritan Woman: The Meaning of συγχράομαι." *Journal of Biblical Literature* 69 (1950): 137–47.

Davey, J. Ernest. *The Jesus of St. John: Historical and Christological Studies in the Fourth Gospel*. London: Lutterworth, 1958.

Davies, John G. "The Primary Meaning of παράκλητος." *Journal of Theological Studies* 4 (1953): 35–38.

Davies, Margaret. *Rhetoric and Reference in the Fourth Gospel*. Journal for the Study of the New Testament Supplement Series 69. Sheffield: JSOT Press, 1992.

Davis, J. C. "The Johannine Concept of Eternal Life as a Present Possession." *Restoration Quarterly* 27 (1984): 161–69.

Dawe, Donald G. "The Divinity of the Holy Spirit." *Interpretation* 33 (1979): 19–31.

de Argandona, P. S. "The Sense of History in the Gospel of St. John." *Homiletic and Pastoral Review* 94 (1994): 62–66.

de Jonge, Marinus. "Jewish Expectations about the Messiah According to the Fourth Gospel." *New Testament Studies* 19 (1972/73): 246–70.

―――. *Jesus: Stranger from Heaven and Son of God. Jesus Christ and the Christians in Johannine Perspective*. Edited and translated by John E. Steely. Society of Biblical Literature Sources for Biblical Study 11. Missoula, Mont.: Scholars Press, 1977.

———. "Son of God and the Children of God in the Fourth Gospel." Pages 44–63 in *Saved by Hope: Essays in Honor of Richard C. Oudersluys.* Edited by James I. Cook. Grand Rapids: Eerdmans, 1978.

———. "John the Baptist and Elijah in the Fourth Gospel." Pages 299–308 in *The Conversation Continues: Studies in Paul and John in Honor of J. Louis Martyn.* Edited by Robert T. Fortna and Beverly R. Gaventa. Nashville: Abingdon, 1990.

———. "Christology and Theology in the Context of Early Christian Eschatology, particularly in the Fourth Gospel." Pages 1835–54 in vol. 3 of *The Four Gospels, 1992: Festschrift Frans Neirynck.* 3 vols. Edited by Frans van Segbroeck, Christopher M. Tuckett, Gilbert van Belle, and Jozef Verheyden. Bibliotheca Ephemeridum Theologicarum Lovaniensium 100. Leuven: Leuven University Press, 1992.

———. "The Conflict Between Jesus and the Jews and the Radical Christology of the Fourth Gospel." *Perspectives in Religious Studies* 20 (1993): 341–55.

de Jonge, Marinus, and Adam S. van der Woude. "11 Q Melchizedek and the New Testament." *New Testament Studies* 12 (1966): 301–26.

de Kruijf, Theodor C. "The Glory of the Only Son (John 1:14)." Pages 111–23 in *Studies in John: Presented to J. N. Sevenster on the Occasion of his Seventieth Birthday.* Edited by M. C. Rientsma, et al. Novum Testamentum Supplements 24. Leiden: E. J. Brill, 1970.

de la Potterie, Ignace. "I am the Way, the Truth and the Life." *Theology Digest* 16 (1968): 59–64.

———. "The Truth in Saint John." Pages 53–66 in *The Interpretation of John.* Edited by John Ashton. Philadelphia: Fortress, 1986.

de Pinto, Basil. "John's Jesus: Biblical Wisdom and the Word Embodied." Pages 59–68 in *A Companion to John: Readings in Johannine Theology (John's Gospel and Epistles).* Edited by Michael J. Taylor. New York: Alba House, 1977.

de Vogel, Cornelia J. "Greek Cosmic Love and the Christian Love of God." *Vigiliae Christianae* 35 (1981): 57–81.

Deeks, David. "The Structure of the Fourth Gospel." *New Testament Studies* 15 (1968/69): 107–29.

———. "The Prologue of St. John's Gospel." *Biblical Theology Bulletin* 6 (1976): 62–78.

Demke, Christoph. "Der sogenannte Logoshymnus im johanneischen Prolog." *Zeitschrift für die Neutestamentliche Wissenschaft* 58 (1967): 45–68.

———. "Das Evangelium der Dialoge: Hermeneutische und methodologische Beobachtungen zur Interpretation des Johannesevangeliums." *Zeitschrift für Theologie und Kirche* 97 (2000): 164–82.

Dennison, William W. "Miracles as «Signs»: Their Significance for Apologetics." *Biblical Theology Bulletin* 6 (1976): 190–202.

Derrett, J. Duncan M. "Why and How Jesus Walked on the Sea." *Novum Testamentum* 23 (1981): 331–48.

———. "The Samaritan Woman in India c. A.D. 200." *Zeitschrift für Religions- und Geistesgeschichte* 39 (1987): 328–36.

———. "The Bronze Serpent." *Estudios Biblicos* 49 (1991): 311–29.

Dettwiler, Andreas. *Die Gegenwart des Erhöhten: Eine exegetische Studie zu den johanneischen Abschiedsreden (Joh 13,31–16,33) unter besonderer Berücksichtigung ihres Relecture-Charakters.* Forschungen zur Religion und Literatur des Alten und Neuen Testaments 169. Göttingen: Vandenhoeck & Ruprecht, 1995.
Dexinger, Ferdinand. "Samaritan Eschatology." Pages 267–76 in *The Samaritans.* Edited by Alan D. Crown. Tübingen: J. C. B. Mohr (Paul Siebeck), 1989.
Dietzfelbinger, Christian. "Paraklet und theologischer Anspruch im Johannesevangelium." *Zeitschrift für Theologie und Kirche* 82 (1985): 389–408.
Dillon, Richard J. "Wisdom Tradition and Sacramental Retrospect in the Cana Account (Jn 2,1–11)." *The Catholic Biblical Quarterly* 24 (1962): 268–96.
Dockery, David S. "Reading John 4:1–45: Some Diverse Hermeneutical Perspectives." *Criswell Theological Review* 3 (1988): 127–40.
Dodd, Charles Harold. *Interpretation of the Fourth Gospel.* Cambridge: Cambridge University Press, 1953. Various reprints.
— — —. "The Prologue to the Fourth Gospel and Christian Worship." Pages 9–22 in *Studies in the Fourth Gospel.* Edited by Frank Leslie Cross. London: Mowbray, 1957.
— — —. *Historical Tradition in the Fourth Gospel.* Cambridge: Cambridge University Press, 1963. Reprints 1965, 1979.
— — —. "John 5:19–35 in Christian History and Interpretation." Pages 183–98 in *Christian History and Interpretation: Studies Presented to John Knox.* Edited by William R. Farmer, et al. Cambridge: Cambridge University Press, 1967.
— — —. "A Hidden Parable in the Fourth Gospel (Jn 5:19–20a)." Pages 30–40 in *More New Testament Studies.* Manchester: University Press, 1968.
— — —. "New Testament Translation Problems II." *The Bible Translator* 28 (1977): 101–16.
Domeris, William Robert. "The Holy One of God as a Title for Jesus." *Neotestamentica* 19 (1985): 9–17.
— — —. "Christology and Community: A Study of the Social Matrix of the Fourth Gospel." *Journal of Theology for Southern Africa* 64 (1988): 49–56.
— — —. "The Paraclete as an Ideological Construct." *Journal of Theology for Southern Africa* 67 (1989): 17–23.
— — —. "The Farewell Discourse. An Anthropological Perspective." *Neotestamentica* 25 (1991): 233–50.
Doohan, Leonard. "Portraits of God in John." *Milltown Studies* 25 (1990): 37–62.
Dowd, S. E. "Toward a Johannine Theology of Prayer." Pages 317–36 in *Perspectives on John: Method and Interpretation in the Fourth Gospel.* Edited by Robert B. Sloan and Mikeal C. Parsons. Lewiston, N. Y.: Edwin Mellen Press, 1993.
Dowell, Thomas M. "Jews and Christians in Conflict: Why the Fourth Gospel Changed the Synoptic Tradition." *Louvain Studies* 15 (1990): 19–37.
Dozeman, Thomas B. "Sperma Abraam in John 8 and Related Literature, Cosmology and Judgement." *Catholic Biblical Quarterly* 42 (1980): 342–58.
Draper, Jonathan A. "The Sociological Function of the Spirit/Paraclete in the Farewell Discourses in the Fourth Gospel." *Neotestamentica* 26 (1992): 13–29.
du Plessis, Isak Johannes. "Christ as the Only Begotten." Pages 22–31 in *The Christ of John: Essays on the Christology of the Fourth Gospel.* Proceedings of the Fourth

Meeting of Die Nuwe-Testamentiese werkgemeenskap van Suid-Afrika. Potchefstrom, South Africa: Pro Rege Press, 1971.

du Rand, J. A. "Perspectives on Johannine Discipleship According to the Farewell Discourses." *Neotestamentica* 25 (1991): 311–25.

— — —. "A Story and a Community: Reading the First Farewell Discourse (John 13:31–14:31) from Narratological and Sociological Perspectives." *Neotestamentica* 26 (1992): 31–45.

du Toit, B. A. "The Incarnate Word—A Study of John 1:14." *Neotestamentica* 2 (1968): 9–21.

— — —. "The Aspect of Faith in the Gospel of John with Special Reference to the Farewell Discourses of Jesus." *Neotestamentica* 25 (1991): 327–40.

Duke, Paul D. *Irony in the Fourth Gospel: The Shape and Function of a Literary Device.* Atlanta: John Knox Press, 1985.

Dumbrell, William J. "Law and Grace: The Nature of the Contrast in John 1:17." *Evangelical Quarterly* 58 (1986): 25–37.

Duncan, Robert L. "The Logos: From Sophocles to the Gospel of John." *Christian Scholars Review* 9 (1979): 121–30.

Dunn, James D. G. *Christology in the Making: A New Testament Inquiry into the Origins of the Doctrine of the Incarnation.* London: SCM Press, 1980.

— — —. "Let John be John—A Gospel for its Time." Pages 309–40 in *Das Evangelium und die Evangelien*. Edited by Peter Stuhlmacher. Wissenschaftliche Untersuchungen zum Neuen Testament 28. Tübingen: J. C. B. Mohr (Paul Siebeck), 1983.

— — —. "The Question of Anti-Semitism in the New Testament Writings of the Period." Pages 177–212 in *Jews and Christians: The Parting of the Ways A.D. 70 to 135*. Wissenschaftliche Untersuchungen zum Neuen Testament 66. Tübingen: J. C. B. Mohr (Paul Siebeck), 1992.

— — —, ed. *Jews and Christians: The Parting of the Ways A.D. 70 to 135.* Wissenschaftliche Untersuchungen zum Neuen Testament 66. Tübingen: J. C. B. Mohr (Paul Siebeck), 1992.

Edanad, A. "Johannine Vision of Covenant Community." *Jeevadhara* 11 (1981): 127–40.

— — —. "Johannine Theology of the Church." *Jeevadhara* 15 (1985): 136–47.

Edwards, Ruth B. "χάριν ἀντὶ χάριτος (John 1.16). Grace and the Law in the Johannine Prologue." *Journal for the Study of the New Testament* 32 (1988): 3–15.

Ehrman, Bart D. *The Orthodox Corruption of Scripture: The Effect of Early Christological Controversies on the Text of the New Testament.* New York/Oxford: Oxford University Press, 1993.

Eller, Vernard. *The Beloved Disciple: His Name, His Story, His Thought. 2 Studies from the Gospel of John.* Grand Rapids: Eerdmans, 1987.

Elliott, James Keith. "John 1.14 and the New Testament's Use of πλήρης." *The Bible Translator* 28 (1977): 151–53.

Ellis, E. Earle. "Background and Christology of John's Gospel: Selected Motifs." *Southwestern Journal of Theology* 31 (1988): 24–31.

Ellwin, Eduard. "Heilsgegenwart und Heilszukunft im Neuen Testament. Auslegung von Johannes 5:17–29." Pages 7–28 in *Heilsgegenwart und Heilszukunft im*

Neuen Testament: Zwei Abhandlungen. Theologische Existenz heute – Neue Folge 114. Munich: Kaiser, 1964.
Eltester, Walther. "Der Logos und sein Prophet." Pages 109–34 in *Apophoreta: Festschrift Ernst Haenchen.* Beihefte zur Zeitschrift für die Neutestamentliche Wissenschaft 30. Berlin: Alfred Töpelmann, 1964.
Emerton, John A. "Melchizedek and the Gods: Fresh Evidence for the Jewish Background of John X.34–36." *Journal of Theological Studies* n.s. 17 (1966): 399–401.
Epp, Eldon J. "Wisdom, Torah, Word: The Johannine Prologue and the Purpose of the Fourth Gospel." Pages 128–46 in *Current Issues in Biblical and Patristic Interpretation: Studies in Honor of Merrill C. Tenney by his Former Students.* Edited by Gerald F. Hawthorne. Grand Rapids: Eerdmans, 1975.
Epp, Eldon J., and George W. MacRae, eds. *The New Testament and its Modern Interpreters.* The Bible and its Modern Interpreters 3. Philadelphia: Fortress, 1989.
Erlemann, Kurt. *Das Bild Gottes in den synoptischen Gleichnissen.* Beiträge zur Wissenschaft vom Alten und Neuen Testament 126. Stuttgart: Kohlhammer, 1988.
Eslinger, Lyle. "The Wooing of the Woman at the Well: Jesus the Reader and Reader-Response Criticism." *Journal of Literature and Theology* 1/2 (1987): 167–83.
Evans, Craig A. "On the Prologue of John and the Trimorphic Protennoia." *New Testament Studies* 27 (1981): 395–401.
———. *Word and Glory: On the Exegetical and Theological Background of John's Prologue.* Journal for the Study of the New Testament: Supplement Series 89. Sheffield: JSOT Press, 1993.
Evans, E. "The Verb ἀγαπᾶν in the Fourth Gospel." Pages 64–71 in *Studies in the Fourth Gospel.* Edited by Frank Leslie Cross. London: Mowbray, 1957.

Fabella, V. "Christology from an Asian Woman's Perspective." Pages 211–22 in *Asian Faces of Jesus.* Edited by Rasiah S. Sugirtharajah. London: SCM Press, 1993.
Farley, E. "Re-thinking the God-Terms-Tradition: The God-Term of Social Remembering." *Toronto Journal of Theology* 9 (1993): 67–77.
Farrell, S. E. "Seeing the Father (Jn 6:46, 14:9) Part I: From Non-Seeing to Relational Seeing and Part II: Perceptive Seeing and Comprehensive Seeing." *Science et Esprit* 44 (1992): 1–24, 159–83, 307–30.
Fascher, Erich. "Christologie und Gnosis im vierten Evangelium." *Theologische Literaturzeitung* 93 (1968): 721–30.
Fee, Gordon D. "On the Text and Meaning of Jn 20,30–31." Pages 2193–2206 in vol. 3 of *The Four Gospels, 1992: Festschrift Frans Neirynck.* 3 vols. Edited by Frans van Segbroeck, Christopher M. Tuckett, Gilbert van Belle, and Jozef Verheyden. Bibliotheca Ephemeridum Theologicarum Lovaniensium 100. Leuven: Leuven University Press, 1992.
Fennema, David A. "Jesus and God according to John: An Analysis of the Fourth Gospel's Father/Son Christology." Diss. Duke University, Durham, N. C., 1979.
———. "John 1.18: God the Only Son." *New Testament Studies* 31 (1985): 124–35.
Fensham, Frank Charles. "I am the Way, the Truth and the Life." *Neotestamentica* 2 (1968): 81–88.
———. "Love in the Writings of Qumran and John." *Neotestamentica* 6 (1972): 67–77.

Ferreira, Johan. *Johannine Ecclesiology*. Journal for the Study of the New Testament: Supplement Series 160. Sheffield: Sheffield Academic Press, 1998.

Filson, Floyd V. "The Gospel of Life: A Study of the Gospel of John." Pages 111–23 in *Current Issues in New Testament Interpretation: Essays in Honor of Otto A. Pieper*. Edited by William Klassen and Graydon F. Snyder. London: SCM Press, 1962.

Fischel, H. A. "Jewish Gnosticism in the Fourth Gospel." *Journal of Biblical Literature* 65 (1946): 157–74.

Floor, L. "The Lord and the Holy Spirit in the Fourth Gospel." *Neotestamentica* 2 (1968) 122–30.

Ford, J. M. "Mingled Blood—From the Side of Christ. Jn. XIX:34." *New Testament Studies* 15 (1969): 337–39.

Forestell, J. Terence. *The Word of the Cross: Salvation as Revelation in the Fourth Gospel*. Analecta Biblica 57. Rome: Biblical Institute Press, 1974.

Fortna, Robert T. "From Christology to Soteriology. A Redaction-Critical Study of Salvation in the Fourth Gospel." *Interpretation* 27 (1973): 31–47.

–––. "Christology in the Fourth Gospel: Redaction-Critical Perspectives." *New Testament Studies* 21 (1975): 489–504.

–––. *The Fourth Gospel and its Predecessor: From Narrative Source to Present Gospel*. Philadelphia: Fortress, 1988.

Fortna, Robert T., and Tom Thatcher, eds. *Jesus in Johannine Tradition*. Louisville, Ky.: Westminster John Knox Press, 2001.

Fossum, Jarl E. *The Name of God and the Angel of the Lord: Samaritan and Jewish Concepts of Intermediation and the Origin of Gnosticism*. Wissenschaftliche Untersuchungen zum Neuen Testament 36. Tübingen: J. C. B. Mohr (Paul Siebeck), 1985.

France, R. T. "The Worship of Jesus: A Neglected Factor in Christological Debate." Pages 17–36 in *Christ the Lord: Studies in Christology Presented to Donald Guthrie*. Edited by Harold H. Rowdon. Leicester: InterVarsity Press, 1982.

Francis, M. "The Samaritan Woman." *Asia Journal of Theology* 2 (1988): 147–48.

Franck, Eskil. *Revelation Taught: The Paraclete in the Gospel of John*. Coniectanea Biblica: New Testament Series 14. Uppsala: Gleerup, 1985.

Freed, Edwin D. *Old Testament Quotations in the Gospel of John*. Novum Testamentum Supplements 11. Leiden: E. J. Brill, 1965.

–––. "Samaritan Influence in the Gospel of John." *The Catholic Biblical Quarterly* 30 (1968): 580–87.

–––. "Did John Write His Gospel Partly to Win Samaritan Converts?" *Novum Testamentum* 12 (1970): 241–56.

–––. "Theological Prelude to the Prologue of John's Gospel." *Scottish Journal of Theology* 32 (1979): 257–69.

–––. "Who or What was before Abraham in John 8:58?" *Journal for the Study of the New Testament* 17 (1983): 52–59.

Frey, Jörg, *Die johanneische Eschatologie*. Vol. I: *Ihre Probleme im Spiegel der Forschung seit Reimarus*. Wissenschaftliche Untersuchungen zum Neuen Testament 96. Tübingen: J. C. B. Mohr (Paul Siebeck), 1997.

———. *Die johanneische Eschatologie*. Vol. II: *Das johanneische Zeitverständnis*. Wissenschaftliche Untersuchungen zum Neuen Testament 110. Tübingen: J. C. B. Mohr (Paul Siebeck), 1998.

———. *Die johanneische Eschatologie*. Vol. III: *Die eschatologische Verkündigung in den johanneischen Texten*. Wissenschaftliche Untersuchungen zum Neuen Testament 117. Tübingen: J. C. B. Mohr (Paul Siebeck), 2000.

Friend, H. S. "Like Father, Like Son—A Discussion of the Concept of Agency in Halakha and John." *Ashland Theological Journal* 21 (1990): 18–28.

Fuller, Reginald Horace. *The Foundations of New Testament Christology*. New York: Charles Scribner's Sons, 1965.

———. "The Jews in the Fourth Gospel." *Dialogue* 16 (1977): 31–37.

———. "Lower and Higher Christology in the Fourth Gospel." Pages 357–65 in *The Conversation Continues: Studies in Paul and John in Honor of J. Louis Martyn*. Edited by Robert T. Fortna and Beverly R. Gaventa. Nashville: Abingdon, 1990.

Fuller, Reginald Horace, and Pheme Perkins. *Who is Christ? Gospel Christology and Contemporary Faith*. Philadelphia: Fortress, 1983.

Funk, Robert W. 'Papyrus Bodmer II (P^{66}) and John 8:25." *Harvard Theological Review* 51 (1958): 95–100.

Gächter, Paul. "Strophen im Johannesevangelium." *Zeitschrift für Theologie und Kirche* 60 (1963): 99–120, 402–23.

———. "Zur Form von Joh 5:19–30." Pages 63–68 in *Neutestamentliche Aufsätze: Festschrift für Josef Schmid zum 70. Geburtstag*. Edited by Josef Blinzler. Regensburg: Pustet, 1963.

Gadamer, Hans-Georg. "Das Vaterbild im griechischen Denken." Pages 102–15 in *Das Vaterbild in Mythos und Geschichte: Ägypten, Griechenland, Altes Testament, Neues Testament*. Edited by Hubertus Tellenbach. Stuttgart: Kohlhammer, 1976.

Gaffney, James. "Believing and Knowing in the Fourth Gospel." *Theological Studies* 26 (1965): 215–41.

Gardner-Smith, Percival. *St. John and the Synoptic Gospels*. Cambridge: Cambridge University Press, 1938.

Garland, David E. "The Fulfillment Quotations in John's Account of the Crucifixion." Pages 229–50 in *Perspectives on John: Method and Interpretation in the Fourth Gospel*. Edited by Robert B. Sloan and Mikeal C. Parsons. Lewiston, N. Y.: Edwin Mellen Press, 1993.

Garnet, Paul. "The Baptism of Jesus and the Son of Man Idea." *Journal for the Study of the New Testament* 9 (1980): 49–65.

Geffré, Claude. "'Father' as the Proper Name of God." Pages 43–50 in *God as Father?* Edited by Johannes-Baptist Metz and Edward Schillebeeckx. Edinburgh: T&T Clark, 1981.

Giblin, Charles H. "Two Complementary Literary Structures in John 1:1–18." *Journal of Biblical Literature* 104 (1985): 87–103.

Gloer, W. Hulitt. "'Come and See': Disciples and Discipleship in the Fourth Gospel." Pages 269–302 in *Perspectives on John: Method and Interpretation in the Fourth Gospel*. Edited by Robert B. Sloan and Mikeal C. Parsons. Lewiston, N. Y.: Edwin Mellen Press, 1993.

Goergen, Donald J. "The Christology of the Johannine community." Pages 9-35 in *The Jesus of Christian History*. Collegeville, Minn.: Liturgical Press, 1992.

― ― ―. *The Jesus of Christian History*. Collegeville, Minn.: Liturgical Press, 1992.

Goppelt, Leonhard. *Theologie des Neuen Testaments: Vielfalt und Einheit des apostolischen Christuszeugnisses*. Göttingen: Vandenhoeck & Ruprecht, 1976.

Gordon, T. "The Paraclete in the Fourth Gospel." *Search* 11 (1988): 72-82.

Gorospe, V. R. "Krishna Avatara in the Bhagavad Gita and Christ Incarnate in John's Gospel." *Dialogue & Alliance* 1 (1987): 53-72.

Grant, F. G. "Only-begotten—a Footnote to the R.S.V." *Bible Translator* 17 (1966): 11-14.

Grant, Robert M. *Gods and the One God*. Library of Early Christianity 1. Philadelphia: Westminster Press, 1986.

― ― ―. *Jesus after the Gospels: The Christ of the Second Century*. Louisville, Ky.: Westminster/John Knox Press, 1990.

Grässer, Erich. "Die antijüdische Polemik im Johannesevangelium." *New Testament Studies* 10 (1964/65): 74-90.

Grayston, Kenneth. "The Meaning of PARAKLETOS." *Journal for the Study of the New Testament* 13 (1981): 67-82.

― ― ―. "Who Misunderstands the Johannine Misunderstandings?" *Scripture Bulletin* 20 (1989): 9-15.

Green, H. C. "The Composition of St. John's Prologue." *Expository Times* 66 (1954-55): 291-94.

Grese, William C. "Unless One is Born Again: The Use of a Heavenly Journey in John 3." *Journal of Biblical Literature* 107 (1988): 677-93.

Grigsby, Bruce H. "The Cross as an Expiatory Sacrifice in the Fourth Gospel." *Journal for the Study of the New Testament* 15 (1982): 51-80.

Gryglewicz, Feliks. "Die Aussagen Jesu und ihre Rolle in Joh 5:16-30." *Studien zum Neuen Testament und seiner Umwelt* A/5 (1980): 5-17.

Guthrie, Donald. *New Testament Introduction*. 3rd edition. Leicester: Tyndale Press, 1970.

― ― ―. *New Testament Theology*. Leicester, Ill.: InterVarsity Press, 1981.

Haenchen, Ernst. "Probleme des johanneischen Prologs." *Zeitschrift für Theologie und Kirche* 60 (1963): 305-34.

Hagner, Donald A. "The Vision of God in Philo and John—A Comparative Study." *Journal of the Evangelical Theological Society* 14 (1971): 81-93.

Hahn, Ferdinand. "Beobachtungen zu Joh 1:18, 34." Pages 239-45 in *Studies in New Testament Language and Text: Essays in Honour of George D. Kilpatrick*. Edited by James Keith Elliott. Novum Testamentum Supplements 44. Leiden: E. J. Brill, 1976.

― ― ―. "The Confession of the One God in the New Testament." *Horizons in Biblical Theology* 2 (1980): 69-84.

Hall, D. R. "The Meaning of συγχράομαι in John 4:9." *Expository Times* 83 (1971/72): 56-57.

Hamann, H. P. "The New Testament Concept of the 'Church' and its Implied Ecumenical Program, with an Appendix on John 17.20–23." *Lutheran Theological Journal* 18 (1984): 117–28.

Hamerton-Kelly, Robert. *God the Father: Theology and Patriarchy in the Teaching of Jesus*. Overtures to Biblical Theology. Philadelphia: Fortress, 1979.

―――. "God the Father in the Bible and in the Experience of Jesus: The State of the Question." Pages 95–102 in *God as Father?* Edited by Johannes-Baptist Metz and Edward Schillebeeckx. Edinburgh: T&T Clark, 1981.

Hanson, Anthony Tyrrell. "John's Citation of Psalm LXXXII." *New Testament Studies* 11 (1964/65): 158–62.

―――. "John's Citation of Psalm LXXXII Reconsidered." *New Testament Studies* 13 (1966/67): 363–67.

―――. "John 1:14–18 and Exodus 34." *New Testament Studies* 23 (1977): 90–101.

―――. "John 1.14: 'became'." *Expository Times* 93 (1981/82): 215.

―――. *The Prophetic Gospel: A Study of John and the Old Testament*. Edinburgh: T&T Clark, 1991.

Harm, F. R. "Distinctive Titles of the Holy Spirit in the Writings of John." *Concordia Journal* 13 (1987): 119–35.

Harner, Philip B. *The "I am" of the Fourth Gospel: A Study in Johannine Usage and Thought*. Philadelphia: Fortress, 1970.

―――. "Qualitative Anarthrous Predicate Nouns—Mk. 15:3 and Jn. 1.1." *Journal of Biblical Literature* 92 (1973): 75–87.

Harrington, Daniel J. "The Jews in John's Gospel." *Bible Today* 27/4 (1989): 203–209.

Harris, Elizabeth. *Prologue and Gospel: The Theology of the Fourth Evangelist*. Journal for the Study of the New Testament: Supplement Series 107. Sheffield: Sheffield Academic Press, 1994.

Harris, J. Rendel. *The Origin of the Prologue to St. John*. Cambridge: Cambridge University Press, 1917.

Harris, Murray James. *Jesus as God: The New Testament Use of theos in Reference to Jesus*. Grand Rapids: Baker, 1992.

Hartin, Patrick J. "Remain in Me (John 15:5)—the Foundation of the Ethical and its Consequences in the Farewell Discourses." *Neotestamentica* 25 (1991): 341–56.

Hartman, Lars, and B. Olsson, eds. *Aspects on the Johannine Literature: Papers Presented at a Conference of Scandinavian New Testament Exegetes at Uppsala, June 16–19, 1986*. Coniectanea biblica, New Testament Series 18. Uppsala: Almqvist & Wiksell, 1987.

Harvey, Anthony E. *Jesus On Trial: A Study in the Fourth Gospel*. London: S.P.C.K., 1976.

―――. "Christ as Agent." Pages 239–50 in *The Glory of Christ in the New Testament: Studies in Christology in Memory of George Bradford Caird*. Edited by Lincoln D. Hurst and Nicholas T. Wright. Oxford: Clarendon Press, 1987.

Hawkin, David John. "The Johannine Concept of Truth and its Implications for a Technological Society." *Evangelical Quarterly* 59/1 (1987): 3–13.

Hayward, C. T. Robert. "The Holy Name of the God of Moses and the Prologue of St. John's Gospel." *New Testament Studies* 25 (1978/79): 16–32.

———. "Memra and Shekhina: A Short Note." *Journal of Jewish Studies* 31 (1980): 110–18.
Hedrick, C. W. "Unreliable Narration: John on the Story of Jesus: The Chronicler on the History of Israel." Pages 121–44 in *Perspectives on John: Method and Interpretation in the Fourth Gospel*. Edited by Robert B. Sloan and Mikeal C. Parsons. Lewiston, N. Y.: Edwin Mellen Press, 1993.
Heer, J. "Johanneische Botschaft (IX). Jesus offenbart sich der Samariterin (Joh. 4,1–26)." *Sein und Sendung* 33 (1968): 51–64.
———. "Johanneische Botschaft (X). Die Mission in Samaria (Joh. 4,27–42)." *Sein und Sendung* 33 (1968): 99–112.
———. "Johanneische Botschaft (XII). An Jesus entscheidet sich das Heil (Joh. 5:1–30)." *Sein und Sendung* 33 (1968): 243–61.
Hegermann, Harald. "Er kam in sein Eigentum: Zur Bedeutung des Erdenwirkens Jesu im vierten Evangelium." Pages 112–31 in *Der Ruf Jesu und die Antwort der Gemeinde: Exegetische Untersuchungen. Joachim Jeremias zum 70. Geburtstag von seinen Schülern*. Edited by Eduard Lohse et al. Göttingen: Vandenhoeck & Ruprecht, 1970.
Hengel, Martin. *The Johannine Question*. London: SCM Press; Philadelphia: Trinity Press International, 1989.
———. "The Old Testament in the Fourth Gospel." *Horizons in Biblical Theology* 12 (1990): 19–41.
Herzog, Frederick. *Liberation Theology—Liberation in the Light of the Fourth Gospel*. New York: Seabury Press, 1972.
Hickling, Colin J. A. "Attitudes to Judaism in the Fourth Gospel." Pages 347–54 in *L'Évangile de Jean*. Edited by Marinus de Jonge. Bibliotheca Ephemeridum Theologicarum Lovaniensium 44. Leuven: Leuven University Press, 1977.
Higgins, Angus John Brockhurst. "The Words of Jesus According to St. John." *Bulletin of the John Rylands University Library* 49 (1967): 363–86.
Hodges, Zane C. "Grace after Grace—John 1:16." *Bibliotheca Sacra* 135 (1978): 34–45.
Hoffmann, Paul. "Er ist unsere Freiheit: Aspekte einer konkreten Christologie." *Bibel und Kirche* 42 (1987): 109–15.
Hofius, Otfried. "Struktur und Gedankengang des Logos-Hymnus." *Zeitschrift für die Neutestamentliche Wissenschaft* 78 (1987): 1–25.
———. "Der in des Vaters Schoß ist: Joh 1,18." *Zeitschrift für die Neutestamentliche Wissenschaft* 80 (1989): 163–71.
Hofrichter, Peter. *Im Anfang war der "Johannesprolog": Das urchristliche Logosbekenntnis, die Basis neutestamentlicher und gnostischer Theologie*. Biblische Untersuchungen 17. Regensburg: Pustet, 1986.
Hollis, H. "The Root of the Johannine Pun—ὑψωθῆναι." *New Testament Studies* 35 (1989): 475–78.
Homcy, S. L. "You are Gods? Spirituality and a Difficult Text." *Journal of the Evangelical Theological Society* 32 (1989): 485–91.
Hooker, Morna D. "John the Baptist and the Prologue." *New Testament Studies* 16 (1969/70): 354–58.
———. "The Johannine Prologue and the Messianic Secret." *New Testament Studies* 21 (1974/75): 40–58.

Hübner, Hans. *Biblische Theologie des Neuen Testaments.* Vol. 3: *Hebräerbrief, Evangelien und Offenbarung. Epilegomena.* Göttingen: Vandenhoeck & Ruprecht, 1995.
Hunt, B. W. "John's Doctrine of the Spirit." *Southwestern Journal of Theology* 8 (1965): 45–65.

Ibuki, Yu. *Die Wahrheit im Johannesevangelium.* BBB 39. Bonn: Hanstein, 1972.
Inch, M. "Apologetic Use of 'Sign' in the Fourth Gospel." *Evangelical Quarterly* 42 (1970): 35–43.
Irudayraj, K. "Christ(ology) as Creative Mystery." *Jeevadhara* 2 (1972): 222–29.

Jackayya, B. H. "ἀλήθεια (Truth) in the Johannine Corpus." *Concordia Theological Monthly* 41 (1970): 171–75.
Jeremias, Joachim. *The Central Message of the New Testament.* London: SCM Press, 1965.
John, M. P. "Johannine mysticism." *Indian Journal of Theology* 5 (1956): 15–21.
Johnston, George. *The Spirit-Paraclete in the Gospel of John.* Society of New Testament Studies Monograph Series 12. Cambridge: Cambridge University Press, 1970.
— — —. "Ecce Homo! Irony in the Christology of the Fourth Evangelist." Pages 125–38 in *The Glory of Christ in the New Testament.* Edited by Lincoln D. Hurst and Nicholas T. Wright. Oxford: Clarendon Press, 1987.
Judge, Edwin Arthur. "The Social Identity of the First Christians: A Question of Method in Religious History." *Journal of Religious History* 11 (1980): 201–17.
Judge, P. J. "A Note on Jn 20,29." Pages 2183–92 in vol. 3 of *The Four Gospels, 1992: Festschrift Frans Neirynck.* 3 vols. Edited by Frans van Segbroeck, Christopher M. Tuckett, Gilbert van Belle, and Jozef Verheyden. Bibliotheca Ephemeridum Theologicarum Lovaniensium 100. Leuven: Leuven University Press, 1992.
Juel, Donald, and Patrick Keifert. "I Believe in God: A Johannine perspective." *Horizons in Biblical Theology* 12 (1990): 39–60.

Kappen, Sebastian. "Jesus and Transculturation." Pages 173–88 in *Asian Faces of Jesus.* Edited by Rasiah S. Sugirtharajah. London: SCM Press, 1993.
Karris, Robert J. *Jesus and the Marginalized in John's Gospel.* Collegeville, Minn.: Liturgical Press, 1990.
Käsemann, Ernst. "Aufbau und Anliegen des Johanneischen Prologs." Pages 155–80 in vol. 2 of *Exegetische Versuche und Besinnungen.* Göttingen: Vandenhoeck & Ruprecht, 1964.
— — —. *The Testament of Jesus: A Study of the Gospel of John in the Light of Chapter 17.* Translated by Gerhard Krodel. The New Testament Library. London: SCM Press, 1968.
Keck, Leander E. "On the Ethos of the Early Christians." *Journal of the American Academy of Religion* 42 (1974): 435–52.
Kehl, Medard. "Der Mensch in der Geschichte Gottes: Zum Johannesprolog 6–8." *Glaube und Leben* 40 (1967): 404–409.
Kelber, Werner H. "The Birth of a Beginning: John 1:1–18." *Semeia* 52 (1990): 121–44.

Kennard, Douglas Welker. *The Doctrine of God in Petrine Theology*. Diss. Dallas Theological Seminary, 1987.

Kim, Seyoon. *The 'Son of Man' as the Son of God*. Wissenschaftliche Untersuchungen zum Neuen Testament 30. Tübingen: J. C. B. Mohr (Paul Siebeck), 1983.

King, J. S. "Sychar and Calvary: A Neglected Theory in the Interpretation of the Fourth Gospel." *Theology* 77 (1974): 417–22.

Kippenberg, Hans G. *Garizim und Synagoge: Traditionsgeschichtliche Untersuchungen zur samaritanischen Religion der aramäischen Periode*. Religionsgeschichtliche Versuche und Vorarbeiten 30. Berlin: de Gruyter, 1971.

Klinger, J. "Bethesda and the Universality of the Logos." *St. Vladimir's Theological Quarterly* 27 (1983): 163–85.

Klumbies, Paul-Gerhard, *Die Rede von Gott bei Paulus in ihrem zeitgeschichtlichen Kontext*. Forschungen zur Religion und Literatur des Alten und Neuen Testaments 155. Göttingen: Vandenhoeck & Ruprecht, 1992.

Knight, G. A. F. "Antisemitism in the Fourth Gospel." *The Reformed Theological Review* 27 (1968): 81–88.

Knöppler, Thomas. *Die theologia crucis des Johannesevangeliums: Das Verständnis des Todes Jesu im Rahmen der johanneischen Inkarnations- und Erhöhungschristologie*. WMANT 69. Neukirchen-Vluyn: Neukirchener Verlag, 1994.

Koester, Craig R. *Symbolism in the Fourth Gospel: Meaning, Mystery, Community*. Minneapolis: Fortress, 1995.

Koester, Helmut. "The History-of-Religions School, Gnosis and the Gospel of John." *Studia Theologica* 40 (1986): 115–36.

Kohler, Herbert. *Kreuz und Menschwerdung im Johannesevangelium: Ein exegetisch-hermeneutischer Versuch zur johanneischen Kreuzestheologie*. ATANT 72. Zurich: Theologischer Verlag, 1987.

Kooy, V. H. "The Transfiguration Motive in the Gospel of John." Pages 64–78 in *Saved by Hope: Essays in Honor of Richard C. Oudersluys*. Edited by James I. Cook. Grand Rapids: Eerdmans, 1978.

Koyama, Kosuke. "The Crucified Christ Challenges Human Power." Pages 149–62 in *Asian Faces of Jesus*. Edited by Rasiah S. Sugirtharajah. London: SCM Press, 1993.

Kremer, Jacob. "»Nimm deine Hand und lege sie in meine Seite!«. Exegetische, hermeneutische und bibeltheologische Überlegungen zu Joh. 20, 24–29." Pages 2153–82 in vol. 3 of *The Four Gospels, 1992: Festschrift Frans Neirynck*. 3 vols. Edited by Frans van Segbroeck, Christopher M. Tuckett, Gilbert van Belle, and Jozef Verheyden. Bibliotheca Ephemeridum Theologicarum Lovaniensium 100. Leuven: Leuven University Press, 1992.

Krentz, Edgar. "The Spirit in Pauline and Johannine theology." Pages 47–65 in *The Holy Spirit in the Life of the Church*. Edited by Paul David Opsahl. Minneapolis: Augsburg Publishing House, 1978.

Kügler, Joachim. "Der andere König. Religionsgeschichtliche Anmerkungen zum Jesusbild des Johannesevangeliums." *Zeitschrift für die Neutestamentliche Wissenschaft* 88 (1998): 223–41.

Kümmel, Werner Georg. *Theology of the New Testament according to its Major Witnesses: Jesus, Paul and John*. Translated by John E. Steely. London: SCM Press, 1974.

———. *Introduction to the New Testament*. Translated by Howard Clark Kee. New Testament Library. London: SCM Press, 1975.

Kysar, Robert. "Rudolf Bultmann's Interpretation of the Concept of Creation in John 1,3–4." *The Catholic Biblical Quarterly* 32 (1970): 77–85.

———. "The Background of the Prologue of the Fourth Gospel: A Critique of Historical Methods." *Canadian Journal of Theology* 16 (1970): 250–55.

———. "Johannine Metaphor—Meaning and Function: A Literary Case Study of John 10:1–8." *Semeia* 53 (1991): 81–111.

Kyung, C. H. "Who is Jesus for Asian Women?" Pages 223–46 in *Asian Faces of Jesus*. Edited by Rasiah S. Sugirtharajah. London: SCM Press, 1993.

Ladd, George E. *A Theology of the New Testament*, Guildford, etc.: Lutterworth, 1975.

Lähnemann, Johannes. "Jesu Rede von Gott—als christlicher Beitrag im Gespräch mit Menschen anderen Glaubens." Pages 443–56 in *Jesu Rede von Gott und ihre Nachgeschichte im frühen Christentum: Beiträge zur Verkündigung Jesu und zum Kerygma der Kirche. Festschrift für Willi Marxsen zum 70. Geburtstag*. Edited by Dietrich-Alex Koch, Gerhard Sellin, and Andreas Lindemann. Gütersloh: Mohn, 1989.

Lamarche, Paul. "The Prologue of John." Pages 36–52 in *The Interpretation of John*. Edited by John Ashton. Philadelphia: Fortress, 1986.

Langbrandtner, Wolfgang. *Weltferner Gott oder Gott der Liebe: Der Ketzerstreit in der johanneischen Kirche; eine exegetisch-religionsgeschichtliche Untersuchung mit Berücksichtigung der koptisch-gnostischen Texte aus Nag-Hammadi*. Beiträge zur biblischen Exegese und Theologie 6. Frankfurt am Main: Peter Lang, 1977.

Lategan, Bernard C. "The Truth that Sets Man Free: John 8:31–36." *Neotestamentica* 2 (1968): 70–80.

Lattke, Michael. *Einheit im Wort: Die spezifische Bedeutung von "agape", "agapan" und "filein" im Johannesevangelium*. Studien zum Alten und Neuen Testament 41. Munich: Kösel, 1975.

Lee, Bernard J. *Jesus and the Metaphors of God: The Christs of the New Testament*, New York: Paulist Press, 1993.

Lee, Dorothy A. *The Symbolic Narratives of the Fourth Gospel: The Interplay of Form and Meaning*. Journal for the Study of the New Testament: Supplement Series 95. Sheffield: JSOT Press, 1994.

Lee, Edwin Kenneth. *The Religious Thought of St. John*. London: S.P.C.K., 1950.

Lee, Jung Young. "The Perfect Realization of Change: Jesus Christ." Pages 62–74 in *Asian Faces of Jesus*. Edited by Rasiah S. Sugirtharajah. London: SCM Press, 1993.

Leibig, J. E. "John and 'the Jews': Theological Antisemitism in the Fourth Gospel." *Journal of Ecumenical Studies* 20 (1983): 209–34.

Lemmer, R. "A Possible Understanding by the Implied Reader, of some of the Coming–Going–Being-Sent Pronouncements, in the Johannine Farewell Discourses." *Neotestamentica* 25 (1991): 289–310.

Leroy, Herbert. "Und das Wort ist Fleisch geworden . . . ." *Bibel und Kirche* 20 (1965): 114–16.

Lieu, Judith. "'The Parting of Ways': Theological Construct or Historical Reality?" *Journal for the Study of the New Testament* 56 (1994): 101–19.

Lindars, Barnabas. "ΔΙΚΑΙΟΣΥΝΗ in Jn 16.8 and 10." Pages 275–85 in *Mélanges Bibliques: En Hommage au R. P. Béda Rigaux*. Edited by Albert Descamps and André de Halleux. Gembloux: Duculot, 1970.

———. *Behind the Fourth Gospel*. London: S.P.C.K., 1971.

———. "Traditions Behind the Fourth Gospel." Pages 107–24 in *L'Évangile de Jean*. Edited by Marinus de Jonge. Bibliotheca Ephemeridum Theologicarum Lovaniensium 44. Leuven: Leuven University Press, 1977.

———. "Discourse and Tradition. The Use of the Sayings of Jesus in the Discourses of the Fourth Gospel." *Journal for the Study of the New Testament* 13 (1981): 83–101.

———. "Slave and the Son in John 8:31–36." Pages 167–82 in *Essays on John*. Edited by Christopher M. Tuckett. SNTA 17. Leuven: Leuven University Press, 1992.

———. *Essays on John*. Edited by Christopher M. Tuckett. SNTA 17. Leuven: Leuven University Press, 1992.

Lindemann, Andreas. "Die Rede von Gott in der paulinischen Theologie." *Theologie und Glaube* 69 (1979): 357–76. Reprinted in *Paulus: Apostel und Lehrer der Kirche. Studien zu Paulus und zum frühen Paulus-Verständnis*. Tübingen: J. C. B. Mohr (Paul Siebeck), 1999. Pages 9–26.

———. "Gemeinde und Welt im Johannesevangelium." Pages 133–61 in *Kirche: Festschrift für Günther Bornkamm zum 75. Geburtstag*. Edited by Dieter Lührmann and Georg Strecker. Tübingen: J. C. B. Mohr (Paul Siebeck), 1980.

———. "Das Johannesevangelium in neuer Sicht." *Reformierte Kirchliche Zeitschrift* 133 (1992): 301–309.

———. "Samaria und Samaritaner im Neuen Testament." *Wort und Dienst* 22 (1993): 51–76.

———. "Die johanneische Frage und der Versuch einer Antwort." *Reformierte Kirchenzeitung* 2 (1995): 75–81.

———. "Mose und Jesus Christus. Zum Verständnis des Gesetzes im Johannesevangelium." Pages 309–34 in *Das Urchristentum in seiner literarischen Geschichte. Festschrift Jürgen Becker*. Edited by Ulrich Mell and Ulrich B. Müller. Beihefte zur Zeitschrift für die neutestamentliche Wissenschaft 100. Berlin/New York: Walter de Gruyter, 1999.

Lindsay, Dennis R. "What is Truth? ἀλήθεια in the Gospel of John." *Restoration Quarterly* 35 (1993): 129–45.

Lips, Hermann von. "Christus als Sophia? Weisheitliche Traditionen in der urchristlichen Christologie." Pages 75–97 in *Anfänge der Christologie: Festschrift für Ferdinand Hahn zum 65. Geburtstag*. Edited by Cilliers Breytenbach and Henning Paulsen. Göttingen: Vandenhoeck & Ruprecht, 1991.

Loader, William R. G. "The Central Structure of Johannine Christology." *New Testament Studies* 30 (1984): 188–216.

———. *The Christology of the Fourth Gospel: Structure and Issues*. Beiträge zur biblischen Exegese und Theologie 23. Frankfurt am Main: Peter Lang, 1989.

Locher, Gottfried W. "Der Geist als Paraklet." *Evangelische Theologie* 26 (1966): 565–79.

Lohse, Eduard. "Jesu Worte über den Sabbat." Pages 62–72 in *Die Einheit des Neuen Testaments: Exegetische Studien zur Theologie des Neuen Testaments*. 2nd edition.

Exegetische Studien zur Theologie des Neuen Testaments 1. Göttingen: Vandenhoeck & Ruprecht, 1973.

— — —. "Miracles in the Fourth Gospel." Pages 64–75 in *What About the New Testament? Essays in Honour of Christopher Evans.* Edited by Morna D. Hooker and Colin Hickling. London: SCM Press, 1975.

Louw, Johannes P. "Narrator of the Father—ἐξηγεῖσθαι and Related Terms in Johannine Christology." *Neotestamentica* 2 (1968): 32–40.

Lowe, Malcolm. "Who were the Ἰουδαῖοι?" *Novum Testamentum* 18 (1976): 101–30.

Maccini, Robert Gordon. "A Reassessment of the Woman at the Well in John 4 in Light of the Samaritan Context." *Journal for the Study of the New Testament* 53 (1994): 35–46.

Macdonald, John. *The Theology of the Samaritans.* London: SCM Press, 1964.

Mack, Burton L. *Logos und Sophia: Untersuchungen zur Weisheitstheologie im hellenistischen Judentum.* Studien zur Umwelt des Neuen Testaments 10. Göttingen: Vandenhoeck & Ruprecht, 1973.

Malatesta, Edward. "The Spirit/Paraclete in the Fourth Gospel." *Biblica* 54 (1973): 539–50.

— — —. "We have Seen His Glory." *The Way* 14 (1974): 3–12.

Malik, Alexander J. "Confessing Christ in the Islamic Context." Pages 75–84 in *Asian Faces of Jesus.* Edited by Rasiah S. Sugirtharajah. London: SCM Press, 1993.

Malina, Bruce J. "John's: The Maverick Christian Group the Evidence of Sociolinguistics." *Biblical Theology Bulletin* 24 (1994): 167–82.

Malina, Bruce J., and Richard L. Rohrbaugh. *Social-Science Commentary on the Gospel of John.* Minneapolis: Fortress, 1998.

Manson, Thomas Walter. "The Johannine Jesus as Logos." Pages 33–58 in *A Companion to John: Readings in Johannine Theology (John's Gospel and Epistles).* Edited by Michael J. Taylor. New York: Alba House, 1977.

Marsh, John. "John: A very Different Gospel." Pages 3–32 in *A Companion to John: Readings in Johannine Theology (John's Gospel and Epistles).* Edited by Michael J. Taylor. New York: Alba House, 1977.

Marshall, Ian H. "Incarnational Christology in the New Testament." Pages 1–16 in *Christ the Lord: Studies in Christology Presented to Donald Guthrie.* Edited by Harold H. Rowdon. Leicester: InterVarsity Press, 1982.

Martin, James P. "Toward a Post-Critical Paradigm." *New Testament Studies* 33 (1987): 370–85.

Martin, Raymond A. *Syntax Criticism of Johannine Literature, the Catholic Epistles and the Gospel Passion Accounts.* Studies in Bible and Early Christianity 18. Lewiston, N.Y.: Mellen, 1989.

Martin, Ralph P. "Some Reflections on New Testament Hymns." Pages 37–49 in *Christ the Lord: Studies in Christology Presented to Donald Guthrie.* Edited by Harold H. Rowdon. Leicester: InterVarsity Press, 1982.

Martinez, Salvador T. "Jesus Christ in Popular Piety in the Philippines." Pages 247–57 in *Asian Faces of Jesus.* Edited by Rasiah S. Sugirtharajah. London: SCM Press, 1993.

Martyn, J. Louis. "We have found Elijah." Pages 181–219 in *Jews, Greeks and Christians: Religious Cultures in Late Antiquity. Essays in Honor of William David Davies.* Edited by Robert Hamerton-Kelly and Robin Scroggs. Leiden: E. J. Brill, 1976.

———. "Glimpses into the History of the Johannine Community. From its Origin through the Period of its Life in which the Fourth Gospel was Composed." Pages 149–75 in *L'Évangile de Jean.* Edited by Marinus de Jonge. Bibliotheca Ephemeridum Theologicarum Lovaniensium 44. Leuven: Leuven University Press, 1977.

———. *The Gospel of John in Christian History: Essays for Interpreters.* New York: Paulist Press, 1978.

———. *History and Theology in the Fourth Gospel.* 2nd edition. Nashville: Abingdon, 1979.

———. "Source Criticism and Religionsgeschichte in the Fourth Gospel." Pages 99–121 in *The Interpretation of John.* Edited by John Ashton. Philadelphia: Fortress, 1986.

Mastin, Brian Arthur. "A Neglected Feature of the Christology of the Fourth Gospel." *New Testament Studies* 22 (1976): 32–51.

Matsunaga, Kikuo. "The Theos Christology as the Ultimate Confession of the Fourth Gospel." *Annual of the Japanese Biblical Institute* 7 (1981): 124–45.

Mattam, Joseph. "Modern Catholic Attempts at Presenting Christ to India." *Indian Journal of Theology* 23 (1974): 206–18.

Mattill Jr., Andrew J. "Johannine Communities Behind the Fourth Gospel: Georg Richter's Analysis." *Theological Studies* 38 (1977): 294–315.

Mattison, R. D. "God/Father: Tradition and Interpretation." *Reformed Review* 42 (1989): 189–206.

McHugh, John. "The Glory of the Cross: The Passion According to St John." *The Clergy Review* 67 (1982): 117–27.

———. "In Him was Life: John's Gospel and Parting of the Ways." Pages 123–58 in *Jews and Christians: The Parting of the Ways A.D. 70 to 135.* Edited by James D. G. Dunn. Wissenschaftliche Untersuchungen zum Neuen Testament 66. Tübingen: J. C. B. Mohr (Paul Siebeck), 1992.

McPolin, James. "Mission in the Fourth Gospel." *Irish Theological Quarterly* 36 (1969): 113–22.

———. "Holy Spirit in Luke and John." *Irish Theological Quarterly* 45 (1978): 117–31.

———. "Johannine Mysticism." *The Way* 18 (1978): 25–35.

———. "The Word was Made Flesh." *The Way* 21 (1981): 22–23.

McReynolds, P. R. "John 1:18 in Textual Variation and Translation." Pages 105–18 in *New Testament Textual Criticism, Its Significance for Exegesis. Essays in Honour of Bruce M. Metzger.* Edited by Eldon J. Epp and Gordon D. Fee. Oxford: Clarendon Press, 1981.

Meagher, John C. "John 1.14 and the New Temple." *Journal of Biblical Literature* 88 (1969): 57–68.

Meagher, P. M. "Christ at the Centre of John's Gospel." *Vidajyothi* 52 (1988): 154–59.

Meeks, Wayne A. *The Prophet-King: Moses Traditions and the Johannine Christology.* Novum Testamentum Supplements 14. Leiden: E. J. Brill, 1967.

―――. "Moses as God and King." Pages 354–71 in *Religions in Antiquity*. Edited by John Neusner. Leiden: E. J. Brill, 1968.

―――. "Am I a Jew? Johannine Christianity and Judaism." Pages 163–86 in vol. 1 of *Christianity, Judaism and Other Greco-Roman Cults: Studies for Morton Smith at 60*. Edited by Jacob Neusner. 4 vols. Studies in Judaism in Late Antiquity 12. Leiden: E. J. Brill, 1975.

―――. "The Social Context of Pauline Theology." *Interpretation* 36 (1982): 266–77.

―――. "Breaking Away: Three New Testament Pictures of Christianity's Separation from the Jewish Communities." Pages 93–115 in *To See Ourselves as Others See Us: Christians, Jews, "Others" in Late Antiquity*. Edited by Jacob Neusner and Ernest S. Frerichs. Scholars Press Studies in the Humanities. Chico, Calif.: Scholars Press, 1985.

―――. "The Man from Heaven in Johannine Sectarianism." Pages 141–73 in *The Interpretation of John*. Edited by John Ashton. Philadelphia: Fortress, 1986. [Originally: JBL 91, 1972, 44–72]

―――. "Equal to God." Pages 309–21 in *The Conversation Continues: Studies in Paul and John in Honor of J. Louis Martyn*. Edited by Robert T. Fortna and Beverly R. Gaventa. Nashville: Abingdon, 1990.

Mees, Michael. "Der Text von Jn 8:12–59 bei Origenes." *Augustinianum* 18 (1978): 321–39.

―――. "Das Wunder am Bethesdateich, Joh 5:1–18 und seine Folgen nach Zeugnissen der frühen Christenheit." *Lateranum* 51 (1985): 181–92.

―――. "Joh 1:12–13 nach frühchristlicher Überlieferung." *Biblische Zeitschrift* 29 (1985): 107–15.

Menken, Maarten J. J. "The Christology of the Fourth Gospel: A Survey of Recent Research." Pages 292–320 in *From Jesus to John: Essays on Jesus and New Testament Christology in Honour of Marinus de Jonge*. Edited by Martinus C. de Boer. Journal for the Study of the New Testament: Supplement Series 84. Sheffield: JSOT Press, 1990.

Mercer, Calvin. "ἈΠΟΣΤΕΛΛΕΙΝ and ΠΕΜΠΕΙΝ in John." *New Testament Studies* 36 (1990): 619–24.

―――. "Jesus the Apostle: 'Sending' and the Theology of John." *Journal of the Evangelical Theological Society* 35/4 (1992): 457–62.

Michaels, J. Ramsey. "Origen and the Text of John 1:15." Pages 87–104 in *New Testament Textual Criticism, Its Significance for Exegesis. Essays in Honour of Bruce M. Metzger*. Edited by Eldon J. Epp and Gordon D. Fee. Oxford: Clarendon Press, 1981.

Miller, Donald G. "John 3:1–21." *Interpretation* 35 (1981): 174–79.

Miller, Ed L. "Codex Bezae on John 1.3–4." *Theologische Zeitschrift* 32 (1976): 269–71.

―――. "The Christology of John 8:25." *Theologische Zeitschrift* 36/5 (1980): 257–65.

―――. "The Logos was God." *Evangelical Quarterly* 53 (1981): 65–77.

―――. "The Logic of the Logos Hymn: A New View." *New Testament Studies* 29 (1982): 552–61.

―――. "P^{66} and P^{75} on John 1:3/4." *Theologische Zeitschrift* 4 (1985): 440–43.

―――. *Salvation History in the Prologue of John: The Significance of John 1:3–4*. Novum Testamentum Supplements 60. Leiden: E. J. Brill, 1989.

Miller, John W. "God as Father in the Bible and the Father Image in Several Contemporary Ancient near Eastern Myths: A Comparison." *Studies in Religion* 14 (1985): 347–54.

— — —. "Depatriarchalizing God in Biblical Interpretation: A Critique." *The Catholic Biblical Quarterly* 48 (1986): 609–16.

Minear, Paul S. "Evangelism, Ecumenism, and John Seventeen." *Theology Today* 35 (1978): 5–13.

— — —. "John 17:1–11." *Interpretation* 32 (1978): 175–79.

Miranda, Juan P. *Der Vater, der mich gesandt hat: Religionsgeschichtliche Untersuchungen zu den johanneischen Sendungsformeln.* Europäische Hochschulschriften, Reihe 23: Theologie, vol. 7. Frankurt am Main: Peter Lang, 1972.

Mlakuzhyil, George. *The Christocentric Literary Structure of the Fourth Gospel.* Analecta Biblica 117. Rome: Pontificio Istituto Biblico, 1987.

Mohammed, O. N. "Jesus and Krishna." Pages 9–24 in *Asian Faces of Jesus.* Edited by Rasiah S. Sugirtharajah. London: SCM Press, 1993.

Moloney, Francis J. "The Johannine Son of God." *Salesianum* 38 (1976): 71–86.

— — —. *The Johannine Son of Man.* Biblioteca di scienze religiose 14. Rome: LAS, 1976.

— — —. *The Word Became Flesh.* Theology Today 14. Butler, Wis.: Clergy Book Service, 1977.

— — —. "John 18. In the Bosom of or Turned Towards the Father?" *Australian Biblical Review* 31 (1983): 63–71.

Moltmann, Jürgen. "Theology of Mystical Experience." *Scottish Journal of Theology* 32 (1979): 501–20.

— — —. "The Motherly Father. Is Trinitarian Patripassianism Replacing Theological Patriarchalism?" Pages 51–56 in *God as Father?* Edited by Johannes-Baptist Metz and Edward Schillebeeckx. Edinburgh: T&T Clark, 1981.

Moody, Dale. "God's Only Son: The Translation of John 3:16 in the Revised Standard Version." *Journal of Biblical Literature* 72 (1953) 213–19.

Moore, George Foot. "Intermediaries in Jewish Theology." *Harvard Theological Review* 15 (1922) 41–85.

Moore, Stephen D. "Are there Impurities in the Living Water that the Johannine Jesus Dispenses? Deconstruction, Feminism, and the Samaritan Woman." *Biblical Interpretation* 1 (1993): 207–27.

Morgan-Wynne, John E. "A Note on John 14:17b." *Biblische Zeitschrift* 23 (1979): 93–96.

Morris, Leon. "Love in the Fourth Gospel." Pages 27–43 in *Saved by Hope: Essays in Honor of Richard C. Oudersluys.* Edited by James I. Cook. Grand Rapids: Eerdmans, 1978.

— — —. "The Relation of the Signs and the Discourses in John." Pages 363–72 in *The New Testament Age. Essays in Honor of Bo Reicke.* Edited by William C. Weinrich. Macon, Ga.: Mercer University Press, 1984.

— — —. *Jesus is the Christ: Studies in the Theology of John.* Grand Rapids: Eerdmans, 1989.

Morrison, C. D. "Mission and Ethic. An Interpretation of John 17." *Interpretation* 19 (1965): 259–73.

Moule, Charles Francis Digby. "A Neglected Factor in the Interpretation of Johannine Eschatology." Pages 155–60 in *Studies in John: Presented to J. N. Sevenster on the Occasion of his Seventieth Birthday.* Edited by M. C. Rientsma, et al. Novum Testamentum Supplements 24. Leiden: E. J. Brill, 1970.

Mowery, Robert L. "God, Lord and Father: The Theology of the Gospel of Matthew." *Biblical Research* 33 (1988): 24–36.

———. "Lord, God, and Father: Theological Language in Luke-Acts." *Society of Biblical Literature Seminar Papers* (1995): 82–101.

Mowvley, Harry. "John 1.14–18 in the Light of Exodus 33.7–34.35." *Expository Times* 95 (1983/84): 135–37.

Moxnes, Halvor, *Theology in Conflict: Studies in Paul's Understanding of God in Romans.* Novum Testamentum Supplements 53. Leiden: E. J. Brill, 1980.

Müller, Ulrich B. "Die Parakletenvorstellung im Johannesevangelium." *Zeitschrift für Theologie und Kirche* 71 (1974): 31–77.

Navone, J. J. "We have Seen His Glory." *Bible Today* 21 (1965): 1390–96.

Nayak, A. "Der Stellenwert des johanneischen Logos in indischer Theologie." Pages 9–38 in *Johannes-Studien: Interdisziplinäre Zugänge zum Johannes-Evangelium. Freundesgabe der Theologischen Fakultät der Universität Neuchâtel für Jean Zumstein.* Edited by Martin Rose Publications de la Faculté de Théologie de l'Úniversité de Neuchâtel 6. Neuchâtel: Theologischer Verlag, 1990.

Neirynck, Frans. "John and the Synoptics." Pages 73–106 in *L'Évangile de Jean.* Edited by Marinus de Jonge. Bibliotheca Ephemeridum Theologicarum Lovaniensium 44. Leuven: Leuven University Press, 1977.

———. "The Sign Source in the Fourth Gospel: A Critique of the Hypothesis." Pages 668–77 in vol. 2 of *Evangelica: Collected Essays.* Bibliotheca Ephemeridum Theologicarum Lovaniensium 99. Leuven: Leuven University Press, 1991.

Nereparampil, Lucius. "The Church in the Johannine Literature." *Indian Journal of Theology* 28 (1979): 169–77.

———. "The Johannine Understanding of Salvation and the World Religions." *Indian Journal of Theology* 30 (1981): 146–51.

———. "'A New Commandment I Give You'": Johannine Understanding of Love." *Jeevadhara* 13 (1983): 104–14.

———. "The Spiritual Vision of St. John and the Bhagavadgita." *Bible Bhashyam* 11 (1985): 93–106.

Neugebauer, Johannes. *Die eschatologischen Aussagen in den johanneischen Abschiedsreden: Eine Untersuchung zu Johannes 13–17.* Beiträge zur Wissenschaft vom Alten und Neuen Testament 140. Stuttgart/Berlin: Kohlhammer, 1995.

Newbigin, Lesslie. *The Light has Come: An Exposition of the Fourth Gospel.* Grand Rapids: Eerdmans, 1982.

Neyrey, Jerome H. "Jacob Traditions and the Interpretation of John 4:10–26." *The Catholic Biblical Quarterly* 41 (1979): 419–37.

———. "John III—a Debate over Johannine Epistemology and Christology." *Novum Testamentum* 23 (1981): 115–27.

———. "Jesus the Judge: Forensic Process in John 8:21–59." *Biblica* 68 (1987): 509–42.

———. *An Ideology of Revolt: John's Christology in Social-Science Perspective.* Philadelphia: Fortress, 1988.

———. "I said: you are gods: Psalm 82:6 and John 10." *Journal of Biblical Literature* 108 (1989): 647–63.

Nicholson, Godfrey C. *Death as Departure: The Johannine Descent–Ascent Schema.* Society of Biblical Literature Dissertation Series 63. Chico, Calif.: Scholars Press, 1983.

Nickelsburg, George W. E. "Revealed Wisdom as a Criterion for Inclusion and Exclusion. From Jewish Sectarianism to Early Christianity." Pages 73–91 in *To See Ourselves as Others See Us: Christians, Jews, "Others" in Late Antiquity.* Edited by Jacob Neusner and Ernest S. Frerichs. Scholars Press Studies in the Humanities. Chico, Calif.: Scholars Press, 1985.

———. "Jews and Christians in the First Century. The Struggle over Identity." *Neotestamentica* 27 (1993): 365–90.

Nicol, William. *The Semeia in the Fourth Gospel: Tradition and Redaction.* Novum Testamentum Supplements 32. Leiden: E. J. Brill, 1972.

O'Day, Gail R. *Revelation in the Fourth Gospel: Narrative Mode and Theological Claim.* Philadelphia: Fortress, 1986.

O'Neill, John C. "The Prologue to St. John's Gospel." *Journal of Theological Studies* 20 (1969): 41–52.

———. "The Word did not "become" Flesh." *Zeitschrift für die Neutestamentliche Wissenschaft* 82 (1991): 125–27.

———. "'Making Himself Equal with God' (John 5.17–18): The Alleged Challenge to Jewish Monotheism in the Fourth Gospel." *Irish Biblical Studies* 17 (1995): 50–61.

Okure, Teresa. *The Johannine Approach to Mission: A Contextual Study of John 4:1–42.* Wissenschaftliche Untersuchungen zum Neuen Testament 2.31. Tübingen: J.C.B. Mohr (Paul Siebeck), 1988.

Ollenburger, Ben C. "What Krister Stendahl meant—A Normative Critique of Descriptive Biblical Theology." *Horizons in Biblical Theology* 8 (1986): 61–98.

———. "We Believe in God... Maker of Heaven and Earth: Metaphor, Scripture, and Theology." *Horizons in Biblical Theology* 12 (1990): 64–96.

Olsson, Birger. *Structure and Meaning in the Fourth Gospel: A Text-Linguistic Analysis of John 2:1–11 and 4:1–42.* Translated by J. Gray. Coniectanea Biblica: New Testament Series. Lund: C. W. K. Gleerup, 1974.

Osborn, Eric F. "The Unity of God in Pauline Thought." *Australian Biblical Review* 28 (1980): 40–60.

Osei-Bonsu, Joseph. "Anthropological Dualism in the New Testament." *Scottish Journal of Theology* 40 (1987): 571–90.

Ottoson, K. "The Love of God in St. John. Chrysostom's Commentary on the Fourth Gospel." *The Church Quarterly Review* 166 (1965): 315–23.

Pack, Frank. "The Holy Spirit in the Fourth Gospel." *Restoration Quarterly* 31 (1989): 139–48.

Pagels, Elaine H. *The Johannine Gospel in Gnostic Exegesis: Heracleon's Commentary on John*. Society of Biblical Literature Dissertation Series 17. New York: Abingdon Press, 1973.

Painter, John. *John, Witness and Theologian*. London: S.P.C.K., 1975.

— — —. "Glimpses of the Johannine Community in the Farewell Discourses." *Australian Biblical Review* 28 (1980): 21–38.

— — —. "The Farewell Discourses and the History of Johannine Christianity." *New Testament Studies* 27 (1981): 525–43.

— — —. "Christology and the Fourth Gospel: A Study of the Prologue." *Australian Biblical Review* 31 (1983): 45–62.

— — —. "Christology and the History of the Johannine Community in the Prologue of the Fourth Gospel." *New Testament Studies* 30 (1984): 460–74.

— — —. *The Quest for the Messiah: The History, Literature and Theology of the Johannine Community*. 2nd edition. Edinburgh: T&T Clark, 1993.

Pamment, Margaret. "Eschatology and the Fourth Gospel." *Journal for the Study of the New Testament* 15 (1982): 81–85.

— — —. "Is there Convincing Evidence of Samaritan Influence on the Fourth Gospel?" *Zeitschrift für die Neutestamentliche Wissenschaft* 73 (1982): 221–30.

— — —. "The Meaning of Doxa in the Fourth Gospel." *Zeitschrift für die Neutestamentliche Wissenschaft* 74 (1983): 12–16.

— — —. "Son of Man in the Fourth Gospel." *Journal of Theological Studies* 36 (1985): 56–66.

Pancaro, Severino. *The Law in the Fourth Gospel: Moses and Jesus, Judaism and Christianity According to John*. Novum Testamentum Supplements 42. Leiden: E. J. Brill, 1975.

Parker, J. "The Incarnational Christology of John." *Criswell Theological Review* 3 (1988): 31–48.

Parsons, Mikeal C. "A Neglected ΕΓΩ ΕΙΜΙ Saying in the Fourth Gospel? Another Look at John 9:9." Pages 145–80 in *Perspectives on John: Method and Interpretation in the Fourth Gospel*. Edited by Robert B. Sloan and Mikeal C. Parsons. Lewiston, N. Y.: Edwin Mellen Press, 1993.

Parunak, H. van Dyke. "Transitional Techniques in the Bible." *Journal of Biblical Literature* 102/4 (1983): 525–48.

Pazdan, Mary Margaret. *The Son of Man: A Metaphor for Jesus in the Fourth Gospel*. Collegeville, Minn.: Liturgical Press, 1991.

Pedersen, Sigfred. "The Concept of God as Theme of Biblical Theology." Pages 243–66 in *New Directions in Biblical Theology: Papers of the Aarhus Conference, 16–19 September 1992*. Novum Testamentum Supplements 76. Leiden/New York: E. J. Brill, 1994.

— — —, ed. *New Directions in Biblical Theology: Papers of the Aarhus Conference, 16–19 September 1992*. Novum Testamentum Supplements 76. Leiden/New York: E. J. Brill, 1994.

Pendrick, G. "ΜΟΝΟΓΕΝΗΣ." *New Testament Studies* 41 (1995): 587–600.

Perlitt, Lothar. "Der Vater im Alten Testament." Pages 50–101 in *Das Vaterbild in Mythos und Geschichte: Ägypten, Griechenland, Altes Testament, Neues Testament*. Edited by Hubertus Tellenbach. Stuttgart: Kohlhammer, 1976.

Phillips, W. Gary. "An Apologetic Study of John 10:34–36." *Bibliotheca Sacra* 146 (1989): 405–19.
Pieris, Aloysius. "The Buddha and the Christ: Mediators of Liberation." Pages 46–61 in *Asian Faces of Jesus*. Edited by Rasiah S. Sugirtharajah. London: SCM Press, 1993.
Polhill, J. B. "John 1–4: The Revelation of True Life." *Review and Expositor* 85 (1988): 445–57.
Pollard, Thomas Evan. "The Exegesis of John X.30 in the Early Trinitarian Controversies." *New Testament Studies* 3 (1956/57): 334–49.
— — —. *Johannine Christology and the Early Church*. Society of New Testament Studies Monograph Series 13. Cambridge: Cambridge University Press, 1970.
— — —. "The Father–Son and God–Believer Relationships According to St. John: A Brief Study of John's Use of Prepositions." Pages 363–70 in *L'Évangile de Jean*. Edited by Marinus de Jonge. Bibliotheca Ephemeridum Theologicarum Lovaniensium 44. Leuven: Leuven University Press, 1977.
Porsch, Felix. "Der <andere Paraklet>: Das Wirken des Geistes nach den johanneischen Abschiedsreden." *Bibel und Kirche* 37 (1982): 133–38.
Poythress, Vern S. "Analysing a Biblical Text: What are we after?" *Scottish Journal of Theology* 32 (1979): 319–31.
Pryor, John W. "Of the Virgin Birth or the Birth of Christians? The Text of John 1:13 Once More." *Novum Testamentum* 27 (1985): 296–318.
— — —. "Covenant and Community in John's Gospel." *The Reformed Theological Review* 47 (1988): 44–51.
— — —. "Jesus and Israel in the Fourth Gospel—John1:11." *Novum Testamentum* 32 (1990): 201–18.
— — —. "The Johannine Son of Man and the Descent-Ascent Motif." *Journal of the Evangelical Theological Society* 34 (1991): 341–51.
Puthenkandathil, Eldho. *Philos: A Designation for the Jesus–Disciple Relationship. An Exegetico-Theological Investigation of the Term in the Fourth Gospel*. Europäische Hochschulschriften, Reihe 3, No. 475. Frankfurt am Main: Lang, 1993.

Radcliffe, T. "'My Lord and my God': The Locus of Confession." *New Blackfriars* 65 (1984): 52–62.
Randall, J. F. "The Theme of Unity in John 17:20–23." *Ephemerides Theologicae Lovanienses* 41 (1965): 373–94.
Raney, W. H. *The Relation of the Fourth Gospel to the Christian Cultus*. Gießen: Töpelmann, 1933.
Rao, O. M. "Soteriology in the Fourth Gospel." *Bible Bhashyam* 14 (1988): 149–62.
Rayan, S. "Jesus und die Armen im Vierten Evangelium." Pages 81–98 in *Wir werden bei ihm wohnen: Das Johannesevangelium in indischer Deutung*. Edited by George M. Soares-Prabhu. Translated by Ursula Faymonville. Theologie der Dritte Welt 6. Freiburg/Basel: Herder, 1984.
Reim, Günter. *Studien zum alttestamentlichen Hintergrund des Johannesevangeliums*. Society of New Testament Studies Monograph Series 22. Cambridge: Cambridge University Press, 1974.

———. "Jesus as God in the Fourth Gospel: The Old Testament Background." *New Testament Studies* 30 (1984): 158–60.
Reinhartz, Adele. "Jesus as Prophet: Predictive Prolepses in the Fourth Gospel." *Journal for the Study of the New Testament* 36 (1989): 3–16.
Rensberger, David. *Johannine Faith and Liberating Community*. Philadelphia: Westminster Press, 1988.
Reynolds, S. M. "The Supreme Importance of the Doctrine of Election and the Eternal Security of the Elect as Taught in the Gospel of John." *Westminster Theological Journal* 28 (1965): 38–41.
Rhea, Robert. *The Johannine Son of Man*. Abhandlungen zur Theologie des Alten und Neuen Testaments 76. Zürich: Theologischer Verlag, 1990.
Rhodes, S. J. "Christ and the Spirit: Filioque Reconsidered." *Biblical Theology Bulletin* 18 (1988): 91–95.
Richard, Earl. "Expressions of Double Meaning and their Function in the Gospel of John." *New Testament Studies* 31 (1985): 96–112.
Richardson, Alan. *An Introduction to the Theology of the New Testament*. London: SCM Press, 1958.
Richardson, Neil Graham. *Paul's Language about God*. Journal for the Study of the New Testament: Supplement Series 99. Sheffield: Sheffield Academic Press, 1994.
Riches, John. "Recent Developments in Johannine Study." Pages 175–97 in *A Century of New Testament Study*. Valley Forge, Pa.: Trinity Press International, 1993.
Richter, Georg. "Die Fleischwerdung des Logos im Johannesevangelium." *Novum Testamentum* 13/14 (1971/72): 81–126, 257–77.
———. "Präsentische und futurische Eschatologie im 4. Evangelium." Pages 117–52 in *Gegenwart und kommendes Reich: Schülergabe Anton Vögtle zum 65. Geburtstag*. Edited by Peter Fiedler & Dieter Zeller. SBB 6. Stuttgart: Katholisches Bibelwerk, 1975.
Ridderbos, Herman N. "The Structure and Scope of the Prologue to the Gospel of John." *Novum Testamentum* 8 (1966): 180–201.
———. "The Christology of the Fourth Gospel: History and Interpretation." Pages 15–26 in *Saved by Hope: Essays in Honor of Richard C. Oudersluys*. Edited by James I. Cook. Grand Rapids: Eerdmans, 1978.
Riedl, J. "Der Heilige Geist wird Euch in alle Wahrheit einführen (Joh 16,13)." *Bibel & Liturgie* 1 (1971): 89–94.
Riga, P. "Signs of Glory: The Use of 'Semeion' in St. John's Gospel." *Interpretation* 17 (1963): 402–24.
Rissi, Matthias. "Die Logos-Lieder im Prolog des vierten Evangeliums." *Theologische Zeitschrift* 31 (1975): 321–36.
———. "John 1:1–18 (The Eternal Word)." *Interpretation* 31 (1977): 394–401.
———. "Der Aufbau des vierten Evangeliums." *New Testament Studies* 29 (1983): 48–54.
Ritt, Hubert. *Das Gebet zum Vater: Zur Interpretation von Joh 17*. Würzburg: Echter Verlag, 1979.
———. "So sehr hat Gott die Welt geliebt ... (Joh 3,16)." Pages 209–26 in *"Ich will Euer Gott werden": Beispiele biblischen Redens von Gott*. Stuttgarter Bibelstudien 100. Stuttgart: Katholisches Bibelwerk, 1981.

Roberts, J. H. "The Lamb of God." Pages 41–56 in *The Christ of John: Essays on the Christology of the Fourth Gospel*. Proceedings of the Fourth Meeting of Die Nuwe-Testamentiese werkgemeenskap van Suid-Afrika. Potchefstrom, South Africa: Pro Rege Press, 1971.

Roberts, R. L. "The Rendering 'Only Begotten' in John 3.16." *ResQ* 16 (1973): 2–22.

Robertson, P. E. "Glory in the Fourth Gospel." *The Theological Educator* 38 (1988): 121–31.

Robinson, Gesine. "The Trimorphic Protennoia and the Prologue of the Fourth Gospel." Pages 37–50 in *Gnosticism & the Early Christian World: In Honor of James M. Robinson*. Edited by James E. Goehring, Charles W. Hedrick, Jack T. Sanders and Hans Dieter Betz. Sonoma, Calif.: Polebridge Press, 1990.

Robinson, John A.T. "Elijah, John and Jesus: An Essay in Detection." *New Testament Studies* 4 (1957/58): 263–81.

— — —. *The Priority of John*. London: SCM Press, 1985.

Robinson, James M. "The Relation of the Prologue to the Gospel of St John." *New Testament Studies* 9 (1962/63): 120–29.

— — —. "A Formal Analysis of Colossians 1:15–20." *Journal of Biblical Literature* 76 (1957): 270–87.

— — —. "The Coptic Gnostic Library Today." *New Testament Studies* 12 (1968): 372–80.

— — —. "Gnosticism and the New Testament." Pages 125–43 in *Gnosis: Festschrift für Hans Jonas*. Edited by Barbara Aland. Göttingen: Vandenhoeck & Ruprecht, 1978.

— — —. "Sethians and Johannine Thought, the Trimorphic Protennoia and the Prologue of the Gospel of John." Pages 143–62 in *The Rediscovery of Gnosticism*. Vol. 2: *Sethian Gnosticism*. Edited by Bentley Layton. Leiden: E. J. Brill, 1981.

Rodrigo, Michael. "The Hope of Liberation Lessens Man's Inhumanity: A Contribution to Dialogue at Village Level." Pages 189–210 in *Asian Faces of Jesus*. Edited by Rasiah S. Sugirtharajah. London: SCM Press, 1993.

Rose, Martin, ed. *Johannes-Studien: Interdisziplinäre Zugänge zum Johannes-Evangelium. Freundesgabe der Theologischen Fakultät der Universität Neuchâtel für Jean Zumstein*. Publications de la Faculté de Théologie de l'Úniversité de Neuchâtel 6. Neuchâtel: Theologischer Verlag, 1990.

Rowdon, Harold H., ed. *Christ the Lord: Studies in Christology Presented to Donald Guthrie*. Leicester: InterVarsity Press, 1982.

Ruckstuhl, Eugen. *Die literarische Einheit des Johannesevangeliums: Der gegenwärtige Stand der einschlägigen Forschungen*. Freiburg/Schweiz: Paulusverlag, 1951.

— — —. "Und das Wort wurde Fleisch." *Bibel und Leben* 13 (1972): 235–38.

— — —. "Johannine Language and Style: The Question of their Unity." Pages 125–48 in *L'Évangile de Jean*. Edited by Marinus de Jonge. Bibliotheca Ephemeridum Theologicarum Lovaniensium 44. Leuven: Leuven University Press, 1977.

Rudolph, Kurt. "Problems of a History of the Development of Mandaean Religion." *History of Religions* 8 (1969): 210–35.

Russell, Walt. "The Holy Spirit's Ministry in the Fourth Gospel." *Grace Theological Journal* 8 (1987): 227–39.

Sabourin, Léopold. "Who was Begotten . . . of God (Jn 1:13)." *Biblical Theology Bulletin* 6 (1976): 86–90.
Samartha, Stanley J. *One Christ—Many Religions: Towards a Revised Christology.* Maryknoll: Orbis Books, 1991.
Samuel, S. J. "Neither on this Mountain nor in Jerusalem: The Johannine Understanding of Worship." *Bangalore Theological Forum* 19/2 (1987): 121–29.
—— ——. "The Johannine Perspective on Mission in Christ's Praxis." *Bangalore Theological Forum* 20 (1988): 8–16.
Sanders, Joseph N. *The Fourth Gospel in the Early Church.* Cambridge: [s.n.], 1943.
Sanders, Jack T. *The New Testament Christological Hymns: Their Historical Religious Background.* Society of New Testament Studies Monograph Series 15. Cambridge: Cambridge University Press, 1971.
Sandy, D. Brent. "John the Baptist's 'Lamb of God' Affirmation in its Canonical and Apocalyptic Milieu." *Journal of the Evangelical Theological Society* 34 (1991): 447–60.
Schaeder, Hans Heinrich. "Der Mensch im Prolog des vierten Evangeliums." Pages 306–50 in *Studien zum antiken Synkretismus aus Iran und Griechenland.* Hans Heinrich Schaeder and Richard Reitzenstein. Leipzig: Teubner, 1926. Reprint Darmstadt: Wissenschaftliche Buchgesellschaft, 1965.
Schedl, C. "Zur Schreibung von Joh. I:10A in Papyrus Bodmer XV." *Novum Testamentum* 14 (1972): 236–40.
Schelkle, Karl Hermann. *Theologie des Neuen Testaments.* Vol. 2: *Gott war in Christus.* Kommentare und Beiträge zum Alten und Neuen Testament. Düsseldorf: Patmos, 1973.
Schenke, Hans-Martin. "Jakobsbrunnen—Josephsgrab—Sychar. Topographische Untersuchungen und Erwägungen in der Perspektive von Joh 4,5–6." *Zeitschrift des Deutschen Palästina-Vereins* 84 (1968): 158–84.
Schenke, L. "Der Dialog Jesu mit den Juden im Johannesevangelium: ein Rekonstruktionsversuch." *New Testament Studies* 34 (1988): 573–603.
Schlatter, Fredric W. "The Problem of Jn. 1:3b–4a." *The Catholic Biblical Quarterly* 34 (1972): 54–58.
Schmithals, Walter. "Der Prolog des Johannesevangelium." *Zeitschrift für die Neutestamentliche Wissenschaft* 70 (1979): 16–43.
—— ——. *Johannesevangelium und Johannesbriefe.* Beihefte zur Zeitschrift für die Neutestamentliche Wissenschaft 64. Berlin and New York: de Gruyter, 1992.
Schnackenburg, Rudolf. "Das Johannesevangelium als hermeneutische Frage." *New Testament Studies* 13 (1967): 197–210.
—— ——. "Das Anliegen der Abschiedsrede in Joh 14." Pages 95–110 in *Wort Gottes in der Zeit: Festschrift Karl Hermann Schelkle zum 65. Geburtstag.* Edited by Helmut Feld and Josef Nolte. Düsseldorf: Patmos, 1973.
—— ——. "Johannes 14:7." Pages 345–56 in *Studies in New Testament Language and Text: Essays in Honour of George D. Kilpatrick.* Edited by James Keith Elliott. Novum Testamentum Supplements 44. Leiden: E. J. Brill, 1976.
—— ——. "Der Vater, der mich gesandt hat. Zur johanneischen Christologie." Pages 275–91 in *Anfänge der Christologie: Festschrift für Ferdinand Hahn zum 65. Geburtstag.* Edited by Cilliers Breytenbach and Henning Paulsen. Göttingen: Vandenhoeck & Ruprecht, 1991.

———. "Synoptische und johanneische Christologie: ein Vergleich." Pages 1723–50 in vol. 3 of *The Four Gospels, 1992: Festschrift Frans Neirynck*. 3 vols. Edited by Frans van Segbroeck, Christopher M. Tuckett, Gilbert van Belle, and Jozef Verheyden. Bibliotheca Ephemeridum Theologicarum Lovaniensium 100. Leuven: Leuven University Press, 1992..

Schneider, Gerhard. "Auf Gott bezogenes «mein Vater» und «euer Vater» in den Jesus Worten der Evangelien, zugleich ein Beitrag zum Problem Johannes und die Synoptiker." Pages 1751–82 in vol. 3 of *The Four Gospels, 1992: Festschrift Frans Neirynck*. 3 vols. Edited by Frans van Segbroeck, Christopher M. Tuckett, Gilbert van Belle, and Jozef Verheyden. Bibliotheca Ephemeridum Theologicarum Lovaniensium 100. Leuven: Leuven University Press, 1992.

Schneider, Herbert. "The Word was Made Flesh: An Analysis of the Theology of Revelation in the Fourth Gospel." *The Catholic Biblical Quarterly* 31 (1969): 344–56.

Schneiders, Sandra M. "Woman in the Fourth Gospel and the Role of Women in the Contemporary Church." *Biblical Theology Bulletin* 12 (1982): 35–45.

Schnelle, Udo. *Antidoketische Christologie im Johannesevangelium: Eine Untersuchung zur Stellung des 4. Evangeliums in der johanneischen Schule*. Forschungen zur Religion und Literatur des Alten und Neuen Testaments 144. Göttingen: Vandenhoeck & Ruprecht, 1987.

———. "Die Abschiedsreden im Johannesevangelium." *Zeitschrift für die Neutestamentliche Wissenschaft* 80 (1989): 64–79.

Schoonenberg, Piet. "A Sapiential Reading of John's Prologue." *Theology Digest* 33 (1986): 403–21.

———. "Spirit Christology and Logos Christology." *Bijdragen* 38 (1977): 350–75.

Schuchard, Bruce G. *Scripture within Scripture: The Interrelationship of Form and Function in the Explicit Old Testament Citations in the Gospel of John*. Society of Biblical Literature Dissertation Series 133. Atlanta: Scholars Press, 1992.

Schuessler Fiorenza, Elisabeth S. "Wisdom, Mythology and Christological Hymns of the New Testament." Pages 17–41 in *Aspects of Wisdom in Judaism and Early Christianity*. Edited by Robert Louis Wilken. Studies in Judaism and Christianity in Antiquity 1. Notre Dame: University of Notre Dame Press, 1975.

Schultz, N. "St Paul Describes the Spirit as Arrabon: Would St. Luke and St. John have Agreed?" *Lutheran Theological Journal* 11 (1977): 112–21.

Schulz, Siegfried. *Untersuchungen zur Menschensohn-Christologie im Johannesevangelium: Zugleich ein Beitrag zur Methodengeschichte der Auslegung des 4. Evangeliums*. Göttingen: Vandenhoeck & Ruprecht, 1957.

———. *Komposition und Herkunft der Johanneischen Reden*. Beiträge zur Wissenschaft vom Alten und Neuen Testament 5. Stuttgart: Kohlhammer, 1960.

Schwank, Benedikt. "Das Christusbild im zweiten Teil des Johannesevangeliums (XXII)." *Sein und Sendung* 29 (1964): 435–50.

Schwarz, G. "Genesis 1:1, 2, 2a und Joh 1:1, 1a, 3a: ein Vergleich." *Zeitschrift für die Neutestamentliche Wissenschaft* 73 (1982): 136–37.

Schweizer, Eduard. *Ego Eimi: Die religionsgeschichtliche Herkunft und theologische Bedeutung der johanneischen Bildreden. Zugleich ein Beitrag zur Quellenfrage des vierten Evangeliums*. Forschungen zur Religion und Literatur des Alten und Neuen Testaments 56. Göttingen: Vandenhoeck & Ruprecht, 1939.

———. "Zum religionsgeschichtlichen Hintergrund der Sendungsformel. Joh.3:16." *Zeitschrift für die Neutestamentliche Wissenschaft* 57 (1966): 199–210.

———. "Jesus der Zeuge Gottes." Pages 161–68 in *Studies in John: Presented to J. N. Sevenster on the Occasion of his Seventieth Birthday*. Edited by M. C. Rientsma, et al. Novum Testamentum Supplements 24. Leiden: E. J. Brill, 1970.

Scobie, Charles H. H. "The Origins and Development of Samaritan Christianity." *New Testament Studies* 19 (1973): 390–414.

Scott, Martin. *Sophia and the Johannine Jesus*. Journal for the Study of the New Testament: Supplement Series 71. Sheffield: JSOT Press, 1992.

Scouteris, Constantine. "The People of God—its Unity and its Glory: A Discussion of John 17.17–24 in the Light of Patristic Thought." *Greek Orthodox Theological Review* 30 (1985): 399–420.

Scroggs, Robin. *Christology in Paul and John: The Reality and Revelation of God*. Philadelphia: Fortress, 1988.

Segovia, Fernando F., ed. *"What is John?"* Vol. II: *Literary and Social Readings of the Fourth Gospel*. Society of Biblical Literature, Symposium Series 7. Atlanta: Scholars Press, 1998.

Segovia, Fernando F. *Love Relationships in the Johannine Tradition: Agape/Agapan in 1 John and the Fourth Gospel*. Society of Biblical Literature, Dissertation Series 58. Chico, Calif.: Scholars Press, 1982.

———. "John 15:18–16:4a: A First Addition to the Original Farewell Discourse?" *The Catholic Biblical Quarterly* 45 (1983): 210–30.

———. "The Structure, Tendenz, and Sitz im Leben of John 13:31–14:31." *Journal of Biblical Literature* 104 (1985): 471–93.

———. *The Farewell of the Word: The Johannine Call to Abide*. Minneapolis: Fortress, 1991.

Sevenster, G. "Remarks on the Humanity of Jesus in the Gospel and Letters of John." Pages 85–93 in *Studies in John: Presented to J. N. Sevenster on the Occasion of his Seventieth Birthday*. Edited by M. C. Rientsma, et al. Novum Testamentum Supplements 24. Leiden: E. J. Brill, 1970.

Silva, Moisés. "Approaching the Fourth Gospel." *Criswell Theological Review* 3 (1988): 17–29.

Simmons, B. E. "A Christology of the 'I Am' Sayings in the Gospel of John." *The Theological Educator* 38 (1988): 94–103.

Skedros, James C. "The Works of Jesus: A Study of John 10:22–39." *Delton Biblikon* 10 (1991): 51–57.

Slater, Thomas Bowie. "The Paraclete as Advocate in the Community of the Beloved Disciple." *African Theological Journal* 20 (1991): 101–108.

Sloan, Robert B. "The Absence of Jesus in John." Pages 207–28 in *Perspectives on John: Method and Interpretation in the Fourth Gospel*. Edited by Robert B. Sloan and Mikeal C. Parsons. Lewiston, N. Y.: Edwin Mellen Press, 1993.

Sloyan, Gerard S. *What are they Saying about John?* New York: Paulist Press, 1991.

Smalley, Stephen S. *John: Evangelist and Interpreter*. Exeter: The Paternoster Press, 1978.

Smith, Dwight Moody. *The Composition and Order of the Fourth Gospel: Bultmann's Literary Theory.* New Haven: Yale University Press, 1965.
— — —. "John 16:1-15." *Interpretation* 33 (1979): 58-62.
— — —. *Johannine Christianity: Essays on its Setting, Sources, and Theology.* Columbia, S. C.: University of South Carolina Press, 1984.
— — —. "The Contribution of J.Louis Martyn to the Understanding of the Gospel of John." Pages 275-94 in *The Conversation Continues: Studies in Paul and John in Honor of J. Louis Martyn.* Edited by Robert T. Fortna and Beverly R. Gaventa. Nashville: Abingdon, 1990.
— — —. *The Theology of the Gospel of John.* New Testament Theology. Cambridge: Cambridge University Press, 1995.
— — —. *John among the Gospels: The Relationship in Twentieth-Century Research.* 2nd edition. Columbia, S. C.: University of South Carolina Press, 2001.
Smith, M. D. "The Life Setting of the Gospel of John." *Review and Expositor* 85 (1988): 433-44.
Smith, Taylor Clarence. *Jesus in the Gospel of John.* Nashville, Tenn.: Broadman Press, 1959.
Smothers, Edgar Raymond. "Two Readings in Papyrus Bodmer II." *Harvard Theological Review* 51 (1958): 109-22.
Snodgrass, Klyne R. "That Which is Born From ΠΝΕΥΜΑ is ΠΝΕΥΜΑ: Rebirth and Spirit in John 3:5-6." Pages 181-206 in *Perspectives on John: Method and Interpretation in the Fourth Gospel.* Edited by Robert B. Sloan and Mikeal C. Parsons. Lewiston, N. Y.: Edwin Mellen Press, 1993.
Soards, Marion L. "The Psalter in the Text and the Thought of the Fourth Gospel." Pages 251-68 in *Perspectives on John: Method and Interpretation in the Fourth Gospel.* Edited by Robert B. Sloan and Mikeal C. Parsons. Lewiston, N. Y.: Edwin Mellen Press, 1993.
Soares-Prabhu, George M., ed. *Wir werden bei ihm wohnen: Das Johannesevangelium in indischer Deutung.* Translated by Ursula Faymonville. Theologie der Dritte Welt 6. Freiburg/Basel: Herder, 1984.
Söding, Thomas. "War Jesus wirklich Gottes Sohn? Die neue Debatte um Jesus und die Christologie." *Zeitschrift für Neues Testament* 4 (2001): 2-13.
— — —. "Die Wahrheit des Evangeliums: Anmerkungen zur johanneischen Hermeneutik." *Ephemerides Theologicae Lovanienses* 77 (2001): 318-55.
Song, C. S. "Oh, Jesus, Hear with Us!" Pages 131-48 in *Asian Faces of Jesus.* Edited by Rasiah S. Sugirtharajah. London: SCM Press, 1993.
Spielmann, Kent. "Participant Reference and Definite Article in John." *Journal of Translation and Textlinguistics* 7 (1995): 45-85.
Spiro, Abram. "Stephen's Samaritan Background," in Johannes Munck, *The Acts of the Apostles* (Anchor Bible 31; New York: Doubleday, 1967), 285-300.
Sproston, Wendy E. "'Is Not This Jesus, the Son of Joseph...?' (John 6,42) Johannine Christology as a Challenge to Faith." *Journal for the Study of the New Testament* 24 (1985): 77-97.
Stenger, Werner. "Δικαιοσύνη in Joh 16,8.10." *Novum Testamentum* 21 (1979): 2-12.
Stevens, C. T. "The 'I Am' Formula in the Gospel of John." *Studia Biblica et Theologica* 7 (1977): 19-30.

Stibbe, Mark W. G. '"Return to Sender": A Structuralist Approach to John's Gospel." *Biblical Interpretation* 1 (1993): 189–206.

Strack, Hermann Leberecht, and Paul Billerbeck. *Kommentar zum Neuen Testament aus Talmud und Midrasch*. 7 vols. Munich: C. H. Beck, 1922–1961.

Sturch, R. L. "Can one say 'Jesus is God'?" Pages 326–40 in *Christ the Lord: Studies in Christology Presented to Donald Guthrie*. Edited by Harold H. Rowdon. Leicester: InterVarsity Press, 1982.

Suggit, John N. "Exegesis: The Eucharistic Significance of John 20.19–29." *Journal of Theology for Southern Africa* 16 (1976): 52–59.

― ― ―. *The Sign of Life: Studies in the Fourth Gospel and the Liturgy of the Church*. Pietermaritzburg, South Africa: Cluster Publications, 1993.

― ― ―. "John 13–17 Viewed through Liturgical Spectacles." *Neotestamentica* 26 (1992): 47–58.

Sugirtharajah, Rasiah S. "Reconceiving Jesus: Some Continuing Concerns." Pages 258–67 in *Asian Faces of Jesus*. Edited by Rasiah S. Sugirtharajah. London: SCM Press, 1993.

Sundberg Jr, Albert C. "Isos to Theo Christology in John 5:17–30." *Papers of the Chicago Society of Biblical Research* 15 (1970): 19–31.

Swetnam, James. "The meaning of πεπιστευκότας in John 8:31." *Biblica* 61 (1980): 106–109.

Talbert, Charles H. "The Myth of a Descending-Ascending Redeemer in Mediterranean Antiquity." *New Testament Studies* 22 (1976): 418–40.

― ― ―. "Worship in the Fourth Gospel and in its Milieu." Pages 337–56 in *Perspectives on John: Method and Interpretation in the Fourth Gospel*. Edited by Robert B. Sloan and Mikeal C. Parsons. Lewiston, N. Y.: Edwin Mellen Press, 1993.

Taylor, J. "The Johannine Discourses and the Speech of Jesus, Five Views." *Scripture Bulletin* 14 (1984): 33–41.

Thangasamy, D. A. *The Theology of Chenchiah with Selections from his Writings*. Bangalore: Christian Institute for the Study of Religion and Society, 1966.

Theobald, Michael. *Im Anfang war das Wort: Textlinguistische Studie zum Johannesprolog*. Stuttgarter Bibelstudien 106. Stuttgart: Katholisches Bibelwerk, 1983.

― ― ―. *Die Fleischwerdung des Logos: Studien zum Verhältnis des Johannesprologs zum Corpus des Evangeliums und zu 1Joh*. Neutestamentliche Abhandlungen, Neue Folge 20. Münster: Aschendorff, 1988.

Theron, S. W. "ἵνα ὦσιν: A Multifaceted Approach to an Important Thrust in the Prayer of Jesus in John 17." *Neotestamentica* 21 (1987): 77–94.

Thomas, Madathilparampil M. *The Acknowledged Christ of the Indian Renaissance*. London: SCM Press, 1969.

Thompson, Marianne Meye. *The Humanity of Jesus in the Fourth Gospel*. Philadelphia: Fortress, 1988.

― ― ―. "Signs and Faith in the Fourth Gospel." *Bulletin for Biblical Research* 1 (1991): 89–108.

― ― ―. "God's Voice You Have Never Heard, God's Form You Have Never Seen: The Characterization of God in the Gospel of John." *Semeia* 63 (1993): 177–204.

Thurmer, John A. "The Analogy of the Trinity." *Scottish Journal of Theology* 34 (1981): 509–15.

— — —. *The Son in the Bible and the Church*. Exeter: Paternoster, 1987.

Thüsing, Wilhelm. *Die Erhöhung und Verherrlichung Jesu im Johannesevangelium*. 3rd edition. Neutestamentliche Abhandlungen 21/1–2. Münster: Aschendorff, 1979.

Thyen, Hartwig. "Aus der Literatur zum Johannesevangelium." *Theologische Rundschau* 39 (1974): 1–69, 222–52, 289–330; 42 (1977): 211–79; 43 (1978): 328–59; 44 (1979): 97–134.

Tobin, Thomas H. "The Prologue of John and Hellenistic Jewish Speculation: A Comparative Study." *The Catholic Biblical Quarterly* 52 (1990): 252–69.

Tolmie, D. François. "The Function of Focalisation in John 13–17." *Neotestamentica* 25 (1991): 273–87.

— — —. "A Discourse Analysis of John 17:1–26." *Neotestamentica* 27 (1993): 403–18.

Trumbower, Jeffrey A. *Born from Above: The Anthropology of the Gospel of John*. Hermeneutische Untersuchungen zur Theologie 29. Tübingen: J. C. B. Mohr (Paul Siebeck), 1992.

Tsuchido, Kiyoshi. "Tradition and Redaction in John 8:12–30." *Annual of the Japanese Biblical Institute* 6 (1980): 56–75.

Turner, George Allen. "Soteriology in the Gospel of John." *Journal of the Evangelical Theological Society* 14 (1976): 271–77.

Turner, M., and Gary M. Burge. "The Anointed Community: A Review and Response." *Evangelical Quarterly* 62 (1990): 253–68.

Ukpong, J. S. "Jesus' Prayer for his Followers (Jn. 17) in Mission Perspective." *Africa Theological Journal* 18 (1989): 49–60.

Untergaßmair, Franz Georg. *Im Namen Jesu: Der Namensbegriff im Johannesevangelium. Eine exegetisch-religionsgeschichtliche Studie zu den johanneischen Namensaussagen*. FB 13. Stuttgart: Katholisches Bibelwerk, 1973.

Uprichard, H. "God's Glory in God's Son."*Evangel* 2 (1984): 5–6.

Urban, L., and P. Henry. "Before Abraham was I am: Does Philo Explain John 8:56–58?" *Studia Philonica* 6 (1979/80): 157–95.

van Belle, Gilbert. *The Signs Source in the Fourth Gospel: Historical Survey and Critical Evaluation of the Semeia Hypothesis*. Bibliotheca Ephemeridum Theologicarum Lovaniensium 116. Leuven: Leuven University Press, 1994.

van Boxel, P. "Die präexistente DOXA Jesu im Johannesevangelium." *Bijdragen* 34 (1973): 268–81.

van der Slijs, P. "John 14:23–29." *Clergy Review* 56 (1971): 381–93.

van der Waal, Cornelis. "The Gospel According to John and the Old Testament." *Neotestamentica* 6 (1972): 28–47.

van der Watt, Jan Gabriël. "A New Look at John 5:25–9 in the Light of the Use of the Term 'Eternal Life' in the Gospel According to John." *Neotestamentica* 19 (1985): 71–86.

Vawter, Bruce. "John's Doctrine of the Spirit: A Summary View of his Eschatology." Pages 177–86 in *A Companion to John: Readings in Johannine Theology (John's Gospel and Epistles)*. Edited by Michael J. Taylor. New York: Alba House, 1977.

Vellanickal, Matthew. *The Divine Sonship of Christians in the Johannine Writings.* Analecta Biblica 72. Rome: Biblical Institute Press, 1977.

———. "The Johannine Concept of Righteousness or Dharma." *Bible Bhashyam* 6 (1980): 382–94.

———. "Discipleship According to the Gospel of John." *Jeevadhara* 10 (1980): 131–47.

———. "Die Kirche im Dialog mit den religiösen und kulturellen Traditionen im Umfeld des Johannesevangeliums." Pages 48–70 in *Wir werden bei ihm wohnen: Das Johannesevangelium in indischer Deutung.* Edited by George M. Soares-Prabhu. Translated by Ursula Faymonville. Theologie der Dritte Welt 6. Freiburg/Basel: Herder, 1984.

———. "St. John and the Advaitic Experience of the Upanishads." *Bible Bhashyam* 11 (1985): 68–94.

———. "Man in the Johanine Writings." *Jeevadhara* 16 (1986): 138–48.

Vermes, Geza. *The Religion of Jesus the Jew.* London: SCM Press, 1993.

Vouga, François. "The Johannine School: A Gnostic Tradition in Primitive Christianity?" *Biblica* 88 (1988): 371–85.

———. "Antijudaismus im Johannesevangelium?" *Theologie und Glaube* 83 (1993): 81–89.

Wahlde, Urban C. von. "The Johannine 'Jews': A Critical Survey." *New Testament Studies* 28 (1982): 33–60.

———. *The Earliest Version of John's Gospel: Recovering the Gospel of Signs.* Wilmington, Del.: Michael Glazier, 1989.

Watson, F. "Is John's Christology Adoptionist?" Pages 113–24 in *The Glory of Christ in the New Testament: Studies in Christology in Memory of George Bradford Caird.* Edited by Lincoln D. Hurst and Nicholas T. Wright. Oxford: Clarendon Press, 1987.

Wead, David W. "The Johannine Double Meaning." *Restoration Quarterly* 13 (1970): 106–20.

———. *The Literary Devices in John's Gospel.* Theologische Dissertationen 4. Basel: Friedrich Reinhart Kommissionsverlag, 1970.

Weiser, Alfons. *Theologie des Neuen Testaments: Die Theologie der Evangelien.* Stuttgart: Kohlhammer, 1993.

Wendland, Ernst R. "Rhetoric of the Word: An Interactional Discourse Analysis of the Lord's Prayer of John 17 and its Communicative Implications." *Neotestamentica* 26 (1992): 59–88.

Wengst, Klaus. *Bedrängte Gemeinde und verherrlichter Christus.* 3rd edition. Munich: Kaiser, 1990.

Whitacre, Rodney A. *Johannine Polemic: The Role of Tradition and Theology.* Society of Biblical Literature Dissertation Series 67. Chico, Calif.: Scholars Press, 1982.

Whittaker, John. "A Hellenistic Context for John 10,29." *Vigiliae Christianae* 24 (1970): 241–60.

Wieser, Thomas. "Community—Its Unity, Diversity and Universality." *Semeia* 33 (1985): 83–95.

Wijngaards, John. *The Spirit in John*. Zacchaeus Studies, New Testament. Wilmington, Del.: Glazier, 1988.
Wilckens, Ulrich. "Der Paraklet und die Kirche." Pages 185–203 in *Kirche: Festschrift für Günther Bornkamm zum 75. Geburtstag*. Edited by Dieter Lührmann and Georg Strecker. Tübingen: J. C. B. Mohr (Paul Siebeck), 1980.
Wiles, Maurice F. *The Spiritual Gospel: The Interpretation of the Fourth Gospel in the Early Church*. Cambridge: Cambridge University Press, 1960.
Wilkens, Wilhelm. *Die Entstehungsgeschichte des vierten Evangeliums*. Zollikon: Evangelischer Verlag, 1958.
— — —. *Zeichen und Werke: Ein Beitrag zur Theologie des 4. Evangeliums in Erzählungs- und Redestoff*. Abhandlungen zur Theologie des Alten und Neuen Testaments 55. Zürich: Zwingli-Verlag, 1969.
Wilson, Jeffrey. "The Integrity of John 3:22–36." *Journal for the Study of the New Testament* 10 (1981): 34–41.
Wilson, M. P. "St John, the Trinity, and the Language of the Spirit." *Scottish Journal of Theology* 41 (1988): 471–83.
Wilson, Robert McLaughlin. "The Trimorphic Protennoia." Pages 50–54 in *Gnosis and Gnosticism*. Edited by Martin Krause. Nag Hammadi Studies 17. Leiden: E. J. Brill, 1977.
Wilson, S. "Anti-Judaism in the Fourth Gospel?" *Irish Biblical Studies* 1 (1979): 28–50.
Wind, A. "Destination and Purpose of the Gospel of John." *Novum Testamentum* 14 (1972): 26–69.
Winter, Martin. *Das Vermächtnis Jesu und die Abschiedsworte der Väter: Gattungsgeschichtliche Untersuchung der Vermächtnisrede im Blick auf Joh. 13–17*. Forschungen zur Religion und Literatur des Alten und Neuen Testaments 161. Göttingen: Vandenhoeck & Ruprecht, 1994.
Witherington, Ben. "The Water of Birth: John 3:5." *New Testament Studies* 35 (1989): 155–60.
Witkamp, L. Th. "The Use of Traditions in John 5:1–18." *Journal for the Study of the New Testament* 25 (1985): 19–47.
Woll, D. Bruce. "The Departure of 'The Way': The First Farewell Discourse in the Gospel of John." *Journal of Biblical Literature* 99 (1980): 225–39.
— — —. *Johannine Christianity in Conflict: Authority, Rank, and Succession in the First Farewell Discourse*. Society of Biblical Literature Dissertation Series 60. Chico, Calif.: Scholars Press, 1981.
— — —. "The Logos Concept in the Prologue to the Gospel According to John." *The Theological Educator* 38 (1988): 85–93.
Wright, Nicholas Thomas. *The New Testament and the People of God*. London: S.P.C.K., 1992.

Xavier, A. "John's Gospel in the Indian Context." *Indian Journal of Theology* 21 (1984): 347–65.

Yagi, Seiichi. "Christ and Buddha." Pages 25–45 in *Asian Faces of Jesus*. Edited by Rasiah S. Sugirtharajah. London: SCM Press, 1993.

Yamauchi, Edwin M. "Jewish Gnosticism? The Prologue of John, Mandaean Parallels and the Trimorphic Protennoia." Pages 467–97 in *Studies in Gnosticism and Hellenistic Religions: Presented to Gilles Quispel on the Occasion of his 65th Birthday*. Edited by Roelof van den Broek and Marten Jozef Vermaseren. Études préliminaires aux religions orientales dans l'empire romain 91. Leiden: E. J. Brill, 1981.

Zeron, A. "Einige Bemerkungen zu M. F. Collins 'The Hidden Vessels in Samaritan Traditions'." *Journal for the Study of Judaism* 4 (1973): 165–68.

Zimmermann, Heinrich. "Struktur und Aussageabsicht der johanneischen Abschiedsreden (Jo 13–17)." *Bibel und Leben* 8 (1967): 279–90.

– – –. "Christushymnus und Johanneischer Prolog." Pages 249–65 in *Neues Testament und Kirche: Für Rudolf Schnackenburg*. Edited by Joachim Gnilka. Freiburg/Basel: Herder, 1974.

Zwaan, Johannes de. "John wrote in Aramaic." *JBL* 57 (1938): 155–71.

Select Index of References

1. Old Testament/Hebrew Bible

Genesis
1:1–5	159
1:1	167
2:2	53
3:5, 22	58
15:17–21	111
17	111
18	111
19:19	202
22	111
22:2, 12, 16	200
30:22	65n50
33:2	198
33:19	234
47:29–30	202
49:10	245

Exodus
2:24	262
3:6	183
3:14ff.	140
3:14	114
4:16	58
6:5	262
7:1	58
12:1	125
12:3–5	27
12:5, 6	21
12:6	26
12:10	23
12:22	22
12:36	24
12:46	23
13:2	143
13:21–22	85
14:19–25	85
15:1, 6, 11, 21	198
17:2	235
20:11	53
23:21	180n76
25:8ff.	197
28:41	143
31:17	53
33–34	202n139
33:7	197
34:6	138, 202
40:13	143

Leviticus
8:30	143
12:3	55
14:6–7	22
14:57	215
26:42	262

Numbers
9:12	23, 24, 26
11	227
14:22	98
15:39–40	262
16:28	61
19:6	22
21:4–9	227
21:16	235
24:17	32n51

Deuteronomy
1:15–18	125
5:26	70
7:9	203
8:2	262
18:15	257
18:18	249n45
28:12	65n50
32	133
33	133

Joshua
2:12–14	202
24	246
24:14	246n44
24:15	246n44
24:33	233

Ruth
2:15	202
3:10	202

1 Samuel
2:6	65n50
20:8, 14–15	202

2 Samuel
7:14	203, 221
9:1, 3, 7	202

2 Kings

5:7	65n50
17:24ff.	240n30
17:34–41	246
17:34	242, 243

1 Chronicles

22:8	125
29:1	57
29:28	198

2 Chronicles

5:11	143
6:14	203

Esther

2:9	203

Job

1:21	228
10:41	196n123
12:8	215
23:29	142n29
28	164
28:27	215

Psalms

2	42
2:7	221
5:3	26
7:9–11	109
8:2, 10	180n76
8:23, 30	139
14:7, 15–18	181
20:2	180n76
22:21	200
23	122
24:8	198
25:4–5	270
27:1	85
27:2, 13	20
33:6, 9	181
34 LXX	24
34:21 LXX	23
34:23	16
34:27c	16
35 (36):10	164
35:17	200
35:22–28	109
36:9	70
42:2	70
42:12	246
43:4	246
44:3	85
50:9	22
56:10, 14	20
78:21	227
78:39	196n123
80:1–7, 14–19	85
82	128–29
82:6	58, 123, 126, 127n24, 129
89	203
89:27	221
90:2	114
104:2	183
105:8	262
105 (106):24–25	164
106:45	262
116:13	20n26
118 (119):89	164
119:105	183
143:10	270
148:5	181

Proverbs

1:20–30	189
3:19	181
4:3	200
4:13	182
6:23	183
8:21	164
8:23	173
8:27–30	181
8:31	164
8:32–35	182
15:12	266
20:27	86
30:4	226

Ecclesiastes

11:5; 16:21	226

Isaiah

6	143
6:1–2	198
8:7	198
11:3a–4	266
12:37–41	111
14:12–21	58
16:14	198
26:9	183
26:19	65n50
30:27	180n76
37:20	138
38:17	29
40:26	181
42:1	57
42:6, 9	270
43:10	88
43:11–13	115
45:7	164
46:4	115
47:8, 10	58
48:3	181
48:12	115
52:6	140
52:13	198
53	26, 27
53:3	32
53:7–8	25
53:7	26, 27
53:10ff.	27
55:12	142n29
60:19–22	86
60:19–20	183

Jeremiah		37:7	197	Amos	
1:4	125	39:7	140	8:10	200
1:5	143	43:7	164, 197		
1:11	125				
5:1	99	Daniel		Micah	
6:26	200			1:1	125
10:10	70, 99	7,13ff.	73	5:1–3	122
14:14	187	7:13	72	6	267
17:4	196n123	7:14	72		
19:14	187	8	28		
24:7	137	10:21	100	Habakuk	
31:33–34	137, 260	12:2	65n50	1:12	266
				2:14	137
		Hosea		3:3–4	85
Ezekiel		1:1	125		
1:4	85	2:2, 7, 16	238	Zechariah	
3:26–28	85	2:25	15	1:1	125
6:1	125	4:1	203	6	31
16:60	262	6:2	65n50	6:12	31, 32n51
17:1	125			9:9	197
31:1	125			12:10	200
34	28	Joel		14:5b–7	86
34:23–24	122	4:17	197		
36:25–36	223				
37:1–14	65n50				

2. Deuterocanonical Writings and Septuagint

Baruch		1 Maccabees		Odae	
3:9–4:4	164	1:54	117	11:17	29
3:20–21	189				
3:31, 37	189	2 Maccabees		Sirach	
4:1	182	6:1–7	117	4:10	222
4:2	183	14:36	141	4:12	182
				7:33	203
2 Esdras				18:13; 19:14	266
4:5–11	226	3 Maccabees		23:1, 4	222
5:26	28	2:2	141	24	164
6:58	200	6:27, 37	190	24:8	197
		7:8	190	24:10	197

26:15	206n152	3:9	100	9:9–18	189
40:17	203	5:5	222	9:9	181
50:25–26	244	6:12–11:1	164	9:10	139
		6:18–19	182	10:9–10	155
		7:12	181	11:8	155
Tobit		7:25	139	12:2	266
3:15; 6:14	200	8:4–6	56	15:3	137
		8:4	181	16:20	227
		8:4b	57	18:4	183
Wisdom of Solomon		9:1–4	155	19:9	28
2:13, 16, 18	222	9:1	181		

3. Old Testament Pseudepigrapha

2 Baruch
48   133

1 Enoch
5:9   142n29
37–41   65n51
38:1   29
42   164
42:2   189
46:4   29
49:4   65n51
61:9   65n51
62   73n68
62:2ff.   65n51
63:11   65n51
69:27   65n51
85–90   28n44
89:41–50   28n44

3 Enoch
10:4–5   62
11:1–3   62
16:1   62

4 Ezra
8:19b–36   133

Jubilees
1:19–21   133
1:23–25   224
2:1   164
10:3–6   133
20–22   133
36:11   133

Odes of Solomon
41:16   140
42:20   140

Psalms of Solomon
8:23   28
17:20–21   29
17:30   29, 222
18:4   200

Pseudo–Philo
Liber antiquitatum biblicarum
19:8   133
24:3   133

Testaments of the Twelve Patriarchs 184
Testament of Benjamin
3:8   28
5:3   184n88

Testament of Gad
5:7   184n88

Testament of Levi
4:3   184n88
7   244
18:3–4   184n88
18:9   29
19:1   184n88

Testament of Joseph
19:8–11   28

4. New Testament

Matthew

10:6	231
10:22	137
11:2ff.	205
12:18	57
16:16	42n82
18:3	222
18:15	266
25	77n78
27:46	38
27:50	38
28:17	13

Mark

2:1–12	51n22
2:23–3:6	53n27
10:15	222
12:1–9	201
14:24	144n36
15:34	38
15:37	38

Luke

7:18ff.	205
9:51–56	231
9:52–56	252n56
10:22	137
10:33–37	252n56
12:11–12	264
17:11, 19	252n56
18:17	222
22:19	144n36
23:46	38
24:11, 21ff.	13
24:37–38	13
24:39–41	14

John

1:1–18	151–217
1:1–8	158
1:1–5	159, 163, 186
1:1–2	96
1:1	18, 113, 115, 173–79
1:2	179–80
1:3–5	180–86
1:3	180–82
1:4	182–83
1:5	183–86
1:6–18	159
1:6–8	157, 162, 163, 186–87
1:9–13	158, 174n50, 187–94
1:9	187–88
1:10–13	160
1:10	188–89
1:11	153n7, 189–91
1:12–13	160, 163
1:12	153n7, 191–94
1:12c–13	157
1:13	160, 194
1:14–18	158, 160n32, 162, 194–215
1:14	96, 163, 173, 174n50, 175, 194–204, 259, 279
1:15	157, 162, 163, 204–206
1:16	206–207
1:17	203, 207–208
1:18	18, 174, 201, 208–215, 275
1:29	25, 26
1:30	205
1:31–34	205
1:36	25, 26
1:49	36
1:50–51	36
1:51	34, 74n73, 281
2:13	25
2:17	262
2:19–22	25
2:22	262
3:1–21	219–30
3:3–6	221–25
3:7–8	225–26
3:9–15	226–27
3:16–17	227–29
3:16	67, 69, 189, 199, 201, 210, 277, 284
3:18–21	229
3:18	201, 210
3:19	185
3:30	206
3:36	67, 69
4	37, 287
4:1–42	231–54, 277
4:5–6	233–35
4:7–15	235–37
4:16–26	238–51
4:16, 17–18	238
4:18	243n37
4:19	241
4:20	241–43
4:21	243–44
4:22	244–45
4:23–24	246–48
4:24	197, 275
4:25	248–50
4:26	250–51, 283
4:27–38	251–53
4:31–34	234n12
4:39–42	253
4:46–5:9	67, 69
5	46
5:1–6	64
5:9b–18	47
5:12	31
5:16	51
5:17–30	45–80
5:17–18	52–59
5:17	18, 51
5:18	31

5:19–30	59–79	8:31	110, 115	13:19	91, 283
5:19–25	49	8:35–36	107	13:20	278, 283
5:19–20	59–64	8:37–47	107–108	13:31–16:33	255–56
5:19–20a	48, 49	8:40	33	13:34	33
5:21ff.	64	8:45–46, 47	33	14:5	14
5:21–29	49	8:48–59	108–115	14:6	258
5:21–22	64–67	8:48–50	108–109	14:9	40
5:21	110	8:51–55	110–11	14:16–17	256–60
5:23	67–68, 109, 280	8:56–57	111–13	14:16	14
5:24–25	67, 69–70	8:58–59	113–15	14:26	260–63, 269, 270
5:24	48, 280	8:58	283	14:29	41
5:26–30	49	9	287	15:13	144
5:26	70–71, 183	9:11, 16, 24, 29, 33	31	15:26	264–66
5:27	71–74	10:3	33	16:2	264
5:28–29	49, 73, 74–79	10:10	123, 284	16:7–8	30
5:28, 29	48	10:11, 15	144	16:7b–8	266–68
5:30	79, 280	10:16	33	16:9	267
5:44	138	10:18	38	16:10–11	268–69
6	46	10:22–39	117–31	16:12–13	269–272
6:4	25	10:22–30	118–23	16:33	70
6:14–15	37	10:22–24	118	17:1–26	133–49
6:39	20	10:24–30	119–23	17:1–5	134–39
6:51	25, 144	10:24	42	17:5ff.	147
6:54	27	10:27	33	17:6–10	139–41
6:69	144	10:29a	120–21n11	17:11–15	141–43
7:7	33	10:31–39	123–30	17:12	20
7:15–8:59	81–82	10:31–33	123	17:14ff.	70
7:22–24	55	10:31	115	17:16–19	143–45
7:27	42	10:33	18, 31	17:20–23	145–48
7:31	42	10:34–36	123–30	17:23b–26	148
7:37–38	85, 86	10:36	70, 144	18:4–9	19
7:42–52	219	11:4	70	18:5	21, 283
7:42	42	11:15, 40	41	18:6	21
8:12–59	81–116	11:47	31	18:8	21, 283
8:12–20	84–89	11:48	242	18:9–11	20
8:12	185	11:50–53, 55	25	18:11	21
8:18	282	12:16	262	18:20–23	26
8:21–30	89–98	12:20–26	277	18:27	31
8:21–22	89	12:20	25, 287	18:31	124
8:23	32n53, 90, 275, 282	12:24	25, 33	18:33–38	30
8:24	91–92	12:32	97	18:33	32
8:25–27	92–94	12:35, 46	185	18:34–38	32
8:28–30	94–98	13:1ff.	199	18:34–37	26
8:28	282, 283	13:12–17	199	18:36	34
8:31–34	98–107	13:13–17	33	18:37	33

Deuterocanonical Writings and Septuagint

18:38	21, 34
19:4	21
19:5	30, 31–34
19:6	21, 30
19:9–11	30
19:14	21, 30, 35–37
19:15	30
19:27, 28	38
19:29	22
19:31–32	23
19:34	24
19:34a	14
19:36	23, 24
20:8	40
20:19–29	15
20:19–23	14
20:19	15
20:20	40
20:21, 22, 23	15
20:25	14
20:26	15
20:27	17
20:28	15, 18
20:29	15, 39, 40n72
20:30–31	19, 39–43
20:31	70

Acts
1:8	252n56
2	242
7:15ff.	234n8
8	252n56
8:9ff.	240
8:32	25
9:31	252n56

Romans
3:25	200
8:3	201, 221
8:32	200
11:36	181
14:17	142n29

1 Corinthians
1:16	181
3:8	120
11:24–25	262
11:24	144n36
12:29–30	271
13:12	137
14:24	266

Galatians
4:4	201
4:25	221
5:22	142n29

Ephesians
1:13	260

Philippians
2:5–11	109
2:6ff.	58n40
2:6–11	139, 151
2:7	135, 196

Colossians
1:15–20	151
1:16	181

1 Timothy
1:17	138
3:16	151, 196
6,15–16	138

1 Peter
1:18–19	26
3:18–20	151

2 Peter
1:12–13	262

1 John
1:5	248
1:6, 8, 10	289
2:1	257
2:9	288
2:15	289
2:27	261
2:28	49n14
2:29	221
3:2	49n14
3:5, 8	29
3:9	221, 290
4:1–3	289
4:5	288
4:6	289
4:7	221
4:8–10	290
4:8	248
4:9	210
4:17	49n14
4:20	290
5:1	221, 289
5:4	221
5:5–7	289
5:18	221, 290

Hebrews
1:2–5	151
1:2	181
11:17	200

Jude
5	262

Revelation
6:10	138

5. Dead Sea Scrolls

1QS			VIII, 9–10	247	VI, 25	247
III, 20–21, 25		184n90	IX, 6–7	247	XI, 7, 8–9	247
IV, 2–12		184n90	IX, 26	184n90	XI, 10–14	224
IV, 19–21		224	X, 17	247	XIV, 12	247
IV, 20–22		100–101	XI, 3–4	137, 184n90	XV, 25	247
IV, 20–21		143	XI, 5–6, 9–19	184n90		
V, 2		147n42			1QM	184
V, 7		147n42	1QH			
VII, 25		184n90	I, 30	247	11QMelch	126n22
VIII, 4		247	III, 21	224		
VIII, 5–6		247	IV, 40	247	11QTemp	
VIII, 6		247	VI, 8–9	247	XXIX, 8–10	247

6. Philo

De Abrahamo		*Quod deterius potiori insidiari soleat*	
119–122	166	54	202
121–122	65n52		
124–125	65n53, 66n55	*De ebrietate*	
168, 194	200	44, 132–133, 157	166
262	265n30		
		De fuga et inventione	
De cherubim		95	65n53, 66n55, 181n81
27–28	66n55	98	66n55
27	65n53	100	65n53, 66n55
36	166	101	66n57
86	142n29		
87	54n29	*Quis rerum divinarum heres sit*	
125ff.	181n81	2–4	166
		166	65n53, 66n55
De confusione linguarum		187	202
44	265n30	207	261
146	166	230–231	166
De congressu eruditionis gratia		*Quod Deus sit immutabilis*	
171	66n55	57	181n81
		138	166

Philo

Legum allegoriae	
1.5–6	53n29
1.16	54n29
1.21	166
1.44	202
1.45	142n29
1.49	58n39
3.81	142n29
3.82	206n152
3.96	181n80
3.209	200

De migratione Abrahami	
35	166
42	261
140	200

De vita Mosis	
2.99	65n53, 66n55
2.263	265n30

De mutatione nominum	
18	261
27	202

De opificio mundi	
16–44	166
18–19	166
20	181n80
24	181n80
139	166, 181n80

De plantatione	
85–89	65n52
86–87	65n53

De posteritate Caini	
132, 140–142	261
145	206n152
148	261

De praemiis et poenis	
45	166

Quaestiones in Exodum	
2.13	166
2.67	166
2.68	66nn55.57
2.94	166
2.122	166

Quaestiones in Genesim	
1.4	166
2.62	166
4.2	65n54, 66n56, 166
4.4	166

De sacrificiis	
8	181n81
9	202
59	65n53, 66n55
80–83	166
83	181n80
119	166

De somniis	
1.75	181n80, 202
1.102–114	166
1.162–163	65n53
1.239	166
1.241–242	181n81
2.45	166
2.172	265n30
2.223, 245	202

De specialibus legibus	
1.48	166
1.59	65n53
1.81	181n80
1.209, 307	65n53
1.323	166
2.53	202
3.1–2	166
4.107	261

7. Josephus

Antiquitates
1.13.1	200
2.8	133
11.288	240n30
12.258–264	244
18.85–86	249
18.116–119	204n144

8. Rabbinic Literature

Mishna

Yoma
VIII:9	224n13

Midrasch

Genesis Rabbah
11:10	53n28

Exodus Rabbah
30:6, 9	53n28
41 (48a)	224n13

9. Apostolic Fathers and New Testament Pseudepigrapha

Acts of Thomas
124	190

Barnabas
12:2	262
19:4	267

1 Clement
49:2	215

Didache
4:3	267
10:2	141
15:3	267

Gospel of Philip
54:5–13	140
110, 123	104

Gospel of Thomas
18, 19, 85	110n75

10. Nag Hammadi Codices

Allogenes (NHC XI, 3)	169n42	*Marsanes* (NHC X, 1)	169n42
Apocalypse of Adam (NHC V, 5)	169n41	*Paraphrase of Shem* (NHC VII, 1)	169n41
Eugnostos the Blessed (NHC III, 3 and IV)	169n41	*Plato's Republic – 588A–589B* (NHC VI, 5)	169n42
Gospel of the Egyptians (NHC III, 2 and IV, 2)	169n41	*Prayer of Thanksgiving* (NHC VI:7)	140
Gospel of Truth (NHC I, 3)		*Sophia of Jesus Christ* (NHC III, 4)	169n41
1:32	55		
22:3ff.	90n25	*Three Steles of Seth* (NHC VII, 5)	169n42
25:35–36	90n25		
35:1–2	90n25		
38:6–31	140	*Zostrianus* (NHC VIII, 1)	169n42

11. Other Ancient Writings

Aristotle

Metaphysics
Λ 1072a, 25, 26, 29, 30   54 n30

Corpus Hermeticum
V:10–11   140
IX:9   54n31

Suetonius

Domitian
13   15

Index of Modern Authors

Abbott, Edwin   17, 52n26, 175, 209n160, 212n171, 241n31
Ackerman, James S.   126-27n24
Alter, Robert   4
Anderson, Gary   167n39
Appold, Mark L.   42n81, 145n37, 146, 250n51, 284n14
Ashton, John   7n21, 164n37

Bacchiocchi, Samuele   56n32
Ball, D. M.   84n7, 91n27, 114n85, 284n13
Barrett, C. Kingsley   3, 15, 22n33, 24n38, 28n45, 31n51, 34, 47nn3.6, 53n28, 55n32, 61nn44.46, 65n50, 73n70, 89n23, 93nn34.36, 97, 100n55, 111n78, 112n82, 118, 119n6, 121n11, 124nn16.18, 126n24, 136, 153n7, 154n8, 157, 158n25, 206n152, 210n165, 213n177, 219n1, 240n30, 255n1, 258, 260n17, 264n28, 267n37, 270, 271
Bauer, Walter   17n19, 40n72, 53n28, 93n33, 213n177, 214n181, 239n25, 245, 267n37
Beare, Francis Wright   259n14, 261n18
Beasley-Murray, George R.   15n2, 17nn18.19, 35n60, 38n66, 39n69, 40n72, 72n66, 86n11, 110n75, 111n78, 133n2, 141n27, 145n38, 175n57, 204n143, 225n15, 240n30, 253n57, 255n1, 264n29, 270n48, 272n58, 280n9
Becker, Heinz   81, 82
Becker, Jürgen   9n24, 40n72, 145n38, 156, 220n5, 256n1, 277n7, 290n21

Berger, Klaus   158
Bernard, J. H.   31n48, 40n72, 53n28, 73n71, 93n35, 117, 118n2, 120n9, 122, 125n20, 151n2, 155, 206n151, 210n165, 271
Bertram, G.   227n20
Betz, Otto   238n21, 244n39, 245n41, 249n47, 261, 269, 271n55
Bietenhard, Hans   140n25
Birdsall, J. Neville   121n11
Blank, Josef   34, 48n8, 64, 73n69, 86n13, 88n19, 93n33, 114n86, 267n37, 268n41
Blomberg, Craig L.   9n23
Boers, Hendrikus   252n54
Boismard, Marie-Émile   7, 8, 49, 160, 208n155, 210n164
Borgen, Peder   68n60, 109n72, 159, 160n30, 166n38, 167n39, 277n7, 280n9
Boring, M. Eugene   271
Botha, J. Eugene   233n4
Bover, José María   206n151
Brown, Raymond E.   7nn18.21, 15, 17n19, 21n28, 22nn30.32, 24n38, 28n45, 31n51, 38n67, 39, 47n6, 48n11, 49, 71n62, 73n71, 82n5, 91n27, 93, 94n41, 102n61, 117n1, 118n3, 125n20, 135, 137n16, 139n19, 147n42, 151n1, 155, 156, 180n78, 185n92, 186n94, 190, 193n114, 195nn118.120, 208n154, 210n165, 212n173, 220nn3.4, 228n23, 238n22, 240n30, 242nn33.36, 245, 250n52, 255n1, 257nn6.7, 258, 260, 267n37, 270n49, 271, 272n56

Bruce, Frederick Fyvie 107n70, 111n77, 125n20, 206n152, 210n165
Buchanan, George W. 231n1
Büchsel, Friedrich 17n20, 140n24, 200n132, 210n166, 236n16
Bühner, Jan-Adolf 280n9
Bull, Robert J. 234n9
Bultmann, Rudolf 3-5, 9, 15n2, 22nn29.33, 24n38, 30, 31n46, 32n54, 34, 35n60, 37n63, 38n65, 40nn72.73, 42n79, 46, 49, 61n46, 63, 67, 73n69, 75, 81, 82, 84n6, 86n14, 89, 93n33, 94n41, 95, 97, 99, 100n52, 101, 103n63, 105n66, 106, 107, 113, 114n84, 118, 119n6, 121n11, 122, 125n21, 128, 134n4, 135, 136, 138n17, 139, 142n29, 143nn30.33, 144, 145n38, 146n39, 148n43, 152, 153, 155, 157, 164, 167, 168n40, 170, 175, 176n63, 177n68, 178n74, 179, 180, 182nn82.83, 186n94, 189, 190nn100.102, 195n121, 202, 203, 204n143, 205n146, 206n152, 209nn160.163, 210n166, 211n164, 212n174, 215n182, 223n7, 224n14, 228n22, 232n3, 235nn13.15, 237n20, 239, 242, 245, 255, 259n12, 261nn19.21, 265n31, 267, 268n43, 269n47, 270, 272
Burge, Gary M. 223n11, 257n7, 258n9, 262n22, 270n51
Burkett, Delbert 71n63, 72n67, 227n19
Burney, Charles F. 26n40, 112, 124n19, 152, 154, 155, 175

Carl, K. J. 137n14
Carson, Donald A. 39n70, 176n62, 266
Charlesworth, James H. 28n45, 167n39, 168n40
Chilton, Bruce D. 167n39
Colwell Ernest C. 71, 72, 129n28
Conzelmann, Hans 3, 85, 155

Cook, W. Robert 135n6
Cullmann, Oscar 55n32, 73n71, 102, 198n127, 210n165, 231n1, 252n56
Culpepper, R. Alan 6, 7, 160nn31.33, 161, 168n40, 193n110, 288n19

Dahl, Nils Alstrup 1, 126n24
Dahms, John V. 200n131
Daube, David 235n15
Davies, Margaret 19n25, 85n8, 227n18
Deeks, David 168n40
de la Potterie, Ignace 100n54, 213
Delling, Gerhard 191n104
Demke, Christoph 154, 156, 168n40
Dettwiler, Andreas 256n1
Dexinger, Ferdinand 249n48
Dodd, Charles Harold 9, 15, 16n6, 24n34, 26n41, 28n45, 34, 37, 38n65, 48, 53n28, 57n37, 59, 60, 66n58, 86n14, 92n30, 93n33, 96n46, 100n52, 101, 107n70, 118n3, 121n11, 129, 135n6, 137nn14.15, 154n11, 157, 165n37, 166n38, 178n72, 203, 204n143, 212n173, 226n17, 253n57
Drijvers, Hendrik W. 169n41
Duke, Paul D. 220n3
Duncan, Robert L. 166n38
Dunn, James D. G. 164n37, 168n40, 174n50

Ehrman, Bart D. 210n166, 212n170
Eltester, Walther 159
Emerton, John A. 126n22
Epp, Eldon J. 164n37
Erlemann, Kurt 3
Eslinger, Lyle 234n12
Essar, H. H. 207n153
Evans, Craig A. 165n37, 167n39, 168n40, 169n41

Fascher, Erich 168n40
Fee, Gordon D. 41n78, 42n80

Fennema, David A. 3, 177n69, 210n165
Feuillet, André 160
Fischel, H. A. 168n40
Foerster, W. 191n106
Ford, J. M. 24
Forestell, J. Terence 24n34
Fortna, Robert T. 9n24, 24-25n39, 232n3
Franck, Eskil 257n5, 259n11, 260n16, 263n26, 265n32
Freed, Edwin D. 24n35, 114, 124n19, 126n22, 164n37, 231n1, 236n17, 249n48
Frey, Jörg 50n21, 55n32, 70n61, 78n80, 79n81, 223n9, 227n20, 257n6, 267n37, 272n58
Friend, H. S. 68n60
Fuller, Reginald H. 178n72
Funk, Robert W. 93n37

Gächter, Paul 47n5, 48, 61, 156
Gaffney, James 137n14
Gardner-Smith, Percival 9, 10
Geffré, Claude 276n5
Gnilka, Joachim 206n152, 207n153, 255n1
Green, H. C. 156
Greeven, Heinrich 242n35
Grigsby, Bruce H. 24n35

Haenchen, Ernst 40n72, 53n28, 72n66, 110n74, 112n79, 122n13, 156, 157, 173, 177n69, 198n127, 207n153, 212n175, 223n8, 239n25, 240n30
Hagner, Donald A. 166n38
Hall, D. R. 235n15
Hamerton-Kelly, Robert 276nn2.4
Hanson, Anthony T. 16n15, 24n37, 31, 32n51, 56n33, 57, 86n11, 88n18, 126n23, 127n24, 129n29, 197n126, 202n139
Harm, F. R. 263n27
Harnack, Adolf von 168
Harner, Philip B. 19n25, 72, 91, 284n13

Harris, J. Rendel 154
Harris, Murray James 17n18, 173n48, 175nn53.55, 176n65, 212n175, 213n179
Harvey, Anthony E. 68n60
Hayward, C. T. Robert 167n39
Hendriksen, William 75n74
Henry, P. 111n76, 112n81
Hofius, Otfried 156, 167n39, 178n73, 210n165
Hollis, H. 227n20
Holtzmann, Heinrich Julius 40n72
Homcy, S. L. 129n29
Hooker, Morna D. 92n30, 161, 202n139
Hoskyns, Edwyn C. 17n19, 31n48, 47n6, 48n8, 55n32, 72n66, 89n23, 93n39, 98n51, 113n83, 119n5, 157, 194n117, 210nn166.167, 213n177, 239n24, 267n37, 272
Hunter, Archibald Macbride 71n63

Jackayya, B. H. 100n53
Jeremias, Joachim 26n40, 27n42, 155n13, 208nn154.155
Johnston, George 267n38, 271n55
Jonas, Hans 169n41
Jonge, Marinus de 37n62, 42n81, 126n22, 200nn3.5, 241n32, 280n9
Judge, P. J. 39n70, 41n74
Juel, Donald 275n2

Käsemann, Ernst 3, 135, 146, 155, 156, 179n75, 196n122, 198, 199n128, 285n16
Keifert, Patrick 275n2
Kennard, Douglas W. 3
Kippenberg, Hans G. 243n38, 249nn46.48, 250n50
Kleinknecht, H. 166n38
Klumbies, Paul-Gerhard 3
Koester, Helmut 168n40, 169n44
Kohler, Herbert 14
Kremer, Jacob 18
Kruijf, Theodor C. de 200n133, 215n183

Kümmel, Werner Georg 97n47
Kysar, Robert 125n20, 142n28

Lamarche, Paul 160
Langbrandtner, Wolfgang 7n18
Lategan, Bernard C. 101n56
Lee, Dorothy A. 276n3, 277n6, 278n8, 284n15
Lee, Edwin Kenneth 97n49, 100n52
Lightfoot, Robert Henry 48n8, 71n63, 93n39, 138n18, 157, 210n166
Lindars, Barnabas 7n18, 17n19, 24n38, 31n51, 48nn8.11, 73n69, 93, 107n70, 110n74, 112n79, 125n20, 164n37, 184n87, 189n98, 200n131, 206n152, 210n165, 220n3, 237n18, 238n22, 239n24, 252n55, 268n42
Lindemann, Andreas 1, 2nn2-4, 155, 156, 208n155, 227n20, 232, 266n33, 267nn39.40, 268n44
Loader, William R. G. 178n72, 212n174, 277n7
Lührmann, Dieter 139n22
Lund, N. W. 160

Macdonald, John 233nn5.7, 234n10, 241n32, 242n33, 249n48
Macgregor, Gregor H. C. 47n4, 71n63, 81, 82
Mack, Burton L. 166n38
Marsh, John 73n71, 75n74, 93n36, 157
Martyn, J. Louis 7-9, 51, 73n68, 92n29, 109n71, 219, 220n4, 232, 264n28
Masson, C. 174n52
Mattill Jr., Andrew J. 7n20
McHugh, John 135n6
Meagher, John C. 197n126
Meeks, Wayne A. 6, 24n39, 31nn47.51, 32n53, 35n59, 36n61, 37, 92n30, 128, 208n155, 220n3, 231n1, 233n5, 241n32, 249n48, 250n51, 282n10
Metzger, Bruce M. 22n31, 41n76, 121n11, 180n78, 211n168

Michaelis, Wilhelm 209n162
Miller, Ed L. 176n60, 180n78
Moloney, Francis J. 72n66, 213nn177.179, 214n180
Moody, Dale 200n134
Moore, George Foot 167n39
Morris, Leon 17n19, 40n72, 72n66, 93, 125n20, 210n165, 212n172, 213n177, 228nn23.24, 238n22, 251n53
Moule, Charles Francis Digby 18, 71n64, 175n57, 213n178
Mowvley, Harry 197n126, 202n139
Moxnes, Halvor 3, 5
Müller, Ulrich B. 262nn23.24, 266n35

Neirynck, Frans 10, 39n68
Neyrey, Jerome H. 3, 50, 66n58, 109n73, 117n1, 120n8, 127n24
Nicol, William 9n24, 232n3

O'Day, Gail R. 3, 4, 233n4, 237n18
Odeberg, Hugo 61, 62n47, 86n14, 90n24, 93n39, 228n21, 245, 249n48
Oepke, Albrecht 213n177
Okure, Teresa 237n19, 239, 240n28, 245n42
Olsson, Birger 232n4, 234nn8.9.11, 238n21, 240n30, 243n37, 250n50

Painter, John 151n2, 154–56, 164-65n37, 256n1, 259n15, 264n28
Pamment, Margaret 135n6, 199n129, 231n1
Pancaro, Severino 207n153
Parunak, H. van Dyke 47n6
Pendrick, G. 200n134, 201n136
Phillips, W. Gary 125n20
Pollard, Thomas Evan 119n7, 164n37, 210n165
Pryor, John W. 191n103, 227n19

Randall, J. F. 133n2, 146n39

Reim, Günter   21n28, 24n35, 56n33
Rensberger, David   287n18
Richardson, Alan   207n153
Richardson, Neil G.   3
Richter, Georg   7, 8, 195n118
Ridderbos, Herman N.   198n127
Rissi, Matthias   158, 164n37
Roberts, J. H.   27n43
Robertson, P. E.   135n6
Robinson, Gesine   168n40
Robinson, John A. T.   205n146
Robinson, James M.   151n1, 168nn40.41
Ruckstuhl, Eugen   158, 159n28, 161
Rudolph, Kurt   168n40

Sanders, Joseph N.   40n72, 48n8, 54n30, 55n32, 72n66, 82, 122n13, 156, 157, 176, 177n68, 202n138, 210n164, 240n30
Sandy, D. Brent   28n45
Schaeder, Hans Heinrich   154
Schenke, Hans-Martin   232n3, 234n8
Schlier, Heinrich   57n34, 103n63
Schmithals, Walter   7n18, 153n6, 155, 156
Schnackenburg, Rudolf   9n24, 17n19, 24n38, 35n60, 38n67, 40n72, 41n77, 47n3, 48n11, 49n13, 60, 61n46, 65n50, 66, 73n72, 75, 76, 87nn15.17, 89n21, 90n24, 93n33, 94n40, 95n44, 97, 102, 114, 115n87, 117n1, 118n3, 119n6, 121n11, 126n24, 130, 134n3, 136, 140n26, 143nn32.33, 145n38, 147n42, 151n1, 155, 156, 178n71, 179n75, 181n79, 184n89, 185n91, 186n94, 188, 189n96, 198n127, 203n141, 204n145, 206n152, 210n166, 213n177, 220n3, 223n9, 224n13, 234n9, 239nn23.24, 240n30, 250n52, 251n53, 256n1, 259n13, 268n43, 269n46, 283n12
Schneider, Gerhard   275n2
Schneider, Johannes   118n3

Schneiders, Sandra M.   240n29
Schnelle, Udo   39, 40n72
Schoonenberg, Piet   165n37
Schrenk, G.   212n176
Schuchard, Bruce G.   124n19, 125n20, 126n23
Schüssler Fiorenza, Elisabeth   172n47
Schulz, Siegfried   31n48, 48n8, 49n13, 73n72, 84, 152, 153n5, 156, 190n100, 210n166, 232n3, 255n1
Schweizer, Eduard   84n7, 195, 196n124, 282n11
Scobie, Charles H. H.   231n1
Scott, Martin   165n37
Segovia, Fernando F.   256n1
Smith, Dwight Moody   6, 7, 10n25, 46n2, 81n1
Smothers, Edgar Raymond   93n37
Spiro, Abram   242n34
Suggit, John   15
Sundberg, Albert C.   50

Talbert, Charles H.   168n40
Tasker, Randolph V. G.   210n167, 267n37
Theobald, Michael   164n37, 200n131, 236n17
Thompson, Marianne M.   4, 38n67, 285n17
Thüsing, Wilhelm   271
Thyen, Hartwig   179n75, 195n118
Tobin, Thomas H.   166n38

Untergaßmair, Franz Georg   140n25
Urban, L.   111n76, 112n81

van der Watt, Jan Gabriël   78n80
Vellanickal, Matthew   192n109, 193nn110.115
Vouga, François   290n21

Wahlde, Urban C. von   9n24, 232n3
Wead, David W.   235n14
Wengst, Klaus   7n22
Whitacre, Rodney A.   289n20, 290n21

Whittaker, John	121, 122n12
Wikenhauser, Alfred	31n48, 48n8, 95n43, 178n71, 239n23, 271n55
Wiles, Maurice F.	119n7
Wilkens, Wilhelm	7n18, 24n39, 232n3
Wilson, Robert McL.	168n40
Winter, Martin	133nn1.2, 256nn1-4, 259n11
Witherington, Ben	223n10
Witkamp, L. Th.	51n22
Woll, D. Bruce	263n25
Woude, Adam S. van der	126n22
Wright, Nicholas T.	3
Yamauchi, Edwin M.	168n40, 169n41
Zahn, Theodor	210n165, 212n174, 239n24
Zimmerli, Walther	207n153
Zwaan, Johannes de	112